IN SEARCH OF IDENTITY:
JEWISH ASPECTS IN ISRAELI CULTURE

Cass Studies in
Israeli History, Politics and Society
ISSN 1368-4795

General Editor: Efraim Karsh

1. Peace in the Middle East: The Challenge for Israel
   edited by Efraim Karsh

2. The Shaping of Israeli Identity: Myth, Memory and Trauma
   edited by Robert Wistrich and David Ohana

3. Between War and Peace: Dilemmas of Israeli Security
   edited by Efraim Karsh

4. U.S.–Israeli Relations at the Crossroads
   edited by Gabriel Sheffer

5. From Rabin to Netanyahu: Israel's Troubled Agenda
   edited by Efraim Karsh

6. Israel at the Polls 1996
   edited by Daniel Elazar and Shmuel Sandler

7. In Search of Identity: Jewish Aspects in Israeli Culture
   edited by Dan Urian and Efraim Karsh

IN SEARCH OF IDENTITY
Jewish Aspects in Israeli Culture

Edited by
DAN URIAN
and
EFRAIM KARSH

FRANK CASS
LONDON • PORTLAND, OR

First published in 1999 in Great Britain by
FRANK CASS AND COMPANY LIMITED
Newbury House, 900 Eastern Avenue, London IG2 7HH, England

and in the United States of America by
FRANK CASS
c/o ISBS, Inc.
5804 N.E. Hassalo Street, Portland, Oregon 97213-3644

Copyright © 1999 Frank Cass & Co. Ltd.

British Library Cataloguing in Publication Data

In search of identity: Jewish aspects in Israeli culture.
 – (Israeli history, politics and society)
1. Jews – Israel – Civilization. 2. Subculture – Israel.
3. Jews – Attitudes towards Israel. 4. Jews – Israel –Identity
I. Karsh, Efraim II. Urian, Dan

ISBN 0 7146 4889 2 (cloth)
ISBN 0 7146 4440 4 (paper)
ISSN 1368-4795

Library of Congress Cataloging-in-Publication Data

In search of identity: Jewish aspects in Israeli culture / edited by Dan Urian and Efraim Karsh.
    p. cm. – (Israeli history, politics, and society, ISSN 1368-4795)
  Includes bibliographical references and index.
  ISBN 0-7146-4889-2 (hb). – ISBN 0-7146-4440-4 (pb)
   1. Jews–Israel– Identity. 2. Judaism – Israel. 3. Israel–Intellectual life. 4. Popular culture–Israel. 5. Israel–Social conditions. I. Urian, Dan. II. Karsh, Efraim. III. Series.
DS113.3.S43   1998
306'.095694–dc21   98-21761
                                                              CIP

This group of studies first appeared in a Special Issue,
In Search of Identity: Jewish Aspects in Israeli Culture in *Israel Affairs*,
[ISSN 1353-7121] Vol.4, Nos.3&4 (Spring/Summer 1998).

All rights reserved. No part of this publication may be reproduced, stored in or introduced into a retrieval system, or transmitted, in any form or by any means, electronic, mechanical, photocopying, recording or otherwise, without the prior written permission of the publisher of this book.

Contents

Introduction	Efraim Karsh and Dan Urian	1

CULTURAL TENSION

Judaism in Israeli Culture	Eliezer Schweid	9
Secular Judaism and Its Prospects	Charles S. Liebman	29
Between Hegemony and Dormant *Kulturkampf* in Israel	Baruch Kimmerling	49
Shall We Find Sufficient Strength? On Behalf of Israeli Secularism	Gershon Shaked	73
Between Rabbi Shach and Modern Hebrew Literature	Dan Miron	86

THE JEWISHNESS OF ISRAELI IDENTITY

Spiritual Rootlessness and Circumscription to the 'Here and Now' in the Sabra World View	Avraham Shapira	103
The Shdemot Circle Members in Search of Jewish Sources	Gad Ufaz	132
Jewish Education in the Jewish State	David Zisenwine	146

ARTISTIC REPRESENTATIONS OF JEWISH IDENTITY

Sisera's Mother and the Trojan Women: On Universal Aspects of the Jewish/Israeli Theatre	Eli Rozik-Rosen	159
From Jew to Hebrew: The 'Zionist Narrative' in the Israeli Cinema of the 1940s and 1950s	Nurit Gertz	175
The Theme of Jerusalem in the Works of the Israeli Fathers of Conceptual Arts	Mordechai Omer	200
The Dybbuk Revisited: Images of Religious Jews on the Israeli Stage	Shimon Levy	219

Baalei Teshuva ('Returnees to the Religious Fold')
in Israeli Theatre   Dan Urian   230

From Rejection to Recognition: Israeli Art and the
Holocaust   Dalia Manor 253

Index   279

Introduction

EFRAIM KARSH and DAN URIAN

As Israel reaches its fiftieth year of statehood and peace with the Palestinians and the Arab states seems ever closer, Israeli society faces a deepening crisis of identity. On the face of it, an inexplicable paradox. Why should Israelis have any self-doubts about their collective identity at a time when even their most implacable enemies are resigning themselves to the existence of the Jewish State in their midst? Besides, such has been the success of Zionism that most Israelis have always taken the Jewish identity of their state for granted.[1] Not in a predominantly religious sense: for not only did Zionism conceive of the prospective Jewish State as a modern, chiefly secular entity, but it was as much a revolt against the reign of the rabbis as against Diaspora life itself. Rather, given its fundamental belief that the Jews constitute a distinct nation, not a mere religious community, and hence deserve a state of their own, Zionism has always subordinated the religious aspect of Jewish identity to the national one. Its recourse to the Bible as a source of legitimacy and its harping on religious sentiments – notably the millenarian yearning for Return embedded in Jewish religious practices from antiquity – were all geared to the overriding goal of reconstituting Jewish statehood in their ancestral homeland.

This was to be a Jewish State – a state of the Jews and for the Jews. Not in the sense of being exclusively Jewish: contrary to a commonly held misperception, from an early stage Zionism had reconciled itself to the existence of a sizeable Arab minority in the Jewish state-to-be. As David Ben-Gurion put it in December 1947: 'In our state there will be non-Jews as well – and all of them will be equal citizens; equal in everything without any exception; that is: the state will be their state as

---

Efraim Karsh is Professor and Head of the Mediterranean Studies Programme, King's College, University of London. Dan Urian is Associate Professor of Theatre Studies at Tel-Aviv University.

well.'[2] Rather, the prospective state was to be Jewish in its national ethos – historically, culturally, religiously – just as France was French and England was English. The various minorities would enjoy equitable treatment, with their religions and cultures even given official status by the state – something that is not yet applicable to the most advanced Western democracies;[3] but as minorities they would *ipso facto* have to acquiesce in the majority's national ethos, as is the case throughout the world. And in Israel's case, the existence of a Jewish majority has been a *sine qua non* for both the establishment of the state and its continued existence. For it is the unwavering conviction that only by becoming a majority in a state of their own would the Jews be able to liberate themselves from the perennial weakness and insecurity attending their Diaspora minority existence which lies at the heart of the Zionist ideal. Were this majority to disappear, for one reason or another, the *raison d'état* of the Jewish State would be irrevocably shattered.

Against this backdrop, it is scarcely surprising that the 1967 Six Day War was to set in train the most severe identity crisis experienced by the Jewish State since its establishment in May 1948. On the one hand, the occupation of the West Bank, or Judea and Samaria as they had long been known, reopened the question of Israel's ultimate borders, ostensibly settled in 1947 when mainstream Zionism accepted the partition of Mandatory Palestine into Jewish and Arab states. On the other hand, the coming of the Palestinian population of the West Bank and the Gaza Strip under Israeli control, at a time when the prospects of mass Jewish immigration, or *aliya*, seemed rather dim, raised the question of Israel's Jewish identity, were these territories to be annexed. Exacerbated by a string of corollary developments, such as the rise of religious messianism preaching the settlement of the entire Land of Israel, the corrupting effects of the occupation on Israeli society, and the evolution of Israeli–Palestinian economic interdependence, these dialectical pressures were not long in generating deep schisms within Israeli society.

These conflicts have been most evident in the political field, where the main battle on the future of the territories has been waged. But they have been equally manifest in other walks of Israeli life, not least in the sphere of 'high culture' – literature, theatre, cinema, dance, the plastic arts, music etc. Like most nineteenth and twentieth century national movements, culture played a focal role in the shaping of Jewish–Israeli national identity; and with Zionism being the secular movement that it is, culture became the effective prism through which religious and historical notions of Jewish nationalism were filtered. It was culture that brought to life – in word, sound and motion – the Zionist ideal of a new and heroic Israeli persona, the *sabra,* as an antithesis to the then widely held image of the Diaspora Jew;[4] and it was culture that provided the main mirror through which most Israelis viewed their image: their historical bond to the Land of Israel, their conflict with the Palestinians and the wider Arab World, their intercommunal relations, etc.

During the first two decades of independence, dominated by the heroic establishment of the state and the Sisyphean consolidation of its foundations, including the absorption of mass immigration and the winning of two further wars, Israeli culture tended by and large towards a hopeful and optimistic outlook, with social and political problems raised and 'solved' in books, plays and films. It was only after the October 1973 War, and all the more so after the 1982 Lebanon War, that the cultural emphasis began shifting from the consensual to the controversial. Unsolvable problems and irreconcilable schisms and contradictions in Israeli society and way of life became the regular diet of artists, as the 'mainstream culture' gave way to a growing number of peripheral subcultures. 'The Israeli is no longer the master of his own home', Israeli academic Gershon Shaked lamented. 'His signal language and world of values have lost their significance because they have lost their validity and inner strength. A new, different language is taking the place of that which has breathed its terminal breath.'[5]

An important subculture which has gained rapid momentum in the wake of the Six Day War has been the religious one, with two main branches: the religious Zionist and the ultra-Orthodox (*haredi*). The former's main reservoir lies in the settlements of the West Bank and Gaza, but it also boasts a substantial following among the religious and traditional Ashkenazi middle class within Israel itself. The latter group, historically opposed to the establishment of a Jewish State before the arrival of the messiah, has mellowed its anti-Zionist rhetoric over the past decade in favour of a deepening involvement in Israel's political life. Add to this the establishment and rapid expansion of a new Sephardi *haredi* political party (SHAS), and the growing *haredi* interest in the hitherto blasphemous media of television and theatre, among others, in their struggle to give their cultural and ideological beliefs the widest possible exposure, to understand the steady weakening of the mainstream culture.

The 'culture war' between secular and religious Jews, to be sure, is not new. Its origins can be traced to the late eighteenth century, when the enlightenment movement challenged the Orthodox establishment and its traditional definition of Jewishness along purely religious lines. The Zionist movement, as noted earlier, took this revolt a significant step forward by making the national, rather than the religious, aspect of Judaism the cornerstone of Jewish identity: shared destiny, one ancestral homeland, Hebrew as a national language and, above all, shared national aspirations, should be the defining factors of Jewishness – not the extent of one's religious practice. It is no accident that Israel's Law of Return, turning the Nazi anti-Jewish laws on their head, defines a Jew as any person who claims Jewish ancestry within a three-generation span, in contravention to the halachic, or the rabbinical, definition of Jewishness, whereby only those born to Jewish mothers are considered Jewish.

Hence the unmitigated *haredi* hostility to the Zionist Revolution which not only challenged G-D's will by seeking the establishment of a nation state, but also imperilled the predominantly religious based exilic Jewish identity.

What makes this latest round in the *Kulturkampf* particularly important is that, for the first time in the century-long history of the Zionist movement, the secular-national brand of Jewish identity that lies at the core of the State of Israel seems to be giving ground to a predominantly religious perception of Jewishness. For, not only has the established Israeli–Jewish identity come under growing pressure from a more assertive ultra-Orthodox establishment, but expressions of self-doubt have been voiced by some well known practitioners of 'high culture', probably the most secularized and avowedly anti-religious sector of Israeli society. Thus, for example, according to poet Dalia Rabikowitz, there is no such thing as secular Israeli culture. 'Our secular culture is a "no" culture,' she claimed. 'I do not observe the *mitzvot* and do not believe in the resurrection of the dead or the coming of the messiah. Nor am I familiar with the traditional expressions of joy, bereavement, and their like – yet have no clear alternative to them; and then the high holidays arrive and I have no idea how to spend them apart from filling my refrigerator and getting bored.'[6]

Although indicative of the growing defensiveness of Israeli artists and intellectuals about their Jewish identity, this self-abnegation is by no means the standard view. In the words of the poet and essayist Nathan Zach:

> What has the secular, or liberal (free) culture created here? My answer is rather straightforward: almost everything – for better, for worse. From A.D. Gordon, Y.H. Brenner, Ahad Ha-am and Bialik to S. Yizhar, Yoram Kaniuk, and Dalia Rabikowitz, to Yehuda Amichai, Lova Eliav, Amos Oz, David Grossman, and Yehoshua Knaz. And all this is merely in the field of literature and social conscience. I have said nothing yet on medicine and its eradication of the rampant regional diseases, as well as on the fields of law, journalism, architecture, painting, sculpture, cinema, music, theatre, and sports.[7]

A study of Israeli culture on the eve of the next millennium thus affords a meaningful insight into a society in a state of transition. So, for example, a recent collection of essays on youth culture in Israel makes almost no mention of the Jewishness of Israeli culture, lamenting instead the 'severance from the past and loss of faith in the future, as if culture were imprisoned in a present-continuous of sorts'. This postmodern situation in which one can turn to neither tradition nor ideology for guidance accounts for the muddled state of mind of present-day Israeli society: 'The present becomes a shock since, by virtue of not being perceived as part of a continuum, there is nothing to prepare us for it. It is always new.'[8]

This problematic continuum between past and present, between

Israeliness and Jewishness, lies at the core of this volume. In the first part, Eliezer Schweid, Charles S. Liebman, Baruch Kimmerling, Gershon Shaked, and Dan Miron discuss the nature and characteristics of this cultural tension, while in the second, Avraham Shapira, Gad Ufaz, and David Zisenwine examine the Jewishness of Israeli identity in several spheres such as the ethos of the sabra, and the 'discovery' of Jewish roots by the kibbutz movement. In the final part, Eli Rozik-Rosen, Nurit Gertz, Mordechai Omer, Shimon Levy, Dan Urian, and Dalia Manor examine selected works from the fields of literature, cinema, theatre and art as an interpretative reflection of the Israeli–Jewish reality.

NOTES

1. Thus, for example, in a survey of Jewish Israeli positions and attitudes in the early 1990s, 90 per cent of Jewish Israelis defined themselves as Zionist, and 94 per cent expressed pride at being Jewish. Shlomit Levy, Hana Levinsohn and Elihu Katz, *Beliefs, Religious Observance, and Social Relations among Jewish Israelis* (Jerusalem: Gutmann Institute, 1993) (Hebrew).
2. David Ben-Gurion, *Ba-ma'araha* (In Battle) (Tel-Aviv, 1959), Vol.IV, Part 2, p.260.
3. Thus, for example, Arabic constitutes Israel's official language alongside Hebrew, and Muslim and Christian religious holidays are considered official holidays.
4. See, for example, Oz Almog,*The Sabra – A Profile* (Tel-Aviv, 1997) (Hebrew).
5. Gershon Shaked, 'Light,Shadow, and Plurality: Israeli Literature's Dialectic Struggle with a Changing Reality', *Alpayim*, No.4 (1991), p.130.
6. Dalia Rabikowitz, 'There is no Secular Culture in this State', *Shishi*, 22 Dec. 1995.
7. Nathan Zach, 'There is a Secular Culture in this State', *Shishi*, 29 Dec. 1995.
8. Gadi Taub, *The Bent-Backed Rebellion: On Youth Culture in Israel* (Tel-Aviv, 1997), p.63 (Hebrew).

CULTURAL TENSION

Judaism in Israeli Culture

ELIEZER SCHWEID

The substitution, following the creation of the State of Israel, of the term 'Israeli Culture' for that of 'Hebrew Culture', which had been the accepted one during the pre-State Yishuv period, expresses a transformation in the culture itself. Not only did the political and social institutions of cultural life change, but also the way of life and patterns of human relationships which find their expression in creativity. As a result, the understanding of the nature and function of culture, of spiritual life and of spiritual creation as a uniting and identifying process, likewise changed: these are no longer perceived as the central factor identifying one national society or people, while the society or the nation as a whole no longer seeks all its spiritual needs or the expression of all of the 'selves' of its component individuals within the framework of nationality.

Thus, the totality of creation as constituted by the expressions of all the individuals and groups is no longer understood within the monistic framework of national culture, but is perceived as composed of many different compartments, including the national, the religious and the national-religious, which are not necessarily open to one another, and do not even necessarily connect all of their component individuals to a single national society or to one people. In place of the national society and culture which seek to mix and to connect, there are manifested in retrospect a broad gamut of partial identities and belongings. Not only various communities, ethnic groups or movements, but even each individual can identify partially with several of these, taking from each one his own 'piece' (how much our young people love the expression 'this piece', *ha-keta ha-zeh* as a form of expression typifying their way of thinking!) as he wishes.

In other words, the individual no longer entirely defines his identity within the realm of nationalism, or even that of religiosity. Where then is

---

Eliezer Schweid is Professor of Jewish Studies at the Hebrew University of Jerusalem.

such wholeness to be identified? As mentioned, this definition has been removed to the instrumental and organizational framework of the material culture, described in the universal political terms of the state. This is in fact the significance of 'Israeliness', which for the majority of those who identify themselves as 'Israelis' connotes civil political-linguistic-territorial belonging. This usually incorporates a certain measure of 'Hebraism' as well as of 'Judaism', in the religious, traditional or national sense, but these are generally partial and fragmented. Even when these are to be found at the centre of personal identity, they are not inclusive, but are liable to be limited, marginalized, or externalized in relation – friendly or hostile – to the identity of others in the nation, or even disappear entirely, leaving in their wake, like the smile of the Cheshire cat, a hazy memory of 'origin'.

This reality, which may be seen today with great clarity, was the dialectic result of the establishment of the State. I said 'dialectical result', as it is quite clear that such was not the intention of the founders, who 'after two thousand years of Exile' created a Jewish State to be based upon Hebrew culture. The state was called 'Israel' after the ancient name of the people, for which in turn the land was named, to indicate a distinct cultural and national identity. According to the Declaration of Independence, Israel was intended to be, not only 'the state of the Jews', but also 'a Jewish State', a centre that would symbolize unity and from whence the spiritual heritage would flow to the people as a whole. Based on this approach, laws were introduced shaping a policy of ingathering of exiles and their social-cultural integration, of Jewish-national education, and of the shaping of a Jewish 'public realm'. Moreover, in its early years the state functioned as a 'melting pot', whose purpose was to forge an inclusive cultural-national identity on the basis of the tradition of 'Hebrew Culture' from the period of the Yishuv.

However, the result of this process, which in practice focused upon the establishment and grounding of a modern Israeli 'statehood' (*mamlakhtiut*), in which priority was given to the factors of national security and economic and organizational-instrumental creativity, and with the emphatic desire to shape a civil society based upon a consciousness of statehood, was just the opposite. The unifying national message focused upon the immediate work at hand: the establishment of state institutions and their economic, technological, administrative, socio-professional, legal-professional and political functioning – areas whose development and perfection predominantly required the internalization of knowledge and expertise drawn from external, Western sources, and not specifically from the values of the tradition.

Against the background of these emphases within the formal education frameworks, a process of voluntary rehabilitation of the cultural, religious, traditional, ethnic or modern-national heritages brought by the immigrants from different backgrounds also began. Simultaneously, the quest for identity on the part of young people who had been born and educated in the State began to occur at a growing distance from their parents' old-fashioned cultural sources, and closer to the contemporary outside sources from which originated the scientific and technological tools and contents vital for the defence, building and grounding of the state as a prosperous Western civilization. Thus, the effort to integrate and to unite the people within the 'melting pot' of a national state culture led to the forgetting and decline of the Yishuv culture, and the emergence of the multicompartmentalized and fragmented Israeli culture described above.

As mentioned, the initial factor leading to this change was the establishment of the State as an institutional-governmental system on a suitable basis of modern civilization. However, in the broader sense one may speak of an historical process of consolidation that continued over a generation and was affected by two more factors alluded to above: the demographic transformation, caused by a series of waves of mass immigration from several different countries of origin, and the cultural transformation which took place in the sources of influence of Western civilization following the Second World War. I refer here primarily to the spread of modern and postmodern American civilization, together with its scientific-technological, socioeconomic, institutional-governmental, legal, social-ethic and spiritual characteristics.

The mass aliya rejected the Hebrew culture of the Yishuv as for the most part alien to it, as well as being inadequate and irrelevant, and in the final analysis led to its destruction. The main cause of this was the vast size of this aliya: not only in the sense that within a few years Israel's Jewish population doubled in size, thereafter continuing to grow in similar dimensions to this very day. More importantly, upon its arrival each aliya created a sociocultural reality of uprooted masses of people whose cultural memories had been suppressed and denied expression during the traumatic process of absorption, and who were equally unable to internalize or creatively confront the cultural influences of the absorbing society, beyond absorbing certain material elements and a passive acceptance of the secular values that accompanied them.

This in itself, together with the fact that the Yishuv culture was intended to act as an absorbing and integrating force, namely one that dominated the immigrants who were alien to it and forcibly changed their culture while guiding them towards itself, led to the emergence of the destructive and decadent features of mass culture: social, linguistic, behavioural and spiritual 'gaps' and 'breaks', coupled with material manifestations typical of a culture of poverty, on the one hand, and of a culture of exaggerated wealth (relative to the poorer class), on the other.

It would seem that only after a period of time, once the socioeconomic consolidation of the new aliya had allowed their suppressed cultural memories to begin their rehabilitation, that the long term structural effect of the mass aliya became clear: to wit, the emergence of a wide range of cultural heritages, different and alienated from one another in nearly all their ways of expression, language, manners and values.

If truth be told, the sense of alienation, whose source lay in the strong assimilating influences of the cultures of the various different countries of origin, was already manifest in the initial social encounter between the aliyot and the 'veteran Yishuv', characterized in practice by a rejection that was clearly opposed to the ideology of absorbing aliya and of the 'melting pot'. This sense was expressed in the image of the 'Second Israel' – a comprehensive term used to refer to the *ma'abarot* (absorption camps), 'development towns', *moshavim* and poor urban neighbourhoods in which the olim were absorbed. The assimilatory power of the various different countries upon the new olim was clearly stronger than the common Jewish denominator, which was anchored on the one hand to tradition and religion, and on the other to awareness of origin and destiny and to weak and confused memories of fragments of tradition.

Since we are concerned with the issue of the Judaism of Israeli culture, it is important to emphasize the sense of alienation aroused with the arrival of each new wave of immigration: the 'new olim' came to the country on the basis of their own Jewishness, a fact that isolated them in their country of origin and generally caused their rejection by it. However, during their initial encounter in Israel there stood out specifically their 'non-Jewish' foreignness, to the extent that it completely hid the signs of their common cultural code. The olim who came to the State of Israel were thus viewed by the veteran, absorbing society – including those immigrants who had preceded them by only a few years – as 'Iraqis', 'Moroccans', 'Yemenites', 'Romanians', 'Russians', 'Americans', 'Ethiopians' etc.

This fact could not but delay the process of their acceptance and cultural reconstruction for a long time, leading to the harsh and painful struggles that are documented in the literary and artistic creations of the first years of the State, and that still echo in contemporary Israeli literature. In any event, there is no cause for surprise that the earliest phase of the process of cultural and Jewish reconstruction of the various aliyot, which took place following the acquisition of education and expertise and the internalization of the social norms of the 'general' absorbing culture, did not lead to dialogic meetings in the social-cultural realm. On the contrary, it increased the walls of hostility and alienation, particularly with regard to those values expressing the unique Jewish identity of all those belonging to a particular 'ethnic origin' unto themselves. So much so, that at times it seemed as if the only common Jewish characteristic of Israeli culture was the confrontation, friction and debate among the different forms of Jewish identity – various kinds of religious Jews, traditionalists, ethnics, or alternatively modern religionists or humanists – struggling for their place within a growing sense of alienation both on the 'public street' and within literary and artistic creation.

In the long run, thus, a process of acceptance took place, through self-rehabilitation and painful adjustment to the framework of statehood and its modern educational and civilization framework. But, at least for the present, that sociology which unites by means of material values and external forms of behaviour has not led to the development of a dialogue which will in turn lead to mutual fructification or the creation of a shared culture with a clear distinctiveness of its own, stressing positive 'codes' of a Jewish cultural heritage.

One might pose the question: What is it that prevents mutual opening and fructification on the level of social ethic and spiritual creation? The most obvious answer is the dominating force of the sociological process that levels down different societies in terms of their underlying culture, and which in retrospect expresses the overpowering sweeping influence of a third factor: contemporary Western culture, in its American form, carried by the economic and sociological taking root of the 'society of abundance', marked by external and showy materialism, extreme competitiveness, and self-centred individualism. On this level, cultural socialization challenges the very value of cultural traditions as such. It denies the importance of historic group identities, placing at the centre the value of individual 'self-realization' that draws upon the present alone, and creates an impregnable barrier between an ironic high culture, which tends towards cosmopolitan universalism and is alienated from its own tradition and people, and the majority of society. It would appear that only Orthodox-religious or fundamentalist-religious identities are able to succeed (at the price of extreme closedness) in withstanding this sweeping influence with even partial success, at least for the moment.

One should mention at this point that the Hebrew culture of the Yishuv period was developed by the main streams within Zionism (socialist-pioneering Zionism, general spiritual Zionism, romantic-nationalistic Zionism and religious Zionism) under the influence of European nationalism, humanism and socialism of the first half of the twentieth century. The theoretical models, the ideological messages that guided its 'realization' and ways of life, the educational process in the school, as well as the literary and artistic creations of the Yishuv period – all embodied varied and original means of emulating and applying the patterns, contents, educational processes and movements of cultural creativity of Europe, expressed in the revived Hebrew language and against the background of layers of literary heritage and Jewish tradition, particularly the consciousness of Jewish history.

The transformation that was affected by the shift in the source of influence from Europe to the United States, against the background of the a-historic, a-social-ideological, and a-national 'postmodernism' that characterized the period following the Second World War was immediate and sweeping – albeit for nearly a generation Zionism remained the ideology that shaped the official identity of the State of Israel, and despite the fact that during that period it had actually changed from a controversial minority ideology to a general Jewish consensus.

Against the backdrop of the traumatic memories of the Holocaust, Zionism, as realized within the State, became the central symbol of Jewish unity and identity. It became the accepted ideology among all those Jews who related positively to their Jewishness, whoever they might have been and whatever might have been their relation to the culture of their people or its religion. One could therefore point with pride to the fact that, among all the ideologies that led mass movements in Europe between the two world wars, Zionism remained the only one that after the war demonstrated its correctness and its possibility of realization. On the other hand, immediately after the War of Independence there were also to be heard harsh statements to the effect that Zionism had 'gone into parentheses' – that is, that it had ceased to guide actual actions or to be realized in the individual way of life, and had instead become a kind of 'credo'.

After the creation of the State of Israel, Zionism in effect became the official ideology of the general state education system. From a concrete programme involving elements of settlement, the establishment of an ideal society, and the creation of Hebrew culture, Zionism became an ideological-emotional declaration of faith, realized through means of conscription into the compulsory state framework of Israel Defence Forces (IDF) service (including extended reserve duty), expression of solidarity with the Jewish people, the acceptance of emotional responsibility for the lot of the people after the Holocaust, loyal citizenship to the State and the country (that is, overcoming the temptations of emigration), and a sympathetic attitude to the social absorption of the aliya. There was thus a broad range of everyday social and cultural life that was left open for the absorption of new ideals deriving from that same source from which Israel derived its much-needed economic, political and defence support, and upon which it also drew the scientific education, technology, and expertise vital to its development and prosperity. There was, it is true, a certain delay in the process of absorbing the American sociological models and cultural ethos, due to the economic need of most of the Israeli population during the early years of the State and the socialist-centralized policy followed in confronting this need. However, from the beginning of the 1960s there began a gradual improvement and change in the socioeconomic policy, while the results of the Six Day War led to the breaking down of all barriers. The socialist policy withdrew, and together with it collapsed the institutions of its realization (the Histadrut) and the social frameworks which it had created (the collective settlement). In its place there was created the economic-social foundation required for the individualistic competitive ethos and other characteristics of American mass culture, and particularly of youth culture, involved in this ethos. In terms of the Jewish characteristic of Israeli culture, the value syndrome that developed against this background may be described as a type of assimilation that strives to obscure all unique characteristics of modern national identity, conveying legitimacy only to self-enclosed, sectarian religious units, which are limited to their compartment without influencing the cultural periphery within which they are mixed in an external and alienated manner.

In its most crystallized form, the result was fashioned, on both the theoretical and practical levels, in the realm of education. I would refer to three levels of messages: the message of the learned curriculum, the message of the instructional framework, and the direct ideological messages, both overt and covert, of the 'general school' system. The greatest change in the educational philosophy of the 'general state' school is expressed in its abdication of the functions of cultural-value socialization of its students – what is known as the 'passing down of heritage', in the sense of the creation of a cultural-historic perspective, the conveying of a feeling of belonging and rootedness of the individual in the culture of his origin: his family, his community and his people; and its encouraging of the formulation of an overall personal-social world view that presents the individual with binding and meaningful ideals of human life.

During the early years of education, in kindergarten and the lower elementary grades, such educational messages still stand out; however, as one approaches the high school years, these are gradually neglected and pushed to the margins. In their stead come messages of 'instruction' (not 'education'!), of 'knowledge' and 'expertise', whose main purpose is professional socialization within a broad range of detailed areas, acquired on the basis of individual choice, while diminishing the general, compulsory learning framework that is intended to pass on the heritage, to crystallize a value orientated world view, and to create a circle of cultural, identity-forming dialogue shared by all students.

The educational philosophy of the high school and university is thus primarily directed to 'preparation for life' in the narrow sense of professional socialization: individualistic, contemporary minded and pragmatic-functional. The main goal is to prepare students for the competitive race that awaits them in their adult life after their years of schooling, in accordance with their specific talents and choices, and of course within the framework of the expectations of the marketplace. This being so, greatest encouragement is given during the course of studies in school to the personal competitive motivation, rather than to that of solidarity and belonging: the entire system of educational tracking and of testing (particularly the baccalaureate exams, which symbolize the guiding myth and goals of education) is directed towards outstanding egoistic attainment. (In this it is diametrically opposed to the original humanistic sense of 'outstandingness', which demands prior commitment of the individual to the other and to the group, and the desire to excel in giving to them.)

Against such a background, it is self-evident that there inevitably emerges a serious problem in the realms of social 'values', of the consciousness of personal spiritual 'identity', and in that of orientation towards a life of meaning. It is true that this problem, known in professional jargon as 'the problem of education for values', is being sincerely confronted by the educational leadership. However, precisely that formulation, and the manner in which attempts are made to answer it, indicates the nature of those values: the school curriculum itself, and its manner of instruction, including the teaching of 'humanistic' and 'Judaic' subjects, are themselves understood as collections of information and as professional disciplines, rather than as identifying sources of value education that shape and fashion a world view. For that reason, the need is felt to add alongside them 'education for values', as yet another 'subject' with its own tools of instruction and specialized professional training for its teachers, as if 'values' were a kind of 'knowledge' or 'skill' like all the others. There likewise follows from this an institutionalized consensus: in order to develop 'education for values', one requires special systems, whether within or outside the school framework (generally speaking, outside the school framework, because the school curriculum already seems excessively full!), which need to be presented as a kind of informal, additional enrichment; in other words – study that does not demand any effort, but is absorbed pleasurably, like a kind of entertainment, and certainly not as something that requires exams and marks, like those other kinds of instructional matter that are taken 'seriously'.

The practical implication of this is that even the 'humanistic' and 'Judaic' subjects taught by the school, such as Bible, History, Hebrew language and literature, and even Oral Torah and Jewish thought, as well as the declarative messages of the school *vis-à-vis* identification with Zionism and the Jewish people, and the various additions of 'education for values' (for example, the values of proper behaviour and civic political values, such as 'education for democracy') are not perceived as being connected with the main function of the school, which is its instructional activity, and certainly have no connection with the motivations encouraged in order to strengthen the learning process.

There is thus no real connection between the messages of Zionism, Judaism, humanism and democracy, and the central instructional task of the school, which is in itself defined by and conveys messages of competitive achievement and the desire for private and present-orientated success and happiness. Any relation to the society and the people, to history and to cultural heritage, or to the vision of some historical future of the people and of mankind, are likewise exclusively understood from the utilitarian-functional viewpoint of the individual, and are therefore seen as at most of secondary importance.

Obviously, the issue of the 'Jewish identity' of the student of the general school also arises within the framework of 'education for values', at least in its political context. The leadership of the general educational system seems to have become concerned about it with a kind of compulsive cyclicity at least once every decade. One hears public criticism by spiritual leaders concerning the fact that the general school does not properly meet the Jewish and Zionist expectations that Israeli society wishes to convey to the younger generation to assure its ongoing identification with it. The claim is articulated that the degree of humanistic education, and particularly of Jewish education, received by the students in the school is too weak and that ignorance reigns. They complain that the identification of the students with the Jewish People and with Zionism is superficial, and in particular that it does not enable it to withstand the temptation of *yerida* (emigration from Israel), or that it is insufficient to create a basis for understanding with Jews of the Diaspora and with new immigrants. Nor does it provide youth with a sufficiently convincing answer to the existential questions: Why do I need to carry the burden of responsibility for the realization of Zionism, and particularly, why do I need to sacrifice precious years of my life in military service and to endanger my life for the sake of the People and the State, when the message of the school is consistently directed towards the ideal of individual 'self realization'?

The first 'cycle' of public confrontation with these questions occurred at the beginning of the 1960s at the initiative of Education Minister Zalman Aran. At the time, a programme was launched known as 'Jewish consciousness', whose success began and ended with a tempestuous public debate, hardly reaching the students in their classrooms at all. The Six Day War and the Yom Kippur War led to a spiritual crisis in Israeli culture, two of whose outstanding expressions were the movement of 'return' to religion (*hazara bi-tshuva*) and the 'quest for roots'. The Education Ministry responded to this challenge with extra-curricular programmes carried out in a network of special institutions – the 'Zionist Institutes', 'Gesher' and 'Shorashim'. But again the results were not satisfactory; at the beginning of the 1990s a new warning was issued concerning the widespread ignorance, superficiality of Zionist identification, and increased yerida among those born in the country and who had served in the IDF. A new public commission of inquiry, the 'Shenhar Commission', was appointed, which sat for three years until it proposed a programme for general reform in the teaching of Judaic and humanistic subjects, suitable to the 'general' non-religious public, under the title 'People and World' (*Am Ve-Olam*), based upon the perception of Judaism as an open humanistic culture.

In light of the regularity with which this problem resurfaces, it is difficult to deny the existence of a 'general' wish on the part of the 'general' public in the State of Israel to convey to its children messages of Jewish identity suitable to the cultural reality of our 'postmodern' age. It is nevertheless difficult to deny that most of the families belonging to the public that send their children to the 'general' school system do not wish or do not know how to do so themselves, within the framework of their familial and communal milieu. They expect the school to do it for them. But it turns out that neither does the general school wish, or know, how to do this with its own tools. The answer is that the school is unable to stand up to the pressure of its commitment to other educational and instructional messages, which reflect prior economic, social, security and political 'pressures'.

The educational system is thus hard pressed to find an educational substitute based upon a clear, pan-Jewish consensus acceptable to all that does not weigh down upon an already overloaded programme of study, but will work primarily on the emotional-existential level. An appropriate substitute is found in memories of the Holocaust and the establishment of the State and in the consciousness of a pan-Jewish 'covenant of destiny' which took shape within the people following the Second World War. The members of the generation who witnessed the Holocaust and were saved from it – the remnants of a genocidal act directed against the entire people, including future generations – and who then experienced the establishment of the State of Israel as a miracle of redemption, were united in accepting their identity as Jews against the background of the apocalyptic events which they saw with their own eyes and experienced upon their own flesh. It was incumbent upon them to rebuild the Jewish People and to protect it from the threat of a future Holocaust, whether this was one of physical or of spiritual destruction (that is, assimilation). The State of Israel is the fortress. The younger generations, against whom the Holocaust was also directed, are obligated to know and remember and take upon themselves the same oath and obligation towards their people and their state. This, then, was the answer found to the question 'Why be a Jew?', to the question 'Why live in the State of Israel?' and to the question 'Why serve in the IDF and absorb aliya?' Over and beyond teaching the cultural heritage of the people, and over and beyond systematic instruction in its textual sources and history, the educational system was called upon to give this inclusive and definitive answer. How so? By experiential, traumatic education in the apocalyptic, mythic memory that connected the Holocaust and the establishment of the State of Israel as a contemporary saga of exodus from enslavement to freedom and from subjugation to redemption. The teaching of the history of the Jewish People in the modern period focused primarily upon the Holocaust and upon Zionism, but emphasis was given to it by means of experiences and rituals: visits to Yad Va-shem, the visit to Auschwitz, participation in the March of the Living, and ceremonies for the Day of Remembrance for the Holocaust, Memorial Day for the Fallen of the IDF, Independence Day and Jerusalem Liberation Day. One should also emphasize in this context that literature, art, theatre and the communications media all contributed to underscore these messages to the general public, and particularly its young people.

This is not the appropriate forum in which to describe in detail the development in Israel and the Diaspora of the memorialization of the Holocaust and the establishment of the State, its institutionalization and transformation into the central ecumenical characteristic uniting the Jewish People in our time, leaving its impression upon all levels of Jewish cultural creativity – in literature, art, scholarship, theory, and religious and national ritual. In the context of this discussion, one may emphasize the centrality of the educational consideration involved in the crystallization of this memory as the primary message of identification with the Jewish People and with Judaism, passed down as a sacred 'oath' from parents to children in a chain of three generations. One should also note that this was a deliberate and planned development, intended to provide an answer to the danger of a 'holocaust of assimilation', of obscuration of the national cultural image and the loss of will to identify with the people, with Zionism, and with the state as a Jewish state.

The capture of Adolf Eichmann in 1960 and his bringing to trial in Israel was done with this intention. Indeed, the trial succeeded in raising the identifying and Jewishly-unifying message of the Holocaust to the level of national ecumenical consciousness. It gave the first push to the inculcation of the awareness of 'Holocaust and Rebirth' to all of the educational systems in Israel and the Diaspora; however, the process of crystallization and conveyance of this idea reached its full realization and acceptance in the Six Day War (also in the consciousness of the Western countries in relation to the Jewish People and Israel). It is easily demonstrated that, alongside the power of the actual experiences that caused the return of the memory and its impression upon the second and third generation after the Holocaust, a deliberate decision was made on the part of the political and educational elites to propose a convincing and unquestioned existential substitute for the messages of identity that had been conveyed in the past by systematic study and transmission of the shared tradition: study of the sources of Judaism, study of Jewish history, crystallization of a humanistic-Jewish and national-Zionist world view, and education for realization of Zionism in the project of settlement and in social ways of life. The instructional-spiritual training in the themes of 'Holocaust and Heroism' and 'Independence and Rebirth' came, therefore, as a substitute for, and not necessarily as a complement to, the earlier educational and tutorial messages.

The message conveyed by the religious school system is, of course, different, in that it stresses the transmission of the religious heritage as a central body of knowledge, as faith, and as a way of life, and imposes absolute commitment in its definitions of the religious and national-religious identity of the people. However, it is also worth emphasizing the following: with regard to all other areas of cultural creation, there is no difference between the State-religious and general educational streams in Israel. As a result, the teaching of religious values is seen in the State-religious schools as the only and exclusive message of cultural identity, because whatever does not come under the realm of religion is not seen as belonging within Judaism. This clearly demands a considerable degree of separation, in terms of outlook and in way of life, from non-religious, or even from non-Orthodox-religious, Jews. As a result, an unresolved tension exists in State-religious education between two opposing value orientations: one absolute in terms of Jewish identification, and the second relative but attractive in terms of appealing to the desire for personal success in the various realms of general cultural activity, understood, not as part of Jewish culture, but as a kind of external, 'neutral' area from the viewpoint of values.

The larger question pertaining to the overall Jewish image of Israeli culture is: What shared identifying cultural denominator is created between the students of the State-religious system and those of the general State schools? What unites them as members of a distinct culture? Do they have a common Jewish language? Do they have any unifying cultural contents, apart from the myth of Holocaust and the Rebirth, conscription to the Army and citizenship in the State? There is no convincing positive answer to these questions. The significance of this fact will be clarified further if we turn our attention to the ongoing debate in the State of Israel from the time of its founding until today surrounding the question of 'Jewish identity', in two areas: the Jewish identity of the State itself (especially in contrast to its identity as a democratic state), and the Jewish identity of the individual, namely, 'Who is and what is a Jew?' One might say that the polemic discussion in these two realms encompasses the programmatic thinking that has been created to date concerning the significance of Jewish culture in the State of Israel.

In the political and legal realms, the question of the Jewish identity of the State of Israel has been primarily discussed in the context of the status of established religion in a secular democracy, and the issue of the status of non-Orthodox Jewish religious movements in the State of Israel ('Jewish pluralism'). However, the level of personal and public concern and involvement displayed during the course of this stormy and prolonged debate changed it into a *Kulturkampf* that was well felt in the social milieu and in everyday life, and which in practice shaped the nature of Israeli-Jewish society. This polemic is in fact reflected on all levels of social-cultural creativity, including literature and art.

From the cultural and spiritual viewpoint, the subject of controversy is the degree and manner of the presence of traditional Jewish symbols in the Jewish 'public street' of the State of Israel, on the one hand, and the legitimacy of halachic norms shaping individual Jewish identity and the Jewish way of life in the family and the community, on the other. Due to Knesset legislation, the following cultural characteristics are to be found in the 'public domain' of Israel:

- Hebrew as the official national language, whose acquisition is the act of national-cultural absorption most emphatically demanded of new immigrants (on this point there is general consensus).
- Respect for the Hebrew calendar, its sabbaths, holidays and other dates, through their recognition as official days of rest and by refraining from

their profanation by state institutions, the Army, the municipalities and public corporations, as well as their commemoration in various other degrees and manners within the public street.
- Respect for the demands of kashrut by institutions of the state, the Army and the municipalities.
- Commitment of the state to providing religious needs in a manner stressing the presence of religious institutions and activity in the public realm – particularly synagogues, study houses and other institutions of religious instruction, which exert considerable effort to influence and to affect public life as much as possible.

By virtue of Knesset legislation, halachic norms shape the definition of individual Jewish identity, with regard to both acceptance, conversion and registration as Jews, and family laws pertaining to marriage and divorce. As a result of this legislation, for the majority of the Jewish residents of the State of Israel the ecumenical presence of symbols of Jewish identity and belonging is impressed upon the course of personal life. One should take particular note of the acceptance of central symbolic ceremonies expressing the belonging of the individual to the people: circumcision, bar/bat mitzvah, marriage, and burial and mourning. One might add to these other symbolic customs, such as the placing of a *mezuza* upon the doors of one's homes. All these together join into a cultural web that may be defined as a 'civic religion' or secular tradition.

The legally sanctioned presence of symbols of Jewish belonging in the public domain therefore penetrates into the private realm as well. It is that which shapes the symbolic status of the Orthodox-Zionist and Ultra-Orthodox (*haredi*) religious public, as that community that accepts upon itself the Halacha (Jewish religious law) to the full extent, and that provides necessary 'religious services' to the general public. One might say that Orthodox Jewry in all its streams (which is perceived by the non-Orthodox public as one Jewry) functions as a central symbol representing the Jewish identity of the people in its state, and it is this fact which causes 'Judaism' as a general concept to be understood even by the non-religious public as one whose significance is defined in terms of religion alone, rather than in those of general national culture. The almost inevitable result that follows from this is that, for the majority of the non-religious public, the personal relation to Judaism, and *ipso facto* one's self-definition as a Jew, are not felt as an expression of contents coming from within expressed in a spontaneous manner in everyday life, but as an external expression, emerging only at certain times, of a voluntary or coerced relating to certain cultural features fixed by the religious public. The secular Israeli adopts these for himself at the appropriate times in order to signify his belonging in principle to his public, which as such is Jewish, and to indicate his awareness of this. But to this end he requires the mediacy and help of 'professional Jews', without himself knowing the culture that they represent in a substantive way, nor himself participating therein in an active manner as an expression of his own feelings and thoughts.

This statement is a far-reaching one, which demands explanation. The fact that the ceremonies of 'civil religion' shape the course of personal life at the points of birth, maturity, establishing a family, giving birth to children, and the conclusion of life, indeed echo within the way of life of the family, and have a certain impact upon the everyday consciousness of belonging to a people and state. Moreover, together with the ceremonies of 'civic religion', non-religious Jewish family life typically draws upon further signs of tradition, particularly folkloristic elements and those of sabbaths and festivals, which in varying degrees become part of the cultural milieu. This is demonstrated in an extensive study recently conducted by the Guttman Institute and Keren Avihai. Moreover, that same study observes two additional phenomena characterizing the dynamics of the processes of Jewish cultural identification in Israel: the ceremonies of civic religion are increasingly understood as an external, coercive presence, which are at best conformed to without a feeling of being forced, but in many cases are complied to with open non-willingness and with a feeling of having no option and of rejection. In either event, for most of the non-religious public they are perceived as external rather than as an organic part of the continuity of the milieu of personal, family and communal life. Second, the choice of those signs that are willingly adopted to mark the milieu of the sabbath and festivals is largely performed in terms of their degree of suitability to a secular, present-orientated cultural milieu and way of life, bearing no relation to a tradition that is rooted in religion, but that does bear a certain positive-pleasurable relation to folklore. It is hence clear that the secular milieu created in this manner through the use of traditional 'materials' removes itself progressively from religious meanings, without even being aware of them. Moreover, it is incorporated within the contents and characteristics of a present-orientated mass folk culture which derives from external sources, and has almost completely lost its unique character.

The feeling of coercion, of rebellion against the imposed nature of religious symbols and norms, and in particular the growing feeling of the contradiction between the halachic norms imposed upon the 'general' public by means of the institutions of the Rabbinate, and the liberal-universal values and norms advocated by the secular public – all these sustain the stormy legal and political polemic which has, as mentioned, assumed the coloration of a 'cultural war'.

Thus far, acquiescence in religious norms as an obligatory imposition upon both the 'public street' and private life of the individual in Israel was bolstered by three factors:

- A sense of responsibility towards preserving the unity of the people, particularly so long as the feeling of a security threat against the State of

Israel originating in external enemies continued.
- Political considerations rooted in the party structure of the government of the State.
- The fact that most members of the first and second generations of those who immigrated after the establishment of the state remained traditional, even when they joined the 'general' (that is, non-religious) sector of the Jewish public, and hence related positively to at least some of the religious impositions and did not find it unduly difficult to make their peace with the rest, even accepting their importance for purposes of national unity.

During the past decade a dramatic change has been felt regarding at least two of these three factors. This is the result, first of all, of the passing of the generations – that is, the coming of age of a generation of young Israelis educated in the general school system, whose attitude to the contents of traditional Judaism differs substantially from that of its parents; secondly, the mass immigration from the states of the former Soviet Union, most of whom have neither knowledge of nor connection to Jewish contents of any sort; and, finally, the peace process, which has dispelled the sense of an external threat hanging over the State of Israel and the consequent feeling of an urgent existential need to assure pan-Jewish unity at any cost.

By contrast, a highly polarized debate has flared up concerning the issue of peace and the 'whole Land of Israel'. As this debate tends to overlap the confrontation between the religious-Zionist public and the secular public, the sense of a need for pan-Jewish agreement has become weakened. Likewise, the positive attitude towards tradition, rooted in previous education, has become weakened among most members of the second generation of immigrants from Eastern lands. There thus remains only the third factor, the political-partisan one. But in light of these other factors, it is only natural that its coercive nature would be seen as even more oppressive and, as it also seems unjustified from a democratic viewpoint, it too becomes intolerable. Protest and opposition in the name of democratic values and individual freedom have become stronger, while public support for 'religious legislation' is to be heard exclusively on the part of the religious public and an interested segment of the political leadership, but not on the part of the majority of spiritual leaders and non-religious educators.

Two facts illustrate the transformation that has taken place in the way of life and culture of Israel. First, despite the fact that 'religious legislation' remains as before ('status quo'), and has possibly become even wider, obedience to it is progressively weakening. The Jewish and Israeli 'public domain' have become more and more secularized and 'general', a feature felt particularly on the sabbath and festivals. Religious legislation has thus become an irksome legal fiction, generating dispute and conflict. Its psychological and sociological impact is tangible enough, but is largely negative in terms of the attitude of the 'general' public to Jewish symbols:

rather than eliciting identification and contributing to knowledge and understanding, it provokes a hostile attitude and elicits a debate almost entirely lacking in intellectual content, which tends to slide to verbal and physical violence.

Second, opposition to religious legislation has become a central tenet in the new ideology that has come to displace Zionism as the defining ideology of secular Israeli identity. Whereas Zionism was understood as a form of Jewish national identity, the new ideology styles itself as 'post-Zionist' – apathetic towards national and religious values as such, but intensely opposed to them as values meant to shape the image of the state, placing above them the values of democracy and freedom of the individual, his dignity and happiness, as universal values which are to shape, not only the government, but also the social and cultural ethos. Hence, this ideology is presented to the Israeli Jewish public, not only as an 'option' for a new cultural identity beyond Judaism and Zionism, but as an exclusive and all-encompassing form of identity staunchly opposed to the continued definition of Israel as a Jewish-Zionist State.

The demand for 'separation of religion from state' arose in the very earliest stages of the debate between the 'religious' and 'secularists', even before the establishment of the State (one must remember that Herzl's political vision included this demand as a prerequisite of the 'State of the Jews', even though as a practical statesman he himself laid the groundwork for the later compromise between religious and secular Zionism known as the status quo). But in the past this demand was raised as a legal and political limitation demanding satisfactory solutions to the issues of personal identity, conversion and family life, to which the non-religious public was particularly sensitive and to which religious Halacha did not give adequate consideration. The assumption was that it would be possible to find appropriate solutions to such problems without damaging the Jewish and Zionist identity of Israel *per se*, and without denying the status of the Jewish religion as an influential factor in society and culture.

For that reason, even those who sought changes in the Halacha did not describe the authoritative status granted to religious institutions in Israel in certain areas as expressing a substantive contradiction between 'Jewish identity' and 'democratic identity'. Such has not been the case in recent years. Today this confrontation evokes the claim that there is a substantive contradiction between the terms 'Jewish State' and 'democratic state' and that one needs to choose between them without compromise. Democracy is hence presented, not only as a form of government based upon the decisions of the majority and respect for the freedoms of all its citizens, but as a universal, all-embracing world view intended to shape all aspects of social and cultural life in the state. That is to say, it is also meant to serve as the universal identity of its citizens as individuals, whereas the 'particularistic' values and norms of religions, and of national and social movements, must be subordinated to the values of liberal democracy and to exist beneath them as private, partial relations. It is thus self-evident, according to this view, that the Jewish or Zionist component must be removed from Israeli identity. From now on, these values will be at best a particular, partial 'compartment' within the identity of those wishing it for themselves alone, but not for the whole.

We now turn to the confrontation on the second plane, that of personal identity, beginning with the debate surrounding the question 'Who is a Jew?' This question arose on the legal-political plane against the backdrop of the implementation of 'The Law of Return', which was unanimously accepted in the Knesset as an expression of Israel's Jewish-Zionist identity. However, the debate rapidly expanded to include the spiritual level along the axis of the question 'Who is a Jew?'

The reason for this expansion is self-evident: if the State accepts the ruling that individual Jewish identity is defined by Halacha and based upon religious authority, and not by secular national law and authority (notwithstanding the fact that the religious definition as such is ethnic and does not in substance contradict the national definition), it conveys to its citizens the clear message that Judaism as the contents of personal identity is defined as a religious world view and way of life rather than as a cultural-national one, and specifically in exclusive accord with Orthodox faith and Halacha. This results in a strange paradox: the Jewishness of the secularist, even if he is nationalist and Zionist, and even if he is traditional, is recognized both by the religious establishment and the State, not on the basis of his own criteria and his own cultural characteristics, but on the basis of criteria imposed by religious Jews with whose world view he disagrees and whose way of life he does not share. That is, by recognizing one's Jewish 'existence' (through birth to a Jewish mother), it is presented to the non-religious Jew as an existence that is empty of authentic Jewish contents, yet filled with contents that is not authentically Jewish, or not Jewish at all. The reaction is likely to be a double one: on the one hand, hostile alienation from religion, or externalization of Jewish identity as something that does not determine the form of Jewish identity of the non-religious Jew in his own eyes. On the other hand, there exists the strange phenomenon of Jews by 'identity' who are nevertheless not Jews in 'essence'. It is only natural for such Jews to be asked repeatedly – by religious Jews in tones of rebuke and accusation, and by themselves in confusion that becomes an angry challenge: 'In what sense are you Jewish?', or 'In what sense are we Jewish?'

The change from the reality that existed during the Yishuv is striking and of great significance. During the latter period, the Jewish national community which defined itself as 'secular' (*hiloni*) or as 'free-thinking' attributed importance to the religious definition of Judaism only in so far as one related to religious Jews as one's brothers and as members of his people, seeing them as Jews based upon his own nationalist criteria without any need to accept their specific definitions of Jewishness. In any event, it was one's own clear feeling that Jewish values, Jewish ways of life and Jewish cultural creativity consisted of all the values, folkways and creations of those people who were born as Jews, married as Jews in their own culture, and wished to live within their own Jewish national framework. Thus, whatever they did and created, including those elements that were borrowed from other cultures, was seen as their own 'Judaism', so that the critical attitude of religious people towards their Jewishness did not particularly impress them. On the contrary: they put forward a countercriticism, preferring their own Jewishness to any other kind of Judaism.

It seems reasonable to assume that, had a similar approach pertained to the Jewish public street in the State of Israel, the dichotomy between the 'Israeli' and the Jew within him, or between 'Israelis' as a group and 'religious Jews' as a group, would not have come about. Everything that the 'Israeli' created and made for himself and his society would have been considered by himself and those of his group as 'Jewish', while everything that the 'Jew' did for his own sake and that of his society would be considered 'Israeli' – and each one would have found their own way towards the sources and history of Jewishness. But once a reality was created in which 'Israeliness' came to be considered as something outside of Jewishness, while 'Jewishness' was viewed as being outside of Israeliness, this dichotomy became unavoidable for both 'religionists' and 'secularists' of various types. 'Israeliness' now became a thing unto itself, and 'Judaism' a thing unto itself. The two may indeed make peace with and complement one another (in the case of religious Zionists), or may exist parallel to one another as two adjacent compartments (in the case of national-Zionists or traditionalist-secularists), but they may also entirely contradict one another (as in the case of non-Zionist religionists or secularists holding a negative attitude to religion or to Zionism).

In terms of the sociology of culture, the significance of this phenomenon is that, instead of the syndrome characterized during the Yishuv period as a process of acculturation and cultural renaissance, the State of Israel witnessed the development of a syndrome that may best be described as, on the one hand, assimilation, and on the other, as a split between identity-preserving Jews and assimilating Israelis. Thus, in the State of Israel, created by the Zionist movement in order to serve as a dyke against assimilation, there has gradually come about a cultural syndrome of assimilation and schism comparable to that which developed in the Diaspora.

Regarding those Jews who assimilate to their Diaspora or Israeli culture, Jewish identity is understood, at best, as a marginal 'compartment' within a multi-storied culture and personality, most of whose compartments are non-Jewish but are rather anchored and domesticated to the surrounding cultural environment, Western or Eastern. Hence, they identify as Americans, Frenchmen, or ... Israelis, more than they do as Jews. In the less favourable case (from the viewpoint of Judaism), their Jewish identity is expressed in alienation from the form of external identity that other Jews attempt to impose upon them, which they reject with all their strength. They thereby remain Jewish in a certain sense, their rejection of Jewishness so as to abandon it itself being a form of involvement.

For those Jews who separate themselves from their environment and define themselves as Jews alone, Judaism is an absolutely obligatory cultural identity, albeit the range of its applicability is narrow, while their attitude towards the surrounding culture, whether 'goyish' or 'Israeli' (that is, 'goyish-Jewish') vacillates between openness to a beneficial external environment and withdrawal from one seen as threatening and dangerous.

In the middle, among the religious-Zionist, traditional and secular-national public, there still exist substantial bridging elites that wish the State of Israel to preserve both its Jewish and its democratic identity, its heritage and its relation to modernity, and who wish Israeli culture to renew the processes of adaptation and renaissance that created the Hebrew and Jewish-Zionist cultures within the Land of Israel. These elites wish to renew a multifaceted Israeli culture that conducts an ongoing creative dialogue within itself on the basis of traditional values and cultural language shared by all Jews in Israel and the Diaspora.

Is there any possibility for realizing such a vision? One cannot ignore the great difficulty: 'postmodern' Western culture, which developed following the Second World War (and is the source of 'post-Zionist' and 'post-Jewish' thinking in Israel), expresses a universal syndrome in modern Western culture, whose dominant cultural ideology is assimilation in the form of the 'global village'. The elites representing this tendency on the highest social levels in the West do not ascribe any importance to national and religious traditions, notwithstanding the fact that these traditions are once more struggling for their existence with great vitality on the folk levels of many countries, and even within Western culture. In any event, the academic elites, particularly the technocratic and communication elites, are abandoning these traditions and striding towards a vision of a cosmopolitan secular culture, which is always contemporary and always prepared for futuristic changes, and which inevitably transforms all forms of cultural identity into something transient, external and exchangeable. This 'postmodern' syndrome clearly negates the possibility of halting the process of sweeping assimilation, discernible today among Diaspora Jewry, as not only does this process not encounter the opposition of the environment, but even receives great encouragement from it. It is worth remembering in this context that the Jews of the Diaspora belong by and large to the middle and upper sociocultural classes in the West. Against this backdrop, it seems as if the only way for the Diaspora Jews to preserve their particularistic-partial identity is that of religious Orthodoxy. It alone is capable of creating a workable, effective and particularistic compartment, combined with effective cultural integration within the open secular environment.

By contrast, the Jewish State that preserves its national and cultural identity may provide effective protection against the sweep of an assimilating culture, thereby allowing a creative process of adaptation and revival of elements of its own heritage, dialogic pluralism and openness to the higher values of neighbouring cultures – both Western and Eastern. One must recognize, however, that this is no easy task. It requires 'swimming against the stream' of that which is fashionable and contemporary in the West, and socioeconomic inertia tends to lead to failure.

Thus, if the tendency to be swept along by the materialistic and individualistic-selfish values of the culture of a 'society of abundance' ceaselessly imported from the United States continues, and there is no reorientation in Israeli education in the direction of transmitting the cultural heritage and expression of our own cultural identity, this possibility will be nullified and the split between an encapsulated Orthodox Jewish religious culture and a secular Israeli culture alienated from its Jewish sources will become a conclusive fact.

Secular Judaism and Its Prospects

CHARLES S. LIEBMAN

I want to discuss a variety of meanings one can attribute to the term 'secular Judaism'. I then want to assess the prospects for the development and transmission of secular Judaism in Israel.

Two points merit mention by way of introduction. Much of what I have to say on this topic, indeed much of what I have to say about Judaism in Israel, is a commentary, an elaboration on, and an occasional demurral from, the work of Eliezer Schweid whose brilliant contribution to Jewish intellectual history evokes the work of Yehezkel Kaufman in his epic *Golah Ve-nechar* and in some ways surpasses him. I would be flattered were someone to describe me as a student of Schweid. My only excuse for writing anything at all on this topic is that Schweid and I often address different audiences and that we rely to some extent on different scholarly traditions: he on philosophical and historical-intellectual traditions, I on social science.

Secondly, my interest in the topic is a political one. My concern with secular Judaism stems from my hope that it is capable of generating a national vision with the capacity to animate Israeli society, at least its Jewish sector, and with a level of culture that ennobles its adherents.

I noticed a few years ago that important post-Zionist thinkers were ready to deny the existence of secular Judaism. Post-Zionists, I suspect, are quite content to concede Judaism to the religious since this facilitates the de-Judaization of the State of Israel. If Judaism is basically a 'religion' as Boaz Evron argues,[1] and as Baruch Kimmerling suggests,[2] if civil religion is indistinguishable from traditional religion as is suggested in Shmuel Hasfari's *Hametz* and the popular anti-religious play *Fleischer*,[3] then 'separating religion from State' means separating Judaism from the state. But the former objective has far greater appeal. One may argue

---

Charles S. Liebman is Professor of Political Studies at Bar-Ilan University.

over the meaning of 'separation of religion from State', but as a slogan it attracts support from a majority of Israelis. According to the comprehensive 1993 study by the Louis Guttman Institute, 54 per cent of Israeli Jews favour the separation of religion and state.[4] Post-Zionists and the religious establishment are joined in at least one ideological alliance; both deny or dismiss the positive features of secular Judaism and define it as no more than an ersatz watered down version of Judaism.

Attributing a political agenda to the analysis of secular Judaism is a double-edged sword. I have come to the conviction that the Jewish religion should be separated from the state, if only for its own sake. If that is to happen and Israel is to remain a Jewish State then the content and meaning of secular Judaism is a central order of concern. I do not intend discussing the Jewish parameters of such a state but only to note that to those like myself who believe that the Jewish people are entitled to a state of their own – that is, a state which reflects their ethnopolitical interests and their cultural heritage – it is necessary to establish that this cultural heritage, albeit transformed and transvalued to suit the needs of a contemporary society, is a meaningful category and refers to something more than a state of Jews. On the other hand, Jewish culture, even secular Jewish culture, can never mean the same thing as French culture or English culture, the culture of a national state, for the simple reason that Jews are not the only nation who reside in the territory of the state and Jews also reside outside the territorial state.

Given the importance of demonstrating the viability of secular Jewish culture, the obvious danger is that my own political agenda will dictate my analysis. The reader will have to judge the essay in this light.

THE COMPONENTS OF JUDAISM

I can only approach the question of the meaning of secular Judaism by trying to understand what is meant by Judaism. I believe that Judaism has three components: ethnic, cultural and religious. The components are of course interrelated, but for analytical purposes they are distinguishable. The ethnic component is the easiest to understand. It involves the special concerns and commitments that one Jew feels for another by virtue of the fact that the other is Jewish. The ethnic tie is a family-like tie based on the sense that Jews are, in some way, biologically tied to one another. The fact that the biological ties are mythical and that many Jews are aware of their mythic quality is irrelevant as long as they behave as though the myth expresses a reality.

The cultural component is the most difficult to understand because 'culture' or the 'concept of culture' is the most elusive. Most of us have a common sense notion of what culture means. We do not have a problem understanding one another when we use the term in every day discourse, even though the term is used in two different senses. We talk about culture in the sense of a cultured person; one who is cultivated, genteel, knowledgeable about matters of art, music, literature. Secondly, we talk about the cultures of various societies or various strata by which we mean something else. It is this 'something else' that we have so much difficulty in specifying even when we have a good enough idea about what it means. When Soviet ideological chief Mikhail Suslov declared that Jewish literary expression was no longer necessary since 'there was no point in reviving a dead culture',[5] the term 'culture' was clear. It is equally clear in the letter addressed to President Zalman Shazar by a group of Minsk Jews who explained their wish to live in Israel by 'the natural human desire ... to live in close contact with Jewish national culture and to acquaint one's children with this culture of which we are now deprived'.[6] The relative clarity of the term for purposes of discussion has not resolved the problem of formal definition. In fact, as I discovered to my chagrin, reading what has recently been written by sociologists and anthropologists on the topic (and these are the disciplines upon which I rely most heavily) is more confusing than helpful. And the more recent the literature, the more confusing it becomes. Hence, I was pleased to find a recent definition that relies heavily on the older literature and, unlike some current definitions, does not stray very far from our common sense notion of what culture means. According to Christopher Clausen:

> The word *culture*, when used anthropologically rather than honorifically, refers to the total way of life of a discrete society, its traditions, habits, beliefs and art – 'the systematic body of learned behavior which is transmitted from parents to children' as Margaret Mead summarized it in 1959.[7]

One must also add that the products of the culture which are part of the 'way of life' are symbolic as well as material. As an early textbook in sociology noted: culture is 'a system of socially acquired and socially transmitted standards of judgement, belief, and conduct, as well as the symbolic and material products of the resulting conventional patterns of behaviour'.[8] What this definition lacks, as I indicate at the conclusion of this essay, is a specific reference to the constraints that culture places upon the individual. But this need not bother us for purposes of the immediate discussion.

Given the definition of culture referred to above, one can discuss both Jewish culture and Jewish subcultures over time and over place. Culture is not static. It is both transformed and its symbols are transvalued. But what characterizes a living and self-conscious culture is that many of the changes it undergoes tend to be imposed backwards in time so that the thread of the culture remains identifiable. 'Tradition' is the culture of the past as it is interpreted in the present.

Ethnicity is an important focus of Judaic or Jewish culture. But it stretches the meaning of Jewish ethnicity, as I understand it, to simply subsume it under the rubric of Jewish culture rather than argue, as I do, that the categories are analytically distinguishable. One may find Jews, large numbers in the United States for example, who have a minimal association with Jewish culture but nevertheless retain strong ethnic ties. I cannot dismiss the argument that this is a sign that Jewish ethnicity is the lowest common denominator of Jewish culture and that what one finds, among such Jews, is an attenuated form of Jewish culture. One can argue that whereas ethnicity involves claims of common biological ties, and this distinguishes it quite clearly from culture, these ties are putative or mythical, derivative from cultural definitions. I recognize the thrust of such arguments but nevertheless find it more helpful to distinguish culture from ethnicity than collapse the latter category into the former. More important, for purposes of my argument, is to distinguish Jewish culture as an object of understanding – a Gentile may be more familiar with and knowledgeable about Jewish culture than a Jew – from participation in that culture. Culture is defined in terms of process, 'the total way of life of a discrete society', and in terms of its literary, musical, artistic product. The two, however, may be alienated from each other and I wish to argue that this is the present predicament of secular culture in Israel. In fact, part of the audience for secular Jewish culture in Israel may be Israelis who only participate in Jewish culture in the most marginal manner. On the other hand, there are Jews, in Israel for example, who know little about Jewish culture but whose judgement, beliefs and conduct are permeated by a Jewish way of life that is not necessarily religious.

This brings us to the third component of Judaism: the Jewish religion. I understand religion as a set of beliefs and rituals which relate the religious adherent to the transcendent, to God. In one respect, the distinction between religion and culture is entirely arbitrary. One can define religion as culture. Against this definition, one could argue that the thrust of contemporary Jewish culture has been the distinction between religion and secular culture.[9] The argument that the Jewish tradition, from its very outset, was 'a unique cultural-historical creation' rather than a 'tradition of Divine revelation in its traditional sense'[10] lay at the heart of the efforts to construct secular Jewish culture beginning in the early nineteenth century. And Reform Judaism, on the other hand, was born in an effort to affirm that Judaism constituted a religion, divorced not only from its national but from 'almost all its cultural components'.[11] But one might still argue that religion is culture and what the advocates of secular Jewish culture and Reform Judaism are really doing is defining the content of Jewish culture.

My reason for choosing to differentiate between religion and culture is because in one important respect 'religion as culture' only provides a partial understanding of religion. Viewing religion as culture is an observer's perspective, whether the observer is or is not an adherent of the religion. This view is helpful in describing and analysing religion from a distance. But phenomenologically, this is inadequate. We also need to view religion from the perspective of the religious adherent when he or she is, to use an awkward but telling phrase, 'doing religion'. When the religious adherent is performing a ritual in a self-conscious manner, or praying in a conscious rather than a routine manner, or undergoing a religious experience of one kind or another (and in the Jewish tradition none of this happens routinely and without some effort), then God becomes manifest to the adherent, and the process is so peculiarly religious that it is misleading to describe it as cultural.

THE MEANING OF SECULAR JUDAISM

Once we accept that the Jewish religion can be distinguished from Jewish culture and Jewish ethnicity, it is evident that secular Judaism is possible. It can mean a number of things. Let us look at each of them in turn.

Secular Judaism could mean ethnic and cultural Judaism without any form of religion, either religion as culture or 'doing religion'. This is theoretically possible but difficult to conceive in practice because the overlap between religion and culture in Judaism is so pronounced. To remove all the religious elements from Jewish culture would mean divorcing it from its own tradition. Culture, by its very definition, must be rooted in a past. To quote Schweid:

> The secret of the vitality of culture is its historical continuation and continuity. Culture develops in organic form from its sources, and the national self exists by preserving the continuity of secular national consciousness from generation to generation.[12]

Removing all traces of religion might leave one with a vestige of culture, though it is not clear at all that what was left would be recognizably Jewish. Perhaps this is what some people once meant by the term 'Hebrew culture', but it is difficult for me to conceive of any culture which is meaningful yet which is rooted entirely in the present. I suspect that this is what led the Canaanite movement to invent a mythic past for their Hebraic culture. There are limited circles of secular Jews in Israel who call themselves humanist and who seek ritual and ceremonial alternatives to the Jewish religion. Some of these 'humanists' seek to reinvest traditional Jewish symbols with secular humanist meaning (see below). This is an enterprise that Zionism has engaged in from its earliest years with varying degrees of success. But a few would abolish these symbols altogether.[13]

A more practical and in my opinion attractive definition of secular Judaism is one that retains the religious component but affirms religion as culture rather than religion which mandates a relationship to God. This is, it seems to me, the characteristic approach of the Jewish enlightenment and the non-religious movements that developed out of the enlightenment, including of course Zionism. In other words, secular

Judaism of this kind retains a religious component. It recognizes that religion constituted the major if not exclusive content of the Jewish culture of the past. The inability of the religious culture to provide a credible conceptual framework to explain the Jewish condition in eastern Europe and its consequent inability to mobilize effectively in defence of Jewish ethnic interests, served as a major impetus to the development of secular Judaism in its contemporary national form. Many efforts were made in the period of the Yishuv and the early years of the State to create a series of rituals and ceremonies that affirmed the Jewish religion by reinterpreting it in social and national terms. The most interesting efforts in this direction were made by various kibbutzim,[14] but all of this proved of limited success. Not surprisingly, this form of secular Judaism is all too ready to pay its respects to religion and finds itself hindered by the insistence of contemporary 'religious' Jews to define Judaism in exclusively religious terms and impose its definitions, in practice as well as in theory, on all other Jews.

There is a third mode of describing secular Judaism, one which can embrace the second definition but which lays stress on the popular aspect of culture; on the notion of culture as the total way of life of a society, its traditions, habits and beliefs. This is the culture that characterizes the vast majority of Israeli Jews, according to the recent study by the Louis Guttman Institute of the religious beliefs, attitudes and behaviour of Israeli Jews referred to above.[15] In a summary statement about the results of that survey, Elihu Katz, one of the study's co-authors, reaches four conclusions that are relevant for our purposes. The most observant Israeli Jews constitute 25 to 30 per cent of the sample. The vast majority of Israelis are not 'religious' in the conventional meaning of that term. But, first of all, Katz notes, they do observe many traditional *mitzvot*, and while their observance is partial and selective, it is not random, individual and unsystematic. Second, these observances are not without intent; they may lack 'proper' intent from a religious perspective but they are motivated by a conscious commitment to the continuity of the Jewish People. Third, those who observe these *mitzvot* are not without belief; indeed religious faith is widespread but, and here one finds the greatest evidence for a living form of secular Judaism, the majority of Israelis part company with observant Jews because, in their own minds, that which they do practice is not dictated by God; they are aware of their 'deviations', and are unperturbed by them.[16] In other words, contrary to what is sometimes said, most Israeli Jews observe the tradition in part but do not believe that their pattern stems from laziness, laxity or negligence. They are participating in a patterned form of observance which is not Halacha, but which they have transformed into the folkways of secular Judaism. Whether Israeli Jews can continue to sustain these folkways is another question. Whether they might evolve into patterns that are no longer distinctively Jewish is a question for the future.

At present, however, this form of secular Judaism is alive, though not entirely well. It tends to be overlooked or dismissed because we are looking elsewhere for signs of secular Judaism and we have preconceptions, based on the secular Hebrew culture of the Yishuv, about how it will look. Those who practice secular Judaism are not *halutzim* who plough the land with one hand while they hold a book in the other. They are certainly not the 'enlightened public' in whom Chief Justice Aharon Barak places so much authority. That 'enlightened public', which is in effect Israel's 'new class',[17] is quite alienated from any kind of Judaism though I am not prepared to give up hope for recovering its sympathies. The breeding grounds for Israeli secular Judaism is found among a population group that may be more familiar with *Adon Olam* than with Brenner. Their secularism is neither rebellious nor anti-religious.

THE PROSPECTS FOR SECULAR JUDAISM

My interest in secular Judaism, I stated at the outset, was in its capacity to generate a national vision, to serve as a major mode by which the cultural heritage of the past is transmitted to the present generation. My assumption has been that much of this is done through the medium of or the support of the state; through its public policies, its symbols and ceremonials, its national holidays, its educational system and the financial support and status it provides to cultural activity that accords with its goals. I believe that secular Judaism, its culture in particular, is in danger of being overwhelmed by both Jewishly religious culture (among a minority of Israeli Jews) and Jewishly neutral culture (among a majority). Ruth Gavison in a very important article makes a similar point:

> It is the opponents of *halacha*, committed to the idea of Israel as a Jewish nation-state, who must explain the particular content of Jewish nationalism. They are the ones who must transmit this answer to the new generation of Israelis who didn't arrive here by virtue of the 'Zionist revolution'; as a consequence of a deep existential struggle with their personal identity. If they don't have an answer, we can anticipate two possible developments: the vacuum will be filled with Jewish religious content, with all its separatist principles, or all Israeli-Jews will be a people who speak Hebrew (and among some of them their Hebrew is poor and defective), but lacking any special orientation to the national Jewish culture.[18]

I have little confidence in the ability of secular Judaism to compete, at least at the present, in the open marketplace unless answers are forthcoming and steps are taken to strengthen it.

I have already suggested that if secular Judaism is understood as Judaism less its religious component, it is left virtually bereft of culture.

All that remains is the ethnic component. In the unlikely case that Jewish ethnicity could be sustained in the contemporary world without religion or culture, it would likely degenerate into some form of racism. I may be fooling myself, but I would like to believe that at least some supporters of Beitar Yerushalayim who shout 'death to the Arabs' when Beitar plays the Arab team from Taybeh are ethnic Jews bereft of Jewish culture. My fear, reinforced by the 1994 Carmel Institute study of high school youth,[19] is that most are part of that majority of the culturally traditional albeit non-religious Israelis to whom the Guttman study refers. If that is correct it reinforces my fears about the gap between the artists and intellectuals who produce Jewish culture and the human products of that culture.

The second definition of secular Judaism involved a recognition of religion's formative role in Jewish culture but a rejection of religion's significance to the individual; religion as culture without 'doing religion'. Religion is acknowledged as a critical force in shaping the Jewish culture of the past. We recognize the Jewish religion, religious symbols and religious artefacts, even many religious values as part of our heritage, and we assimilate them into our culture including our political culture. This does not mean that we accept the religious mandates or injunctions or beliefs as compelling in our own lives. And because we are not ourselves 'religious', we transform and secularize religious symbols, artefacts and values. In many respects, this is an ideal form of secular Judaism. For those anxious to preserve a Jewish state without the burden of religious coercion and with a democratic form of government, this would seem to be a perfect solution. In some respects it describes our present society, but in other respects it is misleading because this is not the direction in which Israeli society is headed.

The civil religion of Israel which Don-Yehiya and I describe in our own study fits this description.[20] Religious symbols are utilized in the construction of a system of myths and rituals that serve to legitimate the social order and integrate and mobilize the Jewish population, though the religious symbols themselves undergo transformation and transvaluation and God plays no role in this quasi-religion. Civil religion may not have satisfied the spiritual needs of the individual in the quest to find meaning in one's personal life. On the other hand, those individuals whose personal identity was merged into the collective national identity also found personal satisfaction in the civil religion.

At the conclusion of our study, published in 1983, in the wake of the War in Lebanon, Don-Yehiya and I suggested our own reservations about the level of commitment that the civil religion was capable of evoking. Our reservations of the past are certitudes of today. In the absence of survey research data, the evidence for the decline is admittedly partial and impressionistic. But it cannot be overlooked. For example, the Israeli media have provided extensive publicity in the last few years to studies that question the stature, heroism and motivation of Israel's founders and early pre-state heroes. Television dramas have been produced and shown in the same sceptical vein. These studies may have occasioned some dissent; but their publication in the press and their airing on public TV suggests that Israeli society is far less appreciative today than it once was of civil religion's mythical heroes.[21]

An excellent example of the decline of Israeli civil religion is the recent theatre production of the play *Hametz* by the popular Israeli playwright Shmuel Hasfari. The play, at least on the evening I saw it, was warmly received and to the best of my knowledge it has not been condemned in the media. In fact, it was awarded the Israeli theatre's most prestigious prize for the best Israeli play of 1995. Its theme is that Israeli society ought to forget its past, ignore its ostensible heroes, forget even the Holocaust and the six million who died, and live as a normal society with no special attachments to anything that is peculiarly Jewish.

Israel's willingness to enter into a peace agreement with the Palestinians is attributable at least in part to recognition by the political and military elite that Israel has already been overtaken by the demand for individual autonomy and material comfort – a demand that erodes if not shatters any ideological or symbolic system which provides a communitarian society with meaning. As the Israeli army's Chief of Staff Amnon Shahak noted, commenting on the apparent rise in the number of young Israelis who consider military service 'inappropriate': 'The problem is a preference for individualism over the collective in an age of liberalism'.[22] Minister of Defence Yitzhak Mordecai is quoted as expressing concern with 'the lowered motivation of youth to serve in combat units in the IDF'.[23] Efraim Inbar of Bar-Ilan University describes this continued decline in the percentage of Israeli youth who volunteer for combat units and observes that Israeli leaders realize that their society 'displays signs of fatigue and is more reluctant to pay the price for the protracted conflict with the Arabs'.[24] He notes that former army chief-of-staff Ehud Barak:

> often expressed concern about Israel's social fiber. For example, he described the changes in Israeli society: '... accumulated weariness and cynicism, accompanied by an aggressive and intrusive media, depreciation of the Zionist deeds, the development of a cleavage in the consensus over Israel's political goals, even over the use of force (we have seen it in Lebanon and in the Intifada) – all these create a perception as well as a reality of weakness'.[25]

Sharper tones are present in a more recent article by *Ha-aretz* columnist and television host Dan Margalit, who characteristically phrases himself with care and balance. According to Margalit, there is more than one reason for the reduced motivation among Israeli youth to enlist in combat units:

> Israeli society has become materialistic and consumer oriented. Some of the parents and the media have projected self-fulfillment

and the good of the individual as prior to any public commitment. Zionism has been pushed behind the word 'post', Judaism has assumed an ultra-Orthodox coloration ...[26]

Other signs of the decline of civil religion include the transformation of civil religious celebrations into private events. A good example is the decline of Independence Day as a major national holiday, and the transfer of celebrations from massive events to more intimate family barbecues in public parks.[27]

One way of viewing the decline of civil religion is in its inability to evoke commitment to the Israeli or Jewish collective and to mobilize the population, at least the Jewish segment of the population for social goals. But since our particular concern is with the assimilation of Jewish values into the civil religion – that is, into the political culture – the recent concern over the issue of Judaism and democracy is of special relevance. The notion of a virtually irreconcilable conflict between Judaism and democracy is taken for granted in most of the debate on the topic despite the fact that according to some outstanding scholars this dichotomy is hardly as sharp as the protagonists in the debate suggest.[28] I am not concerned with the issue of who is right and who is wrong. My own opinion is that whereas one finds major themes within the religious tradition that are inimical to democracy, there are minor themes and minority opinions in the sacred texts themselves that affirm almost all the major values of liberal democracy.[29] What is remarkable, therefore, is that the intellectual, political, and cultural elite in Israeli society has ignored rather than sought to transform these elements of the Jewish religion into normative values. Much in the religion was transformed: for example, religious holidays celebrating man's relationship to God were transformed into national holidays celebrating the achievements of 'the nation'. Hence, the failure to adapt the liberal elements within the religious tradition into contemporary Judaism is of significance.

The answer as to why this has not occurred is, in my opinion, a matter of timing. My guess is that had the issue of Judaism and democracy arisen forty years ago, at least one segment of the country's elite, that identified with MAPAI rather than with MAPAM, would have argued forcefully that Judaism and Jewish values were entirely consistent with those of a democratic society. They would not only have cited traditional text but the conduct of the east European Jewish community. I do not think that the religious Zionist elite would have challenged them on this score. But had they done so, the secular elite would have been relatively untroubled because of their own sense that the cultural tradition, as distinct from halachic norms, was as much theirs to interpret as it was that of the religious public; that what they felt in their hearts was of necessity the strains and echoes of the authentic tradition. The story of the argument between David Ben-Gurion and the first Minister of Religion, Yehudah Leib Maimon (Fishman), is instructive in this regard. When Ben-Gurion refused Maimon's demand that government offices be closed on the fast of Esther and Maimon challenged Ben-Gurion on his basis for refusing the demand, the Prime Minister noted that he was as familiar with what went on in the traditional Jewish towns of eastern Europe as was Maimon. Today this kind of Jewish self-assurance is entirely lacking among secular political leaders, not to mention the cultural elite. Their tendency is to defer to the religious elite in terms of what Judaism means. Indeed, much of the cultural elite are happy to defer to the religious elite since it facilitates the construction of polar models for a society; Jewish as opposed to democratic.

The decline not only of civil religion but of national commitment is well reflected in an article by Gideon Samet in *Ha-aretz*. His column reflects what I consider to be a major if not a dominant motif in contemporary Israeli society. According to Samet:

> For some time now, commentators on identity put their finger on our [growing] normalization. They noted the growing tendency to move from nationalist slogans to simple individualism. ... the lust for life.
>
> ... Madonna and Big Mac are only the outer periphery of a far-reaching process whose basis is not American influence but a growing tendency throughout the west, especially among young people. It is a mistake to attribute this to the product of a foreign identity.
>
> On the contrary, the new language is comprised of new forms of cultural consumption and leisure activity that have become supra-national. So it is with popular music, movies, trips abroad, dress and even the style of speech.[30]

Samet's article puts its finger on the problem of secular Judaism. Secular Judaism faces competition on two fronts. One is on the religious front; a point to which I will return. But its more immediate problem at present is that it is also in competition with modern or postmodern western culture. As Schweid points out, the goal of those who created modern secular Jewish culture, especially that which he refers to as Hebrew culture, was to retain an historical continuity with the Jewish past while transforming the cultural identity of the new Jew into modern European forms. I believe as an observer that one, two and even three generations back could have felt assured that secular Judaism was successful in absorbing both traditional Jewish forms as well as modern European forms into an indigenous culture. By culture, I remind you, I refer not only to literature and art and the symbolic productions of culture but to the total way of life of a discrete society, its traditions, habits and beliefs. There is reason to doubt this today. We have not absorbed or assimilated these cultures as much as subjected ourselves to them. As Samet, correctly in my opinion, points out, the dominant culture of many Israeli Jews is not secular Judaism but the kind of hybrid postmodern culture common to all the West with which he feels so comfortable.

This statement raises a number of questions. First, am I not underestimating the power of language in guaranteeing the survival of an independent Jewish culture. Indeed, it is Schweid himself, generally a voice of gloom, who attributes major importance to language as the primary instrument in the creation and preservation of a distinct culture. Much of the concluding section of his study of Jewish culture is a paean of praise to the accomplishments of the Zionists in their revival-transformation of Jewish culture through the medium of Hebrew. Second, if Samet is correct, how does one account for the results of the Guttman study reported above?

With regard to language, I do not find Schweid's analysis entirely persuasive. I certainly reject the notion that anything produced in Hebrew is *ipso facto* a product of Jewish culture. Secondly, were I to concede Schweid's point about the early importance of the Hebrew language in forging a new Jewish culture, his cultural analysis of the past strengthens the importance of the new wave of 'street literature', an attempt to flatten the language in Israeli literature, rid it of all biblical, liturgical or rabbinic allusion.[31] This linguistic post-Zionism, emptying the Hebrew language of its cultural baggage, as Rochelle Furstenberg points out,[32] reflects a major change in contemporary Israeli culture, a point that Yosef Dan made a few years ago in an article in *Ha-aretz*.[33]

But what about evidence from the Guttman Institute survey of Israeli Jews which seems to demonstrate the continuing vitality of secular Jewish culture at the popular level? And there is additional evidence in this regard. The 1994 survey of high school youth conducted by the Carmel Institute asked Israeli Jewish youth if they felt more Israeli or more Jewish. Fifty-one per cent said they felt equally Israeli and Jewish. Twenty nine per cent said they felt more Jewish, whereas 20 per cent said they felt more Israeli.[34] Indeed, the Carmel Institute finds that Jewish identity is about the same as it was in a comparable study conducted in 1984.[35] Furthermore, whatever one may say about the values of Israeli youth in general, the Carmel study finds that they have remained fairly constant compared to those reported in a 1988 study. Similar results were obtained in Guttman Institute studies from 1974 and 1976. So the question about the prospects of secular Judaism remains open. There is evidence for the forceful presence of Jewish culture in Israeli society and contradictory evidence of its gradual diminution. The argument also depends, to some extent, on the kind of evidence one accepts as authoritative. But it is no less important to appreciate that the vast majority of Israelis live with conflicting value systems. The powerful and pervasive nature of the secular, individualistic, consumption orientated values in western society suggests that almost all Israelis, including many of the more observant, will have internalized some of them to some degree. So the set of values which provide an alternative to the tradition are certainly present. The mistake is to believe that they have entirely replaced more traditional Jewish values.

The Guttman Report demonstrates that whereas less than a quarter, and perhaps only a fifth, of Israeli Jews are 'religious', close to four-fifths testify to their observing at least some aspects of the Jewish tradition. Even among the remaining fifth, among those who identify themselves as 'totally non-observant', a majority are at least partially observant. For example, only 6 per cent of the total sample report that they seldom or never participate in a Passover *seder* and 12 per cent that they seldom or never light Hannuka candles. Israelis score quite high on measures of observance. But two caveats must be added. The first is that the non-observant are the best educated and overwhelmingly Ashkenazi. Independent evidence, on the other hand, suggests that the commitment to traditional Jewish practice among Sephardim is declining much more rapidly than it is among Ashkenazim.[36] The non-observant, although constituting a distinct minority of Israeli Jews, probably constitute a large section if not a majority of its academic, intellectual and cultural elite and are firmly ensconced in the media as well.

Secondly, we do not know what difference this orientation to tradition makes in the lives of most Israeli Jews. We have a vast literature on visiting the tombs of holy men. But in general, we do not have studies of how Israeli Jews in general, and the non-religious in particular, celebrate *britot*, *bar* or *bat-mitzvot*, birthdays and weddings, Jewish holidays, national holidays, or non-Jewish holidays such as Christmas and the secular New Year. We do have some limited material on funerals and private memorials but it is insufficient.[37] Such studies need to inform us of similarities and differences by *edah*, by age group, by education, by level of observance, and by generation in Israel. Only then can we pretend to know the manner in which the Jewish heritage is or is not integrated into contemporary Israeli culture. Of course, many matters would still be subject to individual judgement. In August 1996, Aviv Gefen was married in a wedding ceremony which the Israeli media covered in as much detail as they could. I have trouble interpreting the significance of that event. Is the fact that Aviv Gefen got married at all significant? Is the fact that he was married in a Jewish wedding significant? Is the fact that his marriage was Conservative rather than Orthodox significant or is it significant that he chose to have a Conservative wedding which is closer to the tradition rather than a Reform wedding?

We may have overestimated the level of integration of the Jewish tradition in Israeli culture. It is commonplace to observe that virtually all Israelis celebrate the *seder*. The Guttman Report findings confirms this. But we know very little about how the *seder* is celebrated. There is firm evidence that the traditional *haggada* rather than the innovative *haggadot* that characterized kibbutz *seders* from thirty to sixty years ago are used.

But we do not know what role this plays in the *seder*. Shlomo Deshen, in a forthcoming paper based on reports from his own students at Tel-Aviv University, notes that reading the *haggada* is accompanied by disparaging remarks, sometimes of a lewd nature, about the text.[38] Tel-Aviv University students are hardly a cross-section of Israeli society but one has the feeling that at least among a substantial proportion of Ashkenazi Jews, the rituals and ceremonials that are observed are becoming increasingly emptied of significance. But we really do not know enough, as Deshen points out. This is an area that strikes me as critical to understanding Israeli culture, and Israeli sociologists and anthropologists would do well to explore it.

In fact, we may have underestimated the impact of the tradition on contemporary Jewish culture. The 1996 election results are one indication. The overwhelming majority that the religious and right wing parties obtained among the Jewish electorate is attributable in no small measure to the fears of many Israeli Jews that the continuation of a MERETZ–Labour coalition threatened Jewish culture and Jewish values as they are presently expressed in the policies of the state. (Whether these fears were well founded is immaterial to my argument.)

Even the dark side has its bright counterpart. The Shenhar Commission appointed by the Minister of Education in 1991 to examine the teaching of Judaism in the non-religious school system found that the curriculum materials, the training of the teachers, and the number of hours devoted to Jewish subjects was totally inadequate. In other words, the most forceful socializing agency that the state has at its disposal, the educational system, was not being utilized to support Jewish culture. This leaves hope that educational changes can improve the present situation. Had the Shenhar Commission been satisfied with the teaching of Judaic subjects in the school system, my concern about the prospects for secular Judaism would have been far greater.

The Holocaust, Israel–Diaspora relations, the welfare of Jews throughout the world, Jerusalem, a measure of Israeli nationalism, participation in Jewish ritual, affirmation of basic Jewish beliefs, but above all else, a powerful sense of family ties animate Israeli Jews. Indeed, family ties may provide the most important integrating force in Israeli society. The frequent references to Rabin as a 'father' which one heard from Israeli youth following his assassination are significant in this regard. They seem rather tame in contrast to the values of self-sacrifice for the sake of the collectivity, communalism and mutual assistance, and above all the value of physical labour, values that Schweid characterizes as central to the Hebrew culture of the early Zionists. On the other hand, the present set of values do seem better suited to a modern nation. But except for the value of family ties, little of this is reflected in the Israeli media and least of all Israeli theatre. The Jewish-national values that Israelis share, at admittedly varying levels of commitment, are not reflected in the products of Israel's cultural and intellectual elite.

There may be a significant gap between the cultural expression of Israeli life in its music, art and theatre and the level of Jewish concern and commitment found amongst the vast majority of Israelis. I would describe the orientations of the academic, intellectual and cultural elite of Israeli Jews in much the same manner that the late Christopher Lasch describes its American counterparts.[39] Members of the elite, he says, have mounted a crusade 'to extend the range of personal choice in matters where most people feel the need for solid moral guidelines'.[40] The majority of society appears:

> to the makers of educated opinion [as] hopelessly dowdy, unfashionable, and provincial. They are at once absurd and vaguely menacing – not because they wish to overthrow the old order but precisely because their defense of it appears so deeply irrational that it expresses itself, at the higher reaches of its intensity, in fanatical religiosity, in a repressive sexuality that occasionally erupts into violence against women and gays, and in a patriotism that supports imperialist wars and a national ethic of aggressive masculinity. Simultaneously arrogant and insecure, the new elites regard the masses with mingled scorn and apprehension.[41]

It remains to be seen whether this putative gap between Israel's cultural elite and the majority of its citizens can be overcome, and if so in what way. Will the majority of Israeli Jews assimilate the values of its cultural elite, or will the cultural elite find a way to accommodate the Jewish orientations of the masses? In the latter case, perhaps through some combination of an emerging new elite and a change of heart among the present elite, secular Jewish culture may yet flourish in Israel.

This leaves open the question of the level at which secular Judaism is integrated into one's life. For some it is likely to remain a public or collective expression. They may seek spiritual meaning and fulfilment outside the realm of Jewish culture. Others will find aspects of secular Judaism satisfying at a more existential and spiritual level. Many, perhaps a majority, of Israelis do so today.

CONCLUSION

There can be no secular Judaism which is not anchored in the Jewish tradition and there is no Jewish tradition that denies its religious roots. Under these assumptions, what are the prospects for secular Judaism in Israel? The verdict is not yet in. The evidence is mixed. Among the Israeli elite the impression I get is one of a growing ignorance of and indifference towards the Jewish tradition. It is easy to blame the religious establishment itself for this state of affairs. It is easy to argue that the religious elite has appropriated Judaism for itself, interpreting the traditional text and traditional values in a xenophobic, particularist, sexist manner. It has overlooked or rejected values within the Jewish tradition that could have been beacons of visions and moral behaviour for all Israelis. Instead, it has tolerated behaviour that can only be characterized, to use its own frame of reference, as 'a desecration of God's name'. But even if the religious house of Israel is morally rotten this is not enough to explain the feeble character of secular Judaism. It is too easy to blame the religious or the secular politicians as the late Yonathan Shapiro did.[42] This does not answer why the secularists surrendered so easily in the battle over defining the nature of Judaism.

The answer is obvious. Secular Judaism, unlike religion, does not generate the commitment, the passion, the confidence, that religion generates in the hearts of its adherents. Not enough is at stake in the personal lives of secular Jews to activate them in conflicts over the nature of Judaism. And while we might all agree that a great deal is at stake at the public level – indeed the very future of Israel as a Jewish state may be at stake – ideological concerns no longer generate the efforts they once did. The passivity of secular Jews with regard to public issues renders them helpless in the face of the active religious public on the one hand and the assimilatory pressures of a global postmodern culture on the other.

Yet there is a communitarian spirit among Israeli Jews that is probably stronger than the communitarianism that exists in any western democracy. Israel is a small country, which means that friendship or at least acquaintance circles engulf a large proportion of the society. Were we able to list all the acquaintances of Israeli Jews, and then list all the acquaintances of the second group, we would probably find that most Israeli Jews are no more than one step or at most two steps removed from knowing every other Israeli Jew. In this respect Israeli Jews are like Orthodox Jews all over the world. Secondly, Hebrew as a first language is virtually peculiar to Israeli Jews. Acquaintance circles and language peculiarity mean that Israelis, for all that they travel and for all their exposure to the international media, are considerably more comfortable in one another's presence. It is difficult to document my own conviction that Israelis, more than any other people that I know, seek one another's company, feel peculiarly comfortable in one another's presence, and exhibit a sense of responsibility to members of their own group. This responsibility no longer extends to the state, not even to the civil society. This too is a form of Jewish culture. It is hardly a high culture. But it does form the basis and foundation upon which a more ennobling Jewish culture can be built.

The development of such a culture, however, at least at present, needs the religious as well. A.B. Yehoshua talks about the need that the secular have for the religious because of the latter's access to traditional text which forms the basis of Jewish culture.[43] Amos Oz states that he prefers a spiritual alliance with religious Zionism rather than a political alliance with the 'hellenizing' left.[44] David Grossman talks about the 'sense of mission and social commitment' of the national religious, to the great importance they accord education, 'the vitality of learning in the yeshivot ... the ability for debate and complex dialectic analysis; and to the intellectual attraction of abstract thought'.[45] The reason why I believe that secular Judaism needs an alliance with the religious is that secular Jews alone do not have the will or the self-discipline that affirming a culture of responsibility and loyalty requires.

Admittedly, the prospects for secular Judaism appear problematical. But secular Judaism does exist in Israel. Part of the reason it appears so feeble is that we may have been looking for it in the wrong places. We associate secular Judaism with 'Hebrew culture', the new Jew as opposed to the 'galut Jew', with *halutziut* and with the kibbutz, and with values that conform to the noblest of western civilization. Instead, our search may lead us to the masses of Israeli Jews, *edot ha-mizrach* in particular, so many of whom are the carriers of superstitious beliefs and xenophobic attitudes. But are these my people? Unless the artisans of culture recognize them as such, unless they try to learn the sources of their attitudes and convictions, and unless they try to convey to them the sources of their conviction, the alienation between those who are the products of secular Jewish culture and those who produce secular Jewish culture will only continue to grow.

I would be pleased if the masses of Israeli Jews internalized at least some of the values associated with that which was once called 'Hebrew culture', and I certainly believe that this is a major task of our educational institutions and of the cultural elite. But this can only be done by institutions and by people who accept the Jewish tradition and the Jewish past as a starting point in their effort.

Finally, let us consider the non-religious alternative to secular Judaism more seriously. We have defined culture as the total way of life of a society, its traditions, habits and belief. We have suggested that the major alternative to Jewish culture is a de-judaized Israeli culture which absorbs the values of modern western culture with its emphasis on individual autonomy, personalism and universalism and thereby undermines Judaism as a religion and as a national culture. But perhaps we have exaggerated the force of modern western culture because we have misunderstood the nature of culture. Christopher Lasch, relying on Philip Rieff, maintains that at the heart of any culture lie *interdictions*. Quoting Rieff he says that:

> Culture is a set of moral demands – 'deeply graven interdicts, etched in superior and trustworthy characters'. This is why it makes sense to describe the United States today as a 'cultureless society'. It is a society in which nothing is sacred and therefore, nothing is forbidden. An anthropologist might object that a cultureless society is a contradiction in terms, but Rieff objects to the way in which social scientists have reduced the concept of culture to a 'way of life'. According to Rieff, culture is a way of life backed up by the will to

condemn and punish those who defy its commandments. A 'way of life' is not enough. A people's way of life has to be embedded in 'sacred order' – that is, in a conception of the universe, ultimately a religious conception, that tells us 'what is not to be done'.[46]

As Lasch notes, whereas this definition of culture results in a sweeping condemnation of what he calls the American way of life and we call western culture, it also contains a ray of hope. Because:

> if culture rests on willingness to forbid, a 'remissive' culture like our own cannot be expected to survive indefinitely. Sooner or later our remissive elites will have to rediscover the principle of limitation. The modern project may have run its course. The 'idea that men need not submit to any power ... other than their own' is by no means discredited, but it is losing its capacity to inspire heady visions of progress.[47]

The great advantage of living in Israel is that, unlike the *golah*, the opportunity for the recovery of the tradition and of secular Judaism is always close at hand. The literature and the essays of those who forged modern secular Judaism, and the scholarship of those who found its echoes in the distant past, may not resonate as strongly as they once did, but they are accessible to the Israeli public. We must find a way of linking this kind of cultural product to the concerns and interests of the mass of Israelis who need to become more self-conscious about the nature and meaning of their own Jewish concerns.

NOTES

This is a revised version of an article that appeared in Hebrew in *Alpayim*, No.14 (1997), pp.97–116.

1. Boaz Evron, *Jewish State or Israeli Nation?*, trans. with a foreword by James Diamond, (Bloomington, 1995).
2. According to Kimmerling, 'There are secular Jews in the world and in Israel, but there is grave doubt if there is such a thing as secular Judaism'. Baruch Kimmerling, 'Religion, Nationalism and Democracy in Israel', *Zmanim*, Nos. 50–1 (Winter 1994), p. 129.
3. Dan Urian, 'The Stereotype of the Religious Jew in Israeli Theater', *Assaph*, No. 10 (1994), p. 150, notes that within the play, 'many references equate the "Zionist civil religion" with the Jewish tradition'.
4. Shlomit Levy, Hanna Levinsohn and Elihu Katz, *Beliefs, Observances and Social Interaction among Israeli Jews* (Jerusalem: The Louis Guttman Israel Institute of Applied Social Research, 1993). For further elaboration of the meaning of this statement see Ch. five of Charles S. Liebman and Elihu Katz (eds), *The Jewishness of Israelis: Responses to the Guttman Report* (Albany, 1997).
5. Bernard Wasserstein, *Vanishing Diaspora: The Jews in Europe since 1945* (Cambridge MA, 1996), p. 184.
6. Ibid., p. 190.
7. Christopher Clausen, 'Welcome to Post-Culturalism', *American Scholar*, 65 (Summer, 1996), p. 380.
8. G.A. Lundberg, C.C. Schrag and O.N. Larsen, *Sociology* (New York, 1963), p. 761,

cited in William R. Catton, Jr, 'The Development of Sociological Thought', in Robert Faris (ed.), *Handbook of Modern Sociology* (Chicago, 1964), p. 946.
9. Eliezer Schweid, *The Idea of Judaism as a Culture* (Tel-Aviv, 1995).
10. Ibid., p. 63.
11. Ibid., p. 111.
12. Ibid., p. 174.
13. These efforts and their differences of opinion are recorded on the pages of the journal *Yahadut Hofshit* (Free Judaism), a publication of the Secular Israeli Movement for a Humanist Judaism (Tnuah Hilonit Israelit Le-yahadut Humanistit).
14. Shalom Lilker, *Kibbutz Judaism: A New Tradition in the Making* (New York, 1982).
15. Levy, Levinsohn and Katz, *Beliefs, Observances and Social Interaction*.
16. Elihu Katz, 'Behavioral and Phenomenological Jewishness', in Liebman and Katz (eds), *The Jewishness of Israelis*.
17. For an illuminating discussion of this point see Ronen Shamir, 'Society, Judaism and Democratic Fundamentalism: On the Social Sources of Judicial Interpretation', in Ariel Rosen-Zvi (ed.), *A Jewish and Democratic State* (Tel-Aviv, 1996), pp. 241–60.
18. Ruth Gavison, 'A Jewish and Democratic State Political Identity, Ideology and Law', in Rosen-Zvi, ibid., p. 216.
19. A 1994 survey of Israeli high school youth found that 49 per cent of students in state-religious schools reported that they hated Arabs compared to 33 per cent of the students in non-religious state high schools. Yaakov Ezrahi and Reuven Gal, *World Views and Attitudes of High School Students regarding Society, Security and Peace* (Zichron Yaakov, 1995), p. 68 (Hebrew).
20. Charles S. Liebman and Eliezer Don-Yehiya, *Civil Religion in Israel: Traditional Judaism and Political Culture in the Jewish State* (Berkeley, 1983).
21. For a summary of the debate see the cover story of the *Jerusalem Report*, 'Israel's Heroes Under Attack', 29 December 1994. The lead article by Calev Ben-David, pp. 13–19, is subtitled as follows: 'On stage and screen, in the media and history books, the myths and heroes of Israel and Zionism are being criticized, attacked and reevaluated. Is this the healthy historical revisionism of a changing society, or a growing cynicism that is undermining the country's ideological foundations?' (p. 13).
22. *New York Times*, 31 May 1995, p. A10. The quote appears in a feature article by Clyde Haberman titled 'Israel's Army, Once Sacrosanct, Is Now Becoming Deglamourized', which adds evidence to support the thesis of the decline of Israeli civil religion. The army has, heretofore, been its central institution.
23. *Ha-aretz*, 6 Aug. 1996, p. 4.
24. Efraim Inbar, 'Contours of Israel's New Strategic Thinking', *Political Science Quarterly*, Vol. 111, No. 1 (1996), p. 56.
25. Ibid.
26. *Ha-aretz*, 8 Aug. 1996, p. 1B.
27. Eliezer Don-Yehiya, 'Festivals and Political Culture: Independence-Day Celebrations', *Jerusalem Quarterly*, No. 45 (Winter 1988), pp. 61–84.
28. Eliezer Schweid, 'Israel as a Jewish-Democratic State – Historical and Theoretical Perspectives', *Alpayim*, No. 11 (1995), pp. 78–89, and 'The Jewish Religion and Israeli Democracy', *Yahdaut Hofshit*, No. 7 (December 1995), pp. 24–30; Asher Maoz, 'The Values of a Jewish Democratic State', in Rosen-Zvi (ed.), *A Jewish and Democratic State*, pp. 85–169. Although he does not address the topic specifically, much material supporting the compatibility of Judaism and Democracy, especially equal treatment of the non-Jew is found in a variety of essays by the seminal biblical scholar Moshe Greenberg. For example, Moshe Greenberg, *Studies in the Bible and Jewish Thought* (Philadelphia, 1995); see especially, 'Mankind, Israel and the Nations in the Jewish Heritage', pp. 369–93.
29. Charles S. Liebman, 'Attitudes toward Jewish-Gentile Relations in the Jewish Tradition and Contemporary Israel' (Occasional Papers, Kaplan Centre, University of Cape Town, 1984), and more recently with Steven M. Cohen, 'Jewish Political Liberalism', *Commentary*, forthcoming.
30. Gideon Samet, 'The Nation Goes Up a Grade', *Ha-aretz* (28 July 1995), p. 1B.
31. The new literary journal *Rechov* is the ideological flagship of this approach.
32. Rochelle Furstenberg, 'Post-Zionism: The Promises and the Problems', forthcoming.
33. Yosef Dan, *Ha-aretz Supplement*, 3 March 1994, pp. E1, E8.

34. Ezrahi and Gal, *World Views*, p. 124.
35. Ibid., p. 182.
36. Mordechai Bar-Lev and Avraham Leslau, *The Religious World of Graduates of the Public-Religious School System* (Ramat-Gan, Bar-Ilan University, 1994) (Hebrew).
37. Nisan Rubin, 'Social Structure and Patterns of Mourning', *Hevra Ve-revaha*, 5 (1987), pp. 219–31.
38. Shlomo Deshen, 'Secular Israelis on Passover Eve: Continuity, Creativity, Eradication and Profanation of Traditional Symbols', forthcoming (in Hebrew).
39. Christopher Lasch, 'The Revolt of the Elites: Have they Canceled their Allegiance to America?', *Harper's*, 289 (November 1974), pp. 39–49. The essay is adapted, with revision, from a posthumous book *The Revolt of the Elites and the Betrayal of Democracy*, published in 1995 by W.W. Norton.
40. Ibid., p. 40.
41. Ibid., p. 41.
42. Yonathan Shapiro, *Politicians as an Hegemonic Class: The Case of Israel* (Tel-Aviv, 1996), pp. 54ff (Hebrew).
43. *Ha-aretz Supplement*, 29 Dec. 1995, pp. 20–6.
44. *Ha-zofe, Sabbath Supplement*, 8 March 1996, pp. 7, 17.
45. David Grossman, 'I Need You, and You Need Me', *Avar Ve-atid*, 3 Sep. 1996, pp. 7, 8. The article is translated from the Hebrew original that appeared in *Yediot Aharonot*, 23 November 1995.
46. Lasch, *The Revolt of the Elites*, p. 222.
47. Ibid., p.223.

Between Hegemony and Dormant *Kulturkampf* in Israel

BARUCH KIMMERLING

CONSTRUCTION OF A HEGEMONY

Any public realm in modern or modernizing states is a battlefield on which diverse cultures fight to determine the cultural character of the society. Usually, conflicts between different cultures are controlled or mediated by the state through the rules-of-the-game imposed by it, its institutions and agents. On one extreme there are states that possess full control over the cultural character of the society. In this situation the state is an autonomous actor able to impose and maintain a hegemonic situation. Hegemony is a political-cultural phenomenon described by Antonio Gramsci as ideological domination of one segment of a collectivity over other segments, through the possession of a monopolistic cultural power-position which enables the definition and construction of 'realities', as well as the proper rules of the game within a society and state.[1] As formulated by Carnoy,[2] hegemony is a successful attempt of a dominant segment of society 'to use the political, moral and intellectual leadership to establish its view of the world as all inclusive and universal and to shape the interest and needs of subordinate groups'. In political terms, where hegemony is high there is little need for coercion and force.[3]

On the other extreme of the state–society spectrum is the sociopolitical situation in which a weak state loses control over the definitional monopoly of the society's identity, leaving room for different factions within civil society to struggle over alternative identities to be propagated by the state.[4] At a certain point an intermediate stage, a *Kulturkampf*, is reached. In this case, two or more cultural groups in a society struggle – sometimes using violent means (such as in present-day Egypt and Algeria) – for political and cultural

---

Baruch Kimmerling is Professor of Sociology at the Hebrew University of Jerusalem.

domination of the state through the imposition of their ideology and rules-of-the game (for example, Germany by Nazism, or contemporary Iran and Sudan by extreme Islamic movements). Yet another outcome following the breakup of hegemonic control is the institutionalization of cultural pluralism, supported by political tolerance, and a redefinition of the collective identity in a manner that is able to maintain social cohesion despite the multifocal nature of the identity.

The case study presented in this essay looks at the manner in which a hegemonic metaculture was created in Israel, and the reasons why this 'hegemony' of the Zionist culture has declined. Accompanying this decline is the appearance and persistence of competing countercultures and an increasing culture war between them and the still dominant culture. These countercultures are not based on innovative or new ideas, orientations, rules-of-the-game, rituals or practices. In fact, most of them were present within the original Zionist hegemony,[5] gaining increased coherency due to a *divergence* process within Zionist culture in which they regrouped around more clearly defined clusters of beliefs, ideologies, rituals and practices. At the present time, this culture war remains in a dormant phase.[6]

From the inception of Jewish-Zionist settlement in Palestine, a major aim of the Jewish settler-immigrants was to create a secular Jewish society and culture. This aspiration went beyond the different models of society that accompanied the political ideologies of the founding generation (either liberal-nationalists or social nationalists). However, from the beginning, at least on the level of historical consciousness and collective identity, essential elements of the Jewish religion were included in this culture.[7] The target land for immigration and settlement was 'Zion', the language of the secular Zionist movement was modernized Hebrew, and a secularized Bible were all borrowed from the Jewish religion; but, importantly, these religious symbols were reconstructed to suit the interests of Jewish nationalism.[8] In this vein an overemphasis on the Bible was not accidental. Two specific sections of the Old Testament were selected: the conquest of the land and the establishment of Jewish Kingdoms, as well as the universalistic-social message of the Prophets. Both were supposed to grant legitimacy to Zionist settlement and the unique mixture of components maintaining the hegemony. 'Heroes' from the biblical stories were cultivated by the regime, just as 'heroes of labour' (Stachanov cult) were cultivated by the Soviet regime.

Most of the cultural terms included within Zionism were established by the Jewish Enlightenment movement, which preceded Zionism by a hundred years. This movement created a non-territorial, apolitical cultural nationalism, which was the foundation of the politicized nationalism that followed. In this way Zionism is similar to other cases (Germany, Italy, etc.) in which the nation is constructed as an imagined cultural community without a pre-existing political framework.[9] When the settler-immigrant society was later integrated under the British colonial umbrella and challenged by the local Arab population,[10] religious arguments and symbols provided one of the most powerful answers on the question of 'Jewish rights' over the 'Land of Israel'.[11] This Arab–Jewish confrontation raised a permanent external and internal legitimation crisis within the Jewish polity, and religion provided an answer. The reader only has to imagine the chairman of the World Zionist Organization speaking on the UN podium, waving the Old Testament: 'This is our charter for the land' (of Palestine). All of this in spite of the fact that Diaspora Zionism was considered a secular revolution, both by the Zionists and their rivals, Orthodox religious Jewry, which condemned Jewish nationalism as false messianism.[12]

The demographic composition of the Jewish polity (known as the 'organized Yishuv')[13] was mostly secular, and its dominant ideology and rhetoric social-nationalist.[14] While the secular character of Jewish society was secured by the religious foundations of its identity, the image of the 'new Jew' was also embodied in the image of the secular pioneer (*halutz*),[15] the settler society was symbolized by the kibbutz (or the smaller *kvutzah*) secular-communal settlement and the new coastal city of Tel-Aviv 'built on the sand' (that is, lacking any connection with tradition[16] and apart from the holy sites of the core-land of 'Zion').

However, the builders of the initial secular-Zionist culture had no control over worldwide processes and the 'world system'. The Zionist settlement and culture was not constructed within a 'bubble', and some remote but also immediate occurrences interfered to slowly and accumulatively contribute to the breakup of the system. The major events were the Holocaust, the establishment of the State of Israel, and the uprooting of about 750,000 Palestinian Arabs from the territory,[17] and a non-selective mass-immigration[18] in which the demographic composition of the Jewish polity and territory were changed by an influx of a more traditional and religious Jewish population. As long as these immigrants remained in the peripheral areas of the collectivity, their social, political, economic and cultural impact were marginal and for about 25 years the dominance of the political and cultural elites of the pre-state system remained intact. The remaining 150,000 Arabs were located outside the political and cultural boundaries of the polity.

As mentioned above, at its establishment the Israeli state was built on a hegemonic ideology, culture and social order. This ideology was shaped in order to preserve the character of collectivity and the position of the original ruling elites, ethnic and national groups.[19] Through the imposition of this ideology a front of 'continuity' in society was maintained[20] despite fundamental changes in the composition of the population over a very short period of four years that doubled the Jewish population of the collectivity. The basic premises of the hegemonic ideology were:

- The state as a realization of the Zionist idea is a 'Jewish state', but the definition of 'Judaism' is left open to interpretation as a religion, a secular nationalism, or a secular nationalism built on select religious ingredients.
- The state belongs to the whole Jewish People and not just to its citizens, and all of world Jewry is entitled 'to return' as a constitutional right.
- The citizenship of Arabs is limited to access to common goods based on individual rights; as a group they are socially and politically only partial members of the collectivity,[21] and culturally outside the society's boundaries.[22]
- The state's legal system is differentiated between personal status laws, which are based on the Orthodox Jewish legal code – the Halacha – and all the other laws (criminal and civil), which are based on the Napoleonic codex and Western universalistic orientations.[23]
- The state, its laws, institutions (especially the military)[24] and symbols are the centre of a belief system ('mamlachtiyut' or statism) and the base of an eclectic 'civil religion'.[25]

This last characteristic placed the hegemonic ideology close to the fascist conception of the centrality of the state in a political culture and the relations between the state and individual citizens.[26] The centrality of the state led to a drastic limitation of an autonomous public sphere and the degree of freedom granted to individual expression. The efficiency of this regime was, among others, expressed by the lack of coercive power needed for control, at least among the Jewish population despite the deep cleavages that existed.

The state also produced collective civil-symbols that marked the boundaries of this hegemony: the Jewish anthem, the flag, the celebration of the 'nation's birthday' 'Independence Day', and days of commemoration of fallen in the wars and the victims of Holocaust.[27] These civil-symbols excluded from the collectivity two groups of citizens, the ultra-Orthodox Jews and Arabs, despite the state's declaration of a universal recognition to a 'right to culture'.[28] For both groups of the state's citizens these symbols held counter meanings to those experienced by the majority. For the Palestinians and ultra-Orthodox Jewry the constitution of the Jewish State meant their political and symbolic defeat; and in both cases the Holocaust was given a very different interpretation to that of the Zionist hegemony. On the other hand, major Jewish religious holidays and commemorations were also imposed by the state (such as the Sabbath, Jewish New Year, Yom Kippur fast, Passover, etc.), in the process becoming 'statized' as they were enforced by formal and informal statist mechanisms of control and surveillance. Despite the abundance of festivities and ceremonies a new symbol or festival celebrated by all the citizens of the state, *as citizens*, was never created. May Day, the only common Jewish–Arab festivity, alienated many Jews and Arabs alike because of its socialist and communist character. Even this holiday declined in significance during the 1980s.

Gradually this hegemonic culture was challenged and the power of its elite – the veteran Ashkenazi MAPAI and other 'leftist' party members and elite groups – declined.[29] The immigrants of the 1950s, especially those of oriental origins (the *Mizrahiim*), with a higher birth rate, not only increased their proportion in the population, but acquired social and political skills. As a result the state, party and other mechanisms of surveillance and control gradually lost their power over them.[30] Early protest movements were suffocated, but later protests were institutionalized as Israel's political system became more open and flexible. The process by which protest movements were institutionalized gained momentum after the traumatic 1973 War, and exposed some of the weaknesses of the Israeli state, which until that point was considered a strong state.[31] The 1982 Lebanon War, which was openly declared a 'war of choice', led for the first time to the cracking of the 'self-evident' nature of the state's 'morality' and its unquestionable right to define its citizen's duties, among the mainstream of Israeli-Jewish society.[32] All these led to the upheaval of 1977 which brought to power for the first time right wing parties, ending the convention of 'MAPAI as an irremovable party'.

The territories conquered in the 1967 War gradually introduced within the system another sociopolitical cleavage alongside the already existing one between Israeli-Jews and the Arab Palestinian population of the conquered territories.[33] 'Holy sites' that had been out of the Israeli state's control since the 1948 War were once again in Jewish hands, raising strong religious (often messianic) sentiments among most of the Israeli secular and religious Jewish population. The overwhelming victory, after a long and traumatic period of waiting, was frequently presented in terms of divine intervention in Jewish history, a mirror-image of the Holocaust, the continuation of the 'miraculous' victory in the 1948 War, the 'cleansing' of the territory from the vast majority of the Arab population of Palestine, as well as the establishment of a Jewish sovereign state.

These intertwining processes led to the beginning of the breakup of the hegemonic culture. Three competing Jewish countercultures appeared on the scene to challenge the original Zionist ideology. One envisioned Israel as a Jewish state, ruled by the Jewish Orthodox religious codex, the Halacha, and dogma such as Rabbi Joseph Karo's 'Shulhan Aruch' and 'The Thirteen Principles' of Maimonides.[34] The second counterculture aspired to turn Israel into a liberal, secular and civic state for all its present Jewish and Arab citizens. Both countercultures are rooted within the original Zionist hegemonic culture. Each emphasizes particular aspects of the original culture and takes them to their logical conclusions.[35]

The third counterculture, known as traditionalist culture, has less sharply defined boundaries, with a corresponding lack of clearly articulated beliefs and practices. In fact its eclecticism resembles aspects of the original hegemonic culture. Israeli traditionalism is an incoherent set of values, norms, beliefs and practices mainly borrowed from the codified 'high' Jewish religion, but is mixed with many folkloric and 'popular' religious elements (such as cults and holidays dedicated to local ethnic 'saints'). One way to view traditionalism is to describe it as a less rigorous way to observe the precepts of religion, or a middle position in the secularization process presuming the existence of a continuum between 'complete religiosity' and 'pure secularism'. An alternative conceptualization of traditionalism is to regard it as a substantially distinct culture, both *vis-à-vis* religious and secular cultures. The fourth counterculture, Arab culture, was an insulated one, and was and still is considered a completely different culture from the 'Hebrew' or 'Jewish' culture. Almost all 'cultural studies' in Israel simply ignored its existence and impact on the general Israeli culture.[36]

The social and conceptual boundaries of each of these countercultures are often blurred. Thus there are people who define themselves as 'secular who are keepers of tradition', or 'traditional, but obey religious precepts'.[37] However, each of these countercultures possesses rules of behaviour supported by different styles of life, that obligate certain groups of people in the society. Each of these cultures also has institutional and political infrastructures, which sustain the behavioural patterns related to its distinct belief systems, develop them, and from time to time redefine some of their manifestations, content and social boundaries. At least two of these cultures are geographically separate or segregated, with no common 'table manners' and no common market of bridegrooms and brides.[38] Sometimes there are visible and observable divisions marked by garments or other external labels (such as skullcaps, haircuts, accents and even language). However, such differences can also be observed within each of these cultures, which are highly fragmented, including many competing and adversary groups.

Of course, all these countercultures, as well as the complex relationships among them, are by no means unique to Israeli society and most of their characteristics and contents are universal in nature. But, as usual, the 'Israeli case' includes many *sui generis* ingredients as does any other 'culture', rooted in the various mixtures of its components, historical development and background.

THE RELIGIOUS COUNTERCULTURE

Religion, as an ideal type, is an ideology or an aggregate of perceptions that presume the existence of mostly omnipotent transcendental forces that dominate (and even create) the natural and social worlds.[39] The system has a binary character, using a sharp division between 'good' and 'evil' forces, competing over human deeds and souls. The doing and undoing of human (and sometimes non-human) creatures are accountable, and controlled by this-worldly and other-worldly reward. A clear cut codex of behaviour (precepts) – derived from a holy source, usually as scripture – is imposed on a collectivity of believers and individuals within the collectivity. The degree of strictness of observance of these precepts is a reflection of the quality of belief in the 'truth' of the religion. While religions use many terms and words drawn from ordinary secular experience, the ordinary sense of these terms has been expanded and transubstantiated to the sacred sphere.[40] The individual usually is not entitled to add or distract from the precepts or to interpret or reinterpret the scriptures, the values, or the precepts. For this purpose professional authorities exist, such as high priests, rabbis, qadis and imams (or in the case of revolutionary reinterpretation, prophets), usually organized in a bureaucratic ('church'), communitarian or charismatic hierarchy. Religion tends to be conservative and past-orientated (sometimes supporting social or national revolutionary movements). Usually, beliefs and behaviours of real, imagined or invented ancestors are considered not only as the perfection, but also the ultimate holy and unchangeable model. Religion, with some exceptions, is also 'totalistic', providing obligatory models of conduct in many or all realms of individual and collective behaviour. As such, religion is exclusive as it draws sharp boundaries between members and outsiders of the holy community.[41] The public realm grants rights of participation only to true believers, and is mostly a male society. Actual religion varies in great measure from this ideal type presentation, and creates deep differences among particular religions as well as within them.

Historically, the Jews who defined themselves as religious were deeply divided in the stances they adopted towards modernity, Jewish enlightenment and secularism, and their relations towards Zionism,[42] and later the very existence of a secular 'Jewish State'.[43] From the beginning a small religious stream was established within the Zionist movement,[44] and even before the appearance of Zionism there were rabbis who preached for the establishment of a movement 'to return to Zion'. But the real theological revolution occurred in the late 1920s when Rabbi Abraham Issac Kook[45] reversed the whole Jewish-rabbinical paradigm and causal relationship as it was centred on the term 'redemption'. In place of the traditional condition for the return of the Jewish people to Zion with the coming of the Messiah and full redemption, which was the fulfilment by all Jews of all the '613 commandments' listed in the holy scriptures, the actual causality is reversed. On the fulfilment of one commandment to 'settle the holy land' by as many Jews as possible, the Messiah will appear and redeem 'his people' politically and theologically and will make them follow all his commands and precepts. This will follow a cosmic redemption of the 'whole world'. This new religious perception granted to secular nationalism and the so called 'socialist pioneer' Jews a religious meaning and legitimacy by making them 'a tool' of a divine project of religious redemption. The Kookian theological revolution laid the foundation for participation of its followers in the secular Israeli state and society in the *here and now*, and for a collaboration between this segment of religious Jews and the secular Zionists. However, it must be stressed that the Kookian approach never abolished the ultimate goal of transforming the Israeli polity into a theocratic state, ruled exclusively under halachic law.

Orthodox and ultra-Orthodox (*haredi*) religious subculture persisted as a segregated and insulated society.[46] This despite post-Holocaust immigration to the State of Israel and an increase in their numbers, as branches of European orthodoxy were re-established in the Holy Land. Their anti-Zionist stance actually strengthened, and their historiography made secular Zionism fully responsible for the Holocaust, perceiving themselves as the only remnants of the Jewish People. This anti-Zionist brand of Orthodoxy established a parallel double centre system between their American base and the Holy Land. In this system, the American centre was the dominant one, having the greatest and most charismatic rabbinical authorities, some of whom even refused to visit Israel. Within Israel, most of the greatest rabbinical authorities were ultra-Orthodox, organizing themselves into the 'Council of the Great Torah Sages'. The Israeli Chief Rabbinate was considered as a subordinate statist organ, staffed by second-rank rabbis. Even the kashrut-certification given by the Chief Rabbinate was considered suspicious, and a totally separate supervision mechanism was constructed and operated by the ultra-Orthodox. In terms of the food industry, a very strong and self-conscious consumer market developed, which has taken on political implications. Ultra-Orthodoxy established a parallel court-system as means for internal social control and law and order, as well as to avoid the possibility of its adherents going to the state's secular judicial system.

An additional institutional dimension of this Orthodox society is its educational system and curricula that are completely independent of any state intervention – from kindergartens to High Torah Colleges (Yeshivoth and Kollelim). In fact, according to Friedman, ultra-Orthodoxy has developed into 'a society of learners', in which a considerable portion of the males were involved in a lifetime learning process, supported materially by aid from abroad, females working in peripheral markets, and much later by state subsidies.[47] The exemption of the Yeshiva students from military service provided a strong incentive for the younger generation to join and remain within the 'learning society', and emphasized the boundaries between the larger Jewish society and its Orthodox segments. It also emphasized the strong gender divisions and stratified social system.

From their own point of view the Orthodox communities were outsiders to the hegemonic culture, though this was not entirely the case from the hegemonic culture's perspective. This self-imposed definition of 'outsider' eroded over time. The political and military successes of the

'Zionists' (mostly following the 1967 War) did not go unnoticed by Orthodoxy. Some began to wonder if God had not blessed the Zionists after all.[48] Capturing the core Holy Land following the 1967 War, the territory at the centre of Jewish religious myths, triggered a conversion process between them and the Zionist religious population. This was reinforced by the increasing participation of Orthodoxy in the Israeli political game, particularly via political parties, such as the veteran anti-Zionist Agudat Israel. At first, political participation was aimed at safeguarding particularistic interests of the Orthodox parallel society within the state, but later it was also aimed at influencing the wider society.

Two consequent processes occurred. First, the religious-Zionist Ashkenazi middle class youth became increasingly included within the rank and file of the Israeli military and its elite units, mainly after arrangements were made allowing them to spend part of their service learning in Yeshivoth.[49] This granted the religious youth considerable prestige in Israeli society, enhanced their self-confidence, and pushed them from a peripheral to a central societal position.[50] The second process was the establishment of a religious-settler society in 'Judea and Samaria', rooted in the same social background, which used the old Zionist hegemonic combination of nationalism and securitism with religious messianic elements.[51] However, this settler society was different from its parent model, emphasizing the halachic element and its attempt to establish a revolutionary holy community based as much as possible on the Orthodox-religious codex.

Thus, the settlers of 'Judea and Samaria' pushed Rabbi Abraham Issac Kook's teachings to their logical extreme. The reunion of the 'People of Israel' with the whole 'Land of Israel' meant the termination of the first part of the redemption process. All that remained was the implementation of a society, based on halachic rules, 'Israel's Torah' in their terminology. Their religious practices drew them closer to Orthodoxy. The legitimacy of the state and sanctity of its organs were called into question, as its universal and modern character, granting citizenship and democratic rights to Arabs and Jews alike, came to be perceived as non-Jewish. More and more the values of 'Judaism' were perceived as contradicting the values of 'democracy'. The state's authority was contrasted with halachic authority, and religious commands were perceived as unquestionably superior over the state's law.[52]

The gentile world, Arab and non-Arab, is perceived as hostile, and linked to its self-evident and permanent goal of annihilating the Jewish People, as was so well demonstrated by the Holocaust. Thus, an increasing similarity in ideology and practice between the religious-settler society of the West Bank and Jewish ultra-Orthodoxy was observed. The settler's partial adoption of the ultra-Orthodox lifestyle did not remain unnoticed and was welcomed by the latter group. Some have gone as far as joining the settlement effort, building exclusive ultra-Orthodox localities (such as the cities of Beitar and Emanuel) in the occupied territories.

Moreover, the Israeli-Palestinian accord, which is likely to lead to a loss of Jewish control over substantial parts of 'Eretz Israel' to gentiles, and to put a stop to the development of a large territorial Jewish entity ruled according the halachic precepts, has created a new kind of Jewish non-Zionist nationalism. Individual and groups of Orthodox rabbis issued halachic or non-halachic decisions that hold that giving up any part of the holy land to gentiles is forbidden by religious law. This relatively new involvement in political decisions was reinforced by American charismatic authorities, especially the highly respected hasidic Chabad Lubavicher Rabbi Zalman Shnerson, who on his death bed was declared the Messiah.

Thus the coming crisis of 'giving up the land' and the death of the Chabad leader, who unprecedentedly did not leave behind a 'successor', caused an atmosphere of doomsday and redemption. Despite the great variety of religious groups, we observe a fast process of convergence between them, that allows us to refer to them on one hand as a unified and distinct subculture, and on the other as the product of the breakup of Zionist hegemony. The moral entrepreneurs of this newly formed subculture were mainly political. The innovative face of this culture represented by Rabbi Kook, and continued by the original settlers of Gush Emunim, has fallen back into the culturally frozen braces of Orthodoxy.

THE SECULAR COUNTERCULTURE

Secularism as an ideal type is only partially a mirror reflection of religion. Sometimes it appears as 'secular religion', or in its more politicized form as 'civil religion'.[53] Another phenomenon is 'irreligion',[54] which is completely indifferent conceptually from religious categories and ideologies; while secularism is a more or less coherent 'agnostic' or atheistic ideology. Secularism is an ideology, or a system of beliefs, that makes individuals and collectivities responsible for their own fate and destiny, without the intervention of any transcendental power. The cornerstone of secularism is a conviction in human reason, the naturalization of the supernatural and rationality, which is institutionalized by science and various positivistic philosophical streams.[55] Some versions of secular belief (such as liberal secularism) also included the idea of legitimate pluralism and cultural heterogeneity, making room for 'irrational belief' (that is, religion), and for aesthetic and emotional products such as the arts (in religion the arts are recruited as any other human activity for the reinforcement of the faith). The constructive and destructive powers in secularism, 'good' and 'evil' are all rooted in the human traits and an ability for rational decision making.

'Human reason', its 'linear progress' and supposed perfection cohabit with human drives for self-destruction, such as the Freudian 'id'. Emotional and non-calculated behaviour are not the subject of any divine or satanic supervision or grand design but are outcomes of natural and social 'milieux'. Reward and punishment systems are not rooted in any divine or supernatural accounting, but are located within an individual's internalized values and self-esteem, the reaction of other individuals (social control), and a legal-judicial-sociopolitical system embodied by the state. However, the secular world is full of ambiguities and ambivalences,[56] and religion itself is not necessarily in contradiction with urbanization, modernity, rationality and science. The initial agreement amongst social scientists and philosophers about the disappearance of religion in the 'modern world' has been completely refuted.[57] Secularism and religion grew together simultaneously and do not necessarily enter into a zero-sum relation.[58] Historically, secularism was regarded as connected with upper classes, and religiosity, under the influence of Marx ('religion is the opium for masses'), to lower classes. To Frederick the Great is attributed the observation that religion is a necessity to discipline the masses and agnosticism is the privilege of elite groups. Historical-empirical evidence does not validate this generalization, and shows that irreligiosity has existed under many historical and societal circumstances amongst peripheral but not necessarily deviant classes, and that religion is not a universal phenomenon.[59]

The major attribute of secularism is the inclusionary characteristics of the boundaries of its public realm. Thus, diverse religions or religious motifs are included in this belief system, just as are other legitimate man-made ideologies. Religion is considered as subject to the same change, criticism, scepticism and investigation as any other human phenomenon, with its totalistic and exclusionary forms regarded suspiciously at best, and dangerous at worst. In sum: God has not died – as Nietzsche declared – but is a man-made creature, for his/her convenience, and subject to manipulation, shaping and reshaping. Secularism itself can include one or more religions, acting as autonomous cultural spheres within the secular realm, as well as religious symbols and cultural products (such as religious liturgy) which are secularized and universalized.

As was already stated, the Jewish immigrant-settler movement in Palestine, especially since the second wave of immigration (1904), created an almost purely secular self-defined society. Even if many symbols and practices from Judaism as religion were absorbed within this culture, they were secularized and reinterpreted. Perhaps the most striking example of such an adaptation and modification was the place of the Holy Bible (the Old Testament) in the newly formed culture. The Bible was selectively constructed and reinvented as an ancient national history of the Jewish People, and the basic certificate granting title for the Jewish nation to the Land.[60]

Before the Holocaust, the Bible served as the central core narrative[61] and most powerful constitutive myth of the new collectivity, bridging between the glorious past, the problematic present and the desired future. It was included in the school curricula, used as a 'model' in daily life for many practical purposes (finding names for newborns, old names for 'rebuilt' localities, social institutions, and as a source for examples of ideal behaviour). However, the Bible still remained a religious moralistic text, read selectively or accompanied by a modern 'scientific' critical approach or presented as 'cultural heritage' or 'literature'. The multiple meanings of the Bible, as both a religious holy text and a national history, indeed played a key role in the constitution of the core narrative of this culture. However, the pure secular context of the Bible was always challenged not only as the portion of religious people increased among the general population, and following the Zionist hegemony's own needs, but also due to the inherent characteristics of the Bible as a religious and moralistic narrative. The major and most active 'hero' of the Bible as a narrative is a god, and without a deep 'censorship', no matter how it is interpreted, its omnipresence and moral message remains.[62] This double message of the Bible became one of the major ingredients in the hegemonic Zionist culture.

However, despite the 'Hebrew culture's' inability to completely detach itself from religious elements, a strong self-defined local secular culture was created by the Jewish immigrants in Palestine, modelled after the great contemporary western cultural centres. Together with the adoption of Hebrew as a vernacular and a powerful unifying factor was created a variegated 'high culture' system. Generations, groups and 'schools' of writers, poets, composers, painters, sculptures, architects, scientists and journalists – some of them immigrants and some of them native-born – constructed a vital cultural field. The non-Latin origin of the Hebrew language is considered as an obstacle for access to it, its spread and the limited scope of its market; nevertheless the 'peculiarity' of Hebrew culture encouraged many translations, in order to make possible wider access to the 'classics' to the local readership. Within a relatively short period most of the great western 'classics' and 'old masters' were available in Hebrew. Moreover, the emergence of modern Jewish cultural centres, especially in North America, enlarged the market of Hebrew cultural items, almost globalizing it.[63]

Central culture producing institutions were built as a part of the nation building process, such as theatre houses, libraries, philharmonic and other orchestras, ballet companies, choirs, museums and galleries, universities, colleges, publishing houses, movie companies, mass media, etc. Virtually no culture generating institution found in any great centre in the world is absent from the secular cultural map of the Jewish collectivity. The scope of the 'cultural product' of the secular Jewish collectivity, relative to its size, seems higher than any other comparable product of any other collectivity both in terms of quantity and quality.

An extensive Hebrew educational system was developed, with the aim of creating a new 'Hebrew person'. At least two great metropolitan cities – Tel-Aviv and Haifa – are self-proclaimed secularist entities, practising different secular cults and rituals. An elite daily newspaper (*Ha-aretz*) is a traditional bastion of Israeli secularism, replete with a home grown rhetoric and slang, establishing a public realm of its own, with a community of writers and readers who share a common belief in secularism and civil society. However, secularism as a loosely defined ideology and a way of life is still regarded as a prerogative of elite groups, and is a class phenomenon. It is linked with highly educated, Ashkenazi, affluent middle and upper middle classes. Politically, it is mainly identified with the Civil Rights Movement Party; however, the rivals of the Labour Party as well the Orthodox tend to 'accuse' or suspect Labour, and especially its kibbutz constituency, of being 'secular' or 'non-Jewish'.[64]

The great influx of more than a million immigrants from the former Soviet Union threatens not only to change the fragile balance of power that exists in Israel between ethnic groups (so-called Mizrahi versus European Jews) and relations between Jewish and diverse Palestinian groups, but also between secular and religious Jews. In the long run, this immigration will probably alter the basic profile of Israel's political and social spheres, just as the 1948–54 mass immigration changed the social and political situation that had characterized the pre-state Jewish community in Palestine.[65] This is basically the most secular immigration wave ever to reach the country, with a middle class social profile that will soon obtain considerable political power, not only as a reservoir of voters but also in terms of the highly skilled politically orientated persons who represent the immigrants. Among these immigrants exists a considerable portion, or even a critical mass, which according to Halacha are 'non-Jews'. So far, they tend to conduct their social and cultural life within a 'Russian bubble', but as soon as they integrate into the larger Israeli society, the system will no longer sustain the current religion based marriage system.[66]

A distinction needs to be made between the state-produced quasi-secularist civil religion that places the state itself and its institutions (the military, bureaucracy, courts, parliament) and cult at centre, and the secular culture of civil society. Civil society secularism is based on a greater emphasis on individualistic values and self-realization of the individual. The appearance of an individualistic and post-industrial secular culture was only made possible following the decomposition of the Zionist hegemony, but was also this process's catalyst. The increasing weight of individualism is accompanied by feelings of anxiety and perceived as a disintegration of Israeli society and culture, an escape from 'genuine Jewish and Israeli values', and a general sign of weakness.[67]

Not only do the religious and the old Zionist guard ideologues see the new secular individualism as 'decadence' or destructive hedonism, but even some core persons from the secular elite seem threatened. Thus, Dalia Rabikowitz, the prominent Israeli poet, and pillar of Israeli secular culture, wrote an article under the title 'There is no Secular Culture in this Country':

> I must say that I have not as yet found anything that we can call a developed secular culture in this country. I have only seen some pathetic attempts to create one overnight, on the part of the same people who ridicule the idea of the world created in six days...I have not found in the Israeli secular culture any text or guide on how to gladden a bride and her groom, nor one that will console mourners...Actually our secularist culture is a culture of nothingness...I do not observe the commandments, and I am not religious, but the fact is that I haven't a secular alternative.[68]

Rabikowitz's reflections echo the constant claim of Orthodoxy that secular segments of Jewish society lack any authentic culture, except for a decadent hedonism and that the 'secular' are not 'real Jews' but a mixed mob (*erev rav*).

THE TRADITIONALIST COUNTERCULTURE

Traditionalism can be regarded in two different ways. One is in terms of the degree of the distance from religious beliefs and obedience to the fulfilment of religious commandments; or, in other words, the degree to which behaviour has been secularized. Religiosity is judged by the terms set by the most rigorous practice of a particular religion's precepts. In this case, the traditionalist person regards him or herself as a 'partial' or even 'deviant' person when compared to the 'true believers' in their reference group. These perceptions are not necessarily accompanied by 'guilt feelings' or 'shame', as most societal spaces in the life of western societies are morally stratified and encourage 'compromise'.

The second, and not necessarily contradictory, means of traditionalism is a separate belief system that includes many ingredients from formal religions side by side with other beliefs and behaviours (such as popular religion, cults of saints and holy men/women or sites, superstitions, conservative mores, wearing 'modest' clothing, voting for 'traditional parties', etc.), which are considered as 'proper' simply because they are rooted in the past. Generally, an imaginary or constructed past is considered 'glorious', and is always better than the present. The desired future must always be shaped accordingly to the ideals of the past. Traditionalism selectively adopts aspects of modern culture, its values, mores and especially its technical and scientific commodities and comforts.

The initial assumption of the Enlightenment movements and modern social sciences was that humankind is constantly 'progressing' from a 'dark', irrational 'primitive' religious time towards a modern, rational and secular time – equating 'modern' and 'rational' with 'secular'. This assumption proved itself wrong. Various religious forms flourished together with 'modernism', and proved themselves part and parcel of the secular world.

Israeli-Jewish traditionalism is ethnically and partially class based. Its boundaries with religiosity are highly fragmented and blurred. Self-defined traditionalism is anchored to the first, second and third generations of the immigrants from the developing societies of the Middle East and North Africa, the so-called Mizrahi or Oriental Jews.[69] A long period of absorption and 'modernization' efforts through the 'melting pot' ideology promoted by the dominant Zionist system met with only partial 'success'. Most of the immigrants ended up in the lower strata of the class system. Nevertheless, there were sizeable sectors of these immigrants, especially of the second and third generations, who are almost completely acculturized and have adopted the Ashkenazi perception of self- and collective identity. Social, ecological and economic mobility, education and socialization, accompanied by high rates of intermarriage and military service, located other parts of the Mizrahi immigrants within the boundaries of the Israeli social system and middle class.[70]

The Mizrahi population has developed its own version of Israeli culture, mixing up the cultures of their countries of origin with 'local' varieties such as music, food, the Hebrew language spoken with certain types of accents, and local and national festivities and saints (some of them reinvented and replaced from their countries of origin).[71] A vast industry generating a parallel culture of music and songs, movies and garments was established, which in the eyes of the mainly Ashkenazi elite was regarded at best as 'folklore' and at worst as 'low' or even 'deviant' culture.[72]

Another path of paternalistic reculturation was taken, which turned out to be the building of a competing counterculture *vis-à-vis* the secular and religious Israeli Ashkenazi Jews. This was the turn of some Mizrahi religious elite groups towards Ashkenazi orthodoxy. Generations of highly talented Mizrahi youngsters were accepted and welcomed into the 'Orthodox learning society', and aimed for complete assimilation. But their acceptance was never total and they remained peripheral within the internal hierarchy of this culture. Their access to prestigious positions and marriage within the elite Ashkenazi families was restricted. As a consequence they split from Ashkenazi orthodoxy and formed their own version of 'orthodoxy' around the charismatic figure of the Sephardi Chief Rabbi Ovadia Yossef. The Shas ('Sephardim Obey the Torah') Party was created in 1984, and has since struggled to liberate itself from the ambiguous patronage of the (95-year-old) Ashkenazi Rabbi Shach, who is considered by many in this culture as the greatest Orthodox Rabbinical authority in Israel. Rabbi Shach has been accused by Shas of condoning innuendo and incrimination about the halachic and political competence of Shas's and Israel's Mizrahi religious leadership.

Shas's forceful appearance on the Israeli scene was by means of their considerable political and electoral potential and skill in converting access to material resources into very successful institution-building. As they built an efficient political party, they also built a separate school system from kindergartens to teachers' seminars ('El Ha-mayan'), and separate neighbourhoods for their constituents. Shas is a mixture of an ethnic based Orthodox elite, with a large and inclusive periphery of people who obey religious precepts with great variation and flexibility. The Shas periphery (not all of them necessarily vote for Shas, but nevertheless consider Rabbi Yossef as a spiritual leader), mainly tend to define themselves as 'traditional' (and not 'religious'). This definition makes up a central part of their self- and collective identity. The social boundaries of this counterculture, similar to those of the secular culture, are not sharply defined and there is no one way 'to practise' traditionalism. Less-than-strict obedience is not considered a sin, and individual and family have a large degree of freedom to interpret binding 'practices' which are mixed in with popular or traditional customs. The rise of the Shas counterculture liberated many of the second and third generation Mizrahi population from their political and cultural subordination to Ashkenazi non-Zionist Orthodoxy, but more than that from Zionist hegemonic culture, and contributed to the breakup of this hegemony.

THE PRESENT ABSENTEES

The Arab citizens of Israel were for a long time completely excluded from the boundaries of the hegemonic Zionist culture, just as they were confined to a separate bubble politically and economically. The few Arabs (about 150,000) remaining within Israel after the collapse of Palestinian Arab society during the 1948 War[73] were a partial and fragmented society, lacking almost any elite groups, a middle class or political and spiritual leadership. They found themselves abruptly transformed from a powerful and self-confident national majority to a helpless small minority group within a state defined as a 'Jewish nation state'.[74]

The only social institution remaining after the 1948 catastrophe (*al-nakba*) was the nuclear and extended family, which was empowered as a means of control and surveillance by the state and its military government imposed on the Israeli Arabs until 1968. To this was added a state controlled elementary and high school system. The Israeli school curriculum for its Arab citizens was built in order to create a new ethnic identity of a de-Palestinized Israeli Arab. Their history was a general Arab history, which was presented as consonant with the history of State of Israel. They were taught the Qur'an (and the New Testament, for Christian Arabs) but also the Hebrew Bible and Hebrew literature.[75]

Israeli Arabs became a bilingual and bicultural people, educated to obey 'Israeli democracy' but at the same time systematically deprived of their land and access to most social common goods (welfare, jobs, housing and other subsidized merchandise). They were excluded (except for small groups of Druzes, Circassians and Bedouins, as volunteers) from compulsory military service, but at the same time were denied full citizenship rights on the grounds that they had not paid their full citizenship obligations.[76]

Any national or ethnic based Arab political organization or protest movement was suffocated for decades. Only the Israeli Communist Party managed to serve as the major access point to the centre, and as a political entity that channelled the Israeli Arab protests and fought for their rights within the Jewish state.[77] The Communist Party also served as an intellectual hothouse for a new Arab cultural elite who have created an original local counterculture, almost completely isolated from the cultural developments in other Arab countries. The party's newspapers, periodicals and Arabic publishing house hosted and participated in the creation of opportunities for Israeli Arab poets, writers, thinkers and journalists.[78] Later, especially after the inclusion of the Palestinians of the West Bank and Gaza Strip under a unified Israeli control system,[79] this cultural capital was included within the general cultural and political renaissance of the Palestinian people.

Over time, the Arabs of Israel have accumulated not only cultural wealth, but also considerable material wealth and political power. From about 7 per cent of the total population they grew by 1996 to approximately 20 per cent of the population and 17 per cent of the electorate. They have also created a Follow Up Committee that serves as a semi-official leadership of the Israeli Palestinians, based on a joint committee of Arab municipality heads and mayors. The committee also includes many prominent public figures and intellectuals from the Israeli Palestinian community.

Following the 1992 general elections, the Arab parties were for the first time considered part of the left-wing 'bloc' that prevented the right wing from forming their own government and actually granted the victory to Yitzhak Rabin's Labour. In 1992 Emil Habibi won the prestigious Israel Prize for literature, and in 1996 the soccer team of the small Arab town of Taybeh won the second league cup and passed to the top national soccer league. Following the Oslo Agreement and the 'peace process', which is likely to lead to the establishment of a Palestinian state in the West Bank and Gaza, a rapprochement between the Jews and Palestinians seems possible, from the perspective of both peoples. For the Israeli Arabs, who since 1967 have come to feel a part of the Palestinian people, but at the same time an active participant and actor in the Israeli state, involvement in Israeli politics, society and culture now seems desirable, on the basis of equal citizenship rights.[80] On the other hand, active participation of Arabs in Israeli politics has interested many segments of the secular and especially left and libertarian wings of Jewish society. The social construction of the Arab citizens as a Trojan horse and self-evident 'enemy' is now being strongly challenged. This is a part but also an additional cause of the decomposition of the Zionist hegemony. The possibility of political alliances among central segments of Jewish and Arab societies within Israel should lead to new social and cultural coalitions that were previously unthinkable and that have only become possible due to the cracks produced in the hegemonic culture.

SOME CONCLUSIONS

Politics and religion as a part of a culture are inseparable in the public realm.[81] Every religion, especially the three great monotheistic religions and their particularistic versions, have dogmas about the proper ways and rules that the public realm (both in civil society and the state) should be run. The question remains as to how much political power, in a particular historical circumstance is given to the religious actors and institutions *vis-à-vis* other societal forces, and to which types of religious streams or denominations. We may pose the same problem another way, and ask how much religion is part of the collective identity, and its positioning *vis-à-vis* other ingredients of the identity?

As demonstrated in this essay, the secular Zionist movement used and abused the Jewish religion and its symbols for mobilizing Jewish immigration to 'Zion', and a tremendous effort of nation building and culture creation. Religion served as a legitimacy-generating mechanism both inside (the Jewish society) and outside (the non-Jewish 'world').[82] The infusion of Judaism as religion into the initially secular national movement had high payoffs (even if the combination of religion and nationalism is a universal phenomenon observed in many other modern and Western polities).[83] This synthesis created an ideological movement with a strong religious dimension, something that had institutional and constitutional consequences. Thus, when the 'Jewish State' was established, as opposed to a 'state for Jews', the challenge and the struggle over the definition and actual meaning of the 'state's Jewishness' was built in to its collective identity.[84] For the first three decades – as far as the hegemonic culture was able to sustain all the interpretations of 'Jewishness' – the strains between secularism and religion remained dormant, with very few and marginal exceptions.[85] The state was powerful enough to 'play' an inclusionary–exclusionary 'game' needed to maintain the hegemony. Certain symbols, values and social groups were included, while others were excluded from the boundaries.

Thus, despite the potentially considerable stress and conflict of interests between the diverse segments within Israeli society, a *Kulturkampf* was avoided as a direct consequence of the hegemony. The cultural and sociopolitical boundaries were drawn in such a way that 'dissonant' voices were excluded, or rewarded by partial inclusion, in exchange for conformity with the hegemonic values. Of course, another powerful obstacle before waging any internal 'culture war' was the existence of a protracted conflict with the Palestinians in particular and the Arab surroundings in general. As mentioned before, the hegemonic culture included salient militaristic traits, which resulted from the continuation of this conflict, but also caused its persistence.[86] The developments since the 1978 Camp David Accords with Egypt, followed in 1995 by a convenient peace agreement with Jordan, and especially the 'peace process' with the Palestinians,[87] challenged the militaristic component of the hegemony, but has yet to seriously alter it.

The constantly increasing standard of living, combined with the de-escalation of external conflict, has triggered an additional process. Israel is evolving from a highly mobilized and collectivistic society towards an individualistic, consumer-orientated postindustrial society that locates the individual at the centre of the collectivity. In the future this should include demands not only to separate the synagogue from the state, but also a movement to privatize religion, which will include versions of secular and civil religions.

The cultural hegemony was based on a single strong social and political coalition, which regulated many spheres of individual and public life. This coalition now seems to be in the process of dismantlement. Instead of a dominant coalition, we may expect new social and cultural coalitions, which will include groups and segments of the population that initially were outside the hegemonic coalition (such as the ultra-Orthodox and Arabs, Conservative or Reform Jews). Many of these coalitions are likely to be *ad hoc* and built around one issue, or a cluster of issues, of common interest, while on other issues the partners will belong to other and probably opposing coalitions. One major institutional and cultural-ideological consequence of such a change in the rules of the game will be a much greater variation in educational institutions and curricula, and a concentration of the social conflict on resource allocations for education and culture.

NOTES

1. Antonio Gramsci, *Selection from the Prison Notebooks* (New York, 1971).
2. Martin Carnoy, *The State and Political Theory* (Princeton, 1984), p. 70.
3. David D. Laitin, *Hegemony and Culture: Politics and Religious Changes among the Yoruba* (Chicago), p. 105.
4. Baruch Kimmerling, 'State Building, State Autonomy, and the Identity of Society: The Case of the Israeli State', *Journal of Historical Sociology*, Vol. 6, No. 4 (1993), pp. 397–429.
5. Baruch Kimmerling, 'Between the Primordial and the Civil Definitions of the Collective Identity', in Erik Cohen, Moshe Lissak and Uri Almagor (eds), *Comparative Social Dynamics* (Boulder, 1985), pp. 282–6.
6. Hegemonic culture is not only dominant but 'self-evident' and has the power to exclude any other culture from the collectivity's boundaries (Steven Lukes, *Power: A Radical View* (London, 1974)) or to define it as 'deviant'. In contrast, a dominant

culture is the culture of the most powerful elite groups in a society, but which does not hold a monopolistic situation due to the legitimate existence of cultural pluralism.
7. Kimmerling, 'Between the Primordial and the Civil'.
8. It is not accidental that in the Israeli identification card as well as other official documents categorize 'nationality' as 'Jewish' (rather than 'Israeli'), meaning that religion, ethnicity and national affiliation are interchangeable (Don Handelman, 'Contradictions between Citizenship and Nationality: Their Consequences for Ethnicity and Inequality in Israel', *International Journal of Politics, Culture and Society*, Vol. 3 (1994), pp. 441–59). This categorization has passed many Court decisions and legislative action and is at this point safely guarded by the law (Baruch Kimmerling, 'Religion, Nationalism and Democracy in Israel', *Zemanim*, Vol. 50–1 (1994), pp. 116–31 (Hebrew)). In a similar vein it is significant that Jewish religious studies, under the label of 'Jewish conscience', were included in the late 1950s in the curriculum of the secular state school system by the MAPAI Minister of Education Zalman Aran. The assumption was that the foundations of Jewish-Israeli identity are in religion, and a lack of knowledge about religion cripples the loyalty of the youth to Zionism and the State. In the same spirit were the Shenhar Committee's conclusions, even though this report offered a broader definition of 'Judaism'. See Shenhar [Aliza] Committee, *People and World: Jewish Culture in Changing World. Report of the Investigation Committee on the Status of Jewish Education in the General Educational System* (Jerusalem, 1992) (Hebrew).
9. Benedict Anderson, *Imagined Communities: Reflections on the Origin and Spread of Nationalism* (London, 1991).
10. Yehoshua Porath, *The Emergence of the Palestinian Arab National Movement, 1918–1929* (London, 1974); *The Palestinian National Movement: From Riots to Rebellion, 1929–1939* (London, 1977); Baruch Kimmerling and Joel S. Migdal, *Palestinians: The Making of a People* (Cambridge, MA, 1994), p. 105.
11. Baruch Kimmerling, *Zionism and Territory: The Socioterritorial Dimension of Zionist Politics* (Berkeley, 1983).
12. Shlomo Avineri, *The Making of Modern Zionism: The Intellectual Origins of the Jewish State* (London, 1981), and 'Zionism and the Jewish Religious Tradition: The Dialectics of Redemption and Secularization', in Shmuel Almog, Jehuda Reinharz and Anita Shapira (eds), *Zionism and Religion* (Jerusalem, 1994), pp. 9–20 (Hebrew); Walter Laqueur, *A History of Zionism* (London, 1972); David Vital, *The Origins of Zionism* (Oxford and New York, 1975).
13. Dan Horowitz and Moshe Lissak, *Origins of the Israeli Polity: Palestine under the Mandate* (Chicago and London, 1978); Baruch Kimmerling, 'State Building, State Autonomy'.
14. Zeev Sternhall, *Nation Building or a New Society? The Zionist Labour Movement and the Origins of Israel* (Tel-Aviv, 1996)(Hebrew).
15. Shmuel N. Eisenstadt, *Israeli Society* (New York, 1967).
16. Erik Cohen. *The City in Zionist Ideology* (Jerusalem: Eliezer Kaplan School of Economic and Social Sciences, The Hebrew University, 1970).
17. Benny Morris, *The Birth of the Palestinian Refugee Problem, 1947–1949* (Cambridge, 1987).
18. Baruch Kimmerling, *Zionism and Economy* (Cambridge MA, 1983).
19. Kimmerling, *Zionism and Economy*.
20. Eisenstadt, *Israeli Society*, and *The Transformation of Israeli Society: An Essay in Interpretation* (London, 1985); Horowitz and Lissak, *Origins of the Israeli Polity*, and *Trouble in Utopia: The Overburdened Polity of Israel* (Albany, 1989).
21. Yoav Peled, 'Ethnic Democracy and Legal Construction of Citizenship: Arab Citizens of the Jewish State', *American Political Science Review*, Vol. 86 (1992).
22. Yitzhak Laor, *Narratives without Natives: Essay on Israeli Literature* (Tel-Aviv, 1995) (Hebrew); Yerach Gover, *Zionism: The Limits of Moral Discourse in Israeli Fiction* (Minneapolis, 1994); Nurit Gertz, *Captive of a Dream: National Myths in Israeli Culture* (Tel Aviv, 1988) (Hebrew).
23. David Kretzmer, *The Legal Status of the Arabs in Israel* (Boulder, 1990).
24. Kimmerling, 'Religion, Nationalism and Democracy in Israel'; Uri Ben-Eliezer, *The Emergence of Israeli Militarism: 1936–1956* (Tel-Aviv, 1995) (Hebrew).
25. Charles S. Liebman and Eliezer Don-Yehiya, *Civil Religion in Israel: Traditional Judaism*

and Political Culture in Israel (Berkeley, 1984).
26. Yeshayahu Leibowitz, *Judaism, Human Values and the Jewish State*, trans. and edited by Eliezer Goldman (Cambridge MA, 1992).
27. Maoz Azaryahu, *State Cults: Celebrating Independence and Commemorating the Fallen in Israel, 1948–1956* (Sde Boker, 1 995) (Hebrew).
28. Avishai Margalit and Moshe Harbetal, 'Liberalism and the Right to Culture', *Social Research*, Vol. 3 (1994), pp. 490–510.
29. A. Arian, *Politics in Israel* (Chatham NJ, 1985).
30. Kimmerling, 'State Building, State Autonomy'.
31. Joel S. Migdal, *Strong Societies and Weak States: State–Society Relations and State Capabilities in the Third World* (Princeton, 1988).
32. Sara Helman, 'Conscientious Objection to Military Service as an Attempt to Redefine the Contents of Citizenship', Ph.D. thesis, Department of Sociology, The Hebrew University, Jerusalem.
33. Horowitz and Lissak, *Trouble in Utopia*; Asher Arian, Ilan Talmud and Tamar Herman, *National Security and Public Opinion in Israel* (Boulder, 1988).
34. Aviezer Ravitzky, *Messianism, Zionism and Jewish Religious Radicalism* (Tel Aviv, 1993), pp. 60–110 (Hebrew).
35. Some call this process the 'de-Zionization' of Israeli society, calling the present era a 'post-Zionist' one, which is equated with 'postmodernism'. See Laurence J. Silberstein, 'Cultural Criticism, Ideology, and the Interpretation of Zionism: Toward a Post-Zionist Discourse', in Steven Kepnes (ed.), *Interpreting Judaism in a Post-Modern Age* (New York, 1992), pp. 325–58.
36. Even today, the veteran 'Association of Hebrew Writers', which is supposed to be a trade unionist organization, does not accept Israeli Arab writers. In 1995 several Jewish writers and poets established a new association, with membership on an equal basis for all Israeli non-Hebrew writers, poets, etc.
37. A recent national sample of the Jewish population of Israel shows the following distribution of the religious identities in the population in terms of the degree and attitude to which they maintain religious observance: (a) Ultra-Orthodox (*haredi*) 3.9%; (b) Religious (*dati*) 11.0%; (c) Traditional (*mesorati*) 26.8%; (d) Secular but maintains some of tradition (*hiloni hamekayem masoret*) 23.4%; (e) Secular (*hiloni*) 30.3%; (f) Anti-religious 4.4%.
38. Menachem Friedman, *Ultra-Orthodox Society: Sources, Trends, and Processes* (Jerusalem, 1991) (Hebrew).
39. Thomas Luckmann, 'The New and the Old in Religion', in Pierre Bourdieu and James S. Coleman (eds), *Social Theory for a Changing Society* (Boulder and New York, 1991), pp. 166–82; Bryan Wilson, *Religion in a Secular Society: A Sociological Comment* (London, 1966); Bryan Stanley Turner, *Religion and Social Theory: A Materialist Perspective* (London, 1983); James Arthur Beckford, *Religion and Advanced Industrial Society* (London, 1992).
40. David Martin, *The Breaking of the Image: A Sociology of Christian Theory and Practice* (London, 1980).
41. Thomas Luckmann, *The Invisible Religion* (New York, 1967).
42. Ravitzky, *Messianism, Zionism and Jewish Religious Radicalism*.
43. Menachem Friedman, 'The State of Israel as a Theological Dilemma', in B. Kimmerling (ed.), *The Israel State and Society: Boundaries and Frontiers* (Albany, 1989), pp. 163–215.
44. Ehud Luz, *Parallels Meet: Religion and Nationalism in the Early Zionist Movement* (Philadelphia, 1988).
45. Abraham Isaac Kook, *The Lights of Penitence. The Moral Principles. Lights of Holiness: Essays, Letters and Poems*, trans. by Ben Zion Bokser (New York, 1978); Shlomo Avineri, *The Making of Modern Zionism*, and 'The Zionist and the Jewish Religious Tradition' (Hebrew).
46. Menachem Friedman, *Society and Religion: The Non-Zionist Orthodox in Eretz-Israel, 1918–1936* (Jerusalem, 1977) (Hebrew); Friedman, *The Ultra-Orthodox Society*.
47. Friedman, *The Ultra-Orthodox Society*.
48. Friedman, 'The State of Israel as a Theological Dilemma'.
49. Mordechai Bar-Lev, 'Graduates of the High-School Yeshivoth in Eretz-Israel: Between Tradition and Innovation', Ph.D. Thesis, Bar Ilan University, Ramat-Gan, 1986, pp.

175–87 (Hebrew).
50. Baruch Kimmerling, 'Determination of the Boundaries and the Frameworks of Conscription: Two Dimensions of Civil–Military Relations in Israel', *Studies in Comparative International Development*, Vol. 14 (1979), pp. 24–41.
51. Gideon Aran, 'The Beginning of the Road from Religious Zionism to Zionist Religion', *Studies in Contemporary Jewry*, Vol. II (Bloomington, 1985); Ian Lustik, *For the Land and the Lord: Jewish Fundamentalism in Israel* (New York, 1988).
52. A dramatic example is provided by Yigal Amir, the murderer of Prime Minister Yitzhak Rabin. As Sophocles' Antigona, he contrasted the law of states with the law of the conscience – that is, 'halachic law', as interpreted by himself and elements in his social milieu – that led him to the extreme act.
53. Robert N. Bellah, 'Civil Religion in America', *Daedalus*, Vol. I (1967), pp. 1–26, and *Beyond Belief: Essays on Religion in a Post-Traditional World* (New York, 1970).
54. Colin David Campbell, *Toward a Sociology of Irreligion* (New York, 1971).
55. Vernon Pratt, *Religion and Secularisation* (London, 1970); Raimundo Panikkar, *Worship and Secular Man* (London, 1973).
56. David Martin, *The Religious and the Secular: Studies in Secularization* (London, 1969).
57. Rodney Stark and William Bainbridge, *The Future of Religion: Secularization, Revival and Cult Formation* (Berkeley, 1985).
58. Callum G. Brown, 'A Revisionist Approach to Religious Changes', in Steven Bruce (ed.), *Religion and Modernization: Sociologists and Historians Debate the Secularization Thesis* (Oxford, 1992), pp. 31–216.
59. Campbell, *Toward a Sociology of Irreligion*.
60. This must be seen in the context of the counterclaim of the local Arab population to the possession of the exclusive right over the land, and their perception of Jewish settlement as a colonial enterprise and the Jewish immigrants as aliens. See Kimmerling, *Zionism and Territory*; Kimmerling and Migdal, *Palestinians: The Making of a People*. Hebrew, the language of the Bible, was also secularized about one hundred years earlier, by the Enlightenment national cultural movement; see Eliezer Schweid, *The Idea of Judaism as a Culture* (Tel-Aviv, 1986) (Hebrew).
61. Yael Zerubavel, *Recovered Roots: Collective Memory and the Making of Israeli National Tradition* (Chicago, 1995); Moshe Zuckerman, *Shoah in the Sealed Room: The 'Holocaust' in Israeli Press during the Gulf War* (Tel-Aviv, published by the author).
62. See a discussion at the Cherik Institute of Hebrew University on 18 April 1996 on the 'Bible and the Israel Identity', with the participation of Yair Zakowitz, Amnon Ben-Tor, Asher Shkedi, Gidon Aran, Shaul Katz, Michael Heyd and others. For a vivid example of a most recent attempt of revitalization of the Bible in a 'secular' and nationalistic spirit, see Rudi Reisel and Esther Reisel, *A Secular Attachment to Judaism* (Tel-Aviv, 1994).
63. Baruch Kimmerling, 'Boundaries and Frontiers of the Israeli Control System', in B. Kimmerling (ed.), *The Israeli State and Society: Boundaries and Frontiers* (Albany, 1989), pp. 265–84.
64. At a prominent public meeting the well known Lithuanian Rabbi Shach prohibited the Orthodox parties from forming a coalition with the Labour party, accusing them of being 'rabbit eaters'. See Dan Miron's essay in this volume.
65. Kimmerling, *Zionism and Economy*.
66. To date there exist in Israel several hundred persons defined as 'unqualified for marriage' or for burial according to religious rules, due to doubts about their 'Jewishness' caused by 'bastardism' or forbidden Cohen-divorced-women marriages, etc. These were defined as 'marginal cases' and mainly ignored by the political system. The Russian immigration dramatically increased the numbers of these 'untouchables'. This increase must lead to the institutionalization of civil marriages in Israel.
67. The statist secular civil religion cannot be regarded as 'secular' because of the definition of the state as a 'Jewish (nation) state' and the abovementioned difficulties in defining 'Judaism' in secular terms. Shlomo Deshen defined 'secular nationalism' as one of four 'patterns of Israeli Judaism' that excluded 'secular non-nationalists' from the boundaries of Judaism ('The Judaism of Middle-Eastern Immigrants', *Jerusalem Quarterly*, Vol. 13 (1979), pp. 98–110). Deshen also refers to the religiosity of the Oriental Jews as a distinct 'pattern' of Judaism, which we refer to as 'traditionalism' (also see Moshe Shokeid, 'Precepts vs. Tradition: Religious Trends among Middle

Eastern Jews', *Megamot*, Vol. 2–3 (1984), pp. 250–64.
68. Dalia Rabikowitz, 'There Is No Secular Culture in This Country', *Globes* (22 December 1995) (Hebrew).
69. Sammy Smooha, *Israel: Pluralism and Conflict* (Berkeley, 1978); Shlomo Swirski, *Israel: The Oriental Majority* (London, 1989).
70. There are considerable differences among the Mizrahi Jews themselves in their reactions to the Israeli melting pot policies. While the majority from Middle Eastern origins, especially the Iraqi immigrants, demonstrated high mobility and 'adaptation' capabilities, the North African immigrants found themselves in a more marginal social position.
71. Eyal Ben-Ari and Yoram Bilu, 'Saints' Sanctuaries in Israeli Development Towns: On a Mechanism of Urban Transformation', *Urban Anthropology*, Vol. 16 (1987), pp. 243–72.
72. For many years this music was not broadcast on radio stations, or was segregated to particular venues of 'oriental music' and sites such as 'wedding music' or 'bus station cassette music'. However, slowly but selectively it was included within the 'high culture', and some oriental musicians and bands have achieved high respectability in the Israeli cultural field.
73. Kimmerling and Migdal, *Palestinians*.
74. On the position of the Arabs in Israel, see Sabri Jiryas, *The Arabs in Israel* (Haifa, 1966) (Hebrew); David Kretzmer, *The Legal Status of the Arabs in Israel* (Boulder, 1990); Ian Lustick, *Arabs in a Jewish State: Israel's Control of a National Minority* (Austin, 1980); David Grossman, *Present Absentees* (Tel-Aviv, 1992) (Hebrew); Uzi Benziman and Attallah Mansour, *Subtenants: The Arabs of Israel* (Jerusalem, 1992) (Hebrew); Peled, 'Ethnic Democracy'; Sammy Smooha, 'Minority Status in an Ethnic Democracy: The Status of the Arab Minority in Israel', *Ethnic and Racial Relations*, Vol. 3 (1990), pp. 389–413; Dan Rabinowitz, *Overlooking Nazareth: The Ethnography of Exclusion in a Mixed Town in Galilee* (New York, 1996).
75. Sami Khalil Mar'i, *Arab Education in Israel* (New York, 1978); Majid Al-Haj, *Education, Empowerment and Control: The Case of the Arabs in Israel* (Albany, 1995).
76. Dan Horowitz and Baruch Kimmerling, 'Some Social Implications of Military Service and Reserves System in Israel', *Archives Européenes de Sociologie*, Vol. 15 (1974), pp. 262–76. This ambivalent position was expressed by several Arab writers, such as the late Emil Habibi's *The Miraculous Story of Disappearance of Said Abi Nakhs al-Mutashil* (1974), translated to Hebrew by Anton Shammas under the title *The Opsimist*, and by Shammas himself in his *Arabesques*. Shammas, an ex-Israeli poet, writer and journalist, provoked an embittered debate and indignation when he published an article in which he accused Israel of excluding the Israeli Palestinians from participation in the common political cultural and collective identity; 'A New Year for the Jews', *Kol Ha-ir* (13 Sep. 1985). The prominent Hebrew writer A.B. Yehoshua was among the many respondents: 'I am suggesting to Shammas that if you want to exercise your full identity, if you want to live in a state that has a Palestinian character with a genuine Palestinian culture, arise, take your possessions, and move yourself one hundred yards eastward, into the Palestinian state, that will be established alongside Israel' (quoted in Y. London, 'The Quilt of the Left', *Politika*, 4 (1985), pp. 8–13). Also see Anton Shammas, 'Kitsch-22: On the Problems of the Relation Between Majority and Minority Cultures in Israel', *Tikkun*, Vol. 2 (1987), pp. 22–6.
77. Eli Reches, *The Arab Israeli Minority between Communism and Nationalism, 1965–1991* (Tel-Aviv, 1993) (Hebrew).
78. An example is the poetry of Mahmud Darwish, an Israeli Arab in exile, who is considered the 'national poet' of the Palestinians and is the author of the 1988 Declaration of Independence. Darwish, like Habibi, published most of his literary works in *al-Jadida* and *al-Itihad*, the periodicals of the Israeli Communist Party.
79. Kimmerling, 'Boundaries and Frontiers of the Israeli Control System'.
80. Recently, a group of Palestinian intellectuals voiced a demand for 'cultural autonomy' in the framework of the Israeli state. This demand seems to raise a dilemma for the Arabs of Israel, as it appears to contradict the claim for completely equal citizen rights and full participation in terms of access to the public domain. It is not clear what the consequences of this demand are, besides the right to establish separate Arab universities and the ability to determine the curricula for all the Arab schools in Israel,

as is currently the case for the separate ultra-Orthodox Jewish school system (see Azmi Bishara, 'On the Palestinian Minority in Israel', *Teoriya U-bikort*, Vol. 3 (1993), pp. 7–20 (Hebrew)). The claim for cultural autonomy raised fierce resistance in most parts of the Jewish political system, due to the fear that this separatism will easily turn into territorial nationalism.

81. Even in the United States, where religion is constitutionally restrained to the 'private sphere' and is considered a matter of individual choice, religion has a tremendous impact in the public and political realm. See, for example, Ted G. Jelen, 'Religion and the American Political Culture: Alternative Models of Citizenship and Discipleship', *Sociology of Religion*, Vol. 3 (1995), pp. 217–84.
82. This was especially necessary given the conflict with the Arab inhabitants of the country, who perceived the settlers as colonialists and the Zionist settlement as part and parcel of the world political, economic and cultural colonial system (Kimmerling and Migdal, *Palestinians*).
83. Luckmann, 'The New and the Old in Religion'.
84. Kimmerling, 'State Building, State Autonomy'.
85. One salient exception was the series of attempts to form in the 1950s and 1960s 'The League for the Prevention of Religious Coercion', which was an offshoot of MAPAM, a left wing party, and was mainly active during election periods. The other was a larger cultural and political phenomenon, the so-called 'Canaanite' movement. This was a pseudo-nativism movement that aimed at cutting all relations between the 'newly recreated Hebrew nation' and Diaspora Judaism. They claimed the creation of a new separate nation, which includes within it a hierarchic order for other ethnic minorities of the Middle East. The Canaanites constructed a separate and original historiography and legacy of 'Hebrew nations' (Yaacov Shavit, *The New Hebrew Nation: A Study in Israeli Heresy and Fantasy*, London, 1987). In a way, it was taking to its logical extreme some of the original Zionist reasoning for the creation of a 'new' Jewish person and culture, based on ancient pre-Rabbinical (close to pagan) Judaism. The appearance of the RATZ Party – the Civil Rights Movement, with a strong secularistic ideology – was seemingly the first sign of a crack in the hegemony.
86. Even the so-called 'peace process' conducted by the Rabin and Peres governments with the Palestinian Liberation Organization, as well as the establishment Palestinian National Authority, were managed from a power orientated and 'security-militaristic' standpoint (Baruch Kimmerling, 'The Power-Oriented Settlement: Bargaining between Israelis and Palestinians', in Moshe Ma'oz and Abraham Sela (eds), *The PLO and Israel: From Armed Conflict to Political Settlement* (New York, St. Martin's Press, 1977) pp. 223–51.
87. The peace process was not only imposed on the Palestinians from a decisive power position, but also was 'marketed' to the Jewish Israeli population in terms of its security-militaristic cultural ingredients (Kimmerling, 'The Power-Oriented Settlement').

Shall We Find Sufficient Strength?
On Behalf of Israeli Secularism

GERSHON SHAKED

In vain all the toil … . In any eventuality whatever happens the Jews will leave the country and wander off. There is no end of the Diaspora. It is clear today … I can see it. I see in another fifty or a hundred years by which time we will be a majority in the country, built up and with everything your heart desires, they will abandon everything and disperse throughout the world … not at the hands of Nebuchanezzar or Titus but without them. Just like that, without a reason, by their own doing and will.

H. Hazaz, Drabkin, Burning Rocks (1938)

THE REVOLT AGAINST THE GHETTO CULTURE
AND THE WEST

The Ghetto Culture of romantic sadness and passive hope is condemned to destruction. What shall we do before the sun of our new enterprising culture shines forth in all its glory? The protective ghetto forces, those of stagnation are being destroyed before our eyes – Shall we find sufficient new forces for tremendous creation as well as for our national soul in a time of transition? Or are we tragically condemned, God forbid, to the fate of a mother not having sufficient strength to give birth?[1]

These words of Moshe Glickson, published in the Soviet Union some seventy years ago, are a kind of summary of the past culture and a kind of suspended animation waiting for the new culture on its way. Glickson's negative view of ghetto culture was shared by many of his

---

Gershon Shaked is Professor of Hebrew Literature at the Hebrew University of Jerusalem.
[This article was translated from Hebrew by Norman Berdichevsky.]

contemporaries. Yosef Haim Brenner, who evaluated Mendele's essay 'An evaluation of Ourselves in Three Volumes', justified this fatal judgement. According to Brenner, Mendele describes a culture deserving of ruin, and the conclusion of this process is the 'workers' agricultural settlements in the Land of Israel'. Brenner hoped for the flourishing of a new secular culture within the socioeconomic revolution that the Jewish People will undergo (without defining its character). In opposition to Ahad Ha-am, Glickson did not have a cultural forecast of one kind or another (in the article cited). He did not describe the future 'Cultural Centre' but hoped that the newly developed culture would differ from that which had been imposed on the Jewish people in the past. His words may not be just mere description and analysis but rather an expression of a secret and deep longing. For indeed, Zionist culture was born of a yearning to break free of the ghetto culture, and for a large segment of the Zionists this meant a break from the culture of the West as well. As argued by Y. Karni, in his article 'The Artists in the Homeland',[2] the culture developing in the Land of Israel could not depend on Western culture but would have to adapt to the culture of the East (the Middle East). All components brought from abroad would have to adapt to the new regional expanse; and only the tension between what was imported and what was taking shape in the area itself was likely to determine a new cultural existence.

I would like to emphasize this theme from another viewpoint. Zionism sought not only to be redeemed from the ghetto. It also yearned for redemption from the 'Decline of the West'. Herzl's European-Liberal vision, 'Altneuland', did not enchant the immigrants who thought of another reality and society. They wished to see in the Land of Israel a haven from the cultural decadence of Europe, a cultural 'October Revolution' of sorts that would change the face of the regional expanse and the national morale of a society that had escaped from the ghettoes of the declining West.

Many stories and poems speak in praise of the 'Earth's Blessing' and are critical of urban culture. Pioneering opposed not only the ghetto culture, but first and foremost fought against the metropolitan culture. It was perceived as a reaction against the increasing urbanization of Europe. A typical example of a work expressing the anti-western and anti-urban longing of the Pioneer Society is Avraham Shlonsky's poem (the form of the poem is ironically that of a modernist urban poet):

Metropolis

And again I walk like an innocent man sentenced for no crime,
bearing his soul away towards some crater – to see them,
the children of chaos, stepsons
both to Satan and to God.

> Here they are – sons of Moloch and Kemosh.
> To which silo will they carry the reapings of murder?
> Only a glimmer of tree rot in place of head *Tefilin*
> I see shining from every forehead.
>
> City, beautiful with deceit, then as now,
> I imagine: a mushroom rising like a black box.
> I am so ashamed of this empty laughter.
> Among the spires of Metropolis, cold as polar light.
>
> Yes then and yes now: I am between temptations.
> I see but cannot be seen, speak and not hear.
> On this rocking image, brothers,
> an amulet tied to my right arm.
>
> I loved you, my brothers, amidst the stabbing prickly pears,
> under the thumbnails of crushing Hamsin heat and desert rock,
> in revolution and peace undressed to the neck:
> Blessed is the yoke weighing upon us.
> Amen.
> Selah.

Before us is a declamatory poem representing the 'City, beautiful with deceit' as opposed to the 'stabbing prickly pears'. Uri Zvi Greenberg wrote in the same vein in the preface to the expressionist periodical *Sadan* which began to appear in December 1925; and these are his words:

> What is the great happiness of being a Hebrew lyrical poet who was born in Europe and denies his birth there? Because the voice of the race has overcome the Latin rhythm. The voice of the First Hebrew. And here am I – the happy pauper in a torn prayer shawl of Israel, belonging lovingly to the country which is of course more holy than all the others and dearer than seventy kingdoms.

This polar opposition is found in different variations in the poems of Uri Zvi Greenberg, Shlonsky, Y. Lamdan and S. Shalom as well as among a majority of the generation's writers. True, sometimes these poles are not stationed facing each other; but the 'Earth's Blessing' exists in all of these works and one can learn from these contrasts. The combination 'piercing thorns of the cactus shrub' did not just have a pioneering-Zionist significance. This world view was influenced by the Narodniks in Russia and by the transformation of the teachings of A.D. Gordon, and the existential existence was also a romantic one in the vein of Chateaubriand. The Land of Israel was conceived as a refuge from western civilization, and Jewish migration to the country as the return of western man to Nature, a return for the sake of rebirth.

LITERATURE HERE WILL BE DIFFERENT

The creators of the new culture in the Land of Israel apparently stood before a broken trough. They rejected two principal factors that had shaped the history of the Jewish People in modern times. They denied both the traditional culture as well as the opposing one that tended towards assimilation in the urban environment.

The detached Jew was a product of the opposing tensions that characterized the 'heroes' of Jewish culture in the nineteenth century, those who had left the ghetto and had vainly attempted to assimilate into western culture, only to be left stranded in both. These detached individuals turned their dilemma into a source of experience and enthusiasm. They laid the foundations of a new Zionist culture because they were revolted by both the ghetto culture and Western culture, either because this culture did not receive them cordially or because they realized that the values of 'Kmosh and Gammora' were no better than the ghetto culture. This double rejection of the two traditions was perhaps the existential source of longing for a different culture. The yearnings for 'another Genesis' and for a 'Gilboa' (characteristic of Shlonsky's poetry) are a result of the cultural abyss which opened before them. Having accepted the Zionist solution, the question emerged 'What image would the new culture bear? What would shape their portrait after leaving behind the fertile tension that had created the Diaspora world?'

Their stand between Judaism and assimilation, between the ghetto culture and the culture of the West, shaped their destiny and led them to literary and cultural achievements. This was the case whether the tension tended towards the West (in the works of assimilationist individuals of creativity such as Sigmund Freud, Arthur Shnitzler, Isaac Babel) or towards the ghetto culture (in the works of Hebrew and Yiddish writers). In the Land of Israel this tension subsided. Jews immigrated to the Land of Israel in order to get rid of this tension and begin anew. Moreover, they knew full well that their *aliya* was a kind of cultural descent in order to realize a social ascent. The Land of Israel did not hold forth the promise of treasures from a cultural viewpoint and could not, from the outset, compete with the ghetto or the western cultures. It could of course provide something that the other two could not; but it denied individuals and groups values and assets which were ostensibly reserved for them in the West.

Jacob Rabinowitz wrote on the development of literature in the Land of Israel (as representative of culture in general):

> Literature here will be different, that is – not Jewish in the usual sense but human, occupationally diverse and multi-faceted. Its Judaism will also be one that adapts to life here and stems from it. This will also mean negative phenomena as well as a narrowing and fall of a kind. The base will expand and the back suffer somewhat. There will be no crowing and boasting. One only has to see and understand.[3]

Rabinowitz's words nicely reflect the characteristic trends of the leading group. People such as A.D. Gordon, Gershon Hanoch, Meir Ya'ari, David Horowitz and others, the authors of articles on literature and culture, were of the opinion that it was necessary to go forward bit by bit. They objected to both the ghetto culture and imitation of the West. If, however, literature and culture showed a continuing western influence, this was due to the contradictions that literature in the Land of Israel had encountered. (The 'Ktuvim' Group, for example, led by Steinmann and Shlonsky preached at continuing the western tradition although they dreamed of 'A New Genesis'.)

A majority of the creative circles and creators of 'pioneering' culture sought to realize and shape the new tensions which had been woven in the region, and which were influenced by the traditions brought by the different population groups from their past. The new factors which made their mark on Israeli secularization were the 'Narodnik' longing for the culture of physical labour and soil and the dream to be absorbed into the Eastern expanse. They did not create a web of culture out of nothing. The existing European and Jewish experiences were brought to the new region and stood in permanent tension with the circumstances and the longing to break free of what had previously existed. Jacob Rabinowitz and many others as well knew that there was a heavy price to be paid for the new beginning and that the loss would be at the expense of the ghetto culture and culture of the West.

The young pioneers who gathered in Betaniya in the 1920s were the cream of European intelligentsia. They came to the Land of Israel to strike roots, to build and be built. We can already hear from their own mouths that it is a matter of gain requiring concessions; and they often recalled the cultural onions and garlic of Warsaw, Vienna and Paris. 'I once again tied the bonds with the spiritual Europe, the old rejected and accursed Europe in which everyone has found a blemish – how great and beautiful and how I long for her! Is she not indeed the breath of our nostrils, the marrow of our bones!', wrote one of them in the group's journal *Kehilateynu* (1922); and a companion of his competes in the very same journal: 'Can one surrender the thousands of cultural possibilities, give up the glowing impressions of a European city, of the wide world stirring with unknown wonders – everything for the sake of realizing our idea in this country?'

A REVOLUTION IN THE DAILY LANGUAGE AND CULTURE

What did these young people who had given up Jewish tradition and European culture expect? They asked themselves time and again what would be the character of this 'impoverished' culture that would be created here – would it compensate them for what had been lost? The new socioeconomic basis, the experience of independence or the 'political haven' on the way – would these make up for the cultural deprivation, would these be a remedy for all the cultural afflictions? Would they be able to overcome the pain of 'two homelands' – the one abandoned and the one being created? The principal compensation given to them was by the pioneering-cultural experience. They felt they were laying the foundations and the basis of a secular Jewish culture. They believed they were the vanguard of a cultural renaissance, the primary bearers of the secularization process. With their help, the religious culture had become the basis of a secular Jewish culture. Whoever believed that there was no advantage in this (Kurtzweill, for example) did not see, in my humble opinion, how great a cultural transformation the Jewish community in Palestine created from the beginning of the century until the 1940s.

There is no need to expand upon what seems to us today as obvious: the creation of a spoken Hebrew language as an established fact; the transformation of a written language from a holy tongue to a literary language; from a literary language to a spoken language to a written language – a marvellous cultural process! The language itself is evidence of the new system of tensions that was created in the social and cultural life of the community. The vocabulary, syntax and structure of 'Our Hebrew' were all created under the influence of both the written and spoken languages of the Ashkenazi Diaspora (Yiddish), and the influence of the pronunciation borrowed from the stress (*Milra* – last syllable emphasized) of the Oriental Jews and Arabic vocabulary. And of course, both these foundations were influenced by European vocabulary and sentence structure. This strange combination of European syntax and the phonetics of Sephardic Jewry, as it appears in the spoken and literary languages, testifies to an ingathering and mixing of diasporas more genuinely than the attempts to revive the folklore of ethnic communities in an artificial way. Such processes of cultural integration were also evident in other corners of the crystallizing Israeli culture. Dance and song are a strange mixture among the dances and melodies brought from Poland, Russia and Romania (Krakowiak, Polka, Horah) and those of the Yemenite immigrants. Some of the folk dances 'invented' by Gurit Kadman and Sarah Levy are attempts at 'linguistic' mergers between East and West and shaped a local culture that is a kind of integration able to cope with the tensions. Another example of this kind of combination is the fertile cooperation between Nahum Nardi and Esther Gamlielit or Bracha Tzefira: an east European composer trying to form a style appropriate for the Middle East. At 'higher' cultural levels, there were also ambitious attempts to create these types of cultural syntheses: Nahum Gutman in his paintings, Paul Ben-Haim in his music and Yonatan Ratosh and others in their poetry. Even in the field of dress, attempts were made to shape a kind of 'Language of Integration' between the rubashka and the kefiya (Itamar Even-Zohar has already commented on this). In all the 'marginal' cultural levels, attempts were made to formulate the new within a configuration of Narodnik ideas,

East European music and dance, the tradition of the Yemenite Jews, and 'Bedouin' ideals (real and imaginary). Things were joined together in a kind of new culture of the youth movements, where these languages developed much better than in other population groups. These cultural configurations became a positive norm because the youth movements (the elite of Israeli society) adopted them and turned them into an obligatory norm. 'Israeli' cultural signposts were characteristic of the 'leading group', and served the elite in its attempts to assimilate the new immigrants. Whoever sought to belong to the new Israeli culture had to accept the rules of the game of the youth movement culture. Whoever left the youth movements did not belong to the 'leading group'. He or she was on the margins. The marginal youth of the 1920s, 1930s and 1940s continued to assimilate according to a pseudo-western model: instead of going to the 'meeting club' as the venue for Israeli youth ceremonies, marginal youth went to the Central European cafes on the shore of Tel-Aviv.

The attempts at 'integration' were occasionally ridiculous. In the 'Ohel' theatre a Russian play was staged – *Jacob and Rachel* – in Shlonsky's Hebrew translation but with Bedouin costumes and a Yemenite pronunciation; between the scenes a Russian accent would be heard. Whoever thinks that these are 'Canaanite' tactics, that is attempts to strike roots in the region and ignore the past, does not know what he is talking about. 'Canaanism' did not try to create a new configuration by a confrontation with old foundations. It tried to get rid of the tensions through 'integration' in the region, not to 'live' them or to use them to create a new cultural reality. True 'Israeliness' is a product of cultural tensions and not an escape from them, honest attempts to create something within the melting pot, a new ideal in which the previous foundations were cast (east European, original Jewish, Oriental).

The ideal was to shed the Diaspora clothes and put on the clothes of the homeland. People were separated from their original names and preferred to be called Agnon instead of Tchatchkes, Ratosh and not Halperin, Mazur and not Mizrahi. In other words, to create a new identity for themselves, to 'assimilate' in order to be different – to leave the ghetto culture of both the East and the West.

ISRAELI CULTURE

There were also other deeper aspects in the renewed shaping of secular culture in the Land of Israel. Haim Nahman Bialik's idea of the 'Assemblage' (*Kinus*) was one of the most important attempts at national cultural secularization of the religious tradition. Bialik contributed in fact to the concept of renewal much more than Ahad Ha-Am in his ideological essays (the idea of absolute justice, etc.). The Book of Legend by Bialik and Ravnitzky transferred an old cultural tradition in new clothes to both youth and adults (including writers such as Moshe

Shamir). The late Professors Schirman in his Poetry Anthology and Tishbi in 'The Doctrine of the Zohar' followed in Bialik's footsteps in the ways of the Assemblage of Jewish tradition. The segments of Legend (*Agadah*), Learning *(Midrash)* and Sermons *(Darush)*. In their original format these segments are combined in books of religious rules (Halacha) or in the adjacent sermons on portions of the Torah. Bialik took out the segments from their surroundings and organized them according to a clear secular historic, or social and moral order: from Adam to the destruction of the Second Temple and from the relations among men to those between a man and his family. The religious tradition was culled anew according to the needs of the secular individual who has been detached from the Halacha and is no longer confident with the sermons. The secular individual saw in these 'Outlooks' a national heritage that in the past was principally that of a religious community, a tradition that had become part of the secular culture without the new Israeli committing himself or herself to the yoke of the religious commandments (*Ol Mitzvot*) or that of community life. The new secular community was fashioned by these transformations from the Halacha and the *Midrash*, and later from The Song of the Middle Ages ('shirat Yemei Ha-beynaim') and the Doctrine of the Zohar.

The fundamental ideological and practical tenets of the 'Assemblage' idea were formulated in a brilliant manner by one of the spiritual fathers of the renewed Israeli culture, Berl Katznelson. His words on the confrontation between the present and tradition became a theoretical basis for many deeds and projects and they are among the most cited in the formative period of the new Israeli culture:

> A creative and innovative generation does not throw the heritage of past generations on to the rubbish heap. It examines and checks, sorts out what is relevant and what is of no consequence. Sometimes it holds fast to an existing tradition and adds to it and sometimes descends to the piles of junk, uncovers forgotten items, polishes them to remove the rust and returns an ancient tradition to life so that it may nourish the soul of the enquiring generation. (1934)

The Bible became the infrastructure of Israeli education and underwent a total transformation in the secular school. 'The educational values of the Bible' were not necessarily 'religious' values as one might expect. The historical, archaeological and national approaches created for the secular reader of the Bible his own bible with a significant difference from the one he had in the ghetto culture. This also applies to the new approach to history (it is possible to either agree with or reject the Zionist historiography of Ben-Zion Dinur but its influence in the State of Israel has been very considerable). This is the case with the changes in emphasis stemming from a negation of the Diaspora and the ghetto culture and a positive approach to the periods of pre-ghetto and post-ghetto independence.

The secular transformation of the religious tradition is also very pronounced in the changes of sense and significance in the formation of the Jewish holiday and ceremony, which has become Israeli. At the heart of the religious tradition stand typical religious holidays such as Rosh Ha-shana and Yom Kippur. The Israeli tradition transferred marginal holidays in the historical tradition to the centre of community life: Tu Bi-shvat (Arbour Day) and Hag Ha-bikkurim (Harvest Festival) as holidays of nature and the soil. These have begun to capture a central position in public consciousness and in 'ritual' performance. Ceremonies and dances have even been created for these 'revived' holidays: 'The planters have gone out on Tu Bi-shvat' and 'They have brought in a full load of first fruits'. New rituals have been created that are more closely linked with the Jewish National Fund than with God's sacrificial altar. Moreover, for Hannukah and Passover, two essentially religious holidays, a secular meaning has been given: the war of the Maccabees has been preferred over the miracle of the oil, and when in the Haggadah we read that in every generation one has to regard oneself as if one went forth out of Egypt – this has been interpreted as a clear cut Zionist commandment.

Are these transformations negative? Not at all! They form an appropriate connection between Jewish life in the past (which has lost its meaning) to Jewish life in the present. They seek to restore a crown of old from before the ghetto culture to its glory. This is a sincere attempt to adapt a tradition to the new pioneering and anti-urban ideals (hence *agricultural* holidays) and to relate the tradition to the new cultural components that developed in the country (the new songs, the dances, the costumes). The Song of Songs has become an Israeli song of love and courting. Hannukah songs have assumed a national significance and the Pesach ritual meal (Seder) has received a new image. These secular transformations have been supported by the educational system from kindergarten to the youth movements and by the social elite of the rural settlements, and have established the new Israeli and his world view.

Have outstanding works been created in the fields of literature, dance, music and painting? As noted above by Rabinowitz: 'This will also mean negative phenomena as well as a narrowing and fall of a kind. The base will expand and the back suffer somewhat.' The best of modern Jewish culture was not produced in an environment that was all 'ghetto' or in one that was totally 'assimilation in the West'. It was rather created because of the great tension between the two.

Bialik and Agnon, Bashevis-Singer and Manger, Joseph Roth, Saul Bellow and Philip Roth are the fruit of these tensions. They were torn between the polar opposites and their creation was the outcome of this rift before Jews decided to redress the distortion and fashion themselves anew. The renunciation of the 'disease' brought about a kind of limited and proscribed 'health'. This does not mean that the Jews have arrived at the 'promised land' and have been relieved of all their spiritual and social illnesses. They came to fashion themselves (as human beings) in new circumstances and to enter a field of new tensions (perhaps less complex) in order to reduce the previous tension and to achieve a new identity. New horizons have been opened by the new cultural reality: there was both a longing to return to Europe and Judaism as well as the desire to detach oneself completely from all this and integrate into the new region. The former has been expressed in works which cast doubt on the ability of Jews to strike roots in the new country (Hazaz) while the latter tendency can be seen in the works of S. Yizhar. Literary creation at its best does not literally mean processes of integration but rather touches upon spaces and gaps, asks questions and deals with difficult problems. Literature senses the new difficulties, but the strength of the new cultural life is greater than its finished products.

It is incumbent upon us to emphasize again: the new Israeli culture was also produced through rejection and loathing. Its choice was not solely positive. Zionism rejected the ghetto culture and loathed the culture of the West. The source of searching was in the revolutionary experience: an old world being destroyed to its very foundations and from the ruins a new world would be built. One must abandon and destroy in order to build and be built (and here Zionism unconsciously followed Nietzsche and Berdichevsky).

EMIGRATION TO THE WEST AND A RETURN TO THE GHETTO?

What happened to the revolution of Zionist culture? Where has it gone and disappeared to? Why are its creators ashamed of their work (such as former Knesset member Nehemkin who was ashamed of his secular Zionist education)? Why has their resolve weakened and why are they undergoing a religious revival and returning to the ghetto culture or 'descending' from Israel to emigrate to the West and its culture?

Economic and social processes of the achievement-orientated western society, as well as counterprocesses (characteristic of both Israel and Iran) providing a single all-encompassing 'religious answer' to the urban corruption of western culture, gain strength and control over our lives. It is no longer becoming to be an Israeli. It is much nicer to be 'western' or to return to Orthodoxy. Not only have the processes changed but the norms have also changed. An anti-Israeli world view is developing in our Israel. An attempt is taking place to destroy the infrastructure that was created in order to fashion a new Israeli society. There are many reasons for these processes – mostly social. 'Israel' of the Yishuv (Jewish community in Mandatory Palestine) was a land of absorption that accepted people who had been trained towards their *aliya* (immigration) and who brought with them *ideals* of a new society and a new culture. When they turned from being absorbed to become the absorbers, a whole absorption culture was created and norms were established which shaped the face of society. The immigration processes in the 1950s were too swift and the absorbers were unable to 'digest' the new arrivals. Moreover, the urbanization processes and the economic changes turned the absorbing society from a 'pioneering' one into the 'western' type. Not only did the absorbing society fail to make its mark upon the newcomers, but it lost its own distinctive nature. The immigrant society which had made strenuous efforts to form for itself a modern 'Judaism' and reliable Israeliness returned to being a society of immigrants. A significant portion of those who had immigrated to Israel or had been born there no longer see themselves as having an Israel identity.

Everyone is letting us know in good taste that 'Israeliness' is now bankrupt. There are those who have made a full return to the culture of the West and for those whom this does not satisfy, there is the Orthodox return to 'The Holy One – Blessed Be He', and even more far-fetched (and similar!) solutions: from India to Ethiopia. The West has once again become an economic and social ideal and hence a cultural one. If an individual has not reached the ultimate conclusion and emigrated, he is able to bring the West's writing and language here: he is in the East but his culture is in the West.

The norm is no longer simplicity and frankness (one of the anti-western and anti-ghetto norms created here) but ceremonial splendour and pomp that did not spring from this region and from the Israeli situation but were rather brought here in cellophane packaging from Poland. The Israeli parties around the campfire have given way to cocktail parties in the villas of reserve brigadiers and generals. Israeli songs are songs of nostalgia for old people longing for their youth; their age has embarrassed their youth. In moments of truth (not those of nostalgia) we all dance western dances and hum the latest 'hit'. Instead of choir singalongs we have the Eurovision, and instead of dance festivals we will soon dance the last tango in Tel-Aviv. The sad internal conclusion of the loss of Israeli identity is emigration abroad (*yerida*). Anyone who yearns to realize the European–American norm (as a positive cultural norm) does so by emigrating to a 'distant land'. This is a return to the longings of the Betaniya group, which were fought against, while attempting to create a new Israeli culture.

This attachment to the West involves the cancellation of the tension between the West, on the one hand, and Judaism and the local culture on the other; a renunciation of polar opposites in order to abolish the 'Israeli tension'. It is an attempt to leave the Israeli transformation and return to a previous situation. This is a return (or an attempt at a return) to assimilation when the opposing aspect (Judaism) no longer provides for a fertile rift.

Another attempt stemming from the loss of the Israeli identity is a return to Orthodoxy (*hazara bi-tshuva*). At the end of the day, this is nothing more than a return to the ghetto. Rabbi Shach could just as well have said that the People of Israel as a 'Jewish' people does not need the Land of Israel at all. The ghetto culture needs no 'old-new land'. The

'Assemblage' culture is the opposite of the ghetto culture. The return to Orthodoxy is an attempt (an unjustified one in my opinion) to return from the 'Book of Legends' to the sources. If such a return were indeed authentic, it would ultimately lead to the culture of Halacha and *Drasha*, to a religious reality that has no need for a new socioeconomic reality. The ghetto culture is the culture of the *Kollel* – a return to the Yeshiva students whose study is their livelihood, and their livelihood, the Torah. The ghetto culture also relates to the secular environment as 'goyish' (gentile), hence as one that must be exploited for the needs of Torah as livelihood and to ensure the provision of subsistence for the Torah.

Even if attempts are made to impress a national Israeli character on the ghetto culture, one must remember that Israeliness and Zionism were created as a revolt against the culture of the ghetto. Zionism did not look forward to a just messiah. It arose without one. It shaped the cultural revolution by a new *alternative* out of the depths of an old tradition, by a secular decision. A return to orthodoxy is an admission of the failure of Zionism's cultural revolution.

Part of the process of the formation of 'Israeliness' was the attempt at a complex integration of eastern and western folklore, the languages of East and West, an integration that indeed succeeded in several areas. One of the solutions, attempted by Israeli society to offset the disintegration of 'The Israeli Image', has been the cultivation of ethnic communities and their folklore (a feature providing a livelihood to many Ashkenazi Jews). Lo and behold it turns out that this does not encourage integration processes but rather those of fragmentation. The Israeli ideal was to integrate the different diaspora communities and turn them into a People, not to cultivate fragmentation. If the Mimuna festival were meant to become a general Israeli holiday, then that would be fine; but if it is intended to make permanent communal fragmentation, then we have not advanced at all towards Israeli identity but have fled from it to the ghetto culture (an eastern ghetto is also still just a ghetto).

THERE IS A RIGHT TO ISRAELI SECULARISM

The western and ghetto cultures are leading Israelis to emigrate to New York or cause them to return to Kavtziel and Casablanca. The original Israeli culture strove to mediate and integrate diverse factors, to live with the tensions and to engender a new identity, perhaps more limited and impoverished than the identities from which it sprung, but different and independent. Moreover, the Diaspora imitated this culture. In the 'Rama' camps of the Conservative Movement in the United States, they sang Israeli songs, danced Israeli dances and even tried to imitate the simplistic way of life which was still identified with 'Israeliness'.

Israeli society has become a spiritual centre, not because it rebuilt the falling Satmar sukka hut but because it created a new centre worthy of imitation (though not precisely along Ahad Ha-am's model). But if the

Israelis imitate the lives of the Camp Rama youth, whom will the youngsters imitate in the United States?

The struggle for Israeli identity, no matter how synthetic it may be, was a struggle over a norm, over a point to hang on to and a way out for a society that had lost its European and Jewish identity.

One should view this norm as a leaning point and not as a compulsory norm, a kind of imaginary uniformity. Israeli society during the Yishuv period was collective in its thought and demanding with regard to the rules of behaviour. There were those who rebelled against the norm in the name of pure individuality; they could rebel so long as there was an Israeli portrait with which they could vie; but when that norm became a lifeless scarecrow, the baby was thrown out with the water and the bathtub was drained empty. The single Israeli is no longer capable of finding his 'Israeliness', for it has disappeared while he was trying to flee from it. What remains is a people with a blurred image, living a secular life, smitten by guilt feelings for a lost 'Yiddishkeit' which it does not know how to define for itself.

This is not to say that I am longing for an Israeli made on a conveyor belt according to a historic cookbook recipe. There is a place for a religious Israeli, a Sephardi Israeli and an Ashkenazi Israeli, and a 'western' Israeli can reside next to a 'Jewish' Israeli so long as they have a common identity. There is nothing as important for a society rich in human resources as ours as social pluralism, on condition that there is a latch, a common point to lean on and start from. The problem however is that the foundation has been destroyed and the links of the chain are disintegrating. The adjectives (Sephardi, religious, Ashkenazi) outweigh the noun (Israeli).

The emigrants (Yordim) and those who have returned to Orthodoxy now dominate the scene – those with packed suitcases and those with skullcaps, both the black and knitted ones. I have come to speak on behalf of the Israeli foundation that has been lost: one should look for it again. There is a right to exist for Israeli secularism: it is not inferior and impoverished, is not guilty, and does not need to return to orthodoxy or emigrate from the country westwards. It alone is likely to shape an original culture here. Without Israeliness – it is difficult to be an Israeli.

NOTES

1. M. Glickson, 'The Change of the Guard', *Masuot* (Odessa, 1926).
2. *Hedim*, Vol. 1, No. 1 (1912).
3. Yaacov Rabinowitz, 'Our Literature and Life', *Hedim*, Vol. 3 (1924).

Between Rabbi Shach and Modern Hebrew Literature

DAN MIRON

The rallying of Israel's Haredi community behind Benjamin Netanyahu in the 1996 elections took many observers by surprise and played the key role in ensuring his victory. Yet this was not the first instance in which this community, which constitutes a small segment of the Israeli population, determined the identity of the country's prime minister. Six years earlier it was Rabbi Shach, arguably the foremost Haredi spiritual authority in Israel, who dealt the *coup de grace* to Shimon Peres's attempts to bring down the National Unity Government and form a Labour government under his leadership.

The Rabbi's well known speech, which brought the political crisis of 1990 to one of its most grotesque moments, was nothing more than one long insipid and stammering diatribe of cliches. One might have expected to hear such a speech from a third-rate operator of anti-Zionist Orthodoxy rather than from a great scholar and man of the Torah, a spiritual figure who is followed by many. His remarks were shallow even by the standards of the spiritual world from which they emerged. As an expression of a contemporary religious Jew, the speech only produced shallow water from the deep well of Jewish religious thought. His remarks were characterized by anachronisms, a lack of information, demagogic sentimentalism and a senile holding on to the slogans of fifty and sixty years ago.

One has but to return and reread Agnon's *As a Guest He Used to Lodge* – a story written in 1938 that described the atmosphere of a provincial Jewish town in Poland ten years earlier – in order to realize that the claims and replies of the kind that the Rabbi used in his speech were those heard in the period between the two world wars from minor

---

Dan Miron is Professor of Hebrew Literature at the Hebrew University of Jerusalem. [This article was translated from Hebrew by Norman Berdichevsky.]

rabbis and third- and fourth-rate political hacks of Agudat Israel in the backwater towns of Poland and Lithuania. In the meetings and debates of the guest (the narrator) with the town's rabbi – an arrogant narrow minded religious scholar – and with his son, a journalist and Aguda political worker, Rabbi Shach's words seem to float to the surface, including the accusations of desecration of the Sabbath and of eating non-kosher food made against the kibbutzim in the Land of Israel.

Ironically, Agnon as a religious Jew who observed the contemporary Jewish reality rejected these accusations (though not of course the idea of a life in harmony with the Torah commandments, with which he identified; only the use of the Torah as a means to denounce Zionism and deprive its enterprise of legitimacy from a Jewish viewpoint). He presents the Rabbi and his son as part of the spiritual impoverishment and disintegration that destroyed Polish Jewry from within before the murderers' hands put a physical end to its existence.

In any event, the words of the Rabbi and his son from *As a Guest He Used to Lodge* were said in a Galician town sixty years ago, whereas the words of Rabbi Shach were pronounced in Tel-Aviv fifty years after the Holocaust and forty years after the establishment of the State of Israel. The provincialism, the introversion, the stewing in their own juice which one might have forgiven in the case of Agnon's dismal heroes (all the more so since they perished together with all the House of Israel in Poland in the furnaces of Auschwitz and Treblinka), are unforgivable in the case of a spiritual figure, the ostensible leader of a generation, who has not learned anything from what happened to the Jewish People during all those years, has not asked any question or searched for any answer. This was made apparent from the Rabbi's studied disregard of the historical uniqueness of the Holocaust and its fateful destiny, both from the human and universal aspects as well as the Jewish national one.

From the Rabbi's words we understood that in this century of ours, the trials and tribulations of Israel have increased but the problems themselves are well known 'classical' Jewish difficulties. The Holy-One-Blessed-Be-He punishes Israel for its sins and subjects the people to 'trials'. The only legitimate Jewish reaction to these problems and 'trials' was holding firmly to the Torah's commandments down to their smallest detail in the past and still is the same today.

This is it in a nutshell. According to Rabbi Shach, the Holocaust as a unique phenomenon deviating from any known past succession of events not only from an historical viewpoint, but a theological one as well, did not occur at all. Hence it was not specifically mentioned in his sermon, not even once.[1] Since it never happened, the Rabbi is absolved from coming to terms with its religious meaning. To put it more succinctly, the Rabbi does not allow the Holocaust to intrude on his thoughts because he is not ready and is not capable of facing up to it. If he were ready to cope, he would have to ask if it could be possible that the Holy-One-Blessed-Be-He allowed the spilling of the blood of a million Jewish children who had not sinned for the sole purpose of paying stricter attention to the instructions of the *Shulhan Aruch*, and so that the Jewish sinners who had ignored the prohibitions in the Torah learn morality and withdraw from their sinful path. As a believer, he should have asked the Job-like question on the nature of how the world is run under the watchful eye of an omnipotent God who saw Auschwitz and yet permitted it to exist. But the Rabbi refuses to ask questions like these that are likely to disturb his halachic-scholarly environment of 'business as usual'.

Indeed, Rabbi Shach revealed in his speech the refusal of the majority of the religious camp to be exposed to questions that confront them with the post-Holocaust era. From this follows the essential mendacity that has characterized this Jewry (from the internal religious aspect) in general, and its ultra-Orthodox segment in particular, during the past two decades. Many knowledgeable people including those in the ultra-Orthodox religious camp speak, not coincidentally, of the great spiritual aridity characteristic of the world of contemporary Jewish scholarship. It turns out that 'the geniuses of the generation' are mostly 'technical' ones who master the halachic mechanisms quite well but are not capable of drawing conclusions from them which have a spiritual significance. They have added not a single tome to the treasury of religious literature which could stand unashamedly alongside the outstanding works of Jewish religious thought from the time of Philo to the days of Rabbi Kook.

It is clear that as someone who stands at the centre of such a spiritual wilderness, Rabbi Shach is incapable of evaluating – from an internal religious Jewish basis – the idea of Zionism, the establishment of the State of Israel and all that they entail. Whoever looked at his face during the speech and at the mob of black-clad men who listened to him could not but see and feel the intellectual and spiritual poverty of halachic Jewry. Paradoxically, this is all the more so in this generation in which the power of halachic Jewry has not only grown, but also the number of perplexed and lost souls regarding it as 'enlightenment' and searching for guidance and atonement has increased.

The sight was at once pathetic and offensive, ridiculous and trivial. In many ways it was nothing but yet another revelation of a familiar moral and cultural degeneration, the same degeneration that Modern Hebrew Literature described and analysed in all its detail in great depth during a hundred years of creativity and struggle from the time of Yitzhak Erter and Joseph Perl to the days of Y.H. Brenner. It is important and even essential that we look clearly at this revelation and strive to understand the nature of this degeneration; not only because Rabbi Shach's speech had, as is well known, immediate political results affecting the lives of every Israeli (the prevention of Shas's support of a Labour-led government; defeat of Shimon Peres's manoeuvre leading to Likud's retention of power; making peace more remote), but because one understands from the Rabbi's words the significance of Jewish Orthodox's principled stand in regards to the Israeli national public life and its focus. This is the struggle going on between the two rival Zionist conceptions; the one that puts top priority on the continuation of the State of Israel as a democratic and Jewish state and the other that considers continuation of control over the 'Entire Land of Israel' as the most important issue (though the concept 'The Entire Land of Israel' has never been clearly defined).

The first concept strives to secure the physical existence of the state and preserve its democratic and Jewish character by securing peace with the Palestinian-Arab People and by partitioning the Land of Israel between the Jewish State and a prospective Palestinian-Arab State. The other concept is ready to sacrifice not only peace but Israeli democracy as well and to abolish the very functioning of the State of Israel as a viable political entity so long as control of the country, of territory, is not weakened.

It is alleged that Rabbi Shach is ostensibly closer in his political views to the first concept, with its reservations from the territorial fundamentalism of the rival concept; he even included several words to this effect in the body of his speech. But such a view is based on a fundamental misunderstanding of his way of thinking that stands behind his 'dovish' views. The Rabbi is not a 'dove' in any reasonable or tolerable sense of the word. He is one of many Jews who were ready, and still are ready today, to continue an existence without any Jewish sovereignty over territory in spite of all that has happened to the Jewish People through the centuries. They did not join spiritually in any way whatsoever in the fateful decision of the people in Israel to take responsibility for its historical destiny into its own hands and to bear the difficult burden of political independence. They are willing to surrender territories in the state and the land with which they share no common political identity – whether this is done in the name of *Pikuach Nefesh* (Saving of Life) or to preserve the quiet that will allow them the cultivation of the routine of maintaining the Torah with *Derech Eretz* (customary honourable habits and manners).

In contrast with them, even the quintessential Israeli 'dove' is not prepared to give up the principle of Jewish sovereignty over a defined territory in the Land of Israel, a sovereignty which, as a last resort, may require the spilling of blood and self-sacrifice. As someone who believes in the unavoidable necessity of partitioning the country between Jews and Palestinian-Arabs for the sake of physical survival of the State of Israel, let alone its existence as an enlightened and properly functioning state – personally I feel further divorced and more reserved about Rabbi Shach's 'dovishness' than the irresponsible 'hawkishness' of Ariel Sharon and Geula Cohen.

Moreover, the 'dovishness' of Rabbi Shach (and Rabbi Ovadia Yosef) has no real political significance. Indeed, as we have seen, when the moment of truth arrived and ultra-Orthodoxy had to come down with political weight on one side of the scales, the difference between the 'dovish' and sober Rabbi Shach and his hated opponent, the 'hawkish' and Messiah-drunk Rabbi Shneurson, disappeared. The two religious leaders opted for the Likud and did everything in their power to prevent exploring the peace possibility by means of compromise and dialogue. These are the determining factors. From this one has to draw long range conclusions. In order to do so, however, one needs a deeper understanding of the historical basis of the Rabbi's words. This came through most strongly in the most important and turbulent part of his speech – in his acrimonious words against the kibbutzim.

These words, which apparently were not germane to the political part of the speech, were in fact its core. One should not regard them as a sudden explosion or an idiosyncratic distortion that diverted the Rabbi from the majority of the people or from those who support the Labour Party to a small minority among them in the kibbutzim. As already noted, Rabbi Shach's hostility towards the kibbutzim continues a central line in the rhetoric of anti-Zionist Orthodoxy from the 1920s and 1930s. This line expresses Orthodoxy's inability to come to grips with the changes that have occurred in the life of the People of Israel in the modern era and reveals the rationale of its opposition to the Zionist world view.

It is neither the eating of pork products and rabbits nor the desecration of the Sabbath in the kibbutzim which have aroused Orthodoxy's wrath, despite such claims for purposes of propaganda. Its spokesmen know very well that non-kosher food is also found on the tables of many Jews who are not kibbutz members and are not even Zionists. Nor is the desecration of the Sabbath typical just of kibbutz life. What has been disturbing and angering is not the material transgressions in themselves but the social and spiritual context in which they were committed. While ordinary transgressors in Israel are, from the point of view of Orthodoxy, bad Jews, lax Jews who have sinned and are liable to inherit hell unless they repent in time, kibbutz members are neo-Jews who dare to postpone the 'eternal' rule of the Torah and who have dared to institute a new 'usurpatory' code in its place, offering a deceitful *Shulhan-Aruch* in place of the true one. They have offered up pork on the table posing as an altar and in the framework of a feast that the poet described as a holy banquet of the poor ('I was called to the banquet of the poor – and I shall come. I have not brought a slice of bread. I brought a red song'). This same poet, at times the prophet of the Revisionists, declared the sanctity of the kibbutzim that for him comprised 'Jerusalem of below' and announced the abolition of any theological difference between them and 'Jerusalem of above':

> Ein Harod, Tel-Yosef and Beit-Alpha, two vibrant Deganias
> Jerusalem – the tefillin of the head, and the Emeq – of the hand
> A lamed-vav [righteous man] in all the kibbutzim in the glory of the Lord of all kingdoms.[2]

Orthodoxy's representatives probably never read Uri Zvi Greenberg's poems, but the intuition underlying these poems was familiar to them. It demonstrated to them that the true spiritual danger of Zionism as a whole was embodied in the kibbutzim (as they were then in the 1920s and 1930s). It was therefore that kibbutz members were presented as Datan and Aviram, and their enterprise – as the heretical deed of Korach and his sect.

Of course, the kibbutzim were nothing less than the spearhead of socialist Zionism and this is the place to wonder about the developing inclination of anti-Zionist Orthodoxy in the face of a lack of an alternative, to prefer the Zionist Right over the Labour Movement – a kind of preference for cholera over malignant cancer. It is said that this preference has its origin in the alienation of the Labour Movement to 'tradition', compared with the affection of the Zionist Right for this tradition, especially since it came to power. This is a distortion, stemming from unfamiliarity with the historical roots of this phenomenon and from the tendency to explain them according to their surface reflection on public life and the flow of contemporary events alone, which has accompanied us right up to the present.

It is also said that the closeness between Orthodoxy and the radical Right is fixed in a shared predilection for religious mysticism, and this too is a nonsensical supposition as anyone should know who has wondered about the style of thinking of a pronounced anti-mystic such as Rabbi Shach. As far as authentic Orthodoxy is concerned, both the sympathy for tradition of such right-wingers as Menachem Begin and the ritual of 'Jewish Consciousness' by such Labourites as Zalman Aran are ridiculous caricatures – something like the grimacing of a monkey's face trying to imitate the countenance of a true believer. Neither of them is worth a grain of salt. When it comes to mystical experiences of dedicated right-wingers, the pseudo-religious yearning for the Temple Mount or the 'Fountainhead', or mystigogic talk *à la* Yair Stern's 'Principles of Rebirth' and Israel Eldad-Sheib's sermons, authentic Orthodoxy sees them all as akin to idol-worship, pure and simple. The only exception to this pattern is Religious Zionism, which differs from authentic Orthodoxy in the same way as two hostile tribes differ from one another.

In the Orthodox framework, there is no holiness that can be divorced from the Torah and its commandments and from a life of Torah study and maintenance of the Halacha down to its last detail; there is no holy soil, holy grave, holy sacrifice or holy kingdom that is not bound up with the unappealable acceptance of the 'Yoke of Heaven'. When divorced from the Torah, all these are but idols and tainted meat. Indeed, Orthodoxy relates to 'traditionalism' and to the pseudo-religious mysticisms of the Zionists in the same way – with contempt and disgust. In this regard, one can see the attitude of alienation towards a party such as the Tehiya. No matter how hard it has tried to outdo itself in demonstrating a positive attitude towards 'tradition' and in pretending to speak in the name of the 'Values of Israel', it has not won Orthodoxy's trust. To the contrary, Orthodoxy suspects it of precisely what it has long suspected of the kibbutzim: the pretension to 'continue' Judaism while altering its content and transferring the core of the matter from God and his commandments to the land (of Israel) and its control.

Likud, by comparison, does not raise such a suspicion. It is regarded by Orthodoxy as a large camp of simple and unsophisticated Jews. Of course they are sinners and bad Jews – attending football games on the Sabbath and treading upon scores of important commandments in their footsteps – but they at least do not have the audacity to be more than they are – bad Jews. They do not possess the intellectual acumen and independent opinion that are the hallmarks by which Orthodoxy identifies its spiritual opponents. No, the ultra-Orthodox are willing to support Likud, not because of the latter's supposed sympathy for tradition but on another account entirely, which in turn requires clarification.

As a matter of historical truth, the fathers of the Zionist Labour Movement were closer to religious tradition by a long margin than were the fathers of Revisionism. Members of the Ha-poel Ha-tzair arrived at Zionism and the Land of Israel from the *heder* and the *yeshiva*. They were mostly brought up studying in Jewish religious academies, and this childhood memory and its heritage still resonated within them on their arrival in Eretz Israel. Berl Katznelson arrived at Zionism from the depths of the Jewish enlightenment and a feeling of belonging. Nothing in the spiritual and literary past of the people was alien to him. Zalman Rubashov-Shazar reached Zionism from the heart of the Chabad community and he bore within him the Chabad fervour and the wailing over the mystical-Cabalistic messianism all his life. The founders of Ha-shomer Ha-tzair preserved the mark of the Galician and Polish Hasidic experience under the Marxist and Freudian layers of their creed. Only people such as Meir Ya'ari could turn to Moshe Dayan, after the latter had left the Labour Movement and deserted to the Rightist camp, and cry out directly quoting from the prayers of the evening before Yom Kippur: 'Look to the covenant and don't give in to your instincts!'

By comparison, Ze'ev Jabotinsky and his comrades arrived at Zionism from the salons of the Jewish assimilationists in Odessa and Warsaw. They were Russian and Polish Jewish intellectuals, liberals who had grown up in a cultural world devoid of a traditional Jewish layer. They adopted a world view and distinct cultural habits, and brought with them a fluent command of gentile languages and a great interest in the literature and culture of their parents' homes and their study desks. (As is well known, Jabotinsky was not only a master craftsman of the Russian language but also an important figure in Russian culture. He was one of the initiators if not the founding father of the 'Odessa School' of Russian journalism and literature.) Their road to Zionism was parallel to that of Theodore Herzl; hence their constant attachment to his personality and

Zionist method. Like him, they were deeply rooted in the alien gentile culture. Like him, they saw their spiritual world in the liberal *fin de siècle* Europe. Like him, they arrived at the idea of the political redemption of the Jewish People, not through love for Mordechai but out of hatred for Haman, that is from the force of the confrontation with anti-Semitism, whether in its mass-pogrom form or in its cultured refined version. They were proud people, who stood tall and erect, self-confident of their value and talents, and their response to anti-Semitism was one of defiant national pride. But this pride was certainly not tied to the religion of Israel and its scholarly-rabbinical tradition. Quite the reverse: they desired to provide the Jews with political independence in order for them to live in their own land as a proper European nation.

This desire stood out with Jabotinsky even more than with the utopian Herzl. He wished to see the rise of an independent Jewish society, confident of its sovereignty and power to the extent of allowing its citizens to be 'like the rest of the nations' without losing their Jewish national identity. One has only to read *Shimshon* (Samson) to realize how the founding father of the Revisionist Movement saw the priests of Israel and their Torah tradition in a negative light and how great his admiration was for the European spirit as reflected in Samson's attitude to the sons of Crete – the Philistines.

Apparently, a man like Berl Katznelson should have been closer to the heart of the ultra-Orthodox Jew than a 'goy' like Jabotinsky; but it was not so, nor could it even be. This was not due to Katznelson's attachment to socialism and the revolutionary movements in Russia, but ironically because of his deep attachment to modern Hebrew literature – to Bialik, to Feierberg, to Berdichevsky and Brenner, a group in which a man like Jabotinsky did not really feel at home, in spite of his love for Bialik and the great service he did for Bialik with his masterful Russian translations.

It seems to me possible to distinguish between any Zionist view achieved through the mediation of modern Hebrew literature and other approaches whose architects skipped over it. A division of Zionist concepts according to this criterion would place Ahad Ha-am and Berdichevsky together (despite all the differences between them) in contrast to Herzl and Nordau; Nahum Sokolow vs. David Wolfsohn, Chaim Weizmann vs. Ze'ev Jabotinsky, Berl Katznelson as contrasted with Berl Borochov (the Yiddishist), even the present-day Labour Movement, with all its ideological wretchedness and cultural poverty, as contrasted with Likud. In the case of Likud, one of the mechanisms common to all its different and strange component branches is the attachment to a Zionism that did not pass through the melting pot of Hebrew literature and its distinct modern Jewish culture and as a result feels an essential alienation from contemporary Israeli literature. That is the case with the veteran Revisionist layer of 'Herut', as it is with the nativist-'Boazi' layer of the *moshavot* citrus growers and with the oriental communities that leaped straight from the world of religious tradition to Zionism. And this is the case with the ultra-Orthodox who have never left their world and for whom Hebrew literature and its culture are still within the realm of forbidden food.

Modern Hebrew literature was the nucleus of modern Jewish culture which severed itself from the religious faith. It dealt, of course, with the tribulations of the Jewish Diaspora, reacted to murderous anti-Semitic outrages, described the wanderings of migration and the hardships of poverty, envisaged the establishment of a 'safe haven' for persecuted Jews in the Land of Israel. With all this, it did not concentrate on the physical existential 'Problem of the Jews' but rather on the historical-cultural 'Problem of Judaism'. The principal national question that provoked interminable struggles was whether or not a spiritual and worthy Jewish identity could possibly continue after religious faith had retreated. Many among the great personalities of literature wondered whether Judaism, as a spiritual and historical phenomenon, had not indeed reached the end of the line. Nevertheless, they saw in their very activity as Hebrew writers and their vying with the 'To be or not to be' question of the national soul a sign of its continuation. Even those among them who were not avowed Zionists and ostensibly did not believe in the spiritual and moral value of historical Jewish identity, such as Y.H. Brenner, pointed out either directly or indirectly the essential parallelism between creative spiritual activity in the Hebrew language and Zionism's attempt to comprise a continuation of Judaism by what Ahad Ha-am termed 'relocating its centre'.

From the beginning of the nineteenth century, long before the advent of Zionism, modern Hebrew literature identified itself as an alternative Jewish culture that had come to take the place of the scholastic religious tradition. It was to be the 'Watchman of the House of Israel', responsible for discussing all the problems and provide answers for matters occupying the individual Jew both as a human being and as a Jew. From this, authors such as Ahad Ha-am and Bialik, as well as their followers, derived the right to speak to their readers in a prophetic tone. This prophecy was, from the point of view of Hebrew literature, both possible and legitimate in spite of being a prophecy without God, a mission without a transcendental messenger. Hebrew literature was entirely a continuous confirmation of the new Jewish spiritual situation in which the highest authority had been transferred from God to the Jewish heart internally; from the burning bush to the holy flame within the prophet's own heart (see Ahad Ha-am's description of Moses in his well known essay). Zionism had come from the academy of modern Hebrew literature and saw itself as the organizational and political expression of this new internal Jewish authority. It came not only to create a Jewish state as Herzl had demanded, but to provide a 'body' to a new worthy Jewish cultural life.

Members of the Second Aliya were far removed from the school of 'spiritual Zionism' as advocated by Ahad Ha-am but they did subscribe to his perception of Zionism as the continuation of Judaism through its spiritual reorganization around the uniqueness of 'The National Morality' rather than the religion of Israel. Hence their quests for a synthesis between Zionism and Socialism; hence their striving for 'a Human-Jewish Revolution' bound not only to a negation of the Diaspora and an ambition for political independence but, above all, to a change in the moral character of the individual Jew by means of his/her return to 'the universe' (nature) and to the 'work of the universe' (primarily productive work and principally the cultivation of the soil). This revolution, incidentally, was from an intellectual point of view a direct continuation of the demands of the literature of the Hebrew enlightenment.

Ultra-Orthodox Judaism viewed this pretension of establishing a new Jewish culture of values with suspicion and hatred. True, not all of its leaders shared this view. We know, for example, how Rabbi Kook reacted to the emergence of members of the Second Aliya, a group that included such hardened and bitter atheists as Y.H. Brenner. To him, they were messianic Jews, the unwitting messengers of the God of Israel. Rabbi Kook, however, represented that messianic wing of Judaism which retreated before the ultra-Orthodox wing that can be termed 'reactionary' (this term does not necessarily imply a negative connotation, just as the description of Rabbi Kook's orthodoxy as 'messianic' does not necessarily imply a positive trait as evidenced by the case of Gush Emunim). Rooted in nineteenth century Central Europe (Hungary, Germany), this reactionary stream described its function as a defence of the wholeness of Jewish life by withdrawal and isolation from the destructive influences of assimilation and apostasy. It stemmed from the reaction to assimilation and a reticence from contact with the modern world which had produced it, and was characterized by a stronger attachment to the Halacha and opposition to any factor external to it.

In the twentieth century, this ideology of orthodoxy took control of wide sectors of traditional Judaism such as a large part of Hassidism in Poland which was led by tendencies completely different from those of ultra-pious elements ('Hatam Sofer') in Hungary. When, on the eve of the First World War and immediately thereafter, it was time for the political organization of anti-Zionist Orthodoxy, there was already a 'reactionary' common denominator between the Hasidim of Poland and the strictly observant Orthodox in Germany. This reactionary wing gradually gained the upper hand in the entire ultra-Orthodox camp. In *As a Guest He used to Lodge*, the 'guest' conducts his argument with the town's rabbi in a tone that reminds us of Rabbi Kook's debates with Rabbi Sonnenfeld. In other words, this is a debate between an orthodox Judaism ready to acknowledge the internal Jewish significance (even the unconscious one) of the enterprise of rebirth in the Land of Israel and the one denying it. After the Holocaust, however, this debate apparently became less and less possible. Although Agudat Israel distanced itself from its sharp anti-Zionist stand in 1947, this was not due to a decision to consider Zionism a legitimate Jewish phenomenon, but rather because it decided to view it as a neutral governing body with which it was permissible to cooperate in order to reap benefits and advance the interests of the 'Torah Jewry'. It was within this context that Orthodoxy cooperated with the MAPAI regime from the days of Itche Meir Levin to the time of Avraham Shapira.

Nevertheless, Orthodoxy did not reduce its powerful emotional opposition to the revolution embodied in the new Hebrew-Jewish culture, of which the purest expression was Hebrew literature and Zionist activism. It was here that orthodoxy identified its hated opponent – the usurper. It was here that the enemy's true face was revealed. Orthodoxy much preferred ordinary bad and lax Jews or even 'gentile-Jews' – as had been the case with the Polish state and its leader Josef Pilsudski – with whom it was possible to do business. The Zionist Right was therefore a negative rather than a malignant phenomenon. It did not have the audacity to develop its own set of rules or introduce new modern values into the Jewish way of life. Its concept of Jewish identity was limited to the shell, to the framework: an independent powerful Jewish State on both banks of the Jordan. From a 'principled' Jewish point of view, the majority of its members were just 'modern' Jews following their bad impulses. When they ate pork or desecrated the Sabbath it was anything but new.

The same transgressions in a kibbutz, however, were an outrage over which one must cry to heaven. The Zionist Right did not present Orthodoxy with a 'Jewish' challenge. Its principles left a Jewish vacuum into which one could cast any value, at any opportunity, provided that it was compatible with the principle of Jewish independence and sovereignty in the Land of Israel: the absolute secularism of Ze'ev Jabotinsky and his circle of followers; the fighting atheism of his son Ari Jabotinsky; even the seeds of the Semitic-'Canaanite' concept of Adolph Gurewitz (Adia Gur-Horon) and Uriel Shelah-Ratosh. At the same time, Revisionism was also able to embrace the 'Prophetic Socialism' of Yosef Klausner and the mystical-messianic religiosity of Uri Zvi Greenberg and Yehoshua Heshl Yevin. Revisionism was further able to absorb fragments of Hebrew Literature, and even tried in this way to strengthen its political-cultural standing opposite General Zionism (which prided itself on the leadership of Revisionism's bitter foe, Bialik), on the one hand, and the Zionist Labour Movement, on the other. However, these fragments were never able to be incorporated in the Revisionist framework into a continuous literary-cultural complex.

There was no true spiritual connection between the neo-religious messianism of Uri Zvi Greenberg and the tough social Darwinism of A. Reuveni, between Klausner's concept of 'Judaism and Humanity' and the territorial nationalism of Ratosh, between the tough literary conservatism of writers such as Reuveni, Yaakov Horgin and Y. Har-Even and the modernism of Avigdor Ha-Meiri and Uri Zvi Greenberg. The Revisionist World was unable to even supply these writers with a stage for a creative spiritual confrontation such as the one the Labour Movement's journalism had provided for the bitter encounter between the literatures of the Second and Third Aliyot. This was because the intellectual context of the new Hebrew literature was alien to Revisionism. It was in this context that the Revisionist mentality and doctrine occupied a neutral space; by the same token, Revisionist doctrine and mentality remained neutral in its Jewish or anti-Jewish contents or its pseudo-religious and defiantly secular views, introduced by such people as Yonatan Ratosh vs. Avraham Stern, or Israel Eldad vs. Natan Yelin-Mor. Orthodoxy did not find here a clear spiritual foe and its attitude towards the Revisionists was marked with less suspicion and animosity than to the Zionist Labour Movement. It was even already able to cooperate in the 1930s with Revisionism in an opportunistic way (in the Polish Sejm).

Moreover, Orthodoxy identified a basic characteristic of Revisionism that not only indicated a possibility of (limited) cooperation but a certain similarity between them as well. Indeed, in one important respect Revisionism does resemble Orthodoxy: like Orthodoxy, it concentrates entirely on a single priority. For Orthodoxy, it is securing its distinct interests and furthering the process of imposing the Law of the Torah on the life of the people and the state. For Revisionism, it is confirmation and consolidation of Jewish sovereignty over the entire Land of Israel. There is no logical reason why the advancement of these two different priorities cannot go hand and hand. The Labour Movement, by contrast, promulgated a heterogeneous and more complex order of priorities, the realization of which would always clash with the implementation of Orthodoxy's ambitions.

At a later stage, with the appearance of the Likud, Orthodoxy discovered what the oriental communities had found: a body of 'simple' Jews, uninvolved in the modern secular Hebrew culture, not committed to its synthetic formulations (be it humanism or socialism and Judaism) and untouched by the didactic moralistic rhetoric that stemmed from them. From an economic and social aspect, these formulations turned the Labour Movement into a haughty elite incapable of honouring and absorbing whoever did not bear its values and conceptual world. Already in the era of the underground movements before the establishment of the state, the Revisionists were able to absorb both the oriental immigrants and the inhabitants of Meah-Shearim whereas the PALMACH was closed and remote within its own sense of the cultural superiority of the Zionist Labour Movement and its sense of *sabra* nativist belonging. It was thus in the underground that the first intimate link was formed between the migrants of Polish and Lithuanian origin and the 'marginal' groups who had been rejected and oppressed within the pre-state Jewish community.

Menachem Begin, who had been wise enough to recognize the political value of this connection, cultivated it after the establishment of the state during the despotic arrogance of the MAPAI regime and Ben-Gurion, who represented to these marginal groups this closed and haughty 'foreign' culture. Herut did not represent such a culture or else represented it only in such a weakened and diluted form that it posed no real danger. With the rise of a wave of protest by the deprived masses against the ruling Zionist establishment under the aegis of the Labour Movement, the Likud became the natural political force to channel the energy of this wave, and thus smashed Labour's rule.

In this process, Orthodoxy gained a special niche. Its strong internal organization and spiritual coalescence around the Halacha and its teachers clearly differentiated it from the unorganized parts of the 'periphery' population. It preserved its frameworks and internal hierarchical structures. At the same time, its principled and ingrained tendency to prefer the Zionist Right over the Zionist Left increased. And if this in itself was not enough, the deep emotional identification of many of its supporters (especially among the non-Ashkenazi population) with Likud as the anti-establishment movement of protest compelled this preference on its leaders, even against their will. Thus the 'brilliant' political 'manoeuvre' of Arieh Deri ended in a total disaster despite Rabbi Ovadia Yosef's support; thus the unhappy ending of the strange alliance between Labour and Agudat Israel, as illustrated by the latter's participation in the Shamir (1990–92) and the Netanyahu (1996–) governments, and its absence from the 1992–96 Labour administration. In any event, Rabbi Shach's 1990 speech revealed the deep historical roots of Orthodoxy's hatred of the idea of Zionism as a new Jewish culture. Unfamiliarity with these roots was responsible more than any other factor for frustrating Shimon Peres's calculations.

An awareness of these roots has a clear political significance. It determines that any stable political strategy of cooperation between Orthodoxy and the Labour Movement is virtually impossible. For such a relationship to succeed, if at all, can only be a tactical temporary stage. Even if politicians can be found in Orthodoxy who strive for a renewal of the alliance with Labour, the natural, historical weight of their movement and culture will inevitably come and sever them from it or threaten to overwhelm them. The proximity of several leaders of Orthodoxy to some of the Peace Camp's positions (as already noted, for reasons that have nothing to do with the national considerations guiding this camp) will always remain secondary and inactive from a political standpoint in comparison to their total cultural repugnance to what they consider the humanistic 'neo-Jewish' basis on which the Zionist Left's culture and ideology are predicated. This means that no ally can be found in the Orthodox camp who will help in creating a parliamentary base for an Israeli peace policy, as evidenced by the term in office of the Rabin–Peres government. A fundamental change in this respect can come, if at all, only after grave developments both within Israel and beyond will convince a large and growing majority of Likud supporters that holding on to the entire Land of Israel will bring about the destruction of the State of Israel or, they will convince the international community and the United States in particular that there is no alternative to imposition of partitioning the Land of Israel and of peace on both Jews and Arabs.

This is the difficult and grave political truth revealed by both the 1990 government crisis and the 1996 elections. It was emphasized in Rabbi Shach's speech, which also had another tragic side to it (not from the speaker's viewpoint). For, Rabbi Shach's war against the kibbutzim and the new Jewish culture of the Zionist Labour Movement is a war against shadows. The Rabbi continues to fight against the kibbutzim of the 1920s and 1930s and the ideology that reigned supreme at the time of Berl Katznelson. He has no idea how the wind has been taken out of the sails of the kibbutzim and how Katznelson's ideology has worn thin. The kibbutzim have been emptied of all authentic sense of a national-cultural mission. The Labour Movement of Shimon Peres, Yitzhak Rabin and their likely successors, is far removed from Berl Katznelson's and David Ben-Gurion's movement – a distance of many eras (from a spiritual standpoint). The Rabbi ridiculed the kibbutzim which in addition to eating pork and desecrating the Sabbath 'are also beggars!' Little did he know that the material beggary of the kibbutzim is nothing in comparison to their cultural and spiritual impoverishment. In his view, this beggary only reveals the danger of the kibbutzim as competitors for state support in a share of the special allocations; of course these allocations must be availed to 'Torah Jewry' and its institutions. The Rabbi felt that the kibbutzim would stand at the door with outstretched hands as if they were a body with moral values, while such a stand should be reserved only for the representatives of Torah study and the custodians of its commandments. Even from this point of view he still saw them as dangerous 'spiritual' enemies. If only there was in this a speck of truth ...

NOTES

1. In the meantime, Rabbi Shach has seen the necessity of addressing the Holocaust. His claim – the Holocaust was nothing more than a punishment from Heaven for the historical deviation of the Jewish People from the way of the Torah (the enlightenment and its successor, modern Jewish secularism) – is in no way distinguished in its intellectual and moral level from Rabbi Yitzhak Peretz's claim that the death of scores of children from Petach Tikva in a train accident was caused by the desecration of the Sabbath by their parents. In fact, Rabbi Shach's assertion falls even below Peretz's ridiculous claim, for it provided a sort of absolution of responsibility to the murderers of the Jewish People: after all, they were only the instrument of God's wrath. The train disaster that Rabbi Peretz spoke about was only a disaster caused by human error without ill will on the part of anyone, whereas the Holocaust was a planned and systematic mass murder, based on an anthropological and political 'theory' and

expressing political, national and even 'religious' intentions. Ironically, it was the 'sinful' Zionist movement that understood its possibility and warned of the danger for several decades. The Holocaust's description as a justified punishment by God is first and foremost a desecration of the Lord's name and the transformation of God himself into a devil. Indeed, Rabbi Shach's words also provoked bitter criticism from other religious figures.
2. Uri Zvi Greenberg, 'Hizdaharut' (Glowing), in *Rising Masculinity* (Tel-Aviv, 1926), p. 13.

ately they stand side by side as symbols of the different identifications in the self-concept and social identity of Israelis." Other, smaller groups within the society show somewhat different patterns.

THE JEWISHNESS OF ISRAELI IDENTITY

Spiritual Rootlessness and Circumscription to the 'Here and Now' in the Sabra World View

AVRAHAM SHAPIRA

Much of the discussion and research on the image of the sons and daughters of the Zionist revolution in the Land of Israel (*Eretz Israel*) are preoccupied with, or centre on, the '1948 Generation' (the 'War of Independence Generation'). The reference here is mainly to those people born during the second and third decades of the twentieth century, sons and daughters of the people who made up the second aliya (or wave of immigration, from 1904 to 1914) and the third aliya (1919–23). The generation in question is customarily called the 'PALMACH Generation' (though it also includes members of the 'Irgun' and 'LEHI', separate underground movements that fought against British rule in Mandatory Palestine).[1] To be realized, supposedly, in the lifetime of this generation unit, were the longings of the founding fathers, creators and carriers of the Zionist project of resurrection. Their dream of a 'new man' was to be fulfilled, a dream of a 'new Hebrew', or, at least, a new and other Jew. This new human specimen would be free of all the afflictions of the Diaspora: 'rootlessness' or a tendency towards spiritualization, 'passivity' and 'helplessness'. In the process, he was also to detach himself from the legacy of generations and eras of historical Jewish culture. The more prominent spokesmen and representatives of this generation are the writers and poets associated, for the most part, with the PALMACH.

The entrenched equation of the 'Sabra' with the 1948 Generation has recently come into question. This generation unit was preceded by generational layers that had evolved in the land since the beginnings of the first aliya. Some of these preceded the formation of a collective mentality of the 1948 Generation, while others emerged in parallel with this process. Rachel Elboim-Dror points out the fallacy of overlooking the culture

---

Avraham Shapira is Associate Professor of Jewish History, Tel-Aviv University.
[This article was translated from Hebrew by Rela Mazali.]

developed by the locally born during the closing decades of the nineteenth century and the opening ones of the twentieth.[2] She presents four portraits of youth culture evolving in the period in question: youth groups, village (*moshav*) youth, urban educated youth, and religious-Zionist youth.[3]

Two characteristics are prominent in the world and make-up of the 1948 Generation. While not exhaustive or unique to this group, they are very central to it:

1. Containment within the Joint Generation Experience
The collective self is a central axis in the identity of this generation; it does not override personal selfhood but it often arrests the path of individual growth. It is a basking, as it were, in a 'togetherness' excluding those who do not 'belong'. I am referring here to the 'ever we' (the title of a novel by Nathan Shaham) to which one is proud to belong but which also, at the same time, provides an easy 'escape' from the individual's private tests of self. This mode of being is possibly epitomized in a line from an autobiographical poem by Haim Guri, '1923–58: People spoke in First Person Plural'. The poem deals mainly with the polarity between this chummy collectivism and the possibility of individuation. Originally published in the daily *Ha-aretz* in 1958, it underwent transformations or, more precisely, excisions, in preparation for its inclusion in two integrative collections of Haim Guri's poetry: *Ad Kav Ha-nesher* (Till the Eagle's Line), *1949–75* (Tel-Aviv, 1975), and *Heshbon Over* (Fluid Account), *1945–87* (Tel-Aviv, 1988). In these collections Guri omitted the last three lines of the section of the above quoted poem, lines that characterize many of his contemporaries even in their advanced years:

> Meaning remained far
> Behind the deeds
> And din touched din

The shared social self of the 1948 Generation was carved and woven out of joint generation-specific imbibings (among them mental ties to landscape and terrain and to the Hebrew language), out of incessant existential-defence tensions, out of the binding power of ideological stands that also became a kind of 'secular (civic) religion' or a political theology.[4] The private sphere, pushed and repressed inside, in this generation's mode of being, found an outlet in the writing of both personal journals and intimate letters. When this hidden, 'shadowy' side was revealed through the estate literature – a broad literary field comprising memorial collections that preserve the personal statements and styles of those killed in the military actions of the Hagana (in the years preceding statehood) and in the battles of the War of Independence – it aroused a sense and consciousness of discovery.[5] This growing stream acquired high public-cultural visibility, especially in the first and second decades following Israel's declaration as a state. Almost each and every one of the memorial books provides some evidence of the dual tensions in the world of the local born Jews: (a) between the familiar and known image – the mask formed and worn by the individual – and the tumult of the repressed interior; (b) between the commands of the collective and the secular religion, along with the social norms these entailed, and the personal path of the individual. In other words, these were tensions between the public spheres where one spoke 'in first person plural', and a communality or public togetherness providing a space for self-expression and partly informed by the essential axes of mutual relations between individuals. In a personal letter to a friend (27 February 1945), Raffi Meletz of kibbutz Ein Harod (born in Jerusalem on 3 March 1927 and killed in the War of Independence on 22 February 1948), writes:

> Where is that cold Raffi, sarcastic, cynical, laughing at people, the whole hard and ruthless shell that I wrapped myself in without knowing and without any clear intention? Too soft, emotional, the inner Raffi, who must not be seen in such way as to be crushed by the same spirit of ridicule and self-confidence encompassing the whole of our lives. Don't show your inside if it be weak, for you'll burn.[6]

Especially notable in this passage is the language of the generalization ('encompassing the whole of our lives'). Personal expressions of the speaker's character, as it were, cry out from the memorial collections for the sons who fell in battle in the first and second decades of statehood, and in those published later to commemorate the dead of the 1973 Yom Kippur War.

Expressions of this dual tension are already intimated in the early works of the 1948 Generation authors (Yigal Mossinson, Aaron Meged, Shlomo Nitzan, Hanoch Bartov and others). Avner Holtzman defines it as 'the tension ... between the needs of an enlisted, ideological society and the individual's longing to realize his separateness and difference'.[7] This polarity was manifest in the worlds created by these authors, among other things, in the fluctuations, at changing intervals, between the axes of individuality and the 'we'. 'The literature of the "War of Liberation" was born', says Gershon Shaked, 'in the circumstances that formed it, under the sign of the "we", and sought a way towards the "I", and when its creators reached the "I", they once again asked where they stood before the "we", and what right the "I" had to exist out of relation to some kind of social reality (Aaron Meged's *The Living on the Dead*, Moshe Shamir's *The Border*, S. Yizhar's *Plain Stories*).'[8]

2. Definite Circumscription to the Here and Now
The local born 1948 Generation, as well as their younger siblings and the young people maturing into the first and second decades of statehood, for whom they served as role models, are characterized by an excessive attachment to the 'ground of the present'.[9] This comprised an unmistakable

emphasis upon place, a deep connection to the land and its landscapes which also replaced relations with the Diaspora of the Jewish People and the legacy of its past; an adherence to contemporary Hebrew with its shifts and changes, rather than its living ties with historical layers; a pronounced earthiness manifested, among other things, in a practical businesslike attitude to life, and engendered by a rejection of Diasporic spiritualization which, at the time, was fully equated with spirituality. These locally born Jews kept their distance from everything they identified as 'Diasporic' Judaism, including, in the process, Judaism as culture and historical legacy.

The first pioneers, creators of the projects of the second and third aliyot, were totally preoccupied with the experience of the 'new life' and with the 'new man' being forged in the land to which they had emigrated. They came from the environs of the 'Jewish street' of eastern Europe, with its combination of Hasidim and Misnagdim, of Orthodox Jews and non-believers, of 'emancipated' Jews alongside Bundists, Zionists and revolutionaries. Mental custom and patterns bred by the culture of generations were still present and potent among members of movements and schools which had supplanted transcendentalist Orthodoxy with the passion of contemporary political messianism. Even assimilated Jewish families or those totally detached from Jewish community were permeated by remnants of tradition.[10]

The rebelling pioneers who emigrated to Eretz Israel tried to obliterate the scenes imbibed in their fathers' homes, and the spiritual residue of shtetl childhoods. Their 'Negation of the Exile' was not merely ideological. It swept with it the values of life in the 'Jewish neighbourhood' and those of Jewish family life. In the process they tried to dissociate themselves from the 'historical-Jewish book shelves' and from the multiform legacy of Jewish culture. Many of them were forced to deal with a repressed tension between the 'there' and the 'here', between the heritage of parents' homes and the pioneering mode cultivated in the new land. Within them, murmuring, were scenes and tunes, as well as suppressed substance, which failed to conform to the new ideologies. They 'lived them [that is, these voices and habits of the world they had left behind] but did not admit to them'.[11] The sons of these builders, and the young people they educated, were no longer aware of anything other than the 'new man', the new society, the new life, in the ostensibly new land. The ideal figures of generations of Jewish culture – some of the most important of which were the scholar, the righteous man and the Hasid[12] – were supplanted in the new land by the ideal of the 'pioneer'.[13]

The beliefs and life values of those who created pre-state, Jewish, 'Yishuv' society were imprinted upon their children – native to the land; these children internalized and adopted their fathers' dreams. Even if they had wished to be different, they would have lacked the enabling background conditions needed to develop into something else, something other than their fathers. They knew no mode of being other than the one of Eretz Israel. The mythical Sabra, born of this milieu, was cast as the new 'Hebrew' – come into being out of nothingness. Indeed, 'Hebrew' was a prevalent label for projects of the Zionist revolution. 'It is no coincidence that the founding fathers of Zionism preferred the earliest epithet for our people: "Hebrew"', writes Meir Pail; 'for instance: Hebrew labour, the Herzlia Hebrew Gymnasium, the Hebrew Battalions in the First World War, the Hebrew University in Jerusalem, the Hebrew Technion in Haifa, the First Hebrew School in Rishon Le-zion, the General Union [Histadrut] of Hebrew Workers in Eretz Israel, and even the main slogan of the anti-British campaign: "Free Immigration, Hebrew State".'[14] In this context he also notes that it was only after the Holocaust that the term 'Jewish' came to be used more commonly.

In the world of the 1948 Generation, the national, ideological and social values of the founding fathers also play the role of world views which extend beyond the dictates of the times. In the absence of a cultural fabric guiding the conduct and habits of the individual and his social environment, the ideologies of the pioneer group, along with the symbols and rituals it engendered, were perceived as a 'secular religion' (on which I elaborate further below).

THE RESTRICTEDNESS OF 'A REALITY WHICH IS AN END IN ITSELF'

> In a reality which is an end in itself there is no before and no after; nothing is necessary to the whole or unnecessary to the whole; nothing is eminent or base ... there is no 'reason why' for which the hand would toil putting this before that. There is no beckoning harbour towards which the narrator would introduce a regime and an order into the flow spilling before his eyes from the springs of life.[15]

The background within which the Sabra youth grew up combined with the trends of their mental and ideological formation to produce their excessive preoccupation with historical present. However, like their parents and teachers, they failed to discern in a reality which is an end in itself, any factor of restrictedness, of deprivation. On the contrary, many of the fathers of Zionism and their disciple-students, and not only those representing its catastrophic-political trend,[16] viewed Zionism as a movement of redemption.[17] Consequently, concrete realization of the vision, complete with snares and obstacles, was identified as a longed-for historic move. Prominent in the history of Zionism are messianic or secularized messianic actualizations, which are manifested through ideological and social phenomena, and also through all manner and shades of belief.[18]

Many of the spokesmen and the leaders/form-givers of Yishuv society perceived the establishment of the State of Israel not only as the attainment of a longed-for visionary climax, but also as the start of a redeemed mode of being. The Hebrew prose and poetry that accompanied the project of resurrection in Eretz Israel reflect this messianic consciousness.[19] And some of the foundations of this consciousness were understandably internalized by the native born who grew to adulthood in its environs. These Sabras did not adopt the pathos of redemption used by the writers of their parents' generation, or by leaders such as David Ben-Gurion. However, they experienced the reality of Eretz Israel as an all encompassing mode of being, without sensing the degree of its limitation and restrictedness. A characteristic expression of this is already evident in the early work of the central 1948 Generation writers, which elevates existence to the level of an end in itself. Confinement within the limited local environment, in temporal as well as spatial terms, was perceived by such as a world replete in its own right. And when longings arose, from time to time, for other worlds – at least other geographical worlds – these were instantly repressed and anaesthetized:

> Hell, how can you get abroad, there are roads there thousands of kilometres long. I never saw thousands of kilometres. Actually, there aren't any thousands of kilometres in the world. That's propaganda.[20]

Sparks of awakening combine with self-directed irony, in these words of Amos Kenan's. Notably, he was one of the few to deviate from the sacred conventions of his generation and their times.

The people of the second and third aliyot and their followers displayed no conscious awareness of the double detachment typical of the mode of existence in which their sons and disciples were raised:

- The Zionist redemptive project's shedding of, and uprooting itself from its generative sources in the eastern European 'Jewish street', and in the heritage of historical-Jewish culture in general.
- The barriers between the 'collective mental world'[21] in which the Sabras were formed, and the ethnic cultures surrounding Eretz Israel and also, apparently, more distant cultures. Each of these barriers is worth scrutiny.

Revolutionary Change Lacking Dimensions of Continuity

While the Sabras were raised and formed in a society equating its revolution with the creation of a 'new man', free of the continuity and evolution of a cultural-historical tradition, this usually failed to arouse in them any wonderment or hesitating objections. Very few exceptions among them experienced a consciousness of cultural deprivation or superficiality resulting from a dissociation with their traditional culture. Nevertheless, their personal texts, their polemic and parts of their literary writings contain flashes or embers of revealing self-scrutiny. S. Yizhar (Yizhar Smilansky) is one of the few who has taken notice of, and described, the narrowness and limited horizons of his generation:

> The millennia dividing the days of the Bible from the days of Nahalal – he [Moshe Dayan] and his friends knew little of them and were uninterested in them. This enormous heavily-weighing distance closed up and was no more, as it were. As if the entire yesteryear of the Jews and all the years of the Exile, had been nothing but a long dark unnecessary night, and now they were waking from it straight into this rising morning.[22]

These words, focused on Moshe Dayan, also serve at the same time to characterize the internal worlds of many of the spokesmen and symbols of the 1948 Generation; as stated elsewhere by Smilansky in a later and equally revealing formulation:

> People such as Yigal Alon or Moshe Dayan, and many many others like them, what did they learn of Judaism, what did they know of Judaism, other than Bible chapters, and between the Bible and Bialik all they had was a cultural desert and a frozen Antarctic of nothingness and thus came a detachment from the continuum and an inward turn into an insular bubble, lacking any ties with the before or the after. And thus began a life of single individuals alongside each other, without a people, without the togetherness of a people, without the history of a people.[23]

Not only the generation of 1948, but also those children who grew up in their wake, related to this detachment as a fact of existence which is also, equally, an ideological goal and a symbol. When one of the most central members of the former generation says 'Between me and my father – the sea',[24] it is a statement bearing no connotations of crisis.

Although there were members of this generation who provided it with more than glimpsed expressions of discontent and a consciousness of spiritual poverty, they were incapable of comprehensive soul-searching, of taking full stock of their world, or of the conclusions these might entail; moments of reflection did not turn into a consciousness of crisis with the abysmal depths and generative power that may accompany such an awakening.

Even Yizhar Smilansky, although he repeatedly uncovered and depicted the spiritual poverty of a native born son of the land, did not go beyond a lamenting description of the rootless and superficial Sabra, until the 1980s. While dwelling on the problematics of past and present, or present and past, as well as past and future, his readers were not guided towards a recognition of the significance of recasting an anchor in the past. Noteworthy among his articles and writings on this subject, prior to the 1980s, is 'Yesterday and the Day after Tomorrow'. He says there:

> I cannot ... see the dimensions of time as criteria for creative work, but rather the opposite: the drive to utter – [is and contains] a criterion for all the rest: times, places and forms.[25]

And these are his words in the closing chords of that comprehensive speech:

> We are trapped by responsibility. And with everything we know and do not know, not knowing tomorrow is what permeates. – What will become of us when the night is over and the sun comes up. Will it, then, be too much to say in conclusion that the coming day means more to me than all the yesterdays of yesterdays?[26]

As stated, it is only since the early 1980s that this outlook of Smilansky has truly undergone a change, of which his abovementioned article 'Master of the Short and Straight Line' is one of the first substantial embodiments.

There is perhaps, only one other exception, in the sense under discussion, among the organized groups of the 1948 Generation: Eliezer Schweid. Exceptional though he may be in this sense, it should be noted that Schweid was definitely an integral member of that generation: a member and counsellor in one of the youth movements of labour Zionism, a member of a PALMACH brigade who ran the gamut of its battles, one of the founders of a kibbutz after the War of Independence, along with his youth movement and PALMACH comrades.

Since the eve of the 1950s he examined issues of cultural identity, tradition and transmission, continuity and variety, the process of the Midrash and other related subjects.

Towards the end of the first decade of statehood he still adhered to the hopeful assumption that his contemporaries would change, would undergo a transformation. And so he wrote, in his article 'Before Locked Gates', which scrutinized the meanings of the novel *Yemei Ziklag* (Days of Ziklag), by S. Yizhar:

> The generation emerging from the test of battle in the War of Independence will no longer be able to mend the rift, to see in the national and social goals for which it seemingly fought, either an exclusive aim or a central objective. And when it continues to do so by virtue of the historical reality in which it lives, this is due to other motives and for the sake of other ends.[27]

Several years later he discussed the literature of the 1948 Generation as a mirror of its spiritual world, in the final part of his book *Shalosh Ashmorot* (Three Shifts). In this case he illuminates what he calls 'the sorrow of the slashed roots'. The fourth of the five sections in the chapter bearing this title is subtitled 'Face to Face with the Void'. The last and final section bears the title of the whole chapter: 'The Sorrow of the Slashed Roots'.[28] The substance of his discussions in these and the previous chapters reveal a distinction between 'sorrow' and an awareness of the void, which leads to a reckoning or at least to a spiritual drive-search:

> The comfortable disappointment with which the author discovers – long after the fact – the reality of cultural disconnectedness, is not a

spiritual event containing inside it a great creative drive. The author and his hero are not imbibed in the mode of being whose absence they sense. This mode itself ... is totally distant from their intimate sphere of existence and therefore causes no reaction – not even that of rejection or criticism ... . the hollowing out and growing vacuousness are evident not only through their intentionally explicit formulations by protagonists in the young Hebrew literature, but also through the very diminution of the literary work itself.[29]

The critical insights presented by Schweid in 1964 are still just as true of many of the writers of that generation, today in their 70s and 80s.

Restriction to the Native Locality

The political-geographical insularity of the Yishuv within the confines of the Eretz-Israeli 'pale' approximated the degree of its cultural and social dissociation from the surrounding cultures; Hebrew society in Eretz Israel conducted no interaction with these cultures in any field (whether religious, cultural, class-ideological etc.). The same was true of their pronounced segregation from societies within the area of Eretz Israel: Arab, Druze, Armenian, and so forth.[30] These circumstances grew even worse following the founding of the State of Israel. Israelis became a people who dwell alone among their enemies. The Sabras were raised with a clearly ethnocentric orientation, behind them and all around them hostile and threatening borders and underneath their feet 'a long dark unnecessary night' – so they saw the historical culture of their people.[31]

The patterns of collective beliefs imprinted the childhood landscapes of the Sabras with dominant normative directions. And these were hardly 'disrupted' by winds of any kind from outside. Those born and raised in the land experienced neither intercultural tensions nor friction with the threatening other, nor any of the self-nurturing aspects of such experiences. In the absence of any exposure at close quarters to 'foreign' worlds, they did not even experience the drives of self-scrutiny in the face of the 'other'.[32]

Jewish history, it seems, provides hardly any instances of such insular community life as isolated from the contexts of its surroundings as were successive generations of native born Jews in Eretz Israel, since the time of the first aliya and onwards.

Some made the claim that the Sabras experienced other cultures, and were exposed to other ways of life and world views, through the 'library' at their disposal which comprised a variety of Hebrew translations of world literature from different cultures.[33] 'Paradoxically, as they read only Hebrew, what they read was in fact the best of world literature, for that was what was available in Hebrew translations', says Dan Horowitz, reconstructing the reading of his generation, the youth of the 1940s.[34] 'Actually', he points out, 'we mostly read translated literature. European and Anglo-Saxon literature was translated into Hebrew in gradually broadening circles, the best of the nineteenth century writers and right up to the quality literature of our times.'[35] Translated literature broadened the horizons of knowledge and implanted the experiences of faraway worlds. As Horowitz puts it, 'The translated literature brought to us the scents of the world out there.'[36] However, a distinction should be drawn between the scents of other worlds, accompanied by a broadened knowledge, and an actual, concrete meeting or friction with other cultures. It is pertinent to ask whether the intellectual curiosity and the habit of reading world literature (in Hebrew translation), could generate any cracks in the flat one-dimensionality of a small and extremely insular society – in its very obvious parochialism.

The treasures of knowledge and literary learning, and also a knowledge of art in its various forms, enriched the spiritual world of the local community and fertilized the experience of childhood and youth here. But it is questionable whether they also became components of a world view, or informed an outlook. For those immersed in a homeland to the exclusion of all else, could such input, in itself, prove capable of rooting them in other cultures?

It would seem that beyond any external effects, in the words of Moshe Shamir,

> This generation [of 1948] is principally and essentially involved in the true, authentic experience of Eretz Israel, which begins in muteness, which begins in speechlessness... The generation of the PALMACH represents the first generation that lived in the land before speaking it. And it is this that is typical of the PALMACH as a human group too, as a social and national background – that within it there grew an authenticity, a combined ideological and physical life force.[37]

Regardless of the scope of personal reading (and the openness, through other channels, to manifestations of faraway cultures and art) and its function in constructing single intellectual personalities, these were marginalized by the common beliefs and norms. It is unlikely that they could have provided components of the Eretz Israel authenticity to which Moshe Shamir refers so proudly, and which characterized not only the 1948 Generation but also those preceding and succeeding it,[38] whether knowingly or not. The world of the Sabra contained a split that was clear, even if it was unseen and implicit, a split between hidden personal growth and the concepts and values of the collective.[39]

The restrictiveness of this Eretz Israel 'authenticity' of the Sabra stands in interesting contrast to a mode of life open to the pluralism of various spheres of identity (allowing contradictions and struggles as well as mutual enrichment); the autobiographical testimonies and literature of Jews from throughout the Diaspora introduce the existential tensions of dually and multi-rooted lives and environments. They allow a view of creative friction and of fertile syntheses, and also of tragic and irreconcilable contradictions;

of openness to the other and the stranger on the one hand, emanating from a spiritual identity not yet undermined, and on the other hand, a weak, numbed identity, crumbled by processes of erosive assimilation into the surrounding cultures; of aspirations to a symbiosis between cultures and traditions alongside a sense of Jewish rootlessness with no visible solution.[40]

An acquaintance with 'otherness', with the different other, through a fictional literary mirror, cannot replace living contact, concrete encounter – and even less so when it takes place through barriers of insularity or a sense of uniqueness.

The biographical testimonies of immigrants and survivors – those who came to the country from outside the Sabra milieu – reveal how shielded the native born were from the 'other', the 'Jew of the Exile', an attitude that forms a major topic in its own right. Similarly, another significant topic is the pressing 'need' of 'the shadow children' (the title of a play depicting the obstacles barring the entry into Israeli society of immigrant children survivors of the Holocaust) to obscure the details of their past, so as to gain a hard-to-come-by sense of belonging and 'Israeli-ness'.

THE PRIMARY ROLE OF THE YOUTH MOVEMENT

It is pertinent here to discuss in brief the major formative factors which left their marks on the collective portrait of native born Jews in Eretz Israel: the parents' home (the nuclear family), school, and the youth movement.

The Parents' Home

The parents' home did not constitute a central cultural agent in Yishuv's Jewish society in Eretz Israel. Since the time of the second aliya, the emigrant pioneers' rebellion against their fathers' homes was normative; the founding fathers' decisions to leave their parents' homes was accompanied by conflicts and, at times, by temporary break-offs of strong family bonds. Upon emigrating to Eretz Israel, and after the emigration, many of the young pioneers abandoned the heritage of traditions from the 'Jewish home' of eastern Europe. Remnants or traces of traditional conduct and echoes of inherited mentality were common even among non-religious sections of the 'Jewish street of eastern Europe' (the culture of the shtetl). The Jewish family continued to form the fundamental social unit even in those circles that had abandoned their world of beliefs, both in the shtetl and towns of Russia and Poland, though such communities showed visible scars of crisis caused by loss of their sources of authority. None of this was true of the conduct of the pioneer-sons. By the time the people of the second and third aliyot started families and became parents, they usually did not have before them a normative model for the establishment of a code of 'family' conduct. In addition, this was not among the topics that occupied the pathfinders of the emerging Yishuv society. The ideologies and norms of the pioneering society seemed to supplant the values of the

'Jewish family' as well.⁴¹ Moreover, Yishuv society showed no awareness of the place-role of the 'Jewish community' as a mode of social-traditional belonging bridging the gap between family unit and relations with Yishuv society in general.

The new Hebrew literature has produced a number of family sagas, tracing the processes of change and disintegration of the 'Jewish family' in eastern and western Europe, in the old Jewish community in Eretz Israel, etc.⁴² There are similarities and analogies between the features of crisis revealed by Jewish families in separate and very different Jewish centres. They may indicate that the disintegration of the family in Eretz Israel and in Israel reflects not only internal, locally Israeli, processes but also, and perhaps primarily, historical processes that are typical of modern Jewish history.

Zichron Dvarim (Past Continuous) by Jacob Shabtai offers an exaggerated reflection of the decomposition of the nuclear family on the one hand, and of the clan on the other, processes that are analogous and concurrent in the book, and that represent a fundamental problem permeating the world of the individual, the family and its extended ties:

> These were his peers, except that this closeness, and the closeness between him and most of the rest of his family, had turned over the years to a mode of being devoid of any living meaning and had become something embarrassing, and at times even oppressive, for besides the given fact of the family tie, that existed in the mind as a system of duties and commitments that could only be escaped through heresy and turning one's back, they were strangers ...
>
> ... and Goldman, who went on holding the emptied cup of tea in his hand, felt sadly and powerlessly how everything was wearing out and ending – the body and the people and the people's relationships, while he himself was part of this process of erosion ...⁴³

The basic truth to life that this work elicited from the depths of the 1930s, the 1940s and the 1950s, is one of the reasons for its enormous success both immediately following its publication and in 1994, when a new edition came out.

The factors and means that secured the bonds of social cohesiveness may be said to constitute the very causes that emptied the family of content and undermined its roles.⁴⁴

Jewish culture, over its broad, varied temporal and geographical range, views the personal identity of the individual as formed primarily in the family, through rootedness in the nuclear unit:

> Personal biography begins with the family. But the family is not a unit in itself and doesn't begin and end with itself ... . It expresses a commonality which precedes it and a commonality which extends beyond it as well ... . thus, when someone identifies himself ... as his parents' son, he also identifies himself as the son of his people and his historical culture.⁴⁵

As stated, in practice, the parents' home relinquished this role and purpose in Yishuv society. The social agent which stepped into the vacuum created when the 'Jewish family' faded away was, at least during late childhood and adolescence, 'the movement' as it was called, that is the youth movement (see below).

School

The primary and secondary school played a role which was considerable in terms of time investment and required tasks. However, the children and youth of Eretz Israel were mainly preoccupied with the world of after school hours. The Hebrew school teacher, and especially at urban schools, did not usually present the figure of an educator or a bearer of social values. In the literature of the 1948 Generation, the teacher is usually depicted as a contemptible, foreign figure, cut off from the issues at the centre of the very down to earth reality of each individual youth, who is usually a member of the youth movement. In one of his latest works, Yizhar Smilansky draws a group portrait of the main teachers at a prestigious high school in Jerusalem during the 1940s:

> Revered people teachers and just what is it that we have in common, where are they at and where are we at. They are in the middle of the nineteenth century and we are, obviously, already hatching and branching out from the first third of the twentieth. They were born and raised there and cast here unluckily and became teachers because they had no other choice instead of becoming the best of the world's researchers, and all their worlds are foreign no less than old-fashioned no less than laughable, and all of us are just like Indians to them, Indians whose Hebrew is full of mistakes, wild, who want only to torment their gray heads, such ignoramuses, uncouth, and primitive, with no respect for culture or education ...[46]

Smilansky goes beyond the collective portrait to a series of individual vignettes of teachers, from the point of view of his childhood friend from Jerusalem. Thus, for instance, the Talmud teacher, 'our teacher Master Doctor Bruchin'. As the writer says, in the voice of his childhood friend (one of the main protagonists here), Yechiam Weitz,

> The sermons he tries, if he is not interrupted, dry me out, how much the distance between us, a hundred years, three generations, in his lifetime there were not yet spades or rifles or even simple bicycles, and cinema, for him, means bad, cheap popular culture and bad manners, ... when the commotion in the classroom rose to unbearable levels, poor Dr. Bruchin with the Talmud open before him, used to stretch his scrawny neck out of his empty collar, one of those old wrinkled necks, like a used purse, and like a crane he used to take a short breath, still rasping out of humiliation, and raise the remnant of his cracked and broken voice.[47]

The students' attitude to this teacher of Talmud also conveys their attitude to the Talmud itself and to the whole heritage of their Jewish past. These teachers are indeed 'like salesmen of a great culture that is not selling any more',[48] whose time and relevance are past and gone. They came from the grovelling, despicable, repulsive world of the shtetl. And the native born sons included the entire 'historical-Jewish book shelves' in this Exile-identity of their teachers. School and teachers were perceived as an antithesis to the Yishuv-typical pioneer youth movement – where the children found space for self-expression, role models and norms to adhere to.

The Pioneering Youth Movement

The Eretz Israel youth movements, evolving since the late 1920s and the early 1930s, were imbued with the world of pioneering-labour Zionism. In the course of the 1930s and more pronouncedly since the 1940s, they drew elite sections of Yishuv society youth. The youth subcultures that developed in the pioneering youth movements clearly took precedence, in movement members' view, over the parents' homes and even more so over school.[49] These were new circumstances, born of Yishuv society. In the Jewish youth movements founded in eastern Europe, Ha-shomer Ha-tzair, Gordonia and others, rebellion against the parents' home and its traditional roles were already widespread. 'The peer groups formed in the [Jewish eastern European] youth movements', writes Zvi Lamm, 'were "cultural islands", so to speak, islands of a culture different from the one surrounding them'.[50] The feeling of belonging to a movement and of identification with its course stepped in to fill the void left by a disintegrating culture and to replace the deteriorating Jewish family. This was only partly true of the youth movements active here in Eretz Israel. They identified with the values of Yishuv society and with the visions of the labour movement leading it. However, their rebellion added a dimension of passion and creative dynamism where their parents had made compromises with the values of their original societies or had – at least in their sons' view – failed the test of fully realizing their goals. A degree of rapprochement between the home and the youth movement was present only in some homes. Many members of the multi-branched labour movement adhered to a hidden petite bourgeoisie ideal. Many parents were torn between their ideological beliefs and the age old ambitions of Jewish parents for their sons. Even at the time of the second aliya Aaron David Gordon stated that workers did not necessarily wish their sons to follow in their footsteps.

The youth movements constituted 'young people's "yeshivas", as it were, preparing their students to take upon themselves "the burden of the mitzvot"'[51] of pioneering society. The formative authority of the youth movement collective prevailed over the role of 'the home' (the family) on the one hand, and over that of the formal educational authorities (school) on the other. Dan Horowitz, combining personal testimony and a researcher's perspective, explains that 'the youth movement, that is, any and every actively pioneering youth movement', served, in the world of his contemporaries, as 'a kind of organizational and ideological umbrella'. The units of membership in the youth movement (the 'group', 'battalion', 'layer', etc.) formed 'the meaningful unit determining the individual's way of life ... the "reference group" as sociologists term it'.[52]

The ideological principles of the pioneering youth movements and their orientative axes were harshly delineated. Within their boundaries there was considerable space for self-expression, but not necessarily for intellectual growth, for initiating spiritual search or cultural creativity, neither of which complied with the 'movement-like' way. The 'movement-like' way, claiming to pioneering-Zionist objectives, hardly presumed to fill out the spiritual world of the youthful member. The hyper-collectivism typical of membership in the movement obstructed the expression of a personal path and left almost no space for the productive fermentation of spiritual resources that failed to conform to the 'way of the movement'.[53] This hothouse disallowed the growth of individuals in their own individuality.

The deeper the sense of 'rebellion' in the youth movement and the more pronounced the movement's status as a competitor against home and school for the time and spiritual energies of its members, the more pronounced and intense was the sense of belonging. School made scholarly demands and sometimes also established norms of conduct. 'Home', on the other hand, relinquished its role from the outset.[54] In cases where there were family customs and conduct or family norms and traditions, the 'home' was forced into fierce competition with the youth movement and its 'sacred' values. This situation, originating during the Yishuv period, was still fully intact in the first decade and even, in many cases, in the second decade of statehood.[55]

Notably, the contrast between the youth movement and the family (the 'home') and the deep sense of belonging to the youth movement did not entail an emotional split between the sons and their parents or defects in the loving relationships between them. Even in warm families it was, as it seems, understood that some areas were suspended from family authority and belonged to the (youth) 'movement'. It would seem that this dialectic of father–son relationships has not yet been comprehensively researched.

A large body of studies, documentation and polemic which does, however, exist already, deals with the history of the youth movements in question, with their role in Yishuv and Israeli society, with their explicit goals, and so forth.[56] And yet, little seems to have been said to date on the spiritual world of the movements, the components of the system – or fragments – of ideological beliefs which they presented to their young members.[57] The active disinterest or the deprivation of the Sabra, described above in the subsections discussing the phenomenon of 'double detachment', finds their fullest manifestation in the pioneering movement youth cultures. In this sense, common ground was shared by Ha-mahanot Ha-olim, Ha-no'ar Ha-oved, Ha-shomer Ha-tzair, Gordonia, Ha-tnu'ah

Ha-me'uhedet, Hativot Ha-no'ar (the last operated by two kibbutz movements, Ha-kibbutz Ha-meuhad and Ihud Ha-kvutzot Vehakibbutzim), Ha-tzofim (Scouts), and others as well.

THE 1948 GENERATION REFLECTED IN THE PIONEERING YOUTH MOVEMENT

An examination of the belief system of the pioneering youth movements would seem to entail a separate discussion of each of them. This is a complex research project which might also include a comparative analysis of the distinct 'movement way' practised by each different movement. Such a study might clarify how deeply these youth movements internalized central value-concepts of the founding fathers and how their rituals, symbols and ceremonies absorbed the pioneering ethos.

Within the limited scope of this essay, I will try to locate the basic components and spiritual possessions of the youth movement called Ha-mahanot Ha-olim – the first pioneering youth movement founded in Eretz Israel.[58] Ha-mahanot Ha-olim evolved out of informal unionizing among high school students, beginning in 1926. From 1931 onwards the movement was affiliated with the faction of the kibbutz movement known as Ha-kibbutz Ha-meuhad and with its political line – that of Si'ah Bet within the MAPAI labour party. The split in MAPAI heightened tensions within Ha-kibbutz Ha-meuhad between a majority which put its faith in Yitzhak Tabenkin and Ha-tnu'ah Le-ahdut Ha-avoda (that is, the Labour Unity Movement, founded after the split) and a minority who maintained loyalty to MAPAI. An analogous tension arose between the youth counsellors and senior members of Ha-mahanot Ha-olim. Towards the end of 1945, the movement split too, when the MAPAI orientated minority among the counsellors and the senior members joined the Gordonia movement (originally affiliated with the Hever Ha-kvutzot faction of the kibbutz movement), and together created the youth movement known as Ha-tnu'ah Ha-meuhedet.[59]

Ha-mahanot Ha-olim was perceived, almost from the outset, as an elitist movement with a pride in its uniqueness and a social atmosphere which evolved into a movement tradition. 'The members of the left-wing youth movements, and especially "Ha-mahanot Ha-olim"', says Netiva Ben-Yehuda in a literary account of the PALMACH mentality, 'were the truest model of the Sabra, the Palmachnic, the new Hebrew youth'.[60]

The difference in political tendencies among the youth counsellors and graduates of Ha-mahanot Ha-olim did not stem from different world views or distinctive fundamental values. An attempt to map the ideas, or spiritual possessions, guiding Ha-mahanot Ha-olim during its formative years may illuminate the nature of the youth culture created in the movement. At issue here, as in the youth cultures of the other pioneering youth movements, was a demand for personal revolution which would direct the movement graduate to a way of life different from the one that was then, and still is today, the standard convention among high school graduates. The youth movement called upon its members to rebel against the natural and unquestioned course of academic studies in preparation for an academic career, a professional or sometimes an artistic career. The movement vision was *hagshama* (realization): in other words, preparing oneself for a life of labour (that is, physical labour and especially agricultural work) on a kibbutz. The central value-concept was 'realization' or 'pioneering' (the connotations of which fell within the realm of the above dream of concrete personal deeds).

In order to ascertain whether 'realization' was in fact the focal point of the movement's educational line and whether it was part of a cluster of values or an inclusive system of ideas, I have chosen to examine the collection *As the Shrub of the Fields*, published by graduates of Ha-mahanot Ha-olim.[61] This collection is intended to summarize the history of the movement over its first twenty years, as reflected in essays, letters, articles and poems assembled from the movement newsletters and archives.

The title of the collection is revealing. It is borrowed from the title of a programmatic article written by Ahuvia Malkin – one of the central figures in Ha-mahanot Ha-olim – which was first published in November 1939. The article likens the movement to the shrub of the fields, sprouting from the nature of Eretz Israel:

> Of its own accord, as the shrub of the fields, without nurturing hand or onlooking eye, without prayers or torments of anticipation our movement rose. No one sowed it in tears and no heart palpitated or hoped for its growth. Of its own accord, as a wild sprout it rose and struck roots in the soil of the homeland.[62]

Ha-mahanot Ha-olim is perceived here as a creature of nature ('a wild sprout'), which struck its own roots into the soil of the homeland, and not as a cultural-historic entity. This implies an almost exclusive tie to the homeland, through the agency of the movement and the channels of its activities, a tie which also supplants the tie to the people and the heritage of its past. The world of the movement is the end-all and be-all here:

> The air of school was stuffy and limp. Everything around – the home, the street, the student community – empty and unsatisfying. The routine and secure path – finish school and become a clerk or go abroad to study – emitted a stale smell of boredom, of pettiness and decay.[63]

The surrender to the movement's 'religion' is again and again supported by the weakness–impotence of all the other possible agents in the world of the youth of Eretz Israel. The visionary ideal depicted here is a unitary one: 'to turn students into workers, pioneers'.[64] No question arises as to how to be workers or as to the substance of the spiritual profile of a book-learned high school student who becomes a worker. The movement is an end in itself and *hagshama* (realization) is an end in itself, and no questions are asked about the nature of this end or the contents to be instilled into it or existing in it and worthy of eliciting. And therefore, in keeping with this line, the article ends with a declaration of grateful loyalty to the movement:

> All of us, each one of us, is given a whole world. How poor would our lives have been, how pointless, if they had not been ignited with the spirit of the movement, and how much life substance and strength of life and what an abundance of belief we have been given! A heart overflowing with love and thanks.[65]

We are dealing with a text central to the world of Ha-mahanot Ha-olim. It is by no coincidence that this text is quoted (almost verbatim) in the collection *As the Shrub of the Fields*, and later in the books *Ha-mahanot Ha-olim Years, Part I* and *Part II* (at the beginning of chapter two, which is titled 'Our Forerunners'). The title of this article has become a term which commonly serves to characterize the movement.

Moreover, the article opening the collection *As the Shrub of the Fields*, written by Avraham Aderet, one of the first members of the movement and a prominent youth counsellor, also depicts the movement as a creature of nature, 'consenting' to the land. 'Eretz Israel' is for him, as for Ahuvia Malkin in the article quoted above, a central value-concept. At times it even seems as if one is reading of nomads belonging to no nation, setting out on a historical course in a new land to which they have come. Even when Aderet refers to the dictates of Yishuv society (and especially to those of the farmers-settlers) he, and others too, formulates them in terms of 'the needs of the land': 'the essence of movement life and its aim: education for the duty of hagshama, in answer to all the needs of the land'. It is thus clear that movement's members are expected to enter into a 'pact for life' not with the people but with the earth, the rocks, the flora, all of which are personified: 'And every year members scattered throughout the land at work-camps and hikes, saw the land in its nudity, its poverty, its enthralling landscape and committed themselves to it in a pact for life.'[66]

This collection is indicative of the 'movement spirit' and of the 'substance of life' which it offers. The above two key pieces in the collection allow a view of some of the foundations of this 'whole world'.

The searching wish to identify additional ideological foundations, interweaving and combining into the 'whole world' that the movement gives its members, leads to the only article, perhaps, in *As the Shrub of the Fields* that deals with the educational methods in Ha-mahanot Ha-olim.[67] The piece introduces the 'main motives' of the movement's educational work, that is 'constructing a pioneer-person'. The objective in question is the formation of a human being who will attain national-social goals set before him as demands. The language is activist, informed by the abovementioned orientation towards 'constructing' the pioneer-person.

The use of the term 'constructing', which verges on the connotation of a spontaneous emergence out of nothingness, is repeated once more: 'Our movement strives to construct people who will have it in their power to build the new working society.'[68] The dictates of the times summoning people to commitment, converge here with the values of spontaneity and close-knit socializing, as the features of social cohesion in the movement: 'Close, warm friendships are among the main factors maintaining the group and therefore the group's assembly is free and independent. At the group's basis is the wish for mutual understanding. This wish determines the internal life of the *hug* (circle) and its responsibility towards all the circles.'[69]

Thus, two contradictory foundations converged in the world of the pioneering youth movements: the internal drive towards friendship and close relationships as a foundation for the cohesion of the movement's basic cells (the *hugim*), and the collectivism, the doctrinarian ideology. The second element, however, was unequivocally assigned precedence or primacy. Personal and social values were, finally, subordinated to the 'goals of the movement'.[70] A long line of traits and personal values are presented in the article on educational methods, as the movement's educational objectives: 'education for equality, freedom, mutual aid, friendship and mutual understanding, frankness with oneself and responsibility towards the collective, courage and patience, loyalty, a love of life and a joy of creation'.[71] None of these, however, is perceived as inherently, independently valuable. They are destined for ends beyond the personality and path of the movement member as a human being. These are values aimed at making the young member 'loyal to the wishes and sufferings of the nation, aware of the pulse of the generation, loyal to himself and capable of combining his psychological truth with the needs of the time and the needs of coming generations'.[72]

Along with the words of movement members and the principles detailed by movement leaders and counsellors, *As the Shrub of the Fields* presents as well the words of David Ben-Gurion at a meeting of movement-graduate activists within the kibbutz movement, held at kibbutz Ma'oz Haim on 8 February 1943. In terms of the circumscription of spiritual horizons there is essentially no difference in content between those texts in the collection written by movement counsellors and graduates, and the ideological outlook expounded by the most prominent and central of MAPAI leaders. 'Two fundamental facts', Ben-Gurion says, 'determine and form our way of life and mode of thought: Eretz Israel and labour ... . This is the whole of our belief in a nutshell, and the rest is nothing more than interpretation and conclusion.'[73] In Ben-Gurion's view, 'all of the values of our movement depend upon these fundamental values'. And he enumerates the former: socialism, Jewish independence, immigration, settlement of the land, *kvutza* (a specific form of the kibbutz), *moshav* (a semi-communal farm), cooperation, agriculture, sea, industry, Histadrut (the national workers' union), workers' unions, Hebrew culture, Hagana, class war and creation, Zionist cohesion, revolution, pioneering.[74]

This representation helps gain a grasp of the centrality of the concept-values of Eretz Israel and labour, which constitute 'the whole of our belief' both here and in the majority of pieces comprising this collection. Worthy of notice are the values that depend, as Ben-Gurion put it, on the two above values, what it is that they stress and what they omit (or marginalize). All of this constitutes an extensive realm in its own right. I would only remark here that Ben-Gurion represented a pronounced line of Diaspora rejection. He opened his speech with a depiction of 'Diaspora life' as 'habits of anarchy and divisive drives' which we 'inherited' from them. As an antithesis to this Diaspora nature he stated that 'our historical destiny commands us to unite'. And this is the whole extent and depth of the Jewish dimension of Ben-Gurion's speech, from which the historical-Jewish side is totally absent.

The list of sources from which *As the Shrub of the Fields* was compiled reveals that most of the collected pieces and articles were written and published in the 1930s or the early 1940s. The piece detailing the educational objectives and means is marked 'From the Archives', apparently referring to the movement archives. Presumably, the article was written in the late 1930s or the early 1940s (like most of the material in the collection). And yet, anyone belonging to a pioneering youth movement in the late 1940s and throughout the whole of the 1950s can testify that the educational objectives and the 'way' of these movements – those of the farming labourers of Eretz Israel – remained unchanged.

Eretz Israel is one of the pivotal value-concepts in the world of Ha-mahanot Ha-olim. As shown above, this was an attitude of worship towards the landscape and the soil. Eretz Israel was to be conquered by foot – hiking its length and breadth, and especially its unsettled, desert areas. The relation to the landscapes, nurtured through a programme of backpacking hikes which spanned several years and became a sacred tradition in Ha-mahanot Ha-olim, also provided motivation for the conquest of the land through *hagshama* – by cultivating the land within the framework of a collective, kibbutz settlement.

In the spirit of the bearers of the Zionist pioneering revolution – the people of the second and third aliyot – and their disciples in the kibbutz movement, the people of Ha-mahanot Ha-olim identified their course with the revolution of the pioneer as a 'new man' or 'new Hebrew'; a course without any roots of tradition and without any formative sources preceding the ethos of the second and third aliyot.

As proposed above, the priorities and hierarchy of values of each of the pioneering youth movements are subjects for separate studies. Nevertheless, it may be said that beyond the mental differences and the variations in emphasis, all of these youth movements internalized the spiritual property and the ideologies of (pioneering) labour Zionism.

There is an almost total overlap between the foci of the ideological world of these youth movements, their main characteristics, and the distinctive features of the 1948 Generation. In many cases, we are dealing with the same individuals. For the enlisted training groups of the youth movements were members of the PALMACH. Thus, the above characterization of the world of Ha-mahanot Ha-olim reflected in *As the Shrub of the Fields* would seem to present a microcosmic examination of the 1948 Generation.

Moreover, the boundaries and circumscription of the spiritual world characteristic of many of the spokesmen and representatives of the 1948 Generation during the 1940s and 1950s have stayed essentially intact throughout their advanced years as well. What they perceived as the 'fundamentals of Hebrew resurrection' still accompanies them, while the basic values of their youth still fail, for them, to mesh with additional value-concepts, and create a comprehensive system. Today, as in their past, they are well versed in 'alternative culture' with no tendency to link their 'Hebrew-ness' with spiritual possessions from the heritage of Jewish culture. In addition, very few of them show any ability to go beyond the experience of their generation and its mental as well as social leanness.

I have chosen to trace the representations of a personal, and a generation-specific 'credo' in the work of Haim Guri – long time poet, writer and journalist who, for several decades now, has been and still is perceived as one of the central representatives of the 1948 Generation. My intention has been to follow any shifts or possible changes that may have occurred over the years in Guri's view of the world.

When Haim Guri took part in a debate about the PALMACH Generation in literature and poetry, from the vantage point of the mid-1990s, he singled out the 'holy trinity' of the 'fundamentals of resurrection': 'Hebrew labour, Hebrew language and Hebrew defence'. In his view, these constitute the central values of the second aliya and its successors – the people of the pioneering aliyot that came after it. His claim was that his contemporaries did not adhere to other alternatives because 'no real social-political-spiritual alternative could arise at the time, because you believed this story'.[75] His speech implies that these fundamentals constituted a comprehensive belief or world view that corresponded with the whole extent of the spiritual world of his generation. They saw themselves as disciples of the founding fathers. 'To rise and rebel is possible and necessary', he said, 'if you have a deeply meaningful spiritual alternative. Let him rise who can say what the total alternative is to the combination of Zionism with Hebrew sovereignty and the Hebrew language.'[76]

A different look was presented by Haim Guri in 1971, in his poetic prose piece *Faces and Names*:

> I have discovered that the sons do not know from whence their fathers come and they come as if anonymous, drawing near out of the mist.

> ... At times it seems to me that these sons have other fathers, that they were born as the progeny of a tough, sword brandishing race. I find it difficult to verify the ties of kinship to understand the family trees. Only the recorded dates and the various documents and oral testimonies can verify what is illogical that these are the fathers and these their sons. Time tables are distorted in me and at times I find it difficult to understand the goings on.[77]

This text deals not with Guri's contemporaries but with all of the Sabras, all of those grown up in the Eretz Israel. The sense of dissociation or mental-cultural barrier is not new to Guri's work. His poem *1923–1958*, some aspects of which were discussed early on in this essay, contains the line 'Between me and my father – the sea'. But the text quoted above reveals more than a sense of severed connections between the parents who have come from 'there' (their many diasporas) and the sons; it also demonstrates the problematics inherent in the way of life of generations of native born, creatures of the new and insular 'Hebrew-ness' and 'Israeli-ness'.

In an article in the late 1980s, Guri attempted to moderate and soften the 'new Hebrew' consciousness displayed by the line quoted above:

> 'Between me and my father – the sea', I wrote as I turned 35. He was born in Russia. I, in Tel-Aviv. But I was born in the 'first Hebrew city' for my father and my mother had immigrated to the country on the ship *Rossalan* that began the third aliya in 1919. I am not the severer committing the patricide of his forefathers, who opens a biography and fate unrelated to them.[78]

Later on, Guri attempts to combine his status as 'owing all the generations as their successor', and his existence as 'the other, a sharer in the secret of the Hebrew Eretz Israel mode of being'. However, the main substance, as well as the title, of the article in question, obscure and dull the marginal sense of 'successor'. For 'Hebrew-ness' is clearly portrayed by Guri as a central feature of the Zionist revolution and he also speaks of it as his current spiritual identity:

> Rise the Hebrews! ... Who are these Hebrews and why and wherefore should they rise suddenly and towards what ends?! O.K. – I direct these two words, then, as a call to my own self, the writer... . We are the Hebrews! It is important that the word be renewed for our existence here, in this land. This precise and true expression has faded, it seems, and been pushed aside between 'Jewishness' and 'Israeli-ness'.[79]

Guri represents the 'Hebrew resurrection' as a total revolution and speaks of it in a combination of past and present tenses. This revolution is for him an exhaustive cultural system:

> The forms created in materials and spirit. The political reality and the

cultural and spiritual longing in philosophy, in literature, in dance and in song and in painting. The meeting with the homeland. The resurrection of the east. The bible as an experience basic to the Hebrew renaissance.[80]

Judaism as culture and generations of the 'Jewish book shelves' (since the emergence of the writings of the sages (HAZAL) till the present, including the Diaspora and its many sites and times) had no place at all in this 'Hebrew-ness'. Guri may be captive of the superficial and mistaken equation of Judaism and Exile in its passive-spiritual sense – the one against which Zionism rebelled at the outset. 'A total revolution', he says, 'a local Hebrew way of being, unlike the worldwide nature of the Jewish Exile'.[81] This impassioned and pathetic call for the renewal of a Hebrew, Canaanite code, on the eve of the 1990s, indicates that almost nothing has changed in Guri's world since the years of his youth and young adulthood, imprinted with the revolution of the new Hebrew, arising, as it were, spontaneously, in Eretz Israel. He is incapable of explaining how a Hebrew culture is to evolve in Eretz Israel, based on the omission of the cultural heritage of Jewish history. He is, it seems, unaware of the difference between Karaism and Judaism. Judaism as a whole is not one of the layers comprising his world view.

In an exhaustive interview, on the occasion of his receipt of the Israel Prize, about a year after publication of the aforementioned article,[82] Guri was unable to better clarify or sharpen his cultural-spiritual world view. His interviewer, Yoram Harpaz, challenged him, saying, 'You [the 1948 Generation] rebelled against religion in the name of nationality, but you did not succeed in creating a new national identity. The national experience of the generation following you is a shallow one.' In reply, Guri stated that he did not believe 'that the only choice is between religious orthodoxy, acceptance of the obligations of orthodox Judaism, or decay and assimilation'. In other words, Guri knew no course offered by Judaism other than the one of orthodoxy. All he could counterpose it with, as purported components of identity, are none other than the features of his outlook as a boy in the youth movement and as a young man in the PALMACH: 'The land, the involvement with the landscapes, with the Hebrew language, with the secular culture created [here] in recent generations, all this is deeply meaningful.'[83] However, he was unable to go beyond these generalizations.

In an article written in the spring of 1996,[84] Guri took issue with what he called 'my Israeli identity', a confrontation significantly more serious than the ones examined above. The article presents two components of his spiritual identity. The first, and more basic, stems from the fact that he is native born, a fact to which he attempts to ascribe a seeming historical depth, one of place alone: 'I was a Tel-Avivian by birth ... I am from here, from Eretz Israel with all its generations, from the Hebrew and Jewish homeland, from this multi-generation locality: from the sculpture

"Nimrod" by Yitzhak Danziger too, which has recently been reacknowledged.'[85] This axis of pronounced Israeli identity is embodied in 'belonging totally to the Jewish people that was killed'; this dimension, of Holocaust, combines in his view with persecution and pogroms that took place in the Diaspora in recent generations (symbolized, for him, in the poem 'Be-ir Ha-hareiga' [In the City of the Killing] by Bialik). In the same breath with which he speaks of Bialik's poetry, Guri speaks too of 'parents and families and personal and cultural memories'. Moreover, he states in the same context that 'even the negation of Exile expressed an enormous spiritual tension, necessary for the Zionist revolution, not an alienated philistine disinterest'.[86] This credo contains not a single clear cut statement concerning ties with the living Jewish people (in addition to the one that 'was killed').

These two aspects of his essence are for him 'the ties of ties that make "Israeli-ness"'. Throughout this entire portrait of his identity, his 'Jewishness' is mentioned only once and then almost in passing – as secondary to his 'Hebrew-ness' ('from the Hebrew and Jewish homeland'). Guri's Jewishness is completely embedded in a single layer of the Jewish fate of our times and its outermost limits are 'personal and cultural memories'. It contains no expression of 'historical memory' or of historical-Jewish identity striving towards levels of Jewish existence which preceded the late nineteenth century. Judaism and its connotations are totally absent from his dual identity. His 'Israeli-ness' includes, as shown above, an element of Jewish fate, lacking any hint of Jewish destiny or of what it is that Judaism may be destined for.

The spiritual-cultural narrowness of the 1948 Generation remains intact in the world of Haim Guri today. There is no echo in his words of the slightest longing to deviate from (or break out of) the clear and structured belonging of a native born adolescence.

The world of the 1948 Generation has, of course, been enriched between the 1950s and the eve of the twenty-first century, by experience and the lessons of life. However, as it seems, not many of the representative figures of this Generation have undergone any change in perspective or attitude, regarding historical-Jewish identity. The roots, then, lacked depth and consequently, the treetops stayed stunted. At the beginning of the 1950s, Shimon Halkin, a central historian of Israeli literature, posed the question of 'the evaporation of a comprehensive-philosophical world view in our [young] poetry'. And in addition he linked the former with 'the question of the disappearance of a sense of the Israeli-Jewish "tradition" in this poetry'.[87] This dual problematic in the work of Sabra writers is no less present today than it was then, nearly five decades ago. Are they a reliable reflection of their generation? People without a history – what kind of future horizon may their spirit forge?

NOTES

1. See G. Shaked, 'Gone from the Heart is that Special Innocence (On the Self-Perception of the Authors of the 1948 Generation)', *A New Wave in Hebrew Prose* (Tel-Aviv, 1971), pp. 11–25; D. Miron, *In Face of the Silent Brother – Readings in the Poetry of the War of Independence* (Jerusalem, 1993); D. Horowitz, *Heaven and Earth – A Self Portrait of the 1948 Generation* (Jerusalem, 1993), pp. 80–2, 94.
2. R. Elboim-Dror, '"He is on his way, from us will he emerge, the new Hebrew" – On the Sub-Cultures of Youth of the First Aliyot', *Alpayim*, 12 (1996), pp. 104–35.
3. Ibid., pp. 109–20.
4. On the meanings of 'civil religion' see C.S. Liebman and E. Don-Yehiya, *Civil Religion in Israel* (Berkeley, 1983). And on preference for the term 'secular religion' see N. Rubin, 'But in a Non-Religious Kibbutz: Use of Sacred Symbols in a Secular Society', *Megamot*, Vol. 31, No. 1 (1988), p. 55 (note 4).
5. One of the first collections in this literary field is *Son of the Land – Excerpts from a Journal, Letters and Poems by Menachem Bergman (Achem)* (Tel-Aviv, 1947). Menachem Bergman was killed on 28 September 1945. For an attempt to examine the world of the 1948 Generation in the light of the estate literature, see B.Y. Michali, *The World of the Sons of the Land* (Tel-Aviv, 1951).
6. See *Biykod* (While Burning): *Letters by Raffi Meletz* (Tel-Aviv and Ein Harod, 1949), p. 63.
7. See A. Holtzman, 'Fifty Years of Israeli Prose: Aesthetic Dynamics and Social Contexts', lecture at the conference 'One Hundred Years of Culture in Eretz Israel', held at the Hebrew University, Jerusalem, 4–7 Feb. 1996.
8. Shaked, *New Wave*, pp. 11–12.
9. This expression originates in the words of Amos Oz, on the occasion of the publication of the second issue of *Yemei Ziklag* (Days of Ziklag) by S. Yizhar (Yizhar Smilansky) (Tel-Aviv, 1989). See A. Oz, 'The Present Ground', *Ha-aretz*, 3 Feb. 1989.
10. The remnants of the Jewish book shelves of parents and grandparents were around in such houses, neglected objects, but not without hidden vitality. A testimony to this type of complexity is evident in the memoirs of the famous Russian-Jewish poet, Osip Mandelstam (1891–1938). His description of the book shelves in his childhood home reveals that only on the bottom shelf, 'cast ... like the rubble of a ruin', were embodiments of his genealogical culture: Humash books with torn bindings, a book about Jewish history in Russian, a folder for studying Hebrew. He recalls this neglected shelf as 'a sort of constant chaos' of an anachronistic existence; he calls it 'the Jewish ruins' (see O. Mandelstam, 'The Book Shelves', *Sheon Ha-zman* (The Drone of Time), 1928, trans. Nili Mirsky (Tel-Aviv, 1988), p. 21). But it only seems that this world is past and gone. Its inner murmurs invade Mandelstam's world with spirited vitality; in the hymns-songs of the Hazan preserved in his childhood memories, they have 'an irresistible power'. Sketched vignettes of his deeply Jewish grandfather on the one hand and his assimilated parents on the other, in combination with the scenes of the poor Jewish quarter of St Petersburg all merge, in his present world, into a collage which he calls 'the Jewish chaos' (see chapter of this name, *Sheon Ha-zman*, pp. 29–34). Rebellion against this residue at the base of the soul is possible but there is no subduing its tastes and smells. As Mandelstam puts it, 'The bookshelf of childhood is a person's companion for life' ('Bookshelf', *Sheon Ha-zman*, p. 20). The world it reflects and presents is an underground vein, as it were, that can be ignored and 'escaped'. But at some unpredictable point it resurfaces and bursts out of its hidden bed. 'Just as a touch of musk is enough to flood the whole house, the tiniest effect of Judaism is enough to fill a whole life. How powerful that smell is! ... I remember to this day', says Mandelstam, 'how this sweetish smell surrounded me in the wooden house in Kalwucubaja in German Riga, at Grandfather's and Grandmother's' (*Sheon Ha-zman*, p. 20). 'Jewish ruins' such as these, or similar ones that retain their inner life in Mandelstam's hidden reality, underwent one more phase of repression in the biographies of the founding fathers after their emigration to Eretz Israel. From then on they were 'buried' in attics or shut up in trunks as useless artefacts. They do not reinsert themselves, they are not elements of the 'fields of memory'. But at times one of the sons of the locally born generation suddenly discovers them; 'a pile of books, worn books, tattered, pages torn, covers weathered, with cloth bundles in between ... I breathed deeply of the smell' – says the boy cast in the image of Aaron Meged – 'an old smell. Wax. Old people's

tobacco. Incense from the Sabbath-closing offering on Saturday nights ...' (A. Meged, 'Shabat' (Sabbath), *Hatzot Ha-yom* (Midday): *Selected Stories* (Tel-Aviv, 1973), pp. 7–13, first published in his book, *Mikreh Ha-ksil* (The Case of the Fool) (Tel-Aviv, 1960)). A story such as this, about a box of religious texts brought here from abroad and shut away and forgotten, is told by one of the heroes of *Yemei Ziklag* (Days of Ziklag) by Yizhar Smilansky. Another and different world of this type – be that in its extinction or the embers of its secret vitality – is usually absent from the one-dimensional existence of the Israeli natives of the land.

11. 'We lived them but did not admit to them,' said Naomi Tzuri, one of the founders of kibbutz Afikim, when asked during the 1960s by adolescents from her kibbutz why they had not observed the traditions of the Passover in their first years on Afikim.
12. G. Scholem, 'Three Types of Jewish Piety', *Ariel*, 32 (Jerusalem, 1973), pp. 5–24.
13. See H. Nir, '"Who's a Pioneer?" Semantic Transformations of the Pioneer Terminology in the Labor Movement of Eretz Israel 1917–1939', in M. Eyali (ed.), *Tura II: A Collection of Jewish-Israeli Research and Thought* (Tel-Aviv, 1922), pp. 228–48; S. Almog, 'Pioneering as an Alternative Culture', *Zion*, 58, III (1993), pp. 329–46. Also see below for this topic.
14. M. Pail, 'Between Zionism and Judaism', *Ma'ariv*, 13 Sep. 1996.
15. Shlomo Tzemach, 'Teshuot Havayatam' (Cheers of their Existence), *Bechinot: Be-bikoret Ha-sifrut*, 2, (Jerusalem, Summer 1952), p. 10.
16. On two fundamental trends of Zionism, see: A. Hertzberg, 'Introduction', to his edited volume *The Zionist Idea* (New York, 1959); D. Vital, 'The Afflictions of the Jews and the Afflictions of Zionism', *Zionism*, IX (Tel-Aviv, 1984), pp. 9–19.
17. Of the abundant literature on this topic I will mention: I. Kollat, 'Zionism and Messianism', in Z. Baras (ed.), *Messianism and Eschatology: A Collection of Essays* (Jerusalem, 1983), pp. 419–32; S. Almog, 'Redemption in Zionist Rhetoric', in R. Kark (ed.), *Redemption of the Land of Eretz Israel – Ideology and Practice* (Jerusalem, 1990), pp. 13–32. See also H. Hazaz, *The Right of Redemption* (Tel-Aviv, 1977).
18. On this question, and especially on the debate between Martin Buber and David Ben-Gurion in this context, see my article 'Political Messianism in Buber's Conception of the Redemption', *Journal of Jewish Studies*, Vol. XLII, No. 1 (Spring 1991), pp. 92–107.
19. This subject requires a separate discussion. Here I will only note that motifs such as these were characteristic of the first years of statehood. Thus, for instance, the words of Haim Hazaz in the twentieth year of statehood, 'Behold the tomorrow is come – today! The tomorrow for which we longed so deeply, which troubled our hearts so, giving no rest. It is come – today. Today, if you hark my words it is come'. (See H. Hazaz, 'Am Nivrah' (People Created), Speech at the Assembly of the Union of Hebrew Writers in Jerusalem, 16 April 1968, in H. Hazaz, *Right of Redemption*, p. 80.)
20. A. Kenan, 'Eretz Hadasha' (New Land), *Aleph* (Tel-Aviv, 1950).
21. This is a reference to ideologies and ideas and their baggage of emotions and values, as well as myths and rituals rooted in the customs and conduct of a society. See R. Chartier, *Cultural History between Practice and Representations* (Ithaca, NY, 1988), pp. 19–21.
22. See Y. Smilansky, 'Master of the Short and Straight Line' (Speech at a Memorial Service for Moshe Dayan, on the Thirtieth Day after his Death, Mann Auditorium, Tel-Aviv, 19 November 1981), *Ma'ariv*, 27 April 1981.
23. Y. Smilansky, 'A State at Midday', *Davar*, 20 April 1988.
24. H. Guri, *1923–1958*, a poem quoted and discussed above (opening this article).
25. Smilansky, Opening Speech at a seminar on 'The Writer and the Past', Hebrew University, Jerusalem, 23 May 1964, as published in *Davar* (5 June 1964, 12 June 1964).
26. Ibid.
27. E. Schweid, 'In Front of Locked Gates', *Molad*, 121–2 (Aug.–Sep. 1958), p. 483.
28. E. Schweid, 'The Sorrow of the Slashed Roots', *Shalosh Ashmorot* (Three Shifts) (Tel-Aviv, 1964), pp. 202–24.
29. Ibid., p. 221.
30. The romanticizing attitude familiar from the periods of the first aliyot was usually accompanied by a sense of cultural superiority and of spreading civilization. For various attitudes to Arab neighbours during the first and second aliyot see Elboim-Dror, *Youth Sub-Cultures*, p. 68.
31. Smilansky, *Master of the Line*.
32. On the generative power of such drives see the personal testimonies of J. Kahanoff, *Mi-*

mizrach Ha-shemesh (From East of the Sun), trans. A. Amir (Tel-Aviv, 1978); R. Matalon, *Ze Im Ha-panim Eleynu* (The One Facing Us) (Tel-Aviv, 1995). And see the combined usage by Nissim Kalderon of this work by Ronit Matalon and the essays of J. Kahanoff: 'Not All the Same Story – On The One Facing Us by Ronit Matalon', *Rehov 2: Literary Magazine* (Aug. 1995), pp. 48–58 about which see also below.

33. Y. Shavit, 'The Legend of the Giants and Their Heirs the Dwarves' (A Review of Y. Shapira, *An Elite without Successors* (Tel-Aviv, 1984)), *Iton 77*, No. 59 (Dec. 1984), p. 50; Anita Shapira, 'Generation in the Land', *Alpayim*, 2 (1990), pp. 185–6.
34. Horowitz, *Heaven and Earth*, p. 101.
35. Ibid., pp. 103, 101–10.
36. Ibid., p. 105.
37. M. Shamir, in *The PALMACH Generation in Prose and Poetry (50 Years with the PALMACH Generation)*, Workshop Proceedings, Centre for the History of the Defence Forces at Yad-Tabenkin-Efal, 1994, addressed by N. Shaham, M. Shamir, H. Guri, p. 14.
38. See the discussion 'Palestinocentrism: Hebrew-Territorial Culture', in Elboim-Dror, *Youth Sub-Cultures*, pp. 125–6. And on the equation of Hebrew-ness with Canaanism, see ibid., p. 123 – based, in this context, on Y. Shavit, *From Hebrew to Canaanite* (Tel-Aviv, 1983).
39. On this topic see above, in the subsection 'Containment within the Joint Generation Experience'. Contesting Y. Shapira whose book *An Elite without Successors* draws the opposition 'non-successors' vs. 'elite' (that is, the founding fathers), Y. Shavit (see above, note 33) disclaims the 'cultural richness' of the masses who emigrated to Eretz Israel from the villages of eastern Europe. The difference between the 'simple masses', some of whom are the founding fathers and the elite of locally born Jews, lies in the fact that the former were burdened with echoes and remnants of the milieu of the 'Jewish family' and the 'Jewish street' (or of Jewish communality) in eastern Europe. Even the simplest and least educated among them didn't usually grow up in a one-dimensional single-tongued mental and social world, totally dissociated from other cultural worlds. Meetings and confrontations with surrounding cultures, both external and internal, were embedded in the code of conduct, the customs, the beliefs and opinions. Traces of this, given from varying points of view, are evident in the many memorial books commemorating the eastern European Jewish communities destroyed in the Holocaust. Further elaboration upon them is beyond the scope of the present discussion.
40. I will list only a few samples of different cultural zones and different genres: F.V. Grunfeld, *Prophets without Honor* (New York, 1979); G. Scholem, *From Berlin to Jerusalem: Memoirs of my Youth* (New York, 1980); G. Scholem, *Walter Benjamin – The Story of a Friendship* (Philadelphia, 1981); *The Diaries of Franz Kafka* (London, 1970); P. Weiss, *Abschied von den Eltern* (Frankfurt am Main, 1961); I. Deutscher, *The Non-Jewish Jew and Other Essays* (London, 1968); A. Memi, *Pillar of Salt* (Tel-Aviv, 1988); S. Michael, *Victoria* (Tel-Aviv, 1993). See also Y. Talmon, 'Jewish History – Its Universal Significance and Uniqueness', *Unity and Uniqueness* (Jerusalem and Tel-Aviv, 1965), pp. 209–45.
41. R. Firer, *Agents of Pioneering Education* (Tel-Aviv, 1985), pp. 157–65. A highly focused manifestation of this aspect can be found in the television series *Language of Mirrors*, which examines central social and spiritual processes in the history of Israel and the Yishuv, through their reflections in literature. One of the episodes, entitled 'Monsters of Redemption', is dedicated to the attitudes of the sons and the founders' generation. It raises and interprets scenes from Amos Oz's *Menucha Nechona* (A Perfect Peace)(1982), and from *Zichron Dvarim* (Past Continuous) by Jacob Shabtai (1977). The booklet accompanying the series reads, 'Goldman grew up in a Tel-Aviv workers' neighborhood. His father was a simple, stubborn construction worker. The principles of the labor movement and the party became the father's primitive religion, cruel and rigid, and he sacrificed his children to it.' (Creators of the series: Gershon Shaked, research, consultation and guidelines; Tamar Lotan, script and editing; Lea Beirach, direction; produced by Educational Television, 1993.)
42. M. Shaked, *Links and a Chain: The Family Saga Novel in Hebrew* (Tel-Aviv, 1990). See also Y. Katz, *Tradition and Crisis* (Jerusalem, 1958), pp. 247–310; Y. Katz, 'The Traditional Jewish Family in Historical Perspective', *Tfutzot Israel* (The Diaspora of Israel), 24 (Winter 1987), pp. 14–19; D. Knaani, *Studies of the Jewish Family* (Tel-Aviv, 1986); G.S. Rosental (ed.), *The Jewish Family in a Changing World* (New York and London, 1970); D. Kraemer (ed.), *The Jewish Family: Metaphor and Memory* (New York, 1989).
43. J. Shabtai, *Zichron Dvarim* (Past Continuous) (1977), new edn (Tel-Aviv, 1994), p. 214.

44. I wish to point out a factor that has not yet been sufficiently studied from the present perspective: the extensive power of boarding school education, the placement of children in Israel. The variety of methods of placement is prominent in Israeli society: agricultural boarding schools, boarding yeshiva high schools, various secondary vocational boarding schools (including military boarding schools affiliated with different branches of the military), youth villages, kibbutz educational centres, and many, many more. Not to speak of orphanages and corrective institutions. The roots of all these, with the exception of the institutions established by the army, are in Yishuv society. The development and branching out of children's placement in Yishuv society resulted, among other things, from the assumption that society, rather than the family, is the primary and central educational agent; see A. Wiener, *Away from Home: The Roots of Child Placement Policy in Israel* (Tel-Aviv, 1984). According to reports from the mid-1980s, the basic approach in this field remained unchanged. In the early 1980s 65,000 Jewish minors were attending boarding schools of all kinds (reported by A. Wiener in an interview, 5 April 1980). An item in *Ha-aretz*, 14 Sep. 1981, reports the placement outside the family home of one in five Israeli youths between ages 14 and 18. Needless to say, boarding schools are not adequate substitutes for homes and nuclear families.
45. E. Schweid, 'Biography, Family, People', *Judaism and the Solitary Jew*, 3rd edn (Tel-Aviv, 1985), pp. 47, 44–59.
46. Y. Smilansky, *Tzahalavim* (Tel-Aviv, 1993), p. 47.
47. Ibid., pp. 48–9.
48. Ibid., p. 49.
49. Y. Shapira, 'Jewish Youth Movements in Eretz-Israel and the Elite', *Jerusalem Quarterly*, No. 36 (Jerusalem, Summer 1985), pp. 17–30.
50. Z. Lamm, *The Zionist Youth Movements in Retrospect* (Tel-Aviv, 1991), p. 81.
51. O. Almog, 'Memorial Sites for Soldiers Killed in Action in Israel: A Semiological Analysis', *Megamot*, 34 (Winter 1992), p. 180.
52. Horowitz, *Heaven and Earth*, p. 40.
53. 'The ethos of the youth movement was essentially collectivist: the individual was of no importance save as part of the group, which strove to act together', says Anita Shapira, who also adds that 'the authority of the group over the individual is all-encompassing and manifested in dozens of ways and means, in major and minor traps, sometimes conscious and sometimes unconscious ... public judgement is quite cruel, and no corner of individual life is exempt from it: ... the built-in expectation is for the individual to accept the authority of the group, willingly, and view this as a normative process'. See Shapira, *Generation*, p. 193.
54. See above in the subsection on the 'family', and also below in the discussion of the collection *As the Shrub of the Fields*.
55. Y. Ben-David, 'Membership in the Youth Movement and Personal Status', *Megamot*, Vol. 5, No. 3 (1954), pp. 227–47; M. Naor (ed.), *The Youth Movements, 1920–1960: Sources, Summaries, Selected Cases and Resource Material* (Jerusalem, 1989).
56. A limited selection of these sources has been listed above. This discussion does not pretend to cover the subject in its entirety. The annotated bibliography 'The Youth Movements, 1920–1960' included in the abovementioned collection edited by Naor is not fully exhaustive either. One of the articles absent from it, for instance, is B. Kurzweil, 'School and the Youth Movement', *Luach Ha-artez* (1994), pp. 113–23. A recent book which deals with the subject is U. Ben-Eliezer, *The Emergence of Israeli Militarism 1936–1956* (Tel-Aviv, 1996). See especially the eighth chapter, 'The Civil Militarism of the Youth Movements', pp. 180–99.
57. For a discussion of the features of the world view of the 1948 Generation, including a discussion of the pioneering youth movements, see Shapira, *An Elite without Successors*, pp. 93–106, 114–21. This book, much of the spirit of which converges with that of the present discussion, aroused critical responses from various parties, including the abovementioned articles by Anita Shapira and Yaacov Shavit.
58. On its beginnings, its history and the 'way' of the movement, see I. Kafkafi, *Ha-mahanot Ha-olim Years, Part I: The First Decade, 1924–1934* (Tel-Aviv, 1975), and *Part II: A Second Decade, 1935–1945* (Tel-Aviv, 1985).
59. See M. Naor, 'Ha-tnu'ah Ha-meuhedet', in Naor (ed.), *Youth Movements*, pp. 92–104.
60. N. Ben-Yehuda, *1948 – Bein Ha-sfeirot (Between the Counts): A Novel on the Beginning of the War* (Jerusalem, 1980), p. 71.

61. M. Tziltzer and A. Aderet (eds), *As the Shrub of the Fields* (Tel-Aviv, 1947), p. 30.
62. Ibid., p. 30.
63. Ibid.
64. Ibid., p. 31.
65. Ibid.
66. A. Aderet, 'Landmarks', *Shrub of the Fields*, p. 8.
67. 'Working Principles for Groups of High School Youth', *Shrub of the Fields*, p. 148.
68. Ibid., pp. 148–52.
69. Ibid.
70. This subordination is expressed from a distanced perspective in an essay written for the sixtieth anniversary of the movement by Y. Kenyuk, a member of 'Ha-mahanot Ha-olim' during the 1940s: 'You were taught to dedicate yourself to the "togetherness", to being "the right thing" for the future. The circles were children who had been raised to be what the poet would later call the silver platter. We were drafted into the movement at age eleven. We went for a hike in Mikve Israel. We slept on the ground and learned that we should love the homeland. We said, "To work, to defence, to the kibbutz, to the training farm [*hachshara*]", in the same intonation that our forefathers recited Shmoneh Esrei'. Y. Kenyuk, 'The Age of Innocence', *Yediot Aharonot* (3 July 1987).
71. 'Working Principles', p. 148.
72. Ibid., p. 148.
73. D. Ben-Gurion, 'Eretz Israel and Labour', *Shrub of the Fields*, p. 52.
74. Ibid., pp. 52–3.
75. *PALMACH Generation*, p. 16.
76. Ibid., p. 17.
77. H. Guri, 'Faces and Names', *Ma'ariv*, 19 Sep. 1987.
78. H. Guri, 'Arise the Hebrews', *Davar*, 27 Nov. 1987.
79. Ibid.
80. Ibid.
81. Ibid.
82. See 'Haim [Life] within the Camp', Y. Harpaz Interviews Haim Guri, *Kol Ha-ir* (Local Weekly, Jerusalem, 1 Jan. 1988).
83. Ibid.
84. H. Guri, 'The Library and the Way', *Davar Rishon* (14 Dec. 1996).
85. Ibid.
86. Ibid.
87. See S. Halkin, 'Collections of Young Poetry in Recent Years', *Behinot*, 1 (Spring 1952), p. 22.

The Shdemot Circle Members in Search of Jewish Sources

GAD UFAZ

This article contains the personal account of one who participated in the search for one's roots. Today, some thirty years later, I re-examine the motives that led me and my companions to seek new ways back to the fabric of Jewish symbols, traditions and content that we knew, if we knew it at all, only in broken and sometimes distorted fragments. Both our own parents and our spiritual fathers had turned their backs on the heritage of generations, striving to mould us, the native born of the country, in the image of the New Jew, people of action, who would fulfil the biblical vision 'every one with one of his hands wrought in the work, and with the other hand held a weapon' (Nehemiah 4: 17).

We were not intended to be Jews of the Book in the sense of the studious hairsplitters of the past, but rather the struggling and conquering people of the frontier. We were not destined to idle away our lives with our eyes raised to heaven, sharpening our brains on the niceties of the Law. We were to live a healthy and natural life in our ancient, renascent homeland, in which every furrow turned would waken memories of our bygone heroic past, and from every mountain top the ancient adventure story would unfold. We were to blend once again into the landscape of Eretz Israel as children returning to their natural homeland after lengthy wanderings. The very memory of the wanderings was to be obliterated from the consciousness of those destined to bring about a new Genesis.[1]

THE SHDEMOT CIRCLE

The Shdemot Circle, as the group was called, emerged around a periodical of the name, *Shdemot*, in the early 1960s. It was the most

---

Gad Ufaz is Lecturer in Education and Jewish Philosophy at Oranim College.

creative, distinctive and significant group within the social sciences and humanities to arise among the second generation of the kibbutz movement. This generation had been called the voiceless generation, made up of mute doers. It was also referred to as the Generation of the State, having come to maturity between the War of Independence in 1948 and the Six Day War in 1967. They were a generation whose childhood was linked to the experience of existential struggle, from the riots of the late 1930s, through the Second World War and the Holocaust, the 'illegal immigration' and the struggle that culminated in the establishment of the State of Israel. Later, they themselves were mobilized again for retaliatory raids, for the Sinai campaign, for the Six Day War, for the War of Attrition and the Yom Kippur War. It was not just the fires of war that seared and formed this generation, but also the tests of pioneering and the demands they made on themselves to be worthy successors to the founding fathers, those giants who immigrated to Israel to devote their entire lives to the country.

The Shdemot Circle had no organizational framework and no formal enrolment procedures. It was a generational group that came together because of spiritual malaise, and was consolidated by Abraham Shapira. Born in Haifa and a member of a pioneering youth movement, he came to Kibbutz Yizrael with the NAHAL, an army unit with a settlement as well as a military programme. After his army service he went to Jerusalem as a youth movement leader. At the same time he attended the Hebrew University and had the privilege of studying with such intellectual luminaries as Gershom Scholem, Samuel Hugo Bergmann and Ernst Simon, who became his mentors. They profoundly influenced his social outlook and his approach to Judaism and education. They introduced him to Martin Buber, the aged philosopher then living in Jerusalem in painful isolation, out of touch with the emergent social, cultural and political reality in Israel and with his former students. Although Buber's Utopian Zionist teachings had led them to come to Israel, they ignored him once they started to carry out the ideas that brought them here and directed them to choose the kibbutz way of life.[2]

In an attempt to bring Buber's philosophy to the entire kibbutz movement, Shapira would take young members to meet Buber in the hope that a dialogue would evolve.[3] While the desired spark was not kindled, an alternative soon appeared. Shapira was asked to edit a periodical that would contain material for the use of youth movement leaders of Ihud Ha-kvutzot Ve-hakibbutzim. Thus emerged the quarterly that in its first stages was called *Shdemot La-madrich* (For the Youth Leader), which appeared to be a product of the movement's educational and ideological establishment.

While dealing intensively with social questions, it contained many and varied areas of interest. It was this rich variety that attracted young kibbutz members, who came from a closed society in a tiny country isolated to the point of siege. *Shdemot* gave off the unfamiliar aroma of mysticism that drew on both the Kabbala and Indian culture, together with existentialist and dialogue philosophy, in the spirit of Buber and his associates from western Europe. Thus all combined, offered a new, open world that had the organic approach of the traditional midrashic style, which imparts new content and significance to old writings, by rearranging and placing them in new contexts.

In addition, *Shdemot* assiduously collected the writings of the continuing generation of the kibbutz, whose members so rarely and so hesitantly expressed their own ideas. Its first issue appeared in April 1960. Three or four years later, discussions began, attended by those who felt especially close to the periodical's unique spirit. These gatherings, of young people mainly, took place every six or eight weeks. Their diverse topics ranged from political issues to art and culture, as well as social and moral problems. A nucleus of regular participants evolved, while others who attended from time to time formed a peripheral group involved with the periodical.

This was the Shdemot Circle, which regarded itself from the beginning as an inter-kibbutz youth group. They felt that the kibbutz needed renewal, both in the realm of ideas and in the way responsibility was passed on to the next generation. They sought to substitute a new social ethos for the prevailing collective, activist approach. Their new approach would put individual and personal self-realization first among intellectual goals. In this respect they were close to the early kibbutz movement philosophy of A.D. Gordon and his followers in the Ha-poel Ha-tzair (Young Worker) movement. A first condition for the desired change was to open up channels of communication in order to create a free dialogue and multilogue that would bring man closer to his fellow man, and raise the spirit of the community.[4]

THE SEVENTH DAY

The Six Day War, a watershed in Israeli life as a whole, took the Shdemot Circle out of its somewhat esoteric obscurity, and transformed it into a widely recognized group with a public point of view. A collection of discussions called *The Seventh Day*, published four months after the war, effected the change.[5] The moving spirits were Abraham Shapira and the Israeli author Amos Oz, together with some members of the group that had come together earlier. Each member interviewed friends and acquaintances who returned from the war. These dialogues, minimally edited, were printed as a collection. The purpose was not documentation, but 'the War as a starting point, by no means as the main thing',[6] as stated in the book's introduction, without defining the main thing. However, there was a hint in the title which described it in the original Hebrew version as 'listening and considering', but few fully understood what the words implied. Only in the final pages did the editors disclose their aim. They placed in apposition to the reality of kibbutz life past and present, as regards expectations for the future, as this passage shows:

> The essence of social cooperation lies in the relations between human beings. This element in our kibbutz life has been sold short in the course of the years due to emphasis on various isms .... When we began to meet in small groups in different kibbutzim we were surprised by the openness, the readiness, by the expectation of a chance for free expression that would alleviate their distress, and liberate hitherto concealed experiences and thoughts. Actually, we were not surprised, because we knew, as Buber said, that, 'Dialogue opens that which cannot be opened in any other way'.[7]

That is to say, the war was, for the continuing generation, a cathartic trauma. It released what they had bottled up within themselves for years because of ideological isms, and created a dialogue situation. There is a hint of an apocalyptic motif in this expression of hidden desires: the turmoil of war roused kibbutz society from years of stagnation, moving it towards renewal.

The ready response of hardened warriors and silent tillers of the soil to the Shdemot Circle dialogue showed that the latter group had been right in assuming that the nature of kibbutz life had choked their generation's impulses towards self-expression. *The Seventh Day* was first published in Hebrew privately, with no intention to distribute it outside the kibbutz movement. However, its appearance became known, and beside several Hebrew editions there were translations, inter alia, into English,[8] French, German, Yiddish, Swedish and Spanish. It is without a doubt a most important documentation of the Six Day War.

When the Shdemot Circle became more widely known, its members were thrust into a period of intensive activity in many social circles. This did the group no good. Publishing their book was a high point after which a decline set in, and the desired change in the kibbutz movement never came about. Shdemot Circle members were on the one hand exposed to sharp criticism from the defenders of the old kibbutz ways, and on the other became the focus of expectations that they could not possibly meet. They were expected to to be the leading force for change in their own settlements and in the wider kibbutz framework. Some hoped they would contribute on the national level, while others hoped they would become involved in relations between Israel and Diaspora Jewry. The focus on teaching and education in Jewish studies grew out of the Yom Kippur War trauma, when the need was felt for deep discussion of the Israeli identity, and its relationship to Jewish sources. Having taken this direction, the Shdemot Circle succeeded in attracting students and perpetuating their ideas among their children's generation.

IN SEARCH OF ROOTS

Of all Shdemot Circle activities, the return to Jewish sources attracted most attention. Most of the critics belonged to the founding generation, who reacted with anger, insult and even fear. They saw the search as a deliberate challenge to them, expressing disbelief in the ethos and the ideology that they had created. This ethos was, among other things, a substitute for religious belief. Omri Lulav of Kibbutz Afikim hurled this indictment at the founders:

> In your early adolescence you underwent a deep personal revolt, involving the whole individual and his understanding of the world around him. The anti-religious sting was not there by chance. It was not only because your parents were perhaps religious and revolt meant doing the opposite.
>
> You took God down from His exalted place, and He was not present except in Man: maybe He even was Man! And in your advancing age, maybe much earlier, you committed the greatest possible sin against yourselves: on God's empty throne you placed, ceremoniously and in holy awe, the values of the kibbutz.[9]

Another son of the kibbutz, Amos Rudner of Giv'at Brenner, said the same thing in somewhat different words:

> The founding generation hungered after ideas, since their spirit was formed in Jewish homes with their human and national values, and it sought to give expression to its spiritual desires. The founding generation, to speak quite clearly, made its own religion – a religion of work, or of Eretz Israel. This may have broken down the old external frameworks, but its source was deep within the Jewish soul that nourished its theory and practice.[10]

On the other hand, the second generation expressed frustration because its roots had been cut, denying them access to the depth and the spiritual wealth nourished within Jewish tradition and history. These complaints filtered through the journalism and the literature that they produced. Some maintained that the silence of their parents was to save their children from 'the burden of the heritage',[11] and no doubt the parents acted with the best and purest of intentions. They wanted to free their heirs from the heavy encumbrance of traditions, beliefs and distortions that the Jewish people had taken upon themselves during the long centuries of exile. On their revolutionary and utopian path, they sought in one daring leap to rid themselves of the historical heritage that they considered to be so much excess baggage. Nonetheless, having acquired the heritage from their forebears, along with a developed consciousness of history, they could not get rid of the burden. What remained was the dream that the next generation would be free of it.

In these desires they were not unlike other revolutionaries with a social and intellectual vision, out to destroy the old world in their longing to build an entirely new one. Herein lies the seed of their failure. Their offspring grows up on a shallow layer of nourishment, without roots in the past, under the delusion that they are a new breed, complete in themselves and perfectly formed. With the awakening come pain and disillusionment: this precious product of the revolution discovers that it is hopelessly green and possibly may never ripen.

Even what was known as the PALMACH Generation complained about the pretensions of the founding fathers.[12] In time, however, complaints sharpened to the point where they became an indictment. This happened principally because of disappointment over the ideology that was to have replaced both tradition and religious belief.

The same anger finds repeated expression in the motif of the Binding of Isaac. Here the founding fathers are described first as having obeyed the commandment to Abraham: 'Get thee out of thy country, and from thy kindred, and from thy father's house, unto a land that I will show thee' (Genesis 12: 1). Later they submitted to Abraham's test when they carried out the commandment to 'Take thy son, thine only son Isaac, whom thou lovest, and get thee unto the land of Moriah; and offer him there for a burnt offering upon one of the mountains that I will tell thee of' (Genesis 22: 2). It often happened that sons were required to sacrifice their lives on the altar of their fathers' beliefs. The sons did not create this belief, but without internalizing it completely, they had to pay for it with their lives. The author Shulamit Har-Even expresses the message, revealed and concealed, that fathers passed on to their sons in an essay she dedicated to 'the Isaac Generation':

> Isaac, Isaac, be handsome and strong and sociable and responsible and honest and wonderful, but don't be like us who turned worlds upside down and shattered frameworks. Do whatever you please within this beautiful world we are making for you, but for Heaven's sake, don't do what we did. Don't smash the framework and don't ever leave us.[13]

Running through works that contain the Binding of Isaac motif is the father as high priest or prophet, or even as God himself. This hints at the presumption of the founding fathers who elevated themselves to the level of new Creators. Yariv Ben-Aharon, a prominent member of the Shdemot Circle, makes this point sarcastically in his war novel:

> Our world was created for us by our Dad. Of course this Dad was God. Nothing less. This was a Dad who could and did create a world from chaos and darkness on the face of the waters.[14]

The presumption contained in any utopia is proportional to its daring. The utopian's attempts to improve on God's world and to fix the Creator's mistakes contain no small measure of effrontery. Man as it were takes the place of God who failed to make creation perfect, and tries to mend God's works, doing better. The theory behind the Binding of Isaac motif is that this leads the father to assume the right to sacrifice his son. Such pride cannot be excused, cannot be forgiven. Thus the father pays with his own life for sacrificing his only son. He hews down his own trunk with his own hands. Put differently, the price the father pays is the loss of his life's work. This is a deeply pessimistic view of what lies ahead, a sharp warning to change, lest the chance for continuity be lost.[15]

As the beliefs that nourished the pioneer generation collapsed, the need for new ones became evident. Or the need could be met by reviving old beliefs and combining them with the new ones, in order to continue to survive and confront problems. No wonder then, that one sided views like Canaanism, nationalism and fundamentalist religion found wide acceptance throughout the intellectual history of the continuing, Sabra generations. A complex approach to Jewish sources, like that of the Shdemot Circle, was far less well received, both by those whose outlook was purely secular, and by the religiously Orthodox. Moreover, the Shdemot Circle preferred long term education over politics and formulated their ideas in ways subject to different interpretations rather than as scintillating slogans: this did not help their cause either. It created no understanding for their path, which deviated from the generational norm of concentrating on material creation anchored in the here and now.

It was difficult to think of an appropriate title for the Shdemot approach to Judaism. Since they did not take the Orthodox, halachic path, the term *hozrim bi-tshuva* (repenting sinners) was inappropriate, as was the phrase *hozrim bi-she'ela* (questioning once more). This is so particularly since they were not raised on a Law that provided an orderly system of answers that they later found wanting, and therefore went on to delve into and question the very foundations of belief. Here we have people who sought to broaden and deepen the Jewish-Zionist-Kibbutz world view. For them, it had not lost its basic validity, but had become shallow and superficial. They sought to give it a spiritual and ideological dimension to replace the immediate, short term ideological message that the kibbutz movement focused on during the years when it poured the foundations, as it were, and raised the framework of the Zionist enterprise.[16]

Calling for a Jewish renaissance, Muki Tzur, one of Shdemot's outstanding thinkers, described a process of accumulating strength, and far reaching change, so as to create 'the ability to survive without walls'.[17] He refers to walls of tradition that serve conservatives to ward off innovation and change and shield revolutionaries against the least contagion from the culture of the past on which they turned their backs. Walls always indicated the insecurity of those who shelter behind them. Courage is required of those who set out in search of the spiritual baggage that their fathers abandoned, without undertaking to adopt it completely – the inner content and the outward forms – and without making its articles of faith and its judgements their sole support and way of life. The call to stand exposed, without walls, is a response to Berl Katznelson, who spoke of 'the right to be confused and to censure attempts to cover up confusion'.[18]

Hence, in the wake of the Six Day War, this explanation of Yariv Ben-Aharon:

> I seem to be living in a spiritual vacuum at this time. Maybe the distress was there in past years, but I have formulated things differently since the war. I had no sense of continuity because I had no sense of attachment to Jewish life, to Jewish history.[19]

Confronting the experience of death in war means confronting the end. One questions the idea of self-sacrifice if one has lost the sense of belonging to a continuity of generations: the individual who has no sense of himself as a link between the past and the future chooses to live out his life in the here and now, not enslaved to remote and unclear aims. Questions like the purpose of human and national existence are then meaningless. No wonder, then, that following the war and the death of friends, some people asked themselves what has sustained the Jewish people through the sufferings of generations. Thus the poet Eli Allon of Kibbutz Ein Shemer wrote:

> I hunger to probe the nature of the belief that, through the generations, Jews were willing to die for ... I am looking for a direct link to the world, to the truth, to God. I do not know if this has a particularly religious significance, and I cannot say what God is for me. This is something I cannot define or explain, and the ongoing search is part of its significance. I feel within myself the ability to live this ... My God may even be the reaction to everything above life, and thinking about Him may even lead to love for the earthly experience and small mortal creatures.[20]

Allon emphasizes two points typical of the Shdemot Circle. One is the desire to discover and examine the secret of the Jewish people's existence and endurance. This meant studying the beliefs that imbued them with the necessary resources for the determined march along the road of persecution and suffering, a demanding way of life stemming from the commandments of the Law. The fact that the founders had severed themselves from this heritage was not accepted as sufficient reason not to return to study the sources so as to gain from them the strength necessary for endurance in future distress, strength that the war had shown to be lacking.

The second point was the implied question that did not seek a final and unequivocal answer. The search itself motivated study and was the source of meaning. There was willingness to set out, with all alternatives valid, and to continue, without determining in advance which ones lead to truth and certainty, since it is unlikely that these exist. The search itself is the source of creative energy and meaning.

This was no easy road, especially since those who took it refused to free themselves of moral responsibility: from the outset there was no nihilistic option. Whoever took the road accepted the challenge of a moral obligation in relationships to family, community and nation. Thus, despite the uncertainty and the danger of a spiritual and intellectual decline, there arose an impetus to an eye-opening meeting with Jewish sources at all levels. Until modern times, all such sources had come from a religious culture. Determination and courage were required of the individual who chose to set out upon such a path of study, which offered no prescribed assurances.

The quest for the roots in order to revitalize the cultural and spiritual life of the individual and the group was the basis of the search that served as the common denominator of Shdemot Circle members and adherents.

THE RIGHT TO INTERPRET

One expression of the Shdemot Circle's desire to return to traditional sources was their demand to become part of the midrashic creative process. The Midrash, as we know, is designed to impart current meaning to the sources of the past, by means of creative and broadened interpretation that makes it approachable. Summing up important segments of the Shdemot Circle's view in his essay 'Jewish Renaissance', Muki Tzur stated:

> One important thing for me in the Jewish tradition is the right to approach it in an interpretative way. The right to interpret recognizes that we accept the yoke of tradition, while reserving the right to resort to it when expressing our own world – this right recognizes the Torah as eternal, and its intepretations as historical ... The *midrash* is the recognition of the whole, and of the organic connection between the sources, a connection that is in fact created by the ordinary person on the outside.[21]

Clearly, then, the strength of the Midrash lies in its ability to form a link between the strata within the sources, and with those who hold different views. We refer specifically to people who have been remote, and are seeking their way back. The Midrash holds within it the possibility of finding new meanings in texts and symbols of the past, thus bridging the gap.

The Midrash means recognizing the sources, along with 'the right and privilege of understanding them in a new way and reviving them'.[22] In other words, accepting the obligation imposed by the sources as authority is at one and the same time a duty to give them new significance in keeping with the commentator's cultural and spiritual needs. This holds true even if the latter day commentator lives in a situation and a time totally different from those that gave rise to the texts s/he interprets and explains. Herein lie the strength and the danger of the

Midrash. For, under the guise of accepting its authority one may empty the source of its meaning, while at the same time fortifying religious Orthodoxy by what appears to be an innovation. That is to say, adapting the source to the here and now may begin a process of enslavement to the past, or of distortion with a view towards the future. Hence both upholders of tradition and self-styled Jewish free thinkers criticized the Shdemot Circle's 'right to intepret' and warned against it.

The question of principle raised by critics from both sides was to what extent those who declare themselves non-religious Jews, educated to the scientific literalist approach, can and should form an organic link with the sources. Moreover, Shdemot Circle members wanted to base both their own studies and their teachings on the integrative midrashic approach.

In all periods, traditional *midrashim* rested on a foundation of empathy and a subjective, personal link throughout all levels of the work. They were created by religious people who unconditionally accepted the authority of the sources and assumed that any new interpretation had been given to Moses at Mount Sinai: they themselves were merely recalling what had been forgotten or blurred in the course of time. This approach legitimizes new interpretations as, in fact, simply reminders of things past. The critical scientific approach, on the other hand, is based on a search for the new by means of an approach devoid of any emotional link. This accepts nothing a priori – only what has stood up to rational analysis.

Shdemot Circle members regarded the Second Aliya as the link to the sources of the past. This requires some explanation, in view of the well known trend in Zionism, socialist Zionism in particular, to reject the midrashic approach as it severed itself from the life-style and thinking of the Galut (Exile). In fact, however, the revolutionary acts of the pioneers were fraught with midrashic elements. The return to the ancient homeland was fuelled in many ways: by past memories; by the revival of the Hebrew language, which meant giving current meanings to old linguistic structures and biblical names to places and people; by putting 'self-realization' in the place of the halachic basis of the Jewish religion; and so on in countless other instances from workaday and holiday experience.

Even in the pioneering Zionist revolution that sanctified the work day and belittled holy days like Rosh Ha-shana and Yom Kippur there was a midrashic element. The very essence of Zionism was to work to continue Jewish life, even if this involved radical change. But for such a change to occur and be legitimized in the public eye, it had to be linked with the past. Moreover, the innovators themselves were born into and grew up in a deeply religious environment whose ethos and tradition they never completely abandoned.

To conclude, the Zionist enterprise was full of midrashic elements, accessible to those who looked for them. This is particularly true of the

Second Aliya. The central place of its pioneers in establishing the Hebrew culture before the state was established, and later in determining the state's social ethos, is indisputable. This wave of immigration with its creative daring was a point of departure rather than an end point. It was a most fertile nursery for experiment. It gave rise to all the important beginnings and to countless failures. The tales of adventure that are part of its history make it look larger than life. In its own time it became a legend as the actors in its drama, with their acute historical consciousness, built upon the legend and set themselves up as an example to the generations.

For our purpose two characteristics are important. The first is that the Second Aliya (1904–17) preceded the Balfour Declaration. This is the period from which most of the Zionist philosophy emanated, so that these years, so rich in deeds, were also a time when numerous ideas combined and fused.

The second characteristic is probably the most important for the present discussion: the overwhelming majority of those who came in this wave of immigration were from a traditional religious background – and were the first to challenge the conventions upon which Jewish culture was based. Moreover, because of the pioneering spirit and of the openness of the time, relations between the Zionist enterprise in Eretz Israel and traditional Jewish sources were not yet determined. Contrary to the view of such scholars as David Canaani,[23] the presumption of the Shdemot Circle was not that the Second Aliya should be held responsible for severing Zionism in Israel from the sources of Judaism. To the contrary, as claimed by Yariv Ben-Aharon, the work of the Second Aliya constituted a shining example of midrashic creativity:

> Such is the power of creative interpretation – it draws from the sources and firmly shapes within them, the spiritual reality of the New Jew putting Zionism into practice. This is what the Sages did with what was created in the time of the First Temple, and we would do well to study that transition stage closely. The reconstruction of our spiritual world must allow us to create once again the spiritual situation that informed the creativity of the Second Aliya – deep roots in our heritage and independent creativity in the present and future.[24]

Within this passage, one after the other, are two transitional stages in the history of the Jewish People: between the Written and the Oral Law, and between the exile and national independence in the renascent homeland. Moreover, there is not mere connection between these two periods but also a link between the classic and what is described as its renewal. According to the Shdemot Circle, the people of the Second Aliya, rooted as they were in tradition, added a dimension to midrashic creativity through their own deeds in the material and the spiritual realms. Personalities like A.D. Gordon, J.H. Brenner, A.Z. Rabinovitch, Reb

Benjamin, Shlomo Zemach, Berl Katznelson, Shai Agnon and in another direction Rabbi A.I. Ha-cohen Kook, and their contemporaries, were perceived as the organic continuation of Jewish creativity through the generations – while introducing an element that is clearly a turning point. But such things have happened before; the Midrash has served on more than one occasion as a means of cultural adaptation to changing reality.

In turning to the Midrash, Shdemot Circle members had a purpose beyond the renewed link with an abandoned heritage. They saw in it a way to strengthen the dimension of ideals, which the kibbutz had lost when the weakness of its adopted ideology was exposed. Since from the outset they opposed any attempt to turn ideas into tools in the hands of the political leadership, the Shdemot Circle saw in the failure of the old ideology a historic opportunity for an ideological renewal that would be deep and fruitful.

There was something romantic and fundamentalist about this concept. Here we have a return to the individualistic and possibly even the anarchic tendencies that characterized many participants in the Second Aliya. They longed to bring back to the kibbutz movement and to Israeli society a spiritual dimension that would balance the growing trend towards materialism. Shades of the spirit of the historic Ha-poel Ha-tzair (Young Workers' Party) of the Second Aliya emanated from the work and way of thinking of the Shdemot Circle.

Among its members it was felt that the kibbutz was in essence a creation that stemmed from Jewish sources.[25] Even if similar principles were to be found in socialist and utopian circles in nineteenth century Europe, this does not alter the fact that the *kibbutzim* were established in Eretz Israel by people who were involved, in all the fibres of their being, in Jewish culture. In diametric opposition to the midrashic approach were the views of the kibbutz establishment, as maintained by the founding generation. Some compared the Shdemot Circle to the Flower Children in the United States, to perpetrators of the student rebellions in western Europe and to the Prague Spring of 1968. With great emotion, Senta Yoseftal, secretary of one of the kibbutz movements, asked: 'Are we about to turn the kibbutz into a hippie commune?'[26]

The individualistic tendencies of the group, as well as their return to Jewish sources aroused alarm: the change could disrupt collective life, replacing the pioneering ethos with egotistical individual desires. But those who thought so were mistaken in their assumption. The purpose was to update and improve life-styles that had degenerated, by returning to the foundations of the past. In this philosophical context, the Midrash was both the means for forging the link between the kibbutz to its authentic sources, and the mode for significant expression and reflection. Accordingly, the revival of the Midrash was to have nurtured an enriching spiritual life.

Different members of Shdemot's inner circle had different mentors, chosen according to the individual's upbringing, education and temperament. In this discussion we need not go into variations and changes that took place over the course of time. Broadly speaking, Martin Buber's influence was strongly felt in the beginning, since his teaching guided Shapira, editor of *Shdemot*, who adopted the aged thinker's philosophical-social view. This endeavoured to create multiple dialogue interactions originating with the individual who carries on an inner debate between the various spiritual strata within himself. The individual is the point of departure for the initial connection with his or her direct partner in dialogue, which proceeds in ever widening circles to include the family, community, nation and all humankind. Buber's organic-developmental relationship to Jewish sources supported the midrashic framework. Shapira, a talented editor, created in *Shdemot* a rich mosaic of the writings of the Sages and the Hasidim, which he linked to passages of modern literature and thought. Whoever relates to the general picture emerging from these issues of the periodical and examines the component details, finds a wide ranging Midrash of sources, centred on Buber's theory. The abstracted passages from Buber's letters and writings are the threads on which all the other passages are strung, and the source of their significance.

Muki Tzur, the second central figure in Shdemot, wrote historical articles and philosophical essays in which he examined the present reality and its sources in the perspective of time. His major interest lay in the story of the different aliyot that determined Hebrew and Israeli culture. Hence his work focuses on the Second and Third Aliyot. The stories that he tells are imbued with a moral and presented in a legendary style. Besides his distinctive style, it was Tzur who laid the ideological foundations for his comrades who chose the midrashic mode of expression.

However, Yariv Ben-Aharon went beyond all the others in developing this model. He wrote essays which were characteristically midrashic, debating current issues. They drew material from a rich range of sources, from the Bible to modern authors. In a daring departure, one of his students, Barry Zimmerman, rearranged J.H. Brenner's story 'In Winter', like a page of the Talmud, with its text in the centre, surrounded on all sides by commentaries.[27]

CONCLUSION

The creative impact of the Shdemot Circle is an unfinished story. The present essay outlined certain characteristics of the first stages in its development. People who were young then are now past middle age. In many ways their work has matured and crystallized in the course of time. In a sense, it is still too early to assess Shdemot's activity. Having involved themselves in education, their current students are the offspring of their children's generation, who have continued and developed their work. It is also too early to evaluate its effect on the Israeli cultural and spiritual identity. One can only continue to sketch the outlines that perhaps in the course of time will resolve themselves into a clearer and more complete picture.

NOTES

1. Much has been said and written on this subject. Most important is the battle monologue in S. Yizhar's *Yemei Ziklag* (Days of Ziklag) (Tel-Aviv, 1958), pp. 554–60.
2. See Eliezer Schweid, 'Martin Buber and A.D. Gordon', in Bloch, Gordan and Dorman (eds), *Martin Buber – Meah Shana L-huladeto* (Martin Buber – the Centenary of his Birth) (Tel-Aviv, 1984), pp. 229–43.
3. See Gad Ufaz, 'The Kibbutz in Search of Jewish Sources in the Thinking of the Sdedmot Circle', Doctoral Thesis, Tel-Aviv University, 1986, pp. 213, 363 (Hebrew).
4. Ibid., pp. 309–32.
5. Abraham Shapira (ed.), *The Seventh Day – the Listening and Contemplating Passages*, published by young members of the kibbutz movement (Tel-Aviv, 1967) (Hebrew).
6. Ibid., p. 5.
7. Ibid., p. 282.
8. *The Seventh Day – Soldiers' Talk About the Six-Day War* (London, 1970).
9. Omri Lulav, 'You! And What About Us?', *Shdemot La-madrich*, 17 (April 1965), pp. 6–10.
10. Amos Rudner, 'Some Reflections on Yom Kippur', *Shdemot La-madrich*, 20 (Winter, 1966), pp. 41–2.
11. Martin M. Buber, 'Studying Torah – Why?', *Darcho Shel Mikra* (The Scriptural Way) (Jerusalem, 1964), pp. 359–61.
12. Yizhaz, *Yemei Ziklag*, pp. 554–60.
13. Avishag (Shlomit Har-Even), 'The Isaac Generation', *Shdemot*, 40 (Winter, 1971), pp. 42–9.
14. Yariv Ben-Aharon, *Ha-krav* (The Battle) (Tel-Aviv, 1966), p. 179.
15. Gad Ufaz, 'The Sacrifice Motif as an Expression of Longing to Rebel, of Frustration and as the Accusing Finger', *Shorashim* (Roots), 7 (1992), pp. 279–95.
16. Berl Katznelson, 'Private Grief', *The Works of Berl Katznelson* (Tel-Aviv, 1945–1950), Vol. 6, pp. 327–41.
17. Muki Tzur, *Le-lo Kutonet Passim* (Doing It the Hard Way) (Tel-Aviv, 1976), pp. 207–15.
18. *The Works of Berl Katznelson*, Vol. 9, pp. 336–41.
19. Muki Tzur, Yariv Ben-Aharon and Avishai Grossman (eds), *Bein Tseirim* (Among the Young), Group Discussions in the Kibbutz Movement (Tel-Aviv, 1969), p. 35.
20. Eli Allon, 'Facing the Experience of Death in War', *Shdemot*, 37, pp. 37–41.
21. Tzur, *Le-Lo Kutonet Passim*, pp. 209–10.
22. 'Self-Esteem in Three Dimensions' (a discussion), *Shdemot*, 63 (Spring, 1977), p. 75.
23. David Canaani, *Ha-aliya Ha-shnia Ha-ovedet Ve-yahasa La-dat U-massoret* (The Relationship of Second Aliya Workers to Religion and Tradition) (Tel-Aviv, 1977).
24. Yariv Ben-Aharon, 'Three Stages along the Jewish People's Road', *Shdemot*, 70 (Summer, 1980), pp. 33, 34–39.
25. Ufaz, 'The Kibbutz in Search of Jewish Sources'.
26. Ibid., p. 234.
27. A detailed discussion is in ibid., pp. 294–9.

Jewish Education in the Jewish State

DAVID ZISENWINE

HISTORICAL DEVELOPMENT

As Israel celebrates its fiftieth anniversary of statehood, the question how Jewish is the Jewish State, and its educational corollary – how Jewish is the educational curriculum of the Jewish State – are asked with frequency and intensity. This in turn implies that the 'Jewishness' of the Jewish State and of its educational system are in doubt. This essay will explore the origins and nature of the 'Jewishness' of the curricula of the Israeli educational system and explain why these questions are raised.

Following the 'Emancipation' of the eighteenth century, Jewish life confronted challenges from within and without. Groups from within began to press for a reconceptualization of Jewish life based on the principles of reason. This led to a diminution of the role of traditional religion and to wider participation in general European culture and society. From without, the non-Jewish communities pressed for an abandonment of traditional Jewish life style and religion and for the integration of Jews into the mainstream of Christian European society. One of the responses to this challenge was Zionism, a revolutionary Jewish nationalism seeking to create a 'New Jew'. This New Jew was to be a person who maintained strong ties to the values and folkways of the traditional Jewish community, while incorporating values of western democratic society. Zionism avoided total surrender to European culture, and introduced a new formulation of Jewish life.

A small group of Zionists established a fledgling community in Eretz Israel in the 1880s. This community, the Jewish Yishuv, was an alternative to traditional Jewish communities, both in Eretz Israel and in the Diaspora. The participants were *halutzim* (pioneers) striving to

---

David Zisenwine is Associate Professor of Education, Tel-Aviv University.

create the New Jewish person, 'rooted in the past yet historically self conscious and committed to modern values'.

The roots of this Zionist radical change in Jewish life were the romantic nationalism of nineteenth century Europe and Russian naturalism of Leo Tolstoy with its emphasis on agricultural labour. Romantic nationalism also incorporated 'the notion of "natural wholeness" which was the basis of the image of the New Jew who would be in a state of nature, living in his own land by his own system of values and norms, speaking his own language, creating his own culture, rooted, stable, and content'.[1]

The goals of Zionism were to provide for the continuity of the Jewish people in the modern world. The schools of the Yishuv needed to forge an explicit link with Jewishness. The issue of the Jewishness of the Jewish curriculum was, therefore, at the heart of Jewish revival early in the Land of Israel.

Early in the history of the Yishuv, various approaches to curriculum development evolved. One was religious Zionism – the Mizrahi[2] – favouring a traditional Jewish school curriculum based on Jewish law (Halacha), within the Yishuv and, later, the State of Israel. It shared the vision of renewed Jewish sovereignty, but rejected the vision of the New Jew as conceptualized by the secular Zionists. A second approach was the negation of the theological roots of Jewish life and the development of a New Jew based on secular humanist western values. This became the basic programme of the Labour Party in the early days of the Yishuv, and continues to be its platform to this day. A third approach, articulated by the Zionist philosopher Asher Ginsburg, better known as Ahad Ha-am, and his colleague the Zionist Poet Laureate Haim Nahman Bialik, was the teaching of traditional symbols and texts in conjunction with western humanist values. They felt that a knowledge of Jewish tradition would enable the new generations to develop a culture that would incorporate the past and provide for the future. The religious elements were seen as an anachronism that could be shed without doing damage to the evolving Jewish national tradition. Yet despite their ability to present thoughts clearly and forcefully, neither Ahad Ha-am nor Bialik, nor the historian Yossef Klausner who shared their general approach, ever presented a clear and articulate set of criteria for separating the national from the religious. This legacy of blurred distinctions and lack of criteria has yet to be clarified.

The involvement in curriculum went far beyond the arena of philosophical writings and public debate. The Yishuv had children to educate, and a culture to create. Their expression of the challenge is in the curriculum of their schools. The early Yishuv schools incorporated the study of Bible, Talmud, Aggada, Hebrew literature, and Hebrew language in their curricula. They continued to debate the value of these subjects, and the time that should be devoted to them. However, they included them in the secular schools.

The course of study during the Yishuv period shows that the dominant curriculum programme for Jewish studies was modelled on the cognitive approach of Ahad Ha-am and Bialik. They assumed that the creation of Jewish culture was the function of learning. For people from the religiously observant centres of eastern Europe, with remembered and imagined warmth of the traditional communities, it seemed self-evident that Jewish learning was the guarantor of vibrant and vital new Jewish communities.[3]

The approach to Jewishness developed in the Yishuv continued into the early State period. The newly formed Ministry of Education required Jewish subject matter as a requirement for high school matriculation examinations. Bible, Hebrew literature, Hebrew language and Jewish history were required yearly matriculation examinations. In addition, there was a State mandated requirement for secondary school graduates to study one credit of either Talmud or Jewish thought in the tenth, eleventh and twelfth grades. Thus, continuation of 'Jewishness' as knowledge was central to the sustained evolution of the new Jewish-Israeli culture.

The early statehood years were rife with problems of security, and with the task of absorbing mass immigration from the survivors of the Holocaust and North Africa. The school system was responsible for teaching children the Hebrew language and introducing the *olim* (newcomers) to the cultural codes of Israeli society. These cultural codes were the Jewish components of life as they had evolved from the Yishuv period and were embodied into the curriculum.

The Yishuv had evolved a popular daily Jewish culture. The Jewish calendar set the rhythm of the year, and individuals became absorbed into this Jewish culture by just being there. The school year was part of the greater society which measured its days in terms of the high holidays – Sukkot, Hanuka, Purim, Lag Ba-omer, Pesach, Shavuot – as well as the new, universally observed Memorial Day, Holocaust Remembrance Day and Independence Day. How one marked their observance was a matter of individual choice. The form had been established, but the content of the Jewish year was not as clear to the individual non-Orthodox Israeli. In elementary school the students learned about the history and symbols of the holidays.

By the mid-1960s it became apparent that the Jewish component of school life had not created the New Jew that the early Zionists had envisioned. The parallel evolution of a society based on western humanistic ideology was more attractive to the new Israeli than Jewish folkways. The nineteenth century romantic view of an agricultural society was replaced by the twentieth century world view of an industrial, technological, efficient, democratic society, which participates in a world that is labelled a 'global village'. This had not been anticipated by the early Zionists. The diminution of the uniquely Jewish in Israeli life led to a period of evaluation by the Ministry of Education, resulting in the creation of a public commission to address the issue of the 'Jewishness' of the educational system. Known by its chairman's name, the Ben-Yehuda Commission was mandated to propose ways and means to incorporate 'Jewish Consciousness' into the curriculum of the school system.[4]

The Minister of Education, Zalman Aran, saw this as a central task in his lengthy administration. The Commission was reminded that the National Education Act of 1953 had explicitly stated that 'the purpose of national education is to base education in Israel on the values of Jewish culture, the achievements of science, on the love of country, and loyalty to the State and people of Israel'.[5] The commission set about to delineate the nature and scope of the problem, and to offer operational suggestions. In 1966 its chairman, Dr Baruch Ben-Yehuda, published a booklet summarizing the commission's suggestions and enunciating the programme for fostering Jewish consciousness. Following this booklet, which analysed the problem in terms of the historical changes in the status of the Jewish People, the commission's published syllabuses to aid teachers. In addition, a centre for inculcating Jewish consciousness was established in the Ministry of Education.

A survey of the materials and programmes developed by this centre shows that the original direction of increased Judaica learning set out by Ahad Ha-am, Bialik and their colleagues in the 1920s remained virtually intact. Notwithstanding declarations about the need for effective Jewish education, the centre published additional, albeit better written, subject matter materials. These expanded the course in Zionist history and philosophy, and added materials about the Holocaust and life in Diaspora communities. The Diaspora study materials emphasized in particular the plight of the Jews in the Soviet Union and their ongoing struggle for their right to emigrate to Israel. The materials also highlighted the varieties of Jewish experience and folklore of the various communities without addressing the issue of identity in depth.

Religious observance was carefully avoided. The commitment to the free and democratic choice of religious behaviour was part of the concern about religious coercion. The main stream of non-religious Zionism had fought this battle in covert and overt ways since the early days of the Yishuv. This ideological argument within the Israeli-Zionist community adds another dimension to the task of defining and implementing a coherent, acceptable programme of Jewish education. Despite the continued publication of materials and in-service training programmes, the Jewish Consciousness Programme was considered an educational failure. It thus ended at the close of Aran's term of office in 1969, with the school system maintaining its basic Jewish curriculum. Yet the popularity and value of Jewish subjects has never been properly measured. Conventional wisdom suggests that they are not high priority subjects and that their value decreases as the students progress into the high school period. Preparation for adult life in a secular western society does not place emphasis on these subjects and reduces their worth to students.

Some parents were displeased with this reality. In 1974 a group of parents in the French Hill area of Jerusalem organized to create a school that would be neither religious Orthodox nor completely secular. They took advantage of an ignored section in the National Education Act of 1953, allowing parents the right to request additional curriculum components at any given school. More specifically, Chapter 2, Section 2 of the National Education Act of 1953 states:

> Parents of children in a specific educational institution who want the institution, or any part thereof, to add additional curriculum from that set by the Minister of Education will act as follows: 75 per cent of parents in any specific class may turn to the principal of the institution and specify in writing a proposal of the additional curriculum that they want implemented. They may also indicate in the case of a program already taught elsewhere that it has been authorized by the Minister of Education. In their proposal they should include the subject matter areas affected and the number of instructional hours proposed.[6]

The French Hill parents took advantage of this section and formed the 'Masorti School', placing it in the secular school system. The parents stated their ideology in terms of intellectual-educational, experiential, value laden and integrative education. The intellectual-educational programme included 'Jewish civilization and its intellectual, spiritual, and aesthetic expression over the past three thousand years ... it employs a wide variety of tools and approaches to the understanding of Jewish sources ... not only traditional commentaries ... but modern approaches to the subjects such as archaeology, comparative history, and comparative religion.' In the experiential part of their ideology they claimed that the affective component of Judaism was no less integral to Jewish tradition than the cognitive. Experiencing Jewish traditions and ceremonies was a dimension to which all Israeli children should be exposed. The parents felt that value education should be embedded in all school studies. They also saw integration of subject matter as critical, and planned to integrate Jewish and general subjects. The TALI Programme, as this new programme was called, also advocated parental involvement in policy, and the daily management of the school. This included ritual and ceremony in the school programme without insisting or requiring the parents to agree to these observances at home. This was the first attempt at fusing religious behaviour and subject matter study in the secular schools. The founders conceptualized the school as an independent community, separate from the home, and a laboratory for Israeli-Jewish life. They saw their format as a mature expression teaching a total Jewish culture.[7]

The Masorti School programme was fought by the religious school system as a dangerous misrepresentation of Jewish tradition. The opposition was not successful in preventing the opening of the school, and the subsequent development of the TALI schools during the tenure of Zevulun Hammer. Hammer served as the Minister of Education from 1977 to 1984 and 1988 to 1992, on behalf of the National Religious Party (MAFDAL). The coalition of Hammer and the TALI parents is worthy of serious analysis in and of itself, but is not within the scope of this essay. For our purposes, it suffices to indicate that Hammer and the TALI parents adopted a pragmatic approach to this new expression of Jewish education and avoided ideological conflict. Their goals were different, but the reality of Israeli educational politics had turned them into political bedfellows. Hammer supported TALI and created a department of Jewish Education at the Ministry of Education. Like his predecessor Aran, Hammer dealt with this issue through the formal institutional structure of the ministry.

There are currently 7 TALI schools and 30 TALI classes throughout Israel. The original French Hill School continues to thrive, but to date only one TALI high school has been established. Despite the unique culture of the TALI schools, they have not attracted a wide following. They are a small and interesting alternative model for Jewish education in Israel.[8]

Following Hammer's tenure, the Department of Jewish Education remained part of the Ministry of Education. In 1993 the Rabin Government made Jewish Education a public issue. The new Minister of Education, Amnon Rubenstein, a member of the politically liberal MERETZ party, appointed Professor Aliza Shenhar, then Rector of Haifa University, to head an official commission to make recommendations for teaching Jewish Studies.

In 1994 the Shenhar Commission published its report. It advocated a better curriculum, teacher in-service and pre-service training, and financial support for Jewish Studies at the universities. They also recommended integration of Jewish and secular studies. The emphasis of the Shenhar Report was on subject matter learning and the incorporation of current trends in general educational pedagogy. The affective domain, or religious practice of Judaism, were absent from the report.

ANALYSIS AND SUGGESTIONS

The concern for continued Jewish identification among Israelis has been a central educational issue from the founding of the Yishuv. The combination of political pressure and religious ideology from the Orthodox parties, and the inability of the non-Orthodox and non-religious thinkers to formulate a clear educational philosophy, led to a series of programmes that fell short of their mandate. The affective-behavioural aspect of Jewish life is missing in the secular schools. This is further aggravated by the failure to find a way of looking at learning that appeals to Israeli children and their sense of being Jewish in the Jewish State.

A combination of Zionist secular ideology and political reality have led to a stalemate in implementing any programme to address this issue. The continued emphasis on the cognitive seems to be a 'loss of nerve' on the part of Zionist-Israeli educational leadership. Zionist ideology claimed to bring Jewish life into the arena of modern western life. Establishing a state and political framework has been necessary, but far from sufficient for Jewish identification.

The work of two philosophers of education, Hanan Alexander from the world of the philosophy of Jewish Education, and Charles Taylor of general philosophy, indicate a different direction.[9] In the *Ethics of Authenticity*, Taylor looks at contemporary culture at large and identifies what he calls 'malaises of modernity':

> that is, features of our contemporary culture that people experience as a loss or decline ... a loss of meaning and fading moral horizons ... we live in a world where people have a right to choose for themselves their own pattern of life, to decide in consequence what convections to espouse, to determine the shape of their lives in a host of ways that their ancestors couldn't control ... Very few people want to go back on this achievement... . But this has not come without a price. There is a darker side to individualism that involves self-centeredness which can flatten and narrow our lives, making them poorer in meaning, and less concerned with others.[10]

Alexander points out that the world of education at large has been affected by the philosophy of instrumentalism, in which the goal of education is instrumentalism, 'the kind of rationality we draw on when we calculate the most economical application of means and ends'. Israeli-Jewish education, and perhaps general education, have in great measure adopted this philosophy. Israelis measure their output through testing of specific objectives. Hence, the high school student who receives a high score on his Jewish History or Bible matriculation examination is thought to be a knowledgeable and thus a committed member of Israeli-Jewish society. Israelis 'train' students to perform well, never asking themselves whether this meets the vision of what they thought the 'good' Israeli-Jew should be:

> When educational philosophers such as Richard Peters and John Dewey speak of the self justifying nature or intrinsic value of education, they are giving expression to the idea that education, whatever else it is about, involves initiating people into that which is most valuable. Education is not merely a means to these valuable ends; the process of coming to understand, appreciate and accept a vision of the good is valuable in itself.[11]

By only training students in subject matter areas, the Israeli educational system restricts their ability to engage in decision making and choice. At best, it 'trains' students to read texts without asking them to see these texts as a possible source of meaning for their lives. Hence, Israelis should view Jewish Studies, and practice, as means to an end, and see these studies as part of the process in the search for meaning in the Israeli context. Study as a critical process that makes life meaningful and not just efficient makes Judaism authentic. The Israeli educational system must replace the cognitively orientated programme of Jewish Studies with a study of texts and ideas that contain the collective memory of the Jewish People, allowing each student to search for his/her meaning in these texts. The search – the dialectic, the 'shakla Ve-tarya' – has always been important in Jewish study. Jewish learning was never instrumental or goal orientated. The process of learning was, and should yet again be, a life-long process. It may very well be that after looking at, analysing and contemplating Jewish subject life, with an intent to find individual meaning, the student will say – it is not for me! That is acceptable if the search has been serious and thoughtful. Choice is, after all, the hallmark of modern secular society.

In the practical sense of education, this means that pre-service and in-service training, always advocated in the history of Jewish education in Israel, should be as concerned about confronting the texts as 'covering the material'. The invitation to see subject matter as 'life matter' offering a 'way of looking at things' is the authentic component of Jewish education. The revolutionary aspect of Jewish education is to move it from the instrumental to personal engagement in the search of a meaning. By going beyond 'knowing about' to questioning what does this say 'about how I will live my life', Israelis will be moving the 'revolutionary' Zionist movement into the twenty-first century. The invitation to find oneself in a caring, cultivating and questioning classroom should be a true celebration of Jewish education. The text is not archaic, but an invitation to find meaning in the collective wisdom of the Jewish People. The individual of modern life seeks out and is guided by the historical collective. The educational leaders of Israel and the Yishuv missed the opportunity to fuse a modern need with collective memory. Today's teachers must be trained as guides who ask questions found in the texts. They should present these questions as challenges, fashion a new-old methodology of engaging the text in the idiom of the day, and understand that not every text is appropriate and responsive to the student. If rabbinic Judaism was an appreciation of the dialectic, then modern Israeli Judaism must be devoted to a conversation about meaning, across time.

The failure to include the affective aspects of Judaism in all of the curricular suggestions has been a theme throughout this essay. The work of Piaget should be our guide to the need for practice and affect. His outline of the stages of cognitive and affect development show the need for hands-on activities. One cannot learn chemistry, biology or history without a hands-on experience. Jewish lifestyle in its many forms certainly cannot be learned without hands-on experience. The TALI model of providing a variety of experiences from Sukkah to Seder in the school environment without any obligation to make this part of one's personal lifestyle is what schooling is about. The school should provide the concrete experiences of Jewish life to all students. For their part, the students and their parents must see schools as a laboratory setting that offers – but not forcing them to live by it. If the experiences reflect a variety of customs, approaches to ritual and lifestyles, it will allow new Jewish forms to emerge and old Jewish forms to be renewed. The cognitive that is not enhanced by the affective cannot succeed. The cognitive that does not stimulate thinking and questioning, as well as decision making and resolution, is just not education. It is at best poor training, and at worst indoctrination. One should be able to use the models, some of which, like TALI, are already available, and to modify them to meet the needs of the day. One must also ensure that the process is not replaced by procedure. The invitation to learn through experience of mind and feeling was missing from the previous models. The new Zionist revolution must rid itself of anachronistic battles with religious ideologies. The call to test one's ideas, beliefs and sense of identity is the starting point in the process of Jewish education. This education should allow the formulation of a sense of how one should live through reflection of and involvement with the texts and practices of Jewish life. Israelis must allow their students to appreciate the past and create their present and future with the knowledge that the very quest is a guarantee of a meaningful Jewish life in the Jewish State.

NOTES

1. Marc Rosenstein, 'The New Jew: The Place of the Jewish Tradition in General Zionist Secondary Education in Palestine from its Beginnings until the Establishment of the State' (unpublished doctoral thesis), The Hebrew University of Jerusalem, 1985.
2. A Hebrew acronym for *Mercaz Ruhani*, meaning a spiritual centre. It is also a play on the word *Mizrah* (east), the direction towards Jerusalem faced in Jewish prayer.
3. See, for example, *The Curriculum of the Reali School of Haifa* (1936) (Hebrew); see also *The Decisions of the Sub Committee for the Study of Talmud, Agadda, and Halacha for Secondary Schools* (1938) (Hebrew). These are just a couple of the many examples of published materials on this topic to be found in the Archives of the Ministry of Education, the Zionist Archives, The David Yellin Archives, and Histadrut Ha-morim Archives, as well as local community and school archives throughout Israel.
4. Dr Baruch Ben-Yehuda served as the chair. He was joined by Avraham Arnon, Ben-Zion Ziv, Dr M. Landau, Professor Dov Sadan, Hanoch Paz, and Member of the Knesset Dr Elimelech Rimalt. The Commission was officially convened on 20 July 1964.
5. The National Education Act of 1953 has remained the basic education law of the State of Israel to this day.
6. *National Education Act of 1953*, Ch. 2, Section 2.
7. Lee Levine, *The Tali Schools in Studies in Jewish Education*, Vol. 7 (Magnes Press, 1995), pp. 259–77.
8. Ibid.
9. Hanan A. Alexander, 'Jewish Education and the Search for Authenticity: A Study of

Jewish Identity', Unpublished Paper delivered at the Conference for Jewish Identity, School of Education, Tel-Aviv University, December 1995; Charles Taylor, *The Ethics of Authenticity* (Cambridge MA, 1991).
10. Taylor, *The Ethics of Authenticity*, p. 5.
11. Alexander, 'Jewish Education', p. 10.

ARTISTIC REPRESENTATIONS
OF JEWISH IDENTITY

Sisera's Mother and the Trojan Women: On Universal Aspects of the Jewish/Israeli Theatre

ELI ROZIK-ROSEN

Why is his chariot so long in coming?
(Judges 5: 28)

Because of its relative openness to foreign traditions, as revealed in the tendency to recreate on stage the treasures of classic world playwriting, the Israeli Hebrew theatre probably reflects more than any other art the utter complexity of the developing Jewish identity within the context of the Israeli culture; and because of its appeal to wide audiences, large sectors of Israeli society are thus exposed to extensive and intensive intercultural interaction. This is in line with Zionist ideology which was committed both to preserving Judaism, though of a very anti-Orthodox nature, and to integrating the major achievements of non-Jewish culture into the fabric of a 'renewed' Jewish culture. The proclaimed aim was to blend the values of biblical culture, in which art was created by a sovereign nation, with universal ones. Zionist ideology assumed that prior to canonization of the Jewish religion, Hebrew culture freely created and interacted with foreign cultures, with the confidence which a free nation naturally enjoys. Identification with the nation's independent past has led to an openness to foreign cultures, particularly the Greek culture, which for the last two thousand years has been conceived by Orthodoxy as the arch-enemy of Judaism.[1] A readiness for exposure and a willingness to assimilate – not merely imitate – any cultural achievement thus became one of the central values of Israeli society. Despite the erosion of Zionist doctrines, I believe that this fundamental attitude has remained valid until the present day. Furthermore, this consciously accepted and articulated attitude underlies most, if not all, of the classic plays (in the broad sense of the term) translated and performed on Israeli stages.

Eli Rozik-Rosen is Professor of Theatre Studies and Dean of the Yolanda and David Katz Faculty of the Arts, Tel-Aviv University.

For those who do not endorse the view that only the ultra-Orthodox are the exclusive trustees of Judaism, and who also believe that Judaism is a culture and not necessarily a religion, national creativity is conceived as an open ended process, in which Judaism freely interacts with other cultures. In this sense, the revival of the Hebrew language, as a common spoken language, the possibility of sharing the literary treasures produced in this language throughout the last three thousand years, and the resettlement of the Land of Israel, have provided the necessary conditions for both intracultural and intercultural interaction. It is because of this triangular conception of the foundations of Israeli culture (Hebrew language, Hebrew literature and the Land of Israel) that the Bible enjoys a privileged status in the consciousness of the new secular Judaism. On the ideological level, identification with biblical times thus justified and enabled renewed exposure to foreign cultural values and free cultural exchange, previously excluded by religious dogma.

I intend to explore this type of free intercultural interaction by analysis of a quite recent production of an ancient Greek tragedy, Euripides' *The Trojan Women*, by the National Ha-bima Theatre (1983). I will attempt to explore the means by which an exponent of a once rival culture was made relevant for and assimilated by an Israeli audience, and compare the reception of this production with that of Euripides' original adaptation of the Homeric myth to the contemporary political situation in the Greek world of 415 BC. Subsequently, I intend to draw an analogy between ancient Greek and biblical attitudes to war and the sufferings of the defeated. In very broad lines, I intend to show that the gap between Jewish and Greek ancient cultures was not after all as profound *as we were led to believe*, and that their coexistence within Israeli culture, even in tension, is not as dangerous to the Jewish identity *as we could have been led to believe*. Moreover, the absorption of the Greek classics into the canon of the Israeli new Jewish identity should be regarded as an index of intracultural strength. After all, in intercultural relations, adaptation to the needs and modes of perception of the host culture is the rule.

THE TROJAN WOMEN BY EURIPIDES

The destruction of Troy, which ended a ten year siege of the city, took place *c.* 1184 BC; it was described by Homer in about the ninth century BC, and part of the narrative was used by Euripides for *The Trojan Women*.[2] The play was written and performed in 415 BC within the historical context of the Peloponnesian War, having in mind the cruel punishment of the neutral island state of Melos a year earlier for not joining the Athenian confederacy, and the preparations for the great unprovoked expedition to conquer Sicily. Euripides found in the ancient legend of Troy an obvious analogy to the atrocities perpetrated by the Athenian forces on Melos: all male citizens were slaughtered and all women and children were enslaved.[3] The Homeric narrative can thus be conceived as a metaphorical description of the contemporary wars. However, whereas the target audience was assumed to see in this ancient story a token of the heroic past of the nation, Euripides presents it from the viewpoint of the defeated enemy nation and, in particular, of the women, the only survivors of the war, revealing their sufferings and the vile and vain nature of their Greek conquerors, and indicating thereby his intention to shock the audience. He probably assumed that the fate of those unfortunate women would induce a sense of identification that would outbalance the hatred of the enemy. He did not include any hint of actuality, most likely believing that the audience would understand the obvious metaphor and its relevance to the actual political situation.

The mechanism of self-criticism used by Euripides acts to confront the audience with the suppressed contents of their psyches and, in particular, the anti-heroic nature of their own heroes and the all too human suffering of the enemy. The typical attitude of a society at war is reflected in attempts to dehumanize the enemy, ranging from depicting their alleged monstrosity to merely ignoring their shared humanity. Whereas the presentation of suffering victims of war of any nationality, particularly women and children, is likely to spontaneously elicit fear and pity, identification with the enemy victims assumedly rehumanizes them and is liable to create an inner conflict between genuine human compassion and spurious national identification. Moreover, the victimization of the women is shown as a token of gratuitous cruelty and the killing of Astyanax as a token of the Athenians' fear:

> Hecuba: ... What shall the poet say,
> What words will he inscribe upon your monument?
> *Here lies a little child the Argives killed,*
> *because they were afraid of him.*
> That? The epitaph of Greek Shame. (1188–91)

Euripides even dehumanizes the Greek heroes, Menelaus and Odysseus in particular, and by an unexpected oxymoron, in the words of the barbarian Andromache, Euripides ranks the Greeks as barbarians (764).

It might appear that in attempting to prevent an unnecessary war, showing the suffering of the mothers of the audience's own side would generate a more effective and powerful emotional response. However, a fundamental difference may be suggested: whereas such a fictional world would have elicited uncontrollable fear and, probably, feelings of outrage and fanatical patriotism, focusing instead on the sufferings of the mothers, wives and children of the enemy may have compelled the audience into subliminally and perhaps aesthetically experiencing the possibility of defeat, perceiving themselves from the possible perspective of the enemy's misery, and thus considering the absurdity of such a dangerous game. It may be the case that the members of an audience are prepared to devote their lives to just causes that lead to war, but it may be more difficult for them to confront the horrendous experiences of those who may have survived it, which tend to be suppressed in the euphoria of victory.

Empathy with the defeated implies that the spectator may be reversing his perception of himself by experiencing the fate of the defeated as his own possible fate, under the unpredictable circumstances of war. This is presented by Euripides as a viable course of events in the words of Poseidon who comments on Athena's whimsical 'change of sympathy' (67). The more convincing the picture of suffering, and the more the war is presented as an unjustified affair, the stronger the conflict that the play is meant to induce in the spectators. Empathy with the enemy is used here to compel the audience into revising its attitude regarding the value of a war which is believed to be unjustified, and even into blunt criticism of pseudo-patriotic feelings.[4] The absurdity of war is again epitomized in Cassandra's words: 'For one woman's sake, / one act of love, these hunted Helen down and threw / thousands of lives away' (367–9).

This mechanism of reversing identification is also employed with regard to the gods. In complaining about his bitter fate, Poseidon reveals the sheer absurdity of the notion of 'local protecting gods': 'so I must leave my altars and great Ilium, / since once a city sinks into sad desolation / the gods' state sickens also, and their worship fades' (25–7). In becoming homeless, Poseidon shares the fate of those whom he was believed to and meant to protect, and reveals that in fact he is just as helpless as the human victims. The gods' welfare is thus shown as dependent upon human worship. The bitter irony of the powerlessness of the gods is poignantly reflected in Hecuba's words:

> O gods! What wretched things to call on – gods! for help
> although the decorous action is to invoke their aid
> when all our hands lay hold on is unhappiness.
> ...
> I mourned their father, Priam. None told me the tale
> of his death. I saw it, with these eyes. I stood to watch
> his throat cut, next the altar of the protecting god. (469–83)

Euripides possibly felt that the inhabitants of the Isle of Melos also put their trust in their gods, just as the Athenians did in theirs, and that these let them down.[5] Moreover, Athena, the 'glorious victor' of the war, is most unhappy with its results and is even scheming to severely punish the Greeks for their offences, another demonstration of her cruel and capricious nature. Athena is thus presented as failing to have taken into consideration the possible behaviour of the victorious Greeks after ten years of war. The implication is that the disasters of war are unpredictable and that there is no moral or religious principle that underlies a logic of war. Following the known pattern of Euripidean plays (*Bacchae* and *Hippolytus*), the humans show a kind of dignity and moral standard that the gods fail to emulate.[6] Hecuba, the victim of Athena's wantonness, is more sublime and commands more admiration than the goddess. Identification with the suffering of their victims is meant, therefore, also to induce a revision of religious beliefs: what kind of gods are those who fail to protect the city, or who decide its fate upon a whim? I believe that the main object of Euripides' criticism was not divinity itself, but the absurd notions that people have of divinity.[7]

Criticism of misconceptions of war and divinity, which is the aim of the play, is fuelled by a different approach to reality, based on rationalism. The structure of the fictional world is such as to defy any possible logic. Catastrophe and success are the undeserved fate of the women and the Greeks, respectively. Behind the scenes, events are dictated by Odysseus, well known for his base nature, and described by Hecuba as 'that vile, that slippery man, right's enemy, brute, murderous beast, that mouth of lies and treachery, that makes void faith in things promised and that which was beloved turns to hate' (283–96). This seemingly biased image of Odysseus is amply corroborated by Sophocles in *Philoctetes*. However, the villain of the play has the upper hand. Despite the troubles awaiting him on his way home, the audience knows that he will survive and live happily ever after with his faithful Penelope. The audience also knows that Helen, the unfaithful counterpart of Andromache (and Penelope), will survive and regain her royal status. Above all, there is a fundamental disproportion between a trivial case of abduction-betrayal and the wholesale slaughter of all the male adults, the enslaving of all the women and children and the destruction of an entire city. Such a disproportion was probably meant to induce a sense of absurdity with regard to the annihilation of the state island of Melos in the immediate past and the possible fate of Sicily in the near future. Basically, the mechanism of criticism is the same as in satire; the difference resides in the serious and sublime style of the play. In contrast to Aristotle's dictum, by restructuring the narrative Euripides shows his intention to shock the 'moral sense' of the audience.[8] Aristotle could not have even contemplated the possibility of absurd structures of tragedy.

THE HA-BIMA PRODUCTION OF *THE TROJAN WOMEN*

Sartre's adaptation of *The Trojan Women* by Euripides, in the Hebrew translation by Eli Malka, was produced by Ha-bima Theatre and premiered on 19 February 1983. The production was directed by the German director Holk Freytag; Hecuba was played by Orna Porat, on loan from the Cameri Theatre; the set and costumes, which played a major role in conveying the specific interpretation, were designed by the German Angelica Edingen; the music was composed by Ofer Shlahin.

In making his adaptation, Sartre had in mind the success of a previous production of the ancient play (in the faithful translation by Jacqueline Moatti) during the war in Algeria, for an audience which was in favour of negotiations with the FLN (Front de Liberation Nationale).[9] Although the war ended in 1962, *Les Troyennes* by Sartre was produced by the Théâtre National Populaire and premiered on 10 March 1965 at the Théâtre du Palais de Chaillot, Paris. The success attained by self-criticism during the Algerian War of Independence clearly encouraged Sartre to adopt the seemingly disloyal attitudes of Euripides in *The Trojan Women* to denounce the absurdity of colonial wars, any war and, in particular, an imminent nuclear war.[10] Sartre apparently identified with the enemy in order to shock his audience and confront it not only with its own actual suppressed fears but also with its suppressed positive values of compassion.

Having in mind the colonial wars of the twentieth century, Sartre stressed the paradox in the extreme cruelty of the so-called 'developed' Greek-colonialist culture towards the assumedly more 'primitive' Trojan population, by assigning to Asian Andromache a homily against European Greeks: 'Hommes de l'Europe / vous méprisez l'Afrique et l'Asie / et vous nous appelez barbares, je crois, / Mais quand la gloriole et la cupidité / vous jettent chez nous, / vous pillez, vous torturez, vous massacrez. / Où sont les barbares, alors ? / Et vous, les Grecs, si fiers de votre humanité, /Où êtes-vous?' (p. 81).[11] Sartre implies that from a humanitarian viewpoint the victors were greater barbarians than the vanquished and, morally speaking, they defeated themselves because they lost their own humanity.

By adding an anti-war homily by Poseidon at the end of the play, Sartre foregrounded the theme of the absurdity of war altogether: 'Faites la guerre, mortels imbeciles, / ravagez les champs et les villes, / violez les temples, les tombes, / et torturez les vaincus. / Vous en crèverez. / Tous' (p.130). He did not identify the parties to a possible colonial or nuclear conflict in the play itself, probably assuming that the audience would do so in any case. Moreover, in contrast to Euripides, Sartre finishes the play with an act of heroic rebellion against any form of domination: Hecuba, in a gesture that is meant to command the admiration of the audience, states: 'portez-nous, chiens, tirez-nous, / poussez-nous de force, / Nous n'irons pas de notre plain gré / vers l'exil et l'esclavage' (p. 125).

Sartre marginalized the religious theme, subordinating it to a comprehensive metaphor of the rule of absurdity in the world. He retained some of the original words of criticism against the gods while adding certain expressions of his own, such as 'alliés suspects' (p. 60), 'Dieux sauvages' (p. 120), 'votre stupide injustice' (p. 121), 'nous souffrons l'enfer et vous riez dans votre ciel' (p. 120), and 'Dieux sourds! Sourds, non. Mauvais' (p. 122). Sartre appears to have generalized his criticism to the extent of condemning the rule of the world, whatever the religion or philosophy.

Although Sartre meant to be faithful to Euripides, *Les Troyennes* can in fact be seen as a new play: it presents a different thematic stress; a different structure of dramatic action, which aims at showing the moral victory of Hecuba; and a different intended effect on the audience.

The initial concept of the actualized interpretation by Holk Freytag hinged on equating the Greek troops with the Israeli occupying forces in the West Bank and Gaza Strip, and the Trojan women and children with the Arab women and children in refugee camps. However, during the production a major event occurred – the war in Lebanon – which drastically changed the political situation and naturally became the new referent of the play, having far-reaching consequences on the way the production was perceived by the audience. Before the war, the widespread and conventional perception of the West Bank occupation was that the IDF's presence in the territories was forced upon Israel by the unwillingness of the Palestinians to negotiate peace. In contrast, the Lebanon War was immediately considered by the vast majority of Israelis, of theatregoers at least, as a gross national mistake. Hence, whereas most of the audience would have been shocked if reference had been made to the West Bank, with regard to the war in Lebanon there was a readiness to accept criticism. Although it was clear that the Sabra and Shatilla massacre had not been perpetrated by the Israeli forces, this event exacerbated the sense of general discontent with government policy. This war, officially justified by considerations of national security, was generally perceived as a political adventure, the product of a fantastic plan to solve the problem of guerrilla attacks on northern Israel and force peace upon Lebanon and, therefore, as causing unnecessary suffering, particularly to the Lebanese civilian population. Dead and wounded women and children were foregrounded by the media and enemy propaganda, and used by Israeli critics as evidence for their claims. Although public controversy focused on the validity of the analogy between the local political situation and that referred to by Euripides (Melos and Sicily), the turn of events obviously favoured the transmutation of the same production into an unquestionably apt metaphor. The main change for many a spectator was thus from that of possible shock to profound agreement with the play's message. In the context of this war, only extreme right-wingers were shocked by the allusion. Against this background, it is clear that the Israeli production employed exactly the same mechanism of self-criticism as Euripides: presenting the war from the viewpoint of the vanquished population and eliciting sympathy for their suffering.

The Ha-bima production preserved the absurdist structure of the original play, making a crucial change only on the level of characterization. It preserved the original Greek and Trojan identities of the characters, but added strong hints as to Israeli and Arab identities, by means of elements of costume, set, sound and body language:

- *Costume*: Most of the Trojan women (particularly the chorus) wore long black robes, and flat shoes, reminiscent of both classical and Bedouin garments. They also carried shabby old fashioned suitcases and bundles, tied up in a hurry, reminiscent of refugees in flight. The Greek soldiers wore light khaki uniforms, badges, army boots and guns of various kinds which, although definitely not typical of IDF soldiers, were conceived as reminiscent of them by the audience. Some critics even mistook them as such. The intention probably was to point to the IDF while avoiding explicit identification.

The uniform of Menelaus, the only general on stage, with lavish military paraphernalia, such as badges, medals and binoculars, was caricaturesque and verged on the grotesque. Such an ambiguity can be understood as an attempt to lend an absurdist meaning on a more universal level; but also to reinforce deconstruction of a possible definite national identification.[12] Helen, who appeared in a glass and iron cage, illuminated by neon light, wore a sexy tight blue dress, high heeled shoes and loose blonde hair suggestive of a girl in the red light district of Amsterdam. Such an allusion to prostitution constituted an additional metaphorical dimension.

Astyanax, in his blue shirt, pants and designer sneakers, resembled a typical middle class boy from any Western country, including Israel. His costume was probably meant to correlate the identities of the child and the soldiers and hint at a possible reversal of fate between conquerors and vanquished, and imply that the conqueror can also be a victim of the war. Eventually the boy's body returns to stage wrapped in a bloodstained sheet, probably conveying the loss of national identity in death.

- *Set*: The women actually engaged in erecting a few tents on stage, from wooden sticks and scraps of cloth, in a clear allusion to refugees preparing to shelter in a new refugee camp. The floor was covered with sawdust, resembling sand, which created a cloud of dust whenever stepped upon. The set was equally ambiguous: although reminiscent of a refugee camp, it did not replicate any actual one in the region, whether in the occupied territories or the neighbouring countries.

- *Sound*: There was background of diving jet bombers and electronic noise. The music was a combination of electronic and flute tunes, the latter reminiscent of oriental motifs. There was also a scene of typical oriental drumming.

- *Body language*: In enacting the characters, by using elements of posture, gesture and intonation, the actors indicated a typical oriental behaviour. In a dumb show a seated soldier engaged in meticulously dismantling and cleaning his gun, in the typical manner of an Israeli soldier.

A 12-minute-long dumb and powerful opening scene (Freytag's own invention) combined most of these non-verbal elements and, in a way, epitomized the overall meaning of the play: dispassionate soldiers brutally pushed refugee women carrying bundles and suitcases onto the desolate set;

the women erected the tents, while fighting each other for any available scrap of cloth, to the tune of an oriental-like melody.[13] Critics claimed that this scene, on the grounds of the possible identification of the parties involved, was in itself so powerful that the subsequent enactment of the dramatic action designed by Euripides/Sartre was superfluous. Freytag, under the inspiration of Sartre's heroic final accord, also designed a new end for Hecuba: she attempted to tie herself up with a rope and even poured petrol over her head (from a typical military jerrican) in a vain attempt to set herself alight. Eventually, while the entire set was being destroyed, she was brutally taken away: a non-verbal image matching the sense of devastation of human life which the production intended to convey.

It would appear that the set of all the abovementioned elements, foreign to the original characterization, constitutes an additional metaphorical layer. However, this is actually a case of inverted metaphor in which the seemingly foreign elements act to indicate literally the new referent of the ancient metaphorical predication:[14] instead of the political situation in Euripides' contemporary Athens, we have the Arab–Israeli conflict. This is in contrast to Euripides's approach which, in employing the Homeric story as a metaphorical description of the contemporary war, avoided any clue to the actual referent of the play in the text. Obviously, whereas Euripides relied on his audience to complete the implied metaphor, Freytag did not; and for his indirect but well calculated reference he was heavily criticized. In the ensuing discussion, which reached the Knesset (Israeli Parliament) in December 1983, the right wing was furious. A religious member attacked the theatre for offending 'the basic values of Judaism' and Yosef Lapid, the then Chairman of the National Broadcasting Authority, sarcastically noted that the play should have been performed at a PLO conference in Algeria.[15] The possibility of viewing the production as a mere piece of propaganda favouring the enemy was probably the fate of the first production of the play in ancient Greece too.

In fact, there was nothing in this production which definitely referred to the Arab–Israeli conflict in general or the Lebanon War in particular. It contained an admixture of reference to classical, oriental and western modern cultures. It was claimed that Freytag had 'played safe', but this is a value judgement. In neutral terms, such a directorial decision may also be interpreted as reflecting both the assumption and confidence that the audience would be guided to the correct referent by bridging the gap between the similarity and the identity of garments, set, sound and body language, as they actually did; as well as the attempt to universalize the message of denouncing war crimes anywhere and at anytime. In fact, the two explanations complement one another. However, by 'sheer coincidence' such a directorial solution was also most convenient in order not to compromise the heavily state subsidized National Theatre as well as, perhaps, to minimize the effect of the director's own German identity. In any case, although the stage text did not determine, it clearly induced a definite referential reading and there was no ambiguity on the audience's part.

Freytag's actualization was acutely problematic because of his German nationality, which for many critics evoked an obvious analogy with Nazi Germany. For example, Hava Novak's words: 'I do not know whether or not it was sensible for a German director to stress so vehemently this analogy on the stage of the National Theatre. No doubt that his own personal associations relate to his own national feelings of guilt. If there is any sin here, this is the attempt to attribute Nazi brutality and cruelty to people living in this area, in this land, in the present.'[16] The use of 'Nazi' for any kind of army or police brutality, even for internal Israeli affairs, is quite frequent in the heavily loaded Israeli rhetorical political discourse. Moreover, in the Israeli context, Talthybius, the prototype of the polite and seemingly sympathetic soldier, who shares in perpetrating the most ignominious crimes, claims that he is merely following orders, reminiscent of the self-defence of Nazi commanders in international trials for war crimes after the Second World War and, in particular, Adolph Eichmann's trial in the Israeli court. This depiction of barbarian behaviour by a cultured nation, associated with the Nazi regime, was exacerbated by Freytag's images, which combined a shocking contrast of cruelty with gentle behaviour: for example, Talthybius carrying in Astyanax on his shoulders in an image of fatherly love; playing ball with the child; and taking him to his death in the same manner. This combination of a play depicting barbaric conduct in the war and a German director, thus explains the shock felt by Israeli audiences. Spectators who could have accepted the analogy Greece–Israel could not accept the analogy Nazi Germany–Israel.

'Relevance' is a key notion in Israeli theatre. Many productions of classic plays reflect the tendency to relate their fictional worlds to political actuality, whether rifts within Israeli society (for example, the production of *Tartuffe* at the Haifa Municipal Theatre in 1985, in which Tartuffe is enacted as an ultra-Orthodox Jew);[17] or the Israeli–Arab conflict (such as the production of Beckett's *Waiting for Godot* at the Haifa Municipal Theatre in 1985, in which two Arab actors enact Vladimir and Estragon as Arab builders waiting for the Jewish contractor to hire them).[18] These plays were made explicitly relevant by adding a new layer of characterization on the non-verbal level of staging. However, while this procedure gains in establishing strong ties with the immediate interest and involvement of the audience, it loses in the universality of the message. In particular, by exclusively focusing on the theme of the local war, this production lost poignancy in addressing the absurd nature of war in general.

Furthermore, the Israeli production marginalized the religious theme, which is, I believe, the main theme of the original play. Whereas in Sartre's adaptation the gods, Poseidon in particular, became subordinated to the theme of the absurdity of war, for Euripides the absurdity of war was only one instance of the absurdity of Greek established beliefs. Sartre probably viewed the divine theme as an element of verisimilitude in creating the inner logic of the Greek–Trojan fictional world, and not necessarily in the context of criticism of contemporary religious beliefs. At most, they are used as metaphors of the powers that rule the world for the sake of producing an image of existential absurdity. Freytag maintained the religious theme, but against the background of almost explicit reference to the local conflict and, mainly, because of the hypersensitivity of the audience, it became peripheral. He probably felt that for an Israeli audience, criticism of such beliefs is not an urgent item on the Israeli agenda, in comparison to a possible criticism of the priesthood's involvement in political affairs. On this account, it may be claimed that the Israeli production was reductive in its overall philosophical meaning.

THE BIBLICAL BACKGROUND

Criticism of war and through it of pagan beliefs was a definite achievement of Greek philosophy and playwriting.[19] This was probably the result of the ascent of rationality, the arch-enemy of both war and paganism, as a new value. The alleged pre-Christian nature of Euripides' thinking may well indicate that rationality, although it may have led to agnosticism and atheism, was reflected in initial monotheism as an improvement on pagan beliefs. It may be assumed that in the ancient world changes in attitudes to the world reflected a general tendency to explore and map uncharted lands on the grounds of increasing rationality, and that not only similarity between cultures but also diversity of solutions reflect shared concerns; that is, answers to the same questions.

In biblical theology, war is used by God to administer divine justice among the nations and is well integrated within a cosmic system of sin and punishment that revolves around faithfulness to the true God or flocking after pagan gods. This idea is shared by the chroniclers and prophets. Against this hermetic background, reading the passage that describes the mood of the mother of Sisera in Deborah's Song reveals an unusual concern for the defeated enemy at war:

(28) The mother of Sisera looked out at a window, and cried through the lattice, Why is his chariot so long in coming? Why tarry the wheels of his chariots?
(29) Her wise ladies answered her, yea, she returned answer to herself,
(30) Have they not sped? have they not divided the prey; ...?
(31) So let all thine enemies perish, O Lord: but let them that love him be as the sun when he goeth forth in his might. And the land had rest forty years. (Judges 5: 28–31)

In this passage, the author/ess of Deborah's Song suddenly diverts attention to the mother of the enemy's commander. Attention is captured by the mere focusing on the apprehensive mood of a mother who belongs in the enemy camp. She is described in her concern for her son, who is late in returning home. Her motherly anxiety seems to be autonomous and not affected by whether she belongs to the Hebrew tribes or the enemy, whether her son is justified in his war against the Hebrew tribes or not. Although it was probably not the intention to criticize heroic Yael who killed Sisera, or war in general, the change of perspective seems to indicate that the author/ess was troubled by a humane and universal concern. It is this concern that is employed by Euripides to condemn warmongering by his fellow citizens. He emphasized irony by viewing war in the domain of Chance, 'who can be relied on to be unreliable'[20] and, indeed, against the backdrop of the incertitudes of war, a dead son and a suffering mother present war in its sheerest absurdity.

It may be argued that depicting the anxious mother can be understood as a case of rejoicing at the misery of the Other. However, her attitude should be contrasted with that of the 'wise women' who do not even envisage the possibility of defeat. Their understanding of Sisera's delay is imbued with the joy of an obvious victory, and their minds rejoice in anticipating the booty. The irony thus reflects on these women, and on whoever else may think that victory is guaranteed by might or determination, and not on the mother. The ironic viewpoint and the focus on the mother's anxiety, although not used to criticize war, reflect a genuine humanitarian concern.

Biblical laws of war are exactly the same as those that applied in the Trojan and Peloponnesian wars: 'And when the Lord thy God hath delivered it into thine hands, thou shalt smite every male thereof with the edge of the sword: But the women and the little ones, and the cattle, and all that is in the city, even all the spoil thereof, shalt thou take unto thyself' (Deuteronomy 20: 13–14). An additional example of a diverging attitude is, therefore, the law regarding the female prisoner who is taken for a wife in Deuteronomy 21:

(10) When thou goest forth to war against thine enemies, and the Lord thy God hath delivered into thine hands, and thou hast taken them captive,
(11) And seest among the captives a beautiful woman, and hast a desire unto her, that thou wouldest have her to thy wife;
(12) Then thou shalt bring her home to thine house; and she shall shave her head and pare her nails;
(13) And she shall put the raiment of her captivity from off her, and shall remain in thine house, and bewail her father and her mother a full month: and after that thou shalt go in unto her, and be her husband, and she shall be thy wife
(14) And it shall be, if thou have no delight in her, then thou shalt let her go whither she will; but thou shall not sell her at all for money, thou

shall not make merchandise of her, because thou hast humbled her. (21, 10-14)

From a legal viewpoint this passage merely means that by marriage the female prisoner has become a free woman. However, from a humanitarian viewpoint it is explicitly stated that, despite her having been the booty of war, her feelings should be respected, not because of marriage, but because she has been previously humbled. Against the background of the brutal biblical laws of war, this law certainly implies criticism of the contemporary attitude and appears to reflect a new attitude to or moral code for war. It is this change of perspective which is indicative of the deep processes moral thinking was undergoing in this part of the world, and which underlies the decision made by Euripides, Sartre and subsequent moralists to use it to denounce the absurdity of war and ruling of the world.

The story of Dinah, daughter of Jacob and Leah (Genesis 34), which parallels in structure and details the story of Troy, is another indication of this trend. Dinah was abducted and 'defiled' (34: 2) by Shechem, son of Hamor the Hivite. Jacob's sons, greatly distraught by the affront, planned to avenge it. They suggested to Hamor, who was eager to consolidate the links between the tribes because of his son's love for Dinah, to adopt the ritual of circumcision. Hamor accepted the 'generous' offer and, on the third day, while all the men of his tribe were still under the effect of the operation, and taking advantage of their pain and weakness, Simeon and Levi slew them all, despoiled their city and all their possessions, and took the women and children captive (34: 26-9). However, Jacob rebuked their base behaviour, calling them 'instruments of cruelty', and deprived them of his blessing upon his death, scattering them among the other tribes (49: 5-7).[21] Jacob condemned his sons because of their disregard for peace with his neighbours: 'Ye have troubled me to make me to stink among the inhabitants of the land ... and I being few in number, they shall gather themselves together against me, and slay me; and I shall be destroyed, I and my house' (34: 30). In short, the sequence of the narrative is the same: abduction, revenge (by an artful plot), and complete disproportion between sin and punishment; the laws of war are also the same: killing all the males and enslaving the rest; however, the overall attitude of this story is diametrically different: peaceful means would have been preferred to settle even such an outrageous affront, for the sake of intertribal coexistence.

These three examples indicate the existence of an embryonic dissident tendency within biblical Judaism, which is perhaps best illustrated by stories such as the sacrifice of Isaac (Genesis 22), which should be compared to the sacrifice of Iphigenia, and God's rescue of Ishmael (Genesis 21: 9-20).

Euripides does not condemn war as such. In the words of Cassandra, he suggests a clear distinction between a sensible and an irrational war: 'Though surely the wise man will forever shrink from war, / yet if war come, the hero's death will lay a wreath / not lustreless on the city. The coward alone brings shame' (400–2). This can be translated into the modern notions of 'just' and 'unjust' war. For biblical theology, however, these distinctions appear to be meaningless and superfluous. In its context, war is a legitimate means for God to administrate justice on an international level.[22] Nations are punished or rewarded by their victories or defeats in war. Euripides chose the most senseless war he could have found in order to criticize both humans and gods: a war in which the victors spent ten years of their lives to avenge the abduction of one single frail woman; they killed and were killed in the thousands and suffered even more upon their triumphal return. This is why by referring the Trojan metaphor in any given war, such war is shown as unnecessary, unjust and, in short, absurd. It is interesting to note, therefore, that modern Israeli humanism is rooted more in dissident Euripides and sporadic divergences in the Bible than in canonical Judaism.

CONCLUSIONS

The universality of Euripides is clearly demonstrated by the ability of the play to apply to any war in the fashion of autocriticism. This is made conspicuous by merely mentioning the parties involved: Greece and Troy in Homeric times; Greece and Melos/Sicily in Euripides' times; France and Algeria in Sartre's times; Israel and the Palestinians and Israel and Lebanon in the Middle East; and by mere coincidence (association introduced by the national identity of the director), Germany and the rest of Europe, the Jews and the Gypsies in particular in the Second World War; not to mention other productions of the play in other countries in which reference was made to fit actual political situations and international conflicts.

Obviously, no contemporary audience (of Euripides or other) was really interested in the fate of Troy. In order to ensure the involvement of the audience, therefore, each production had to refer this same metaphor to the actual wars in which the audiences were engaged. In other words, in order to get an audience response similar to that expected by Euripides, the referent of the Trojan metaphor had continually to be actualized. However, it is not necessary for the actual referent to be mentioned in the text. This can be spontaneously supplied by the audience itself, as implied in the original play.

It would appear that indications of a specific war are reductive and conflict with this universality. In fact, such indications of contemporary actuality stress this generalizing capacity which, in addition, proves most effective, in particular if the production preserves the tension between them and the Greek source. Such a production is 'intercultural' in the terms of Erika Fischer-Lichte in the sense that '[t]he starting point for intercultural staging is ... not primarily an interest in the foreign – the foreign theatre or the foreign culture from which it is taken – rather a situation completely specific within its own culture or a completely specific problem having its origin within its own culture'.²³ It can also be considered 'trans-cultural' in the terms of Pavis, in that it 'transcends particular cultures on behalf of a universality of the human condition. Trans-cultural directors are concerned with particularities and traditions only in order to grasp more effectively what they have in common and what is not reducible to a specific culture.'²⁴

It is not at all surprising that the mechanism of self-criticism used by Euripides has become relevant once again in modern times, even in such different cultures as the monotheistic Jewish and Christian ones, since the same rationalistic atmosphere that makes an absurdity of war and spurious ideas of the divine is experienced again. It is this universal sense of morality, rooted in sheer humanity, which lies at the heart of the modern notion of 'war crimes' and absolute rejection of war as a form of solving international conflicts. The universality of humanitarian concern is rooted in ancient Greek and Jewish cultures for which, after all, the gap was not so profound, and their coexistence not as dangerous to the Jewish identity as we have been led to believe.

Since Judaism is a culture, there are various ways to understand its legacy. When viewed from the perspective of an open, confident and free culture, the attempt at synthesis between some forms of Judaism and foreign cultures can be seen as a return to the healthy grounds of autonomy and free exchange, as in biblical times. It is this powerful subversive tradition, reflected in Jewish and Greek cultures, that nourishes contemporary Israeli culture in general, and theatre in particular.

NOTES

1. A similar readiness for intercultural exchange is reflected in Hebrew literature and philosophy in the Middle Ages, particularly under Muslim rule in Spain.
2. All quotations are from Euripides, *The Trojan Women*, trans. R. Lattimore, in David Greene and Richmond Lattimore (eds), *Greek Tragedies*, Vol. 2 (Chicago, 1972 [1960]).
3. *The History of Thucydides*, trans. Benjamin Jowett (New York, 1906), pp. v, 116.
4. Euripides does not criticize war as such, only unjust wars.
5. Philip Vellacott, *Ironic Drama* (London, 1975), p. 163, and Thucydides, V, 104–5.
6. Vellacott, *Ironic Drama*, p. 163.
7. Eli Rozik, 'Generic Transformation of Drama (The Phaedra–Hippolytus Myth)', *Assaph – Studies in Theatre*, No. 1 (1984), pp. 55–70.
8. Aristotle, *Poetics*, in S.H. Butcher (ed. and trans.), *Aristotle's Theory of Poetry and Fine Arts* (New York, 1961), pp. XII, 2.
9. Bernard Pingaud, Interview with Sartre in *Bref*, Journal du Théâtre National Populaire, Feb. 1965. Reproduced as an Introduction to the adaptation: Jean Paul Sartre, *Les Troyennes* (Paris, 1965).
10. Ibid.
11. All quotations from Jean Paul Sartre, *Les Troyennes* (Paris, 1965).
12. See, for example, Shoshana Weitz and Shoshana Avigal, 'Cultural and Ideological Variables in Audience Response: The Case of *The Trojan Women*', Tel-Aviv, 1982–83', *Assaph – Studies in Theatre*, No. 3 (1986).
13. See full description in ibid., pp. 37–9.
14. In my view, it is not a case of 'interplay of literal frames of reference' but a definite case of inverted metaphor (Cf. Weitz and Avigal, ibid.). They read the play as inducing a series of analogies. There is a basic difference, however, between analogy and metaphor:

whereas the former is literal and looks for the common denominator, the latter foregrounds the uncommon non-verbal associations. Freytag wanted to attach associations of brutality and barbarism to the local situation that Euripides associated with the Trojan War.
15. Quoted by Michael Handelsaltz, 'Actuality on the Stage', *Ha-aretz*, 14 April 1993 (Hebrew).
16. Hava Novak, 'The Israeli Shock in Confronting *The Trojan Women*', *Davar*, 28 Feb. 1983.
17. Dan Urian, 'The Stereotype of the Religious Jew in Israeli Theatre', *Assaph – Studies in Theatre*, No. 10 (1994), pp. 137–41.
18. Dan Urian, *The Arab in Israeli Theatre* (Tel-Aviv, 1996), pp. 62–3.
19. *Lysistrate* by Aristophanes is an additional example of criticism of the absurdity of war.
20. Vellacott, *Ironic Drama*, p. 164.
21. All interpreters agree that the deprivation of the blessing was in retribution for their acts against Hamor.
22. In particular see Amos 1–2.
23. Erika Fischer-Lichte, J. Riley and M. Gissenwehrer (eds), *The Dramatic Touch of Difference: Theatre Own and Foreign* (Tubingen, 1990), p. 283.
24. Patrice Pavis, *The Intercultural Performance Reader* (London and New York, 1996), p. 6.

From Jew to Hebrew:
The 'Zionist Narrative' in the Israeli Cinema of the 1940s and 1950s

NURITH GERTZ

Many films produced in Israel before and after the establishment of the state describe the integration of refugees and Holocaust survivors in the country.[1] Although most of them were scripted in English and addressed American audiences, some were created for people who had come to the country for the purpose of settling there.[2] Israeli artists and actors participated in some of them, and local institutions such as the Jewish National Fund and Keren Ha-yesod funded all of them. Thus the films can be viewed as a cinematic effort to persuade Israelis as well as others of the justness of the Zionist enterprise, thereby expressing – directly and explicitly – the 'Zionist narrative'[3] that prevailed, in various forms, in many popular texts of the time (theatrical productions, children's stories, journalistic reportage, commemorative writings).[4] Hence, they will be studied here as 'a case study' in the translation of ideology into the language of cinema and as parallel to similar efforts in other media and genres.

INTRODUCTION

The Jewish Holocaust survivor in the pre-statehood films embodies all the traits that the Israeli identity is meant to contrast. He is persecuted, homeless, at the mercy of non-Jews, and haunted by the terror of the Holocaust. He threatens to dredge up the repressed Jewish past, to turn the equation inside out, to turn the Israeli back into a Diaspora Jew. He is the 'other' that Israelis see when they look in the mirror and expect to see themselves. As a writer in the journal of the Yiftah Brigade put it: 'The men of our brigade have to understand that this is the raw material we are being sent today. We have to get used to it, as if we were longing for the good old days when our camp was unsullied.'[5]

Nurith Gertz is Associate Professor of Literature, The Open University, Tel-Aviv.

According to Homi Bhabha the national narrative rests on yearnings for a pure origin, not threatened by differences in race, colour and culture. Such an origin is unattainable, because beyond the homogeneity are fringes that do not fit in – the loose ends. 'The origin of the nation's visual presence is the effect of a narrative struggle, the narratives of the people and their differences.' The 'loose ends' threaten the uniform identity; they are the exceptions that overstep the limits of the national image, 'disturb the calculation of power and knowledge' and 'antagonize the implicit power to generalize'. To overcome this threat the 'national narrative' either exiles these fringe identities behind its borders or, according to Bhabha, fashions them as a familiar and therefore non-threatening reality, while sustaining their 'otherness' and, consequently, their inferiority.[6]

The pre- and post-independence cinema coped with the 'otherness' of the Holocaust survivor through two opposing well known strategies. The first was to emphasize his difference, his otherness, his being 'not one of us'. This strategy builds a clear partition between him and Israeli society. The second strategy had the opposite aim: to make him 'the same' – a mirror to the typical image of the Israeli. In both cases, the survivor is 'eliminated' as an independent, distinct and different being with his own past, identity and experience. In the first case he is a parable and a metaphor to the identity rejected by the Israelis; in the second, he becomes a parable that illuminates the identity adopted by the Israeli. In both cases, only one identity remains: the homogeneous Hebrew identity. Bhabha would term it as a mere sign whose signified is the Israeli;[7] James Clifford calls this kind of structure a pedagogical allegory.[8]

The first case is that of Holocaust survivors who populate the national heroic cinema as secondary heroes. Semyon, for example, in the film *He Walked in the Fields*, fought the Nazis in the Second World War but is subjected to his comrades' contempt and scorn in the film. He attempts to emulate them and their behaviour, but his efforts are perceived as somewhat ridiculous. The only possible heroism in this film is that of the Israel-born kibbutz member; the only story in the film is his. In the second case, the survivor's Jewishness represents the entire Diaspora; his 'Hebrewness' exemplifies 'Hebrewness' in general; and his transformation of identities is structured along the lines of the Zionist narrative. This essay bases its analysis of this case on films of the 1940s and 1950s that concern Holocaust survivors.

This is also the story of many literary protagonists. For example: the heroine of the novel *He Walked in the Fields*, Mika, who totally erased her past and identity, the identity of an Holocaust survivor, and adopted a new Hebrew identity by her connection with Uri, a kibbutz member. 'Everyone realizes that only the Hagana can educate these "dust-people" and make them into straight-spined youngsters who can hardly be distinguished from our sabras.' Thus a Hagana commander in Europe speaks about the child survivors whom he encountered in the camps.[9]

This attitude was endorsed by the contemporary Israeli cinema. In these films, it was the survivors' duty to progress from 'dust-people' to proud sabras. This path leads them, in the footsteps of the Hebrew pioneers, down the familiar trail: from Jew to Israeli, which is represented metaphorically by the path from death to resurrection, from desert to flowering garden. The Israeli cinema of the 1940s and 1950s, more than any other art form, dramatized this 'narrative', which starts with a transformation from Jew to Hebrew and ends with growth and prosperity. The Jew, resurrected from the ashes of Diaspora Jewry, from desolation, and from death, expands his territory, builds more settlements, buildings and factories, and conquers the land with his muscles and his legs. The survivors make it possible to recount this narrative, in the films, through new protagonists (the quintessential ones – those who personify it in the most dramatic way: from Holocaust to revival) and to new audiences, thereby reaffirming and reviving it vis-à-vis the threat from within, of 'return to exile', and from without – of Holocaust and annihilation.[10] The Holocaust survivor was not the only 'other' through whom Israeli identity defined itself in the movies. He was connected within complex interrelationships with all other outsiders and these relationships I intend to check.

The survivors in these films reach the country bearing the label of the persecuted Jew and representing sterility and desolation. At this stage, they are identified with all of the aspects considered most threatening by the Zionist Israeli as alien and 'other': the barren land, and the Arab who blends into this land. Like it, the Arab has two faces: passive-desolate and wild. Finally, the survivors are identified with irrational women, who, like the desert, are barren but also wild: seductive and alluring – a combination of Eve and Mary. Thus within the hierarchy of others one can distinguish between different roles these others played in the formation of the collective identity and between different degrees of abstraction by which they were described: the Arabs in these films are always more abstract than the Jews, women are presented more metaphorically than men, and both serve as tools in defining and sustaining the transformation of the Jewish boy into an Israeli Hebrew man. The films also make a distinction between those others who can be transformed and become the 'same' (like the survivors) and those who will always remain outside and sustain the national identity either by negation or by affirmation (like the Arabs).[11]

Thus the others who are eligible for transformation are contrasted with the others who are ineligible, and are able to benefit from their privileged status by contrast with the excluded. It seems as if these propaganda films require and sometimes invent an 'underdog' other who is ineligible in order to strengthen the will and the motivation for transformation in those who are eligible.[12] As the plot of the films progresses, the survivors experience a symbolic death and are reborn as Israelis.[13] Their rebirth leads to a process of psychological and sexual maturation: the survivor comes to the country as a child (the protagonists of most of these films are children)[14] who has passive-female traits. When he becomes an Israeli, he becomes a man who demonstrates his virile potency by cultivating the land (in what is portrayed as an erotic act), by going to war, and by having a 'normal' relationship with a woman. At this stage, as the Zionist identity overtakes and dominates him, all the others around him appear attractive rather than threatening, dominated by the Zionist entity and united with it: the desert becomes a fertile settlement and the barren or seductive woman becomes a pure mother. Although the Arab remained the other outside and thus has no place in this metamorphosis, he serves it indirectly either in a positive way – by helping the survivor reach his land and home – or in a negative way – by helping him discover his masculine courageous identity in war. In this fashion, the accounts of the desert that has blossomed, of the Jew who has become an Israeli, and of the transition from death to life, merge into parallel strands in the plot of the survivor's life and are intermingled in the lives of women and Arabs surrounding him. In 1943, in the midst of the Holocaust, David Ben-Gurion defined Israel's role *vis-à-vis* European Jewry as follows: 'We should ... give them the feeling that what is happening to them is not in vain, that the Jewish nation still has hope, still has a future.'[15] His statement expresses a broader conviction that the Holocaust may have significance and meaning when placed within the Zionist narrative.[16] The films translate that faith into reality by transforming the survivor into the main protagonist in this narrative.

In these films, the survivor looks to the Zionist future. His erstwhile identity, his memories, and the world he has left are mainly elements that inhibit the plot from the start and slow its progression to the happy ending – the substitution of Israeli identity for Jewish identity. This discarded Jewish identity, however, being depicted in other texts even then, is still depicted in documentary and fictional texts today, and has been increasingly troublesome to Israeli national identity.

Bhabha describes the national discourse as an ambivalent one that contains its own negation. The minority, he says, exists as 'a referent of the dominant discourse; it is therefore an addition that diminishes the ability of this discourse to generalize and generate social stability'. The minority shatters the coherence of the dominant narrative and pollutes it with inexpressible contradictions and irrationalities, day to day details that do not fit in, and repetitions that inhibit its general progression.[17] The ambivalence of which Bhabha speaks can be translated into terms of plot structure and interaction between elements that advance and retard the plot. From this point of view, arguably, there is no plot that does not undermine its basic assumption, since no plot can reach its end and achieve its goals without overcoming some obstacles. The elements that the plot overcomes are those that express the ideology that the plot strives to suppress, those that the text negates.[18]

In most cases, these obstacles also merge in the course of the plot in the form of contradictions that break its continuity and coherence, in repetitions that inhibit it, and in day to day details that do not coincide with the overall message and deviate from what Bhabha terms the teleological, pedagogical structure of the national discourse.[19]

An analysis of the elements that impede the plot and breach its coherence should help us understand the cinematic, literary, and historical changes that have occurred in Israeli society over the years. Features that suspended or ruptured the coherence of plots in films of the 1950s became major factors in literary and cinematic plots of the 1970s and 1980s. In other words, the repressed past of the Jews resurfaced and made it necessary to create a new version of the Zionist narrative.

MANY QUESTIONS, ONE ANSWER

The film *My Father's House* opens in total darkness, through which the picture can barely be seen. Clandestine immigrants to Palestine are disembarking from a ship; one of them is a boy named David. He has hardly touched the ground when he asks, 'Where is my father?' His father's name is Halevi, and David hopes to meet him here in Palestine. The night scenes are then replaced by day scenes. The camera follows, at a distance, a truck that delivers the immigrants to a kibbutz. It lingers on the landscape, and the soundtrack renders a poem by Rahel that speaks of the poetess's yearning for this country, 'Maybe It Never Happened.'

The boy emerged from the darkness from his old identity, his old name, his old father. The film answers his question, 'Where is my father?' by presenting the space and light of Palestine: Here is your home, birthplace and fatherland. Thus the boy comes to the kibbutz, where he is awaited by a mother (Mirium, who had been with him on the ship), a father (Abraham, a kibbutz member who takes him under his wing), and a sister (a kibbutz girl who wants to adopt him as her brother). The kibbutz gives him not only these but also a new personal history. Shortly after his arrival, his adoptive family takes him to the old kibbutz cemetery, where he is told of the death of old-time members, malaria, and the possibility of conquering death. This is the account of life and death, of which the child will become part. For the time being, he is not ready to accept it. He insists on searching for his own past – his own father.

Almost all films of the 1940s and 1950s that deal with Holocaust survivors focus on child protagonists. In reality, few of the immigrants were children; in the films, they are a large majority. When they arrive in the country, they are portrayed as incomplete people. As the plot progresses, they experience an apprenticeship, in which they learn the Israeli way of life and culture. To illuminate this process of apprenticeship, lengthy segments of these films are structured in the form of questions and answers. Within this form apprenticeship is connected with knowledge – the Zionist knowledge that controls the survivor's life at the beginning of the films and is absorbed by him at their end. In *My Father's House*, the questions are those of a child in search of his father. In *The Great Promise*, the questions and answers are given in the form of a series of lessons. The moment that Tamara, the child survivor, expresses her wish to join the youth group, the youngsters reply 'From now on, you'll understand us'. The camera follows her into the classroom for a series of lessons in geography and history, all of which focus on the Land of Israel and the Yishuv. The questions are numerous and diverse, but the answer is the same in every case: the Zionist narrative, which unfolds during the film.[20]

FROM DIASPORA TIME TO ZIONIST TIME

David, who came to Israel to search for his father, actually has no father. He cannot remember his father's facial features, name or occupation. Any details he provides about his father are riddled with contradictions and sound like a jumble of delusions and fantasies. Now he says his father was a mechanic; then he recalls him as an engineer, a storekeeper, or as a violinist. Never does he disclose any concrete details that may bring him to life or at least shed some light on him and his home before the Holocaust.

The survivor's past in these films is one of exile, suffering, and wandering, all of which are synthesized in the final drama, the Holocaust. 'Where is your family?', a member of the brigade asks the survivor in *The Great Promise*, and the survivor replies 'I have no family. I have been wandering for two thousand years already.' In *My Father's House*, a waiter in a café approaches the boy and asks 'Where are you from? Bergen-Belsen? Buchenwald?' In the first case, the survivor's private life expands into a long national history of suffering. In the second case, it contracts into one dramatic moment that represents the climax and outcome of this history. In both cases, the protagonists' private past is subsumed into the historical past and this historical past is erased by a process of generalization or selection.[21]

This process of contracting and expanding the protagonists' pasts is communicated in the plots of the films, too, by contraction and expansion of the time dimension. Hava and Yaacov, the main protagonists of *End of Evil*, left the kibbutz and the country in the 1920s and perished in the Holocaust in the 1940s. The film encapsulates their twenty years in Europe in a few symbolic shots: the smashing of a windshield, a doll that is run over, the barbed wire fences of a concentration camp, and corpses – nothing more. Their son, who returned to Palestine, is an intellectual who is said to have smuggled books into Buchenwald rather than food, and when on duty in the War of Independence he rests his rifle on a physics book. However, the film makes no effort to depict the intellectual and cultural atmosphere that could produce such a man; it describes the atmosphere as that of the Holocaust only.

This atmosphere, too, is communicated in symbols or statistics, in measures and numbers, but not as a living experience. In *Faithful City*, the children compete over who has been the most seriously deceived and embittered in war. In *My Father's House*, the object of their competition is to have witnessed more dead and burnt people. Thus a proliferation and variety of memories is converted into one and only one memory, which varies from child to child in size and quantity only.[22] The dramatic event that culminates two millennia of exile in these films leads directly to the contrasting dramatic event: the establishment of the Zionist enterprise. Therefore, in every case, the recollection scenes in these films are followed immediately by redemption scenes. In *My Father's House*, the haywagon on which the children sit and exchange reminiscences of the Holocaust lurches into motion, crosses the kibbutz as the camera pans the faces of throngs of children, and exits the courtyard to the sound of happy song and rolling wheels. The static scene of children seated on the wagon is replaced with the dynamism of motion, flow and voices on the farm. The film has made a transition: from the dead and the butchered to the living.

In other cases, the Diaspora past is replaced not by the present-day redemption but by a different past: that of the Land of Israel. The day after they reach the country, the survivors in *My Father's House* sit and chat with the kibbutz members. As one of the survivors, Stefan, begins to describe how he had returned to the ghetto to fight the Nazis, a kibbutznik interrupts him to suggest that he change his name to a new Hebrew one: Maccabi. This gives him a pretext to tell the survivor how the Maccabis drove the Greek invaders off the hills of Naftali. Thus the kibbutz member terminates the survivor's recounting of his past in order to give him a new name and a new past, both Eretz-Israeli, and thus he converts the survivor's experience of failure in the Holocaust into one of triumph and redemption.

The exchange of the Diaspora past for the Israeli past includes an exchange of the survivor's personal, individual past and identity for collective Zionist ones. It is this account that drives the main plot of *My Father's House*. As David hunts for his one personal father, of whom he knows nothing, he is offered various collective substitutes. First he comes to Tel-Aviv and visits the philharmonic orchestra, having heard that a violinist named Ha-levi performs there. He thinks this may be his father. The musician refers him to a labourer in Sodom named Yehuda Ha-levi and remarks, with a smile, that he remembered the man's name because of his namesake, the poet. Thus, in lieu of a personal father who plays a violin, David is offered a national father who likens his yearnings for the Land of Israel to the song of a violin. In Sodom, Yehuda Ha-levi asks the child about his father's name and mentions the possibility that it was Israel. The child confirms this, thus anticipating his Zionist upheaval by taking on the name of a collective father, that of the nation. However, the end is still far off; David will still migrate among many other names before he comes to the name of his true father. In the Old City of Jerusalem, he stops two priests and asks them where he might find 'the names of the fathers'; he is referring to a list of parents who vanished in the Holocaust. The priests tell him about the Christian son who ascended to his father in heaven in this city, but they understand that he is looking for a different sort of father and send him to the Jewish quarter. There, a rabbi attempts to find out which father he has in mind: Abraham, Isaac or Jacob. Like the priests, however, the rabbi realizes his error and sends the boy to the New City, where he discovers that his father has perished in the Holocaust.

Only after exhausting all possibilities and potential fathers, and after foregoing his personal father and acknowledging his death, can David acquire a real father – who is both a symbolic and collective father, the patriarch of his nation, Abraham, and a member of the new Zionist community, a member of a kibbutz. Now that he has adopted a Hebrew father and a Hebrew present – both of whom are strongly connected with the Hebrew past in the Land of Israel – he confirms his attachment to them at the founding ceremony for a new settlement. Only then, at the moment the land is settled, can he also discover his own roots in the Land of Israel. It happens when Abraham shows him something that he has found in the soil: a potsherd inscribed with the name Ha-levi. Now the transformation is complete: if identity is constructed upon past memories so his identity now is Hebrew-Israeli.

FROM THE GHETTO TO THE EXPANSES OF ERETZ ISRAEL

David takes his journey from the personal past to the national past over a special 'road': the geography of the country. The films posit an 'optimistic geography' from the very outset – a country that one can cross, become part of and control by walking, labour and observation. Many elements in Zionist ideology are associated with space – the transition from Diaspora to the Land of Israel, from ghetto to open space, from 'ethereal existence' to a life rooted in the soil. This ideology was the infrastructure on which one of the most basic components of the sabra-persona was mounted: that of a person who 'walks in the fields', is familiar with them, and controls them.[23] With this in mind, one may understand how the films use space to remake the Holocaust survivor into a Hebrew.

In all the films that deal with Holocaust survivors, the children are taken to a flourishing settlement, a kibbutz or a youth village. True, the place is small and encircled with fences, but it represents a large, spacious and open world – the entire country or perhaps the entire globe. *Tomorrow Is a Wonderful Day*, for example, begins with footage shot from the interior of a room. The camera moves towards the window, the shutter is opened, the camera steps out, into the youth village, whence it heads into the countryside and scans it, first horizontally and then vertically, from heaven to earth. Thus, it emerges from the sealed room in the children's residence but focuses on the country's great open spaces. As the film continues, the camera crosses repeatedly from interior to exterior and back again, and the village children move together with it in the context of perpetual motion – of wagons, processions and groups.

The strong interaction of interior and exterior corresponds to the close relationship between details and the whole. In all of his films, photographer and director Helmar Larsky merges close-up and distance shots in order to express the significance of every detail in the 'big picture' – that is, the country and its history. The close-ups in these films are montages of objects and bodily parts, linked to each other in detail after detail, in the sense of 'dunam after dunam'. The distance shots illuminate the setting to which the details belong and position the details in an inclusive geographical and historical context. Pieces of machinery, the shoulders of a man at work, two people ploughing a field – all of them merge into a single progression of building and planting roots in the soil. As the films approach their end, the series of montages become longer and wider, thus portraying a process of development and growth, in which the entire space is filled with settlements, homes, factories and fields. The account, which begins with a transition from death to resurrection and from withering to efflorescence, ends with a process of growth, prosperity and expansion.[24]

In most cases, the survivor becomes a 'filter' of the camera point of view as soon as he is born into his new Hebrew identity. After having observed the Israeli landscapes objectively thus far, the camera now contemplates it through the survivor's eyes. When he comes to the country, the survivor is the object of the gazes of others – sympathetic, compassionate, caring gazes that are also disparaging, judgmental and accusative. They have the power of the look, which is, according to Foucault, the power of knowledge – the power of control. Only after his rebirth – after he acquired their knowledge, their ideological point of view – can he look back at both the landscape and the people.[25]

In the course of the plot, the survivors acquire more than the right to look about; they also acquire the right to move around the country freely, entering its public and private places. These two matters, movement and gaze, are interrelated and attest not only to the protagonist's ability to dominate the space but also to the change he experiences after changing from a passive Jew into an active Hebrew. At first, the survivors identify their new home with the ghetto and the concentration camp; they feel imprisoned there and attempt to escape. After effecting this escape, they acclimatize themselves to the new country and acquire their new identity – the identity of people who inhabit a large, spacious country and not a ghetto, the identity of people who can circulate in their landscape fearlessly and dominate it with their legs and eyes.

Throughout the first portion of the film, the main protagonist in *Tomorrow Is a Wonderful Day* remains static. Incapable of observing, he takes in nothing of his surroundings. Only after his 'Hebraization' does he abandon his static posture. At this point, the camera trails him as he joins his comrades in establishing a new settlement in the wilderness, enters rooms into which he had previously peered from the outside, and takes part in ceremonies and festivities held there, foremost Hanukka. As he explores the countryside, he discards his old identity and past, experiences something like a symbolic death, and is reborn as a new person, a member of a new collective. (Superimposed footage merges him with his comrades and sets all of them in the open spaces of the country.) The camera, panning the expanses in motion through the protagonist's eyes and following him closely on a dolly, and the dynamic editing, which accelerates the camera's motion, attest to the change he has undergone. Indeed, his comrades encourage him: 'Open your eyes, take a look.' He responds in kind: 'The more I see, the better it looks.' Thus the reversal he has undergone leads him from a closed space into open spaces, from a static to a dynamic character, and from 'blindness' to open eyes that observe and contemplate. The eyes are his but the ideological point of view is the Yishuv, Zionist one.

In *My Father's House*, the change is embedded in the geography itself. The boy, David, who has fled the Shefeyya children's village, reaches the Dead Sea and is adopted there by Yehuda Ha-levi, who introduces himself to David as his uncle. As they frolic on the beach, the children and the adults start up a conversation, and David proposes to revive the Dead Sea and use its water to generate electricity. 'If you have plans for the Dead Sea, it is a sign that you are already Palestinian,' a friend of the family tells him. The next conversation takes place among the children only, after the adults have placed themselves at a distance. David mentions the possibility of being reborn to a new father and a new family. The children try to imagine the father they would choose if they were given this opportunity. Thus, a geographical act, a trip, takes the boy to the lowest place on earth, the Dead Sea. There, in the midst of death, the idea of revival surfaces in two senses – of the Dead Sea and of the human being.[26]

It is precisely here, at the driest and most desolate place on earth, that David chooses to begin his journey to rebirth. Other films, too, prefer to stress resurrection and efflorescence in the same place. In *The Great Promise*, the survivor does remain at the fence of his camp throughout the film, but the Zionist soldier, the brigade fighter, tells him a tale concerning the death and rebirth of the Jordan, in the Dead Sea, as a parable of his own resurrection. The water bursting forth in the wilderness is one of the most salient symbols of this process, which is engraved in the country's geography and the history of each of its inhabitants. The survivor merely reconstructs the process. Thus if the bursting of the water in the desert serves as a symbol to his resurrection so does his resurrection serve as a symbol to the Israeli resurrection as a whole; both are signs to the one and same signified – the Israeli new identity.[27]

After David realizes that Yehuda Ha-levi is not his uncle, he flees from the Dead Sea area and begins to ascend through the desert to the Old

City of Jerusalem and thence to the New City. It is a journey from low elevation to high, from old to new, from death to life. The film, however, does not content itself with such delicate symbolism. When the boy discovers in Jerusalem that his father is dead, he collapses, prostrates himself on the floor, and sucks his thumb. He becomes an infant. Only after he recovers can he effect his rebirth. The gap between the Jewish and Israeli Hebrew identity is so wide in these films that only death and rebirth can bridge it.[28]

FROM DESOLATION TO EFFLORESCENCE

David's ascent from the Dead Sea to Jerusalem is a path from desert and wilderness to efflorescence. It is the road travelled by most Holocaust survivors in most of the films. When they reach the country, they are filmed against a background of wilderness and are identified with it. After they change, they integrate into the surrounding fertility and flowering. Where the heroes are heroines, the transition from desolation to fertility symbolizes a changeover from infertility and licentiousness to motherhood.

In *My Father's House*, the changeover is effected in a subplot, the story of Miriam, David's adoptive mother. Miriam was known as Maria in her previous life, but there, in the Diaspora during the Holocaust, she was not allowed to be a holy mother:[29] she was deprived of her children and became a whore of the SS. When she comes to Israel, she refuses to assume the duty of caring for the kibbutz children. She even finds it difficult to promise to care for David, with whom she has become closely attached. In other words, the Holocaust has left her with the negative, threatening images of woman: those of the childless wife and the prostitute. Here, on the kibbutz, she is asked to resume the function of the holy mother, the unsullied mother, a collective person who tends to collective children, either those of the kibbutz or a Holocaust survivor who is not really her son. The film goes out of its way to maintain her pure appearance; therefore, she develops no intimacy with Abraham, the child's intended father. The fact that they are about to become the child's parents allows one to assume the existence of intimacy, but such a relationship is neither consummated nor alluded to in any form in the course of the film. Miriam remains throughout the whole film a mother only, not a lover. Becoming a lover would shift her from her one and only role, which is to support the national existence metaphorically as a sign of fertility.

It is the camera that illuminates Miriam's infertility as part of her inner desolation and that which surrounds her. One of her fateful conversations with Abraham begins with a lengthy, slow panning motion of the camera over the Judean Desert. Then the camera focuses on the couple as they stand on Mount Scopus and contemplate the landscape. Abraham is talking. He loves this wasteland, he says, because one can begin everything anew here. Thus he attempts to persuade Miriam to forget her past, to dedicate herself to David's upbringing and to 'begin a new life'. She refuses. After what they did to her, she explains, she really should have died. She has no strength to embark on a new life. The camera responds to both attitudes, his and hers, by echoing them. It observes Abraham against a background of blossoming trees and captures Miriam against the wasteland. When Abraham tells her 'You want to destroy everything that is feminine in you,' a barren-branched tree is shown in the background, and when he tells her 'What was done to you there does not exist. I believe in you,' a blossoming tree is shown. When he moves away from her and leaves the decision in her hands, she is again filmed against a desert backdrop. In the end, her decision to bring David home and be his mother represents her choice of efflorescence and fertility, and this is confirmed when she joins the circles of dancers at the settlement founding ceremony. In fact, David's first mother in Eretz Israel is mother earth. He dies and is reborn in the depths of the Dead Sea. After this birth, he undergoes an additional rebirth in Jerusalem and acquires an additional mother, who, like his first mother and like himself, has evolved from a wasteland into a blossoming garden. Thus while he becomes a metaphor of the flourishing country she is a metaphor of a metaphor: all her personality is summarized into this one and only trait of fertility, while she also serves as a tool, the function of which is to lead him to his new identity.

FROM A PASSIVE, COWARDLY JEWISH BOY TO A BRAVE HEBREW MAN

The new Hebrew identity of the boy in *My Father's House* is that of the owner of a new past, a new habitat and a new family. The Hebrew identity of the boy in *Faithful City* is that of the Hebrew warrior who has jettisoned the stereotyped traits of the Diaspora Jew, foremost cowardice. In all cases, it is the strong, brave Hebrew identity that permits its possessor to dominate the country's soil by touch and by gaze. By acquiring this new identity he also succeeds in 'purging' himself of the characteristics that identified him with other outsiders: women and Arabs.

The group of children from Europe is the main protagonist of *Faithful City*. However, the point of view in this film, following the convention of the genre, is that of the objective lens. The children become 'filters' of the point of view in two cases only: when this is necessary to underscore their negative 'Jewish' traits, and after they have adopted the Zionist ideological slant.

As the film begins, the camera rides the bus that is bringing the children to the Zionist Youth Village in Jerusalem. Therefore, the British soldier who boards the bus to search it is observed from their point of view; so is the Arab gang that bombards the bus with stones. Thus, the first people the youngsters encounter as they explore the country are threatening aliens: the British and the Arabs. Not only are they shown from the children's physical point of view; they are witnessed through, and personify, the children's terror and fear.

After the stoning incident, the children remain in the bus, quarantined with their fears as in the ghetto. In contrast, the camera sets out to explore the Jerusalem landscape – towers, ramparts and surrounding hills – 'on its own'. The camera discovers something to which the children are still oblivious: the existence of a large, spacious country that the youngsters are as yet unable to see. Only at the end of the film, in the War of Independence, after Max, the main protagonist, has escaped from the village, met with the warriors and helped bring water to the besieged children, is he able to venture into the countryside and observe it. In any case, his valorous masculinity is evidence of his strong rootedness in the soil. In this film, as in all the others, the war illuminates the Israeli's activism in his homeland and thereby confirms his bond with the soil.

The end of the films also reveals the correct masculine identity with respect to women. At the beginning of the films, neither the survivor-child nor survivor-teenager manages to relate to women properly, and all of them display some traits that are regarded in the films as feminine: passivity on the one hand and wilderness on the other hand. In *Faithful City*, Max beats his girlfriend. In *My Father's House*, David flees from women who wish to be his mother and sister. In *End of Evil*, Yaacov is tempted by Hava, and in *Tomorrow Is a Wonderful Day*, Binyamin disregards Miriam, the girl who lures him. Only after he displays dynamism, bravery, strength at labour and strength in combat does the survivor become a man in this additional sense of relations with women and the elimination of his feminine characteristics. Only then can he relate to a woman and experience emotion or love towards her. However, he always applies his virility to the soil or against the enemy, never towards women. The conjugal relationship too is consummated behind the plough, at the harvest or in building a new settlement – not on the wedding night. The masculine body is shown in its full detail and beauty in the erotic act of penetrating the soil, not in the erotic act of touching a woman. The non-sexual morality of these films serves to strengthen the power of the 'Zionist narrative' and to prevent anything from eluding its collective control.[30]

Femininity is not the only obstacle that the survivors need to surmount; they must shed an assortment of other traits that Israeli culture identifies as the baggage of the Diaspora Jew. The main group in *Faithful City*, headed by the protagonist Max, evades field labour, demands payment for every effort and cunningly measures every gain and loss. When the instructor leaves the room, the children play cards, spend their time idly, harass each other, cheat each other and their instructors and, when necessary, engage in theft. First they steal a wagon and a mule, with which they go on an outing to town; later on, Max swipes a watch from the instructor, Sam, and attempts to peddle it in the Old City. These actions taint them with several Jewish stereotypes: guile, deceit, preoccupation with trade and commerce, passivity, and idleness. They acquire additional traits on top of these 'Jewish' ones: they are violent, uncontrolled and sometimes akin to wild animals. They reject the order and regimen of the youth village and threaten to replace it with chaos. The Arabs in these films, like some of the survivor women,[31] are portrayed similarly.

The films attempted to mould something from a specific profile of Holocaust survivors – adults, teenagers and children. However, the markers of this profile were chosen on the basis of their compatibility with the Jewish stereotype and their contrast with the Hebrew one.[32] Therefore, these films fail to portray the full tension that existed between the socialist ideology of the kibbutzim and the youth villages and the values that the survivors brought with them from home. As against the socialist ideology, they present Jewish stereotypes, not various types of liberal or individual values on which the survivors were raised. As against the ideal of farm labour, they depict the young people's idleness, not their wishes to study, engage in intellectual life or acquire an honest occupation.[33] As against the collectiveness of kibbutz society, they present the young people's acquisitiveness and pilfering, not their personal sensitivities.[34]

The films organize the Jewish traits of the survivors into a package that turns inside out as the Jews are reborn as Israeli Hebrews and as the idlers, cheaters and cunning savages become working, fighting, civilized people.

The Arabs who inhabit Palestine promote the reversal-of-identity process by playing two roles. In one, they metaphorically represent desolation and death and, in this sense, correspond to the Jewish Holocaust survivor before his conversion. In their second role, they are expected to support the conversion process and lead the survivor to his new identity – the Hebrew one. In both cases the Arabs serve as background, which emphasizes the transformation of the Jew having become an Israeli.

Films such as *The Great Promise* and *End of Evil* show the Arabs in the exposition. *End of Evil* opens with shots of a desert and Arab convoys with camels; the narrator introduces the Arabs as part of the old Palestinian landscape that the settlers have come to remake. They are 'the thieves and the desert,' he says. They held the country by force. They are part of 'these dead hills', which the settlers have come to revive.

In *The Great Promise*, the Arabs along the Jordan live the savage lives of uncivilized natives who have not accepted the yoke of culture. They are analogous to the Holocaust survivors, who are depicted as untamed, uncivilized native children, and above all to Tamara, who is described as a savage beast. They resemble the children in *Faithful City* and Binyamin in *Tomorrow Is a Wonderful Day*. The Jordan is childish and innocent, the narrator explains, like the simple folk who inhabit its banks. As he speaks, the camera pans the Arabs, the sheep and the buffaloes. The Jew who has come to settle this locality is defined as 'man' and this definition, by negation, relegates the Arab to the category of pre-man. 'Then came the man,' the soundtrack states, 'with a plan on how to use the land.' This definition is also invoked to describe the change that the survivor has undergone: with the help of the soil, he has been transformed from a pre-man to a man.

This dichotomy of Israeli Hebrew versus Arab is especially salient in *End of Evil*, because here it is the Arab, the embodiment of the savage impulse, who warns the group of the inner impulses that will destroy it. Yaacov and Hava prove how telling his warning is. By placing love over devotion to the collective, they collaborate with him, as it were. The Arabs, representatives of the savage world, attack the settlement from without, just as Yaacov and Hava have done from within.

By creating a parallelism between the Holocaust survivor and the Arab, the films suggest by allusion that by changing his identity the survivor has also changed his affiliation: from the Arab side to a Hebrew one. As Max circulates in the Old City in search of someone to buy the watch that he has stolen, the radio broadcasts a report on an Arab threat to invade Israel. After he has 'repented', he joins his instructors, Sam and Tamar, in celebrating the proclamation of Israeli statehood. It therefore seems that on the day of his rebirth as an Israeli, which corresponds to the birth of the state, his identification with the Arab side also vanishes.

When depicted as part of a savage, desolate and infertile world, the Holocaust survivor is given the attributes of the Arab. In contrast, when the Arab is depicted as part of the old bourgeois world that preceded the socialist settlement enterprise, he acquires several classical features of the Jew. 'How could I tell the Arab,' says the shepherd in *End of Evil*, 'that by changing ourselves we lost our path? He would never understand it. He would be rather pleased to live in the old world, not in the new world that we should have built somehow.' The two of them, the survivor and the Arab, should 'take a course' in the new Zionist civilization in order to understand it. 'Let me show you something that has never been seen in this world,' says the settler to the Arab who has come to visit the settlement in *End of Evil*. Then he explains: 'If we Jews want to be more than a memory in this country, we have to try a new path.' The Arab, like the survivor, is an addressee to whom the Zionist story can be retold. Unlike the survivor, however, he is not expected to participate in this story; he merely supports the process in which the Jews are made into 'new men'. It is his fate to admire the Hebrew settler's 'mastery over the land, which is mastery over the water' (*End of Evil*), but he cannot become a master by himself.

In some of the films, such as *End of Evil* and *Faithful City*, the Arab supports the Jew-to-Israeli transformation by enabling the frightened survivor to become a warrior. In several films, his participation in this transformation, like that of other foreign protagonists, is positive. When he reaches the kibbutz, David, the main protagonist in *My Father's House*, befriends a Palestinian and persuades him to flee with him, by donkey, in order to look for his father. In his second escape, a Palestinian shepherd helps him by leading him across the mountains to Caesarea. There he encounters a British officer and a man wearing a Turkish tarbush, who lead him to Tel-Aviv. David makes his way from Tel-Aviv to the Dead Sea by bus, but from the Dead Sea to Jerusalem he is taken by a Bedouin and his camel. There, in the Old City of Jerusalem, two Christian clergymen guide him to the Jewish Quarter, whence religious Jews point him to the New City. Thus he crosses the paths of members of all the country's peoples. However, instead of unfolding a multinational heterogeneity for him to observe, they guide him towards his one and only identity, that of the Israeli. The Israeli music that accompanies this footage attempts to underscore this by trying to impose Israeli culture and identity even where the camera shows other cultures and other plausible identities. The Hebrew culture and identity form the core around which the lives of the Arab protagonists are arrayed. The Arab protagonists precede, like the desert, the Zionist man, personify metaphorically his pre-Zionist traits, or lead him in the direction of his Zionist identity.[35]

The Arab supports Israeli culture not only by what he does but also by his gaze, a gaze that like that of the transformed Jew is a bearer of the Israeli Zionist ideological point of view. In *End of Evil*, this look encapsulates his very essence. The soundtrack opens with an account of the Arab convoys that traversed the country's sand dunes undisturbed until the Jewish settlers came. The convoys are not shown, and a full view of the camel and its rider is not provided. The camera focuses exclusively on the camel's face, its legs and parts of its hump.[36] Then the convoy encounters the fence of a settlement. The camera abandons its objective point of view and switches to that of the convoy, from which it observes in dazzling sunlight the watchtower and the rifle clutching settler who moves towards the gate. The Arab and the camel are utterly non-existent in the picture, both now and before. Therefore, their entire existence boils down to the way they look at the settlement and the conclusion they draw from it: admiration at the courage of the settlers, who place themselves amid the desolate dunes and shatter a desert tradition that has prevailed for millennia. In either case, the Arab supports the Jewish presence, either straightforwardly or in the manner of Balaam, by watching his curse turn into a blessing.

Thus like the women, the Arabs serve in these films as 'the other of the other': like them they represent some of the non-Hebrew non-Israeli traits of the survivors, like them they help the survivors to acquire their new identity. Unlike the women, however, the Arabs would not participate, not even metaphorically, in the process of transformation itself. Their role was thus to stress by contrast the legibility of the survivors for transformation.

FROM TEXT TO 'SUBTEXT'

By analyzing films from the 1940s and 1950s that placed Holocaust survivors in central roles, one may probe the Zionist narrative that the films attempt to engrave in them, and separate elements of the Israeli identity that they wished to preserve in this fashion from those that they wished to expunge.

First, the films attempt to preserve a coherent history of progress[37] that follows one homogenic, progressive path from one origin only, the biblical past in the Land of Israel, to one future only, a flourishing Zionist community in the Land of Israel. Death, desolation and destruction play a mythical role in this account, one of descent into hell preceding an ascent to Eden. It is a cohesive account, and nothing eludes it. Women, Arabs, Holocaust survivors, Christian priests and British army officers – they all have one function: to integrate into the story or drive it forward. It does not offer alternative pasts, identities and possible futures. It has one tradition, one past, one people and one future. Every individual integrates into its causal progression from the reversal to accrual and growth (from curse to blessing, from Holocaust to redemption, from desolation to efflorescence). The plot reflects this process, and the camera dramatizes it.

No one, be he/she a Holocaust survivor or a veteran settler, is given any leeway in this process. The details of the survivors' lives in and before the camps are incorporated into the films only insofar as they can merge into the Zionist narrative, be redeemed by it, and acquire meaning by its merit. The biographies of longer tenured immigrants are treated similarly. The Holocaust survivor in *The Great Promise* pleads that he lacks the strength to begin anew, and a soldier in the Palestinian brigade replies: 'When I came to Palestine, I was a broken man just like you.' In this respect, there is no difference between them. All of them are fated to follow the same path.

The Holocaust survivor accepts the Israeli redemption account so easily because the details of his life, his past, his suffering and his every experience are presented as being devoid of a 'story' that would organize them and invest them with meaning. The films correct this flaw by organizing the details into the 'Zionist narrative'.[38]

However, the 'Zionist narrative' shown in the films is not the only one that existed in the culture of the time. Other narratives existed and would rise to dominance in due course. Initially, they occurred in marginal cultural systems or were integrated, as marginal components, into texts dominated by the 'Zionist narrative'. Some of these were also buried in the films' 'subtext'.[39] A brief review of the literature and cinema at issue will allow us to probe and examine this process of repressed plot.

The past of the survivors, which obstructs the progress of the plot in the initial phases of the films of the 1940s and 1950s and is fated to give way to a Hebrew past, began to redominate the plots of Israeli books and films in the 1960s.[40] In works discussing Holocaust survivors, it becomes the object of the protagonists' inquiries (*Tel-Aviv–Berlin*). It is disseminated, in the form of a late exposition, throughout the works; it erupts time and again and dictates the present lives of all the protagonists – including their children – and obstructs their integration into the Israeli reality (*Avia's Summer* and *Searing Light*). In all of these cases, the survivors' past is judged as superior to the Israeli present, which the plot blurs either through total obfuscation (*Tel-Aviv–Berlin*) or by presentation, along with recollections of the past, as part of a chaotic, brutal and incomprehensible reality.

Films and stories created and written in the 1980s and 1990s are dominated by the survivors' view of space and time from the early films. Till the conclusion of the plot they cling to their memories and refuse to relate to the landscape of Israel as their own. The protagonists' subjective view dominates the plot in all of these cases, and the work as a whole accepts this.

As with time and space, the new works also thread the outlines of the survivors' image in the films of the 1940s and 1950s, but they change the judgement of this image. The trait formerly considered egoism is portrayed as individualism; idle Jewish lassitude is portrayed as spiritual wealth, seeming cowardice is shown as sensitivity, and the feminine traits as well as the affiliation with Arabs are much more appreciated than the masculine traits or affiliation with the Israelis (examples: *Searing Light*, *Our Tree on the Hill*, *Hide and Seek* and *Avia's Summer*). These works do not turn Jews into Hebrews in the course of their plots; they do the opposite: many of the plots induce the Hebrew to admit that he is in fact a Jew, an orphan (*Hide and Seek*) and the son of Holocaust survivors (*Wooden Gun*) who inhabits a Holocaust-survivor society, still enclosed within the Ghetto walls and immersed in the Jewish past (*Wooden Gun*, *Avia's Summer*, *Searing Light*).

On the one hand, the expositions earmarked for change in the old plots become the main engines of the plots in the new works. On the other, the narrative of the old plots, the resurrection of the Hebrew from the Jew, disintegrates into unconnected episodes in the new plots. It is presented as a collection of cliches that the protagonists do not understand (*Searing Light*), is couched in irony (as a laughable attempt to change one's clothing, as for example in *New Land*), and leads not to the beginning of a new Zionist life in Israel but to that of a life of orphanhood, bereft of parents and educators (*Searing Light*). In the early films, the resurrection process ends with the survivors' adoption of Hebrew parents. In the new plots, the Hebrew fathers are unable to function as sources of authority and strength. They are false (*Searing*

Light, Avia's Summer), they are absent (*Hide and Seek*), they communicate false values (*Wooden Gun*), or they are depicted as parodies of paternal authority (*New Land*). Neither do the mothers fulfil the role given them in the early films. The mothers in *Avia's Summer* and *Wooden Gun* are insane, the farm manager in *Searing Light* is an unsavoury unmarried woman, and the mother in *Hide and Seek* is that of an entire children's village, not of her own son.

Consequently, these new works dismantle the narrative that guided the early films, expand the contents shown in the initial stages of their plots, and modify their judgement towards these contents. In most instances, however, they dredge up contents that the earlier films repressed throughout their whole plots.

The point of view in *The Great Promise* is that of kibbutz children who observe the survivor girl, Tamara, and attempt to define, analyse and understand her. Nevertheless, at a certain moment in the film she manages to elude her comrades' gaze and slip in her own point of view. The film anticipates this moment by providing horizontal footage of the kibbutz in the dark and melancholy music that attests to the change of consciousness that filters the account – from that of the kibbutz children to that of Tamara, the survivor. The horizontal footage is followed by a close-up of Tamara's face in the dark. She removes a necklace from a hiding place and contemplates a photograph of her mother. The girls, sleeping next to her, climb out of their beds and observe her, and one of them narrates: 'We don't know what she's going through.' At the critical stage in the account, the spectator sees what the children can neither see nor comprehend: the girl's inner world and past, of which they are allowed to know nothing. The themes of the subsequent films focus on this world and this past.

In *My Father's House*, the boy, David, ostensibly conquers the landscapes of the country and finds his new identity in them. As a matter of fact, he does not acclimatize himself to the Israeli countryside until the end of the plot, and the angle at which this landscape is filmed attests to this. It is true that he crosses the desert, the sea and the mountains; the camera provides splendid footage of all of them. However, they are invisible to him. To the very end, the camera does not adopt – physically, ideologically or psychologically – his point of view. The boy, stubbornly and obsessively preoccupied with the search for his father, is uninterested in Israeli scenery. In most of the films, the hero is given the 'privilege' of looking around after he has forfeited his Jewish identity. No such thing occurs in *My Father's House*. Even at the end, when David runs to his new father, Abraham, and falls into his arms, the camera wanders around the new settlement and observes the builders and tree planters. David is not the observer. In the plot, the boy eventually stops looking for his father and integrates into the Zionist narrative, but in fact his deepest identity, the one illuminated by his look, remains that of a stranger – a stranger in the society he has joined and an alien in the landscapes of the country, which he does not see.

This contradiction between plot and point of view is strengthened by a contradiction between the direction of the plot and its conclusion. The successive episodes introduce David to the Zionist narrative in its various details: working the land, the history of the country, the cemetery where the early pioneers are buried – an attestation to the possibility of resurrection after death etc. He responds to each of the episodes shown him in one way: he searches for his father. His adamancy and his allegiance to his father's memory threaten the Zionist progression of the plot by leading it firmly and coherently in a different direction: to the Diaspora and the past. David's fixation with the past actually guides the major events in the film: his escape from the boarding school, the trek to the desert, the trip to Jerusalem, and so on. The climax of the plot (David's discovery that his father is dead) does lead David to the 'correct' solution: he abandons his parents' memory and exchanges his past for a new past, that of Israel. Until the end, however, the plot leads him down a different path: the quest for his real father. The conclusion of the plot in *My Father's House* gives the child survivor a Hebrew homeland, past, mother and father. However, the point of view, the footage of the countryside, and the progression of the plot to its resolution all leave him in his real past, with his real father, an alien to the country and its landscapes.

This film attempts to portray the multinational Palestinian space as a large and tranquil one, in which Hebrew pioneers, Orthodox Jews, Arabs and Christians coexist, and all other communities support the Hebrew-Israeli one. Unwittingly, however, the footage of the Arab landscape, filmed from its Arab inhabitants' point of view, sometimes clashes with the Jewish patriotic jingles that resound on the sound track: 'Our Itsy-Bitsy Land', 'My Motherland Canaan', and so on. The songs attempt to 'Judaize' the landscape, but the picture refuses to go along. Similarly, the gaze of the Arab in *End of Evil* is meant to express admiration of the Israeli, but subliminally it also confirms that the Jew needs the gaze of the 'other' in order to define himself. The practical strength of the Arabs and other aliens is manifested by the boy, David, in *My Father's House*, when he forms friendships with them. If we observe his interaction with members of other nationalities (the Palestinian boy, the Bedouin, the British soldier, and in a certain sense the religious Jewish children) without considering the purpose assigned to this interaction in the plot (to lead David to his Israeli identity), we may regard these relationships as the kernel of a totally different plot: that of a boy who considers himself a stranger in his own society and finds a bond with those who live outside it. This is the story of the survivors in literature and cinema from the 1980s on – strangers in a strange land. Others within who join the others without in order to deconstruct the national narrative and identity.

At first glance, the later works reverse the old films' hierarchy of judgement by preferring Jewish-survivor characters over the Hebrews. In fact, such preferences are also embedded in the early films. In the very first part of *Tomorrow Is a Wonderful Day*, the camera, the editing and the sound track express the subjective feelings of the protagonist – the young survivor – with great intensity and dynamism, whereas in its second part, after he has become a Hebrew, his persona melts into the collective experience and vanishes there. In fact, he has ceased to live since he was swept by the great change. His entire life has become one large symbolic celebration. First he celebrates a concert, then the founding of a settlement, and then the Sabbath, the harvest festival, and the festival of first fruit. After the first-fruit festival, the film skips over the lengthy summer, in which he presumably experiences difficulties in adjusting to the work and the communal life, and moves on to a Hanukka celebration. In other films, the celebration is merely a final chord; here it dominates the plot. Thus the film seems to identify most strongly with the fearful teenage survivor, whereas the 'new Hebrew' is portrayed more as an ideological peg than a flesh and blood human being. In similar fashion it is the survivor Anna, the impulsive savage, who becomes attractive to the hero of *Faithful City*, and not the ideologically correct Tamar, who is portrayed as anaemic and genderless.

Thus, this analysis of the subtext of the films shows that their overt contours of time, space and characters conceal a covert set of contours that expresses another ideology. This ideology is also manifested in the latent doubts that the films express towards the death-to-resurrection march. At the end of *End of Evil*, Yosef returns to the kibbutz that his parents had left and is given a festive, emotional welcome. The War of Independence erupts in the middle of the revelry, and the text explains: 'Yosef has come home. Yosef had a home to defend.' Although the war allows Yosef to be reborn as a hero and an Israeli, the picture does not exactly confirm this opportunity. The camera shows lengthy close-up montages of terrified faces and shifts from them to close-ups of a tank, rifle muzzles creeping along and Arabs astride galloping horses. These scenes recall the footage of the Arab riots at the beginning of the film. There, too, we are told that the pioneers have come to Palestine to defend it, but the footage belies this message by showing scenes more reminiscent of a pogrom than a war: shredded parchments, shattered eyeglasses, strewn belongings, a prostrate corpse. The film describes the success of the settlement enterprise in Palestine and the rebirth of Yosef, the Holocaust survivor, in the War of Independence, but recurrent scenes of terror and dread contradict both accounts.

In *The Great Promise*, the resurrection account is torn apart by a structure of repetitions. In one episode, the film follows the Jordan River on its journey to the Dead Sea, and from there to show the revitalization of the wilderness. However, it does not content itself with this; it repeats the resurrection story again and again, five times in all. Thus, whenever we think the process has been completed and the desert has indeed been revitalized, we are taken back to the beginning. The reiterations retard the process and return the plot to death whenever death seems to have been overcome. In so doing, they threaten the dynamic, optimistic advancement of the Zionist account and, thereby, anticipate not only the survivors' films that parody it openly but also the literary works of the 1960s and 1970s, which depict the country's history in cycles of death and destruction (*Facing the Forests* is the most salient example).[41]

The hero of *Tomorrow Is a Wonderful Day* builds a fence around the new settlement and explains, to himself and to others, that 'A wall sets a limit for man and place. What lies beyond is sometimes a grave.' The protagonists in the opening stage of the plots of the 1940s and 1950s films have indeed gathered on the other side of this wall. In the subsequent literature and cinema, they display the personal human sensitivities that were silenced in the previous films. They yearn for the distant 'Diaspora' past that the earlier plots had taken pains to obliterate, and they seek a different history and space, for which the previous plots had no room. They expose the possibilities – and the repressed terrors and impulses – that the early plots obfuscated. Wasteland and desert, a strange countryside, the Arabs, the jackals, the non-Jews all around and also seductive, tempting women, everything that had been tamed and silenced by the plots in the survivor films, now evoke terror, allure and inner impulses.

However, as I have tried to show in this essay, they did not invent anything, they have just brought to the fore what was hidden in the plots of the old films and in the margins of the culture of the 1940s and 1950s as a whole.

NOTES

1. These films include *My Father's House* (1946), directed by Herbert Klein and scripted by Meyer Levin; *The Great Promise* (1948), directed by Joseph Leits; *End of Evil* (1946–49), directed by Helmar Larsky and Joseph Krungold; *It Is No Dream* (1948–49), directed by Joseph Krungold; *House on the Hill: A Tale of One Village*, directed by George Lloyd George; *Tomorrow is a Wonderful Day* (1946), directed by Helmar Larsky; and *Faithful City* (1952), directed by Joseph Leits.
2. Examples are Joseph Leits, Meyer Levin, George Lloyd George and Hemlar Larsky.
3. For the term and its uses see Ella Shohat, *Israeli Cinema* (Austin, 1989).
4. This narrative even appears, if only as a motif, in more complex literary texts such as *Each Had Six Wings* by Hanoch Bartov. For a discussion of such literary works, see Gershon Shaked, *A New Wave in Hebrew Literature* (Merhavia, 1971), and *Hebrew Literature, 1880–1980*, Vol. 4 (Tel-Aviv, 1993). An analysis of commemorative booklets can be found in Noa Amit, 'Patterns of Commemoration and Their Association with Cultural Models, A Test Case: Memorial Pamphlets for War Casualties', Master's Thesis, Department of General Literature Studies, Tel-Aviv University. Jad Ne'eman describes the attitude of the Israeli cinema towards the Holocaust, in 'The Empty Tomb in the Post-Modern Pyramid: Israeli Cinema in the 1980s and the 1990s', in Charles Berlin (ed.), *Documenting Israel* (Cambridge MA, 1995), p. 295.
5. See Hanna Yablonka, *Alien Brothers* (Jerusalem, 1994), p. 134.

6. Homi K. Bhabha, 'Dissemination: Time, Narrative, and the Margins of the Modern Nation', in Bhabha (ed.), *Nation and Narration* (London and New York, 1990), p. 80.
7. Homi K. Bhabha, 'The Other Question: Difference, Discrimination and the Discourse of Colonialism', in Russell Ferguson *et al.* (eds), *Out There* (New York, 1990), p. 316.
8. James Clifford and George Marcus (eds), *Writing Culture* (Berkeley, 1986), p. 100.
9. See Yablonka, *Alien Brothers*, p. 86; see also Tom Segev, *The Seventh Million* (Jerusalem, 1992), p. 152.
10. On the pretensions of the western narrative to express the entire nation, see Clifford, *Writing Culture*, and Stuart Hall, *New Ethnicity: Black Film in British Cinema* (London, 1991), pp. 27–31. Bhabha defines this plot as one that tells a progressive story of growth and prosperity ('Interrogating Identity', *ICA Documents* (1990), pp. 5–11). On this subject, see also Shaked, *Hebrew Literature*.
11. See Helen Sixous in Toril Moi, *Sexual/Textual Politics: Feminist Literary Theory* (London, 1985), pp. 104, 195, who claims that all binary opposites in philosophy and western literary thought tend towards the basic 'couple': male and female. On this subject see also Daniel Boyarin, *Unheroic Conduct: The Rise of Heterosexuality and the Invention of the Jewish Man*, (Berkeley, 1997). Yosefa Lushitsky, 'Himo, King of Jerusalem', in Gertz, Orly Lubin and Judd Ne'eman (eds), *Fictitious Views on Israeli Cinema* (Tel Aviv 1999); Yael Feldman, 'Otherness and Difference as Strategies of Subjectivity: The Perspective of Gender Studies', in *The Other as Threat: Demonization and Antisemitism* (papers presented for discussion at the International Conference, The Vidal Sassoon International Centre for the Study of Antisemitism, The Hebrew University of Jerusalem, 1995), pp. 67–98.
12. One can compare this phenomenon to parallel narratives in other cultures, such as immigrants to America (eligible others) versus the American Indians (who are ineligible).
13. See Ne'eman, 'The Empty Tomb'.
14. See Moshe Zimmerman, 'Hebrew Cinema for the Wallet and the Emotion', *Cinematek* (1989), p. 48; Gross, *The Hebrew Film*.
15. Yehiam Weitz, *Consciousness and Helplessness*, Jerusalem, 1994, p. 106 (Hebrew).
16. Concerning this point see Weitz, ibid., for example p. 113.
17. Bhabha, 'Interrogating Identity', pp. 295, 296, 306, 313. See also Bhabha, *The Location of Culture* (London and New York, 1994), p. 49; Elisabeth Bronfen, *Over Her Dead Body* (New York, 1992), p. 105.
18. In all these cases the texts are not really subversive, because the progress of the Zionist narrative is not somuch halted as it is postponed when the difficulties that impede the fulfilment of the plot's driving ideology are only insinuated. However, it is the reader, not the text itself, who reveals these difficulties. See Shaked, *Hebrew Literature*, p. 16, who speaks of postponing the advancement of the Zionist 'superplot', and Orly Lubin, who analyses the role of the reader in fulfilling the subversive dimension of the film (Lubin, 'TheWoman Character in Israeli Cinema', in Gertz *et al.* (eds), *The Israeli Cinema*).
19. Frederic Jameson, *The Political Unconscious* (London, 1981). The prevailing argument is that the narrative articulates the hegemonic ideology and the expressive devices subvert it (see also Jean-Louis Camolli and Jean Narboni, 'Cinema/Ideology/Criticism (1)', *Screen Reader*, Vol. 4, No. 1 (1977), pp. 2–11). The assumption in this article is that the coherent, processed and unifying level is the one that expresses the overt ideology of the work, whereas the less coherent, less processed levels may contain ideological lacunae and contradictions.
20. The message 'These children need love' appears in a collection of letters on matters of communal education in Ein Harod (July 1943, quoted by Segev, *The Seventh Million*, p. 153): 'But above all, they need to learn to love! To love their homeland, mother earth, flora and fauna. This function – teaching them to love – is our responsibility. Will we have the sagacity to discharge it?' The films arrogate this educational function to themselves.
21. The fact that eight of the ten children who came to the country under youth group programmes had been raised in Europe in warm, affluent homes, among caring friends and teachers, does not emerge in the films. See Segev, *The Seventh Million*; Schnitzer, *The Israeli Cinema*18.
22. The survivor's past is actually subjected to fragmentation (see Bronfen, *Over Her Dead*

Body), as the survivor himself is not given the contours of a complete character. Dependent on the Israeli narrative as his source of authority, he has no history, no past and no future of his own.
23. See Amit, 'Patterns of Commemoration'. The Israeli landscape plays a blatantly propagandistic role in films meant to 'sell' the country to American audiences. However, the films also give the landscapes ideological functions.
24. See Jean Cristophe Horak, 'The Penetrating Power of Light', in Gertz *et al.* (eds), *Fictitious Views*.
25. Such a reversal occurs in Tamara in *The Great Promise*. Our discussion of the point of view in the films is based on Seymour Chatman's *Coming to Terms* (Ithaca and London, 1990), who distinguishes among several points of view: that of the narrator (the angle), that communicated through the consciousness of the character (as a filter), that communicated through the dominant presence of the hero in the story, but not necessarily through his consciousness (as a coordinator), and that communicated through the importance of the character in the broader interest of the story (interest). See summary by Kenneth Johnson, 'The Point of View of the Wondering Camera', *Cinema Journal*, Vol. 32, No. 2 (Winter 1993), pp. 49–57. See also M. George Wilson, *Narration in Light* (Baltimore and London, 1986).
26. His journey corresponds to that of the epic heroes, as described by Lotman ('The Origin of Plot in the Light of Typology', *Poetics Today*, Vol. 1, Nos 1–2 (1979), pp. 161–85): from the grave to rebirth.
27. Shohat, *Israeli Cinema*, and Ne'eman, 'The Empty Tomb', describe the role of water in these films. Shohat picks out saliently colonialist elements in Zionist culture and Israeli cinema. In films such as *The Sabra* and *Oded the Nomad*, she identifies the point of view of a Westerner who comes to a new location, crosses its expanses, and strips it of its mystery. The Arabs who live here, in Shohat's view, are treated as extensions of the landscape and are likened to the desert and the marsh, which await the revitalizing advent of Western man (ibid., p. 44).
28. The same reversal of identity occurs in *Faithful City* after the hero flees to Jerusalem. He celebrates the reversal with his instructors on the day Israel declares its independence. The birth of the state, like the founding of the new settlement in *My Father's House* and the first-fruit celebrations in *The Great Promise*, is a ceremonial event that characterizes the survivor's change as a rebirth and emphasizes the metaphoric aspect of this change.
29. On the image of the woman pioneer as a great mother, see Shohat, *Israeli Cinema*, p. 44.
30. Boyarin (*Unheroic Conduct*) refers to the homosexual traits that the anti-Semitic discourse, and the Zionist discourse which allegedly adopted it, applied to the Jew. This article merely notes the two analogical pairings created by these films: 'Hebrewism' and masculinity, Judaism and femininity.
31. As the wild and rebellious Anna, or as Miriam in *My Father's House*.
32. Weitz quotes Eliahu Dubkin, who visited Tehran in 1942 and categorized the Holocaust survivors by three types of population: a minority 'whose terrifying living conditions warped and destroyed their souls. They are willing to do anything: cheat, steal, oppress'; a minority that 'passed through the crucible of hardship and came out physically and psychologically whole'; and the majority, who, although neither thieves nor oppressors, are of 'shattered spirit. They are dispirited people, bereft of hope.' Most of the protagonists in our films belong to the first category, people whose Holocaust experiences warped their psyches and taught them to steal, cheat, and treat others oppressively.
33. Teenage immigrants were interested in higher learning for additional reasons: such schooling was considered a major value in the Jewish world, it reminded them of their parents' home, and it offered them a way to catch up with local youth (Yablonka, *Alien Brothers*, p. 27). Many of them wished to acquire a trade, and many did not consider the kibbutz way of life appropriate for them, having been raised in a more individualistic climate (ibid., p. 155) and rejecting farm labour as a potential path of social advancement.
34. Most survivors who immigrated to Palestine/Israel from Europe were intellectuals (as many of them had post-primary schooling as did the non-immigrant population). 'The survivor did not come to Israel as an empty vessel', says Aharon Appelfeld ('Subtotal',

Yediot Aharonot, 9 May 1994). 'He brought the entire depth of Jewish history, all the mistakes of the Jewish faiths, a thicket of feelings and contradictions, an ardent desire to avoid everything Jewish but to cling to any Jewish reminiscence, disgust with his universal beliefs, Marxism with all of its entrails, assimilation – and concurrently he was all of these.' The survivors in the films show us nothing of this baggage. Instead, they adopt the derogatory Jewish stereotypes by which their hosts define them. 'I had a wife and a son', says Julius from Breslau in *My Father's House*. 'I always wanted to work the soil, but I never managed to be anything but a shopkeeper.' His comrade follows in the same vein: 'Back in Russia, Jews were not allowed to buy land, so we were all just shopkeepers, shoemakers, and lawyers. I am afraid I am not good at anything.'

35. Ella Shohat describes the Orient in the Israeli cinema as lacking any active historical narrative function – a passive object to be studied and observed (p. 43). In fact, the Orient is not passive in most of these films. The Arabs gallop across the countryside, crisscross it, threaten the Jewish settlers or move them from place to place. Nevertheless, their passivity is evident in the plot: everything they do merely sets the stage for the Israeli identity and the Zionist overarching narrative.
36. As we will recall, shots of segments of a picture are an element in the poetics of the film. However, while the Arab remains segmented, shots of Jews come together to form a complete picture.
37. A teleological history, to use Bhabha's term ('Interrogating Identity').
38. According to Appelfeld ('Subtotal'), the survivors indeed accepted this account with little resistance because the beliefs that had informed their lives had collapsed. 'The Jew considered himself immersed in the great march of progress ... in which nationality and sectorialism are nullified and the world is remade in a new human unity of some kind. This belief, of which he was a leading exponent, blinded him. He did not see, and could not see, that forces of darkness and evil, which for years had been lurking for him, were about to spring from the thicket and dismember him alive'.
39. Itamar Even-Zohar ('Polysystem Studies', *Poetics Today*, Vol. 11, No. 1 (Spring 1990)) describes the structure of a culture as a struggle between systems and models that dominate the centre and those that have not yet reached the centre or have been repelled by it. One may detect this struggle also in specific texts as an interrelationship between their overt and covert levels. One presumes that texts based on the dominant models express these models at their overt level and express models from culturally more marginal systems at the covert level. In this sense, the covert level of the text expresses not only a repressed ideology but also an ideology expressed in other sectors of the culture. Changes that occur over the years lead to two reversals of roles: between the central and the marginal models, and, in specific texts, motives that were in the subtext in previous works find their way to the texts themselves and vice versa.
40. This subject is not fully analyzed in this article. It is discussed in my books *Hirbet Hiza'a and the Morning After* (Tel-Aviv, 1983), and *Motion Fiction* (Tel-Aviv, 1994) (both in Hebrew). The present discussion of later works on Holocaust-survivor themes, too, is sketched in outline form only. It is based on my two articles 'From Jew to Hebrew: The Zionist Narrative in *Searing Light*', and 'A New Look at Holocaust Survivors: The Israeli Cinema in the 1980s and 1990s' in Iris Porush and Ezhak Ben Mordechai (eds), Apelfeld Book (Be'er Sheva, 1998).
41. In this matter, see Bhabha, 'Dissemination', p. 297, who speaks of various repetition strategies that inhibit the development and accumulation of time in the national-progress story.

The Theme of Jerusalem in the Works of the Israeli Fathers of Conceptual Arts

MORDECHAI OMER

The year of the city's unification, 1967, gave birth to a renewed and reinvigorated consciousness among Jerusalem's artists. Two artistic groups arose, one after the other: between 1968 and 1969 there was the 'Mashkof' group, whose main concern was to give momentum to the slumbering cultural life of the city's artists (painters, authors, composers, etc.) and art centres. Beside David Ben-Shaul, there were veterans like Zvi Talkowski and Ivan Schwebel, and younger artists like Yitzhak Gaon, Michael Gitlin and Shaul Schaltz.

A more ideological group that emerged from the new social and political reality of post-1967 Jerusalem was undoubtedly the 'Leviathan' group. Its three founders had settled in Jerusalem in the early 1960s and 1970s (Avraham Ofek in 1962, Michail Grobman in 1971 and Shmuel Ackerman in 1973). The quest for a form whose components could be interpreted in the symbols of 'Jewish mysticism' was a clear artistic echo of the awakening of national consciousness during those great hours of Jerusalem's history.

During the same period when the Leviathan group was developing, another movement came into being in Jerusalem, antithetical in character and orientated towards Conceptual Art (its journal, which appeared in the Jerusalem of the mid-1970s and published texts by artists like Joshua Neustein or Spitzer was written in the English language and was called *Artengrade*).

One of the important conceptualist projects executed in Jerusalem early in the 1970s was The Jerusalem River Project, designed by Neustein, with the collaboration of Georgette Batlle and Gerald Marks. Beside these projects, Neustein continues to this very day to use the

---

Mordechai Omer is Associate Professor of Art History at Tel-Aviv University, and Director of the Tel-Aviv Museum.

landscapes and sacred sites of Jerusalem as concrete instantiations of his conceptual thought, especially of problems linked to the disparities that result from Israelis' mode of reception of the time and place around them.

In the Landscape Amendments that Menashe Kadishman created on top of photographs of Jerusalem early in the 1970s, the city appears as an open stage that gives itself to the artist and changes its appearance to suit the artist's hand. At the outset of his career Kadishman operated on the landscape itself – in this context, in 1972, for example, he painted a stone and an olive tree at the Israel Museum; but today Kadishman takes details from the landscape, isolates them in his drawing, and then enriches them by adding dramatic scenes which return us to those myths of 'binding' and 'ritual' that characterize his later works.

The problem of his identity preoccupied Pinchas Cohen Gan even while he was still a student at the Bezalel Art School in the late 1960s. Indeed, his being in Jerusalem only stimulated and enriched this urge which to this day serves as a point of departure for many of his works. To imprint his mark on the landscape – be it on a view of the Valley of the Cross and the Israel Museum, or on a section of cracked Jerusalem wall – this motive always serves as a conceptual component that allows him to grapple directly and concretely with a message that deals with the nature and essence of modes of life in various formal and social contexts.

In this essay I chose to devote special attention to four artists whose work came to be the precursor and basis of Israeli Conceptual Art in the 1970s: Yitzhak Danziger and Arie Aroch, Menashe Kadishman and Pinchas Cohen Gan.

YITZHAK DANZIGER

Danziger's family, which had absorbed the best of German tradition and culture, migrated from Hamburg to Jerusalem in 1923 and set up its home facing Herod's Gate, close to the Muslim cemetery and the excavations of the Third Wall. At that time Herod's Gate stood between the Muslim Quarter of the Old City and the Arab neighbourhood Karem al-Sheikh outside the wall. Each Friday a sheep fair was held there. The motion of the sheep, the colourful identification marks, the strays that fled into the yard of the 'Danziger Clinic' where they were sheltered by the little boy – these sights were engraved deep in Danziger's memory. The excavations of the Third Wall opened the strata of history to him. He used to accompany Yosef Zaritsky on his circuits around the city wall, and to walk with him in search of sights which would become ever more meaningful in his later spiritual and creative development.

The six years of Danziger's stay in Jerusalem concluded in the summer of 1929, when he was sent with his sister to their aunt in Berlin: the 1929 riots had begun, and their home, some distance away from the Jewish Quarter outside the Wall and also from the new Jewish neighbourhoods, was in danger. The family moved to Tel-Aviv.

During the Second World War Danziger lived in Jerusalem. In the early 1940s he joined the Sixth Company of the PALMACH – a Jerusalem military unit, most of whose members were friends of his from Tel-Aviv. Most of his time during the next four years was spent on trips throughout the country, with returns to his Jerusalem base. He recorded his impressions of the city and its outskirts in rapid and concentrated sketches. Its special light and the great power evoked by its quiet landscapes would serve as stimuli for sketches that evoke a visionary sculptural architecture intended to contain all this mighty wealth of life and folklore, belief and ritual, which motivated the lives of the local inhabitants. Later, these landscapes would reappear in taut and fragmented drawings that recall the horizon lines of imaginary oriental cities. These buildings and landscapes, like Bab al-Wad and 'Absalom's Grave', executed in precise and concentrated lines, are painted as if they have gone through the melting pot of residues of memory whose seals of imagery were imprinted in another time and place.

FIGURE 1
YITZHAK DANZIGER
'Zion will you not ask ... ', 1946. Ink on paper, 12.5cm × 12 cm. Private collection. Inscribed (Hebrew) '*O Zion, will you not ask of the peace of your captives Who desire your peace and are the remnants of your flocks?*'

During those ten years of exile and wanderings abroad, from the end of the Second World War to 1955, the year when he returned to his old workshop in Tel-Aviv and started teaching three-dimensional design at the Technion in Haifa, Danziger drew many landscapes in which inscriptions appear identifying the places, like 'Bethel, which is in Judea' or 'Rama' – centres of faith and ritual connected with this country. In these pages there are many passages quoted from the Bible which relate to Jerusalem, like 'Beautiful in situation, the joy of the whole earth', or long lines from the *piyyutim* and excerpts from poems of yearning for Zion or Jerusalem: 'Zion will you not ask of the peace of your captives / who desire your peace and are the remnant of your flocks'. It seems that more than anything these pages reflect the conflicts occuring within the artist because of his absence from the country during the time when his contemporaries, the 'Generation of 1948', were immersed in the difficult processes of the birth of the state.

The yearnings for those biblical landscapes that had so impressed the German-born boy who had grown up within the romantic oriental landscapes of Jerusalem mixed with guilt feelings about his absence from the battlefield. The landscapes and the fauna of the homeland are replaced more and more in the drawings of the late 1940s by 'altars' and 'sacrifices'. The sheep festivals and the shepherds' tents become transformed into ritualistic monuments connected to myths of sacrifice and redemption.

For Danziger, the full embodiment of the sense of sacrifice and faith was to be found in the symbol of 'The Binding of Isaac', which he treated in several of the 1949 drawings, and especially in the sketch for the sculpture comprising an oblong figure with a square head crowned with horns, in the margins of which is written: 'sheepskin stretched over stone with the skull as a crown. Sculpture for Mount Zion, at the entrance to the Jewish Quarter, "The Binding of Isaac"'. This sketch, done in London for a memorial sculpture on Mount Zion a year after the Quarter and its inhabitants had fallen to the Jordanian Legion, is one of many pages done in Britain as a direct continuation of his earlier plans, which included buildings for the shearing festival at Ein Harod. As early as the end of the 1930s, Danziger had done a sketch for a totem-like 'Tent Pole' with a ram's head at the top. The tent was intended to serve as a place for a mythological-folklore performance by kibbutz members in the Valley. The same ram, which symbolized both the return of the Jewish People to their land and the sacrifice of those who fell for the homeland, appeared again in 1964 as a sculpture which Danziger designed for Jerusalem. 'The Shepherd King', intended to stand as the central mast in the Billy Rose Sculpture Garden at the Israel Museum, symbolizes (despite and also by means of its very abstract forms) several of the city's distinctive values: 'The Shepherd's Staff' alludes to the shepherd who chose Jerusalem as the capital of his kingdom; 'The Head Disk' which faces east is supposed to absorb the rays of the sun when it rises over Jerusalem; 'The Horns', which have become a kind of musical instrument, return the viewer to ancient rituals, which sanctify the connection between the believer and the sound of the shofar.

The complicated and historically charged complex of ecological and cultural factors that have given Jerusalem its hallowed standing over thousands of years for such different and distant religions occupied Danziger throughout his entire life. In his aspiration to achieve truer meetings of man with his place, his environment, and nature, Jerusalem had the status of the ultimate example through which it would be possible to expose these complexes with maximum intensity. He firmly believed that man must learn and discover the language of the time and place of the 'pattern of his homeland's landscape' – he has to be in harmony with the law and cyclicality of 'the place' (the *Makom*). The only way to penetrate and to join with those factors that distinguish a 'place' was by creating the conditions for a constant renewal which was focused, in Danziger's later periods, around the concepts of 'rehabilitation' and 'memorialization', in which he saw the main role of the modern artist.

Danziger found an instructive example of this creative path in the existence of gardens and groves throughout the country, especially in the echoes of the living cosmic order of 'the Shulamite gardens' as described by King Solomon in the Song of Songs. Again, in Danziger's drawings in London towards the end of the 1940s, there are many citations from the Song of Songs: 'My dove in the clefts of the rock / My dove, my undefiled'. The garden, for Danziger, is not only a symbol or expression of the notion 'order'. It is a complex, a language, with a mystic significance in its structure and in everything that is part of it – animal, vegetable and mineral – and in their locations. On another plane, the garden has always symbolized a high level of consciousness (in contrast to the 'forest', which is grasped as a place where the subconscious rules) which imbues those who enter its bounds with a sense of security and faith: 'I am come into my garden, my sister, my spouse ...' (Song of Songs 5: 1).

One of the projects that Danziger began planning the year he died was the garden for Kiryat Ben-Gurion – the Government Buildings in Jerusalem. In his letter to the landscape gardener M. Shoshani (10 April 1977), Danziger defines his role: 'The elements, the solution of which is included in the work, will be examined in the light of the following goals: preservation of the distinctive character of the place and its environs, and in parallel – creation of the atmosphere of an oasis in a desert climate.'

Danziger was aware that Jerusalem was situated on the border of the desert, and that it effectively constituted that rare and noble meeting place between nature and man. Believing that this meeting should be restored and cultivated, he placed all the artist in him in the service of this goal. Elizabeth Gassler, in her introduction to her catalogue of the exhibition Modern Gardens in Landscape, notes that 'when men have had a strong shared sense of their place in the universe, their gardens too have tended to be strong and sure, for the making of a garden is always something of an act of faith'.[1] Jerusalem, which began as a holy place, and whose main task has been the defining of an area of existence while cultivating and defending the sources of livelihood, of the fauna and flora in its areas, has become a symbol of ritual and rootedness, of faith and creativity.

ARIE AROCH

Despite Arie Aroch's continuous day by day connections with Jerusalem, at least since he settled there in 1954, it is hard to point to any specific work that marks this distinctive connection. The main reason for this, apparently, lies in the special way in which Aroch chose to work during his last years, in his belief that the 'what' has to disappear and to resurface by means of the 'how', or, as he put it:

> Only after I understood that one must conserve the what – all the experiences that emanate from the objects that I have loved – inside, and that it was forbidden, forbidden to think about it – that one had to give oneself to the how of a work, the love of the touch of the brush, the scribble and the little lines, and then all the necessary and appropriate what will surface of itself – only then did I succeed in making the paintings I had wished to before, without knowing it.[2]

Nevertheless it seems that in the mid-1960s, immediately after his return to Jerusalem after years in Israel's diplomatic service abroad, there is in his works an intensification and integration of memories of the past with present occurrences. During this period, Jerusalem serves as a stage inseparable from the cultural coefficient from which the artist has given birth to his expressions: 'The artist,' Aroch summed this up, 'carries with him a load of forms, which is like a vocabulary ... The love of painting, of creating forms, generally depends on the number of forms one is intimately connected to.'[3]

In an attempt to reconstruct Aroch's Jerusalem from 'the forms hidden inside the artist' for this essay, I have chosen two pictures which constitute central instantiations of Aroch's mid-1960s period. The painting 'Agrippas Street' was begun while Aroch was still Israel's Ambassador in Stockholm (1959–62). Most of the painting, apart from the sign in its upper section, was painted during the period when Aroch was searching for a 'concrete abstract' from which he could convey his messages in a way that was simultaneously personal and conceptual. As he recalled:

> At some point I started cultivating an idea which has been on my mind again lately: the freedom which abstract painting has brought

> to the world seems most sympathetic to me; on the other hand the chaos and the absolute breaking of barriers have brought despair. American Abstract Expressionism (De Koning, etc.) repelled me. I wanted to create objects that would be clear and at the same time detached from the figurative, from reality, in every form you'd find in an abstract painting. I had never drawn, and now I began drawing incessantly. I was looking for a form that could be defined, an 'object', the opposite to anything chaotic. I filled a sketch-book with attempts to test the form, for myself.[4]

The forms born in those drawings and paintings were suffused with his memories and yearnings, especially with those in which he wanted to return home after years of working abroad. The return involved on the one hand nostalgia for the distant past in his parents' home in Russia, and on the other – yearning for and wondering about what was going on in his home in Jerusalem.

Two houses recur in the central works of the period: the house in Russia in the Tzakpar series, and the house in Jerusalem in the painting 'What's New at Home?' In the above interview he explained:

> I remember that in the city of my birth, Kharkov, a shoemaker's sign hung on a wall. There was a boot, and some gold remained on it. I remembered the sign as 'a work of art', but when I tried to paint it from memory, I failed. I began to change the form – in pencil – I deleted and added here and there until a form emerged that satisfied me as the form of a boot. When I looked at the form again, I knew that no one would believe me that it was a boot. On the other hand, the form that had developed from the boot was, in my eyes, a concrete form (as opposed to an abstract one) that had a right to exist, a right to exist that I wanted to embody in the abstract object, as I defined it before. And what is 'Tzakpar'? When I was working on the picture my son Jonathan came to me and I couldn't tell him what it was, or perhaps I was trying to be funny. I told him it was a 'tzakpar'.[5]

The painted oblong area of 'Agrippas Street' was brought from Sweden in 1962 and completed in Jerusalem two years later – only after Aroch had attached to its upper portion a 'found object', a street sign that he had worked up with white and grey paint scribblings. The painted shoemaker's sign from the memories of his father's home in Kharkov was replaced by a Jerusalem street sign dating from the 1920s, from the same decade in the middle of which, while studying at Bezalel, Aroch had worked as a designer of street signs for Weisenberg's ceramic tile workshop in Jerusalem. The choice of the sign was certainly first of all because of the fact that in this *objet trouvé* Aroch found a new painterly means with which to transmit personal contents far beyond its purely literary content.[6] Yet there can be no doubt that the literary content was part of the sensations and sediments with which Aroch wished to grapple during those days in the mid-1960s.

'Agrippas Street' is first of all a reminder of the first Jewish governor who reigned in Jerusalem in ancient times (41–44 CE), testimony to the time when Jerusalem was ruled by a scion of the Hasmoneans (the grandson of Herod and Miriam, son of Aristoble and Berenice) who tried to increase the power of his capital, and of whom tradition has only good things to say – the *Mishna* relates that 'when he came to "thou mayest not set a stranger over thee" his eyes filled with tears. [The Sages] said to him: "Fear not, Agrippas, you are our brother, you are our brother, you are our brother!"' (Sotah 7: 8).

At the same time, Agrippas also marks that period in Jewish history which, with all its good aspects, represents the lull before the storm and the imminent massive destruction. The high expectations created during Agrippas's time, which were dashed with his untimely death, swept the nation into the great revolt that quickly led to the destruction of the Second Temple. The dilemma, between the option represented by Agrippas who sought to serve the Roman conqueror and at the same time to supply the needs of his Jewish brethren, and the uncompromising stance of the 'Jerusalem Zealots', raises a hard historical question – what might have happened to the Jewish people had it not rebelled against Rome, had it remained in its country and its capital and not gone into exile? One of the most fascinating answers to this question had been given by historian Michael Avi-Yonah, who saw in the revolt against Agrippas's dream:

> a surgical operation which separated the Jews from the ancient world, a separation thanks to which we exist to this day. All the other peoples which existed at that time descended into oblivion at the end of the ancient period. The only people which preserved its consciousness and uniqueness was the Jewish people, for the very reason that long before the decline of the ancient world it had brought about this separation.[7]

To return to Arie Aroch and to his paintings of the mid-1960s, I would like to analyse another painting that also relates to the character of a foreign Jewish governor in Jerusalem, and then to sum up what is common to both paintings. 'The High Commissioner' was painted after the portrait of Sir Herbert Louis Samuel (1870–1963) as woven in a Jewish-Persian carpet dedicated to him by Iraqi Zionist Jews (at the bottom of the carpet is the inscription 'Iraqi Zionism 11'). Sir Herbert was appointed first High Commissioner for Palestine in 1920 by the British Government, as a goodwill gesture to the Jewish People and a sign of His Majesty Government's intention to fulfil what had been promised in the Balfour Declaration. As the first Jewish ruler in Jerusalem since the days of the Second Temple, Samuel was received in the country as a harbinger of redemption. Despite the high hopes he raised, Samuel during his term as High Commissioner (1920–25) turned out to be a disappointment both to the Jews, who increasingly saw him as a second-rate British politician for whom his own people's interest was absolutely secondary, and to the Palestine Arabs, who saw in his appeasement policy a sign of weakness and intensified their demands of the Mandate to an extreme.

When Aroch arrived in Mandatory Palestine in 1924 at the age of 16, his first home was in Jerusalem (after several weeks in Tel-Aviv). Those years between 1924 and 1926, when he was studying at Bezalel, coincided with the end of Sir Herbert Samuel's term of office (1925) and his replacement by Viscount Herbert Charles Onslow, the second High Commissioner for Palestine. There is no doubt that his period of study in Jerusalem shaped Aroch's memories of the Mandate period, especially of the first High Commissioner, whose official visit with his family to the Bezalel school in 1924 is documented as one of the important events in that institution's history (photographs from the visit are to be found today in the Israel Museum collection).[8] It is interesting to note that the Bezalel period was linked for Aroch with the Jerusalem landscapes of the painter Haim Gliksberg. When asked about his memories of his early Jerusalem period, he remarked: 'At that time Gliksberg was painting the top of King George Street. He taught me how to lay down oil paint.'

The renewed meeting, via the carpet, with the portrait of Sir Herbert Samuel may be linked to another problem that preoccupied Aroch during the 1960s. In 1964, Aroch, together with Leah Nikel and Yigael Tumarkin, represented Israel at the Venice Biennale. At this exhibition Aroch was impressed by the rise of the Pop movement, and especially by Robert Rauschenberg, America's representative at the Biennale. In 1966, when asked by journalist Heda Boshes about his connections with Pop Art, Aroch replied:

> They opened doors and windows and allowed me to move in another direction, but they don't deal with the things I deal with, and with colour for its own sake. And the fundamental difference – I don't do paste-ups, and I don't make collages. I take the fixed thing, paper that gets thrown away, play with it and continue in another direction.[9]

Engraved in Aroch's memory from the Venice exhibition is the portrait of President Kennedy in Rauschenberg's painting 'Retroactive I' (1964, Wadsworth Atheneum, Hartford, Connecticut). In the same interview with Heda Boshes, Aroch demonstrated by means of the Kennedy portrait how the technique of Pop Art was not only a question of new forms, but also, and especially, of new contents: 'Colour,' he explained,

> can be put down in all kinds of ways. For example, Kennedy, in Rauschenberg's picture, is a plastic part of the painting, one of its

words (and a word has a unity of its own) which combines into the sentence which is the picture. One word is colour, another is form, and another is the portrait of a man in the news. The connection here is not with the event itself, the assassination of the President, but perhaps with a certain atmosphere.[10]

It is interesting to note that in yet another interview two years later, Aroch was to explain the use of the portrait of the High Commissioner in words very similar to those he had used about the Kennedy portrait in Rauschenberg's paintings:

> The double image of the High Commissioner is in fact 'a picture within a picture'. If I had not painted the figures here, or if I had painted other figures, the painting would have had a completely different appearance, even different content, and actually that is what has happened to the image in painting in general: after all the crises it has gone through, it has once more become legitimate, with a new and different function, in the 'pose'.

This is not the place to add parallels between Aroch's 'The High Commissioner' and the American Pop artists, but it is hard not to recall if only briefly Larry Rivers's 'Washington Crossing the Delaware' (1953, today in the Museum of Modern Art, New York). This picture is not only one of the earliest and most important forerunners of the American Pop gospel, but especially in our context it is certainly a prototype of the development of the myth of America's presidents with all the critical and parodic approach so characteristic of these artists of the late 1950s and early 1960s. Rivers's art-historical approach and his preference for a painterly touch over the mechanical reproduction so characteristic of the Pop artists brings him inestimably closer to the works of Aroch during the mid-1960s.

The reproduction of the High Commissioner in painterly technique, its duplication as a print even though it was painted from a full portrait, and its contraction into a kind of emblem or miniature symbol which shows both the man and his double – all this was painted side by side with Aroch's attempts during this period to establish frameworks of primary forms and primary colours that would compose the syntax of his paintings. In 'The High Commissioner', Aroch was to begin dealing with the primary colours red and blue, which appear in these pictures as bands of clothing or as signs of flags, while later, as in 'Red and Blue in a Landscape' (1970, collection of M. Telem, Tel-Aviv), these colours would be liberated totally and become an element 'and it does not matter how you paint them'.[11] In the same interview, Aroch admitted that 'the weakness of the thesis lies in the fact that blue and red are primary colours, and they recur in human thought, in flags'.

As an interim summary, one can say that in the mid-1960s Aroch sought to evoke 'a certain atmosphere' which for him was connected with the two governors of Jewish birth who had been appointed by foreign authorities to reign in Jerusalem: King Agrippas was evoked by means of a textual quotation as memorialized on a street sign; the High Commissioner was recalled by a visual quotation from a carpet which memorializes his portrait in the 1920s. The most relevant common denominator, at least from a historical point of view, between these two governors, is the fact that both aroused great hopes among their subjects upon their appointment, only to end their short terms in office on a highly disappointing note. This, in turn, fomented Jewish turmoil and rebellion, eventually culminating, directly or indirectly, in great upheavals in Jewish history.

As already mentioned, the Jewish People's rejection of the way outlined by Agrippas – that is, the creation of close ties between Roman culture and the Jewish faith – brought about the destruction of the Second Temple, but at the same time served as a catalyst for the preservation and strengthened existence of the people. In the same way, the unwillingness of the modern 'Jerusalem Zealots' to follow in the path of the 'High Commissioner', and their establishment of a Jewish underground against the British occupation, may have proven, perhaps in a more 'optimistic' way, to be more right.

The comparison between these two periods in Jewish history was recently invoked by Nathan Shor:

> For the sake of comparison let us turn for a moment to the recent past. When the LEHI began its activities against the mighty British Empire, in 1940, and to the majority of the Jewish population in the country this seemed like a completely hopeless project, only half a century passed and this Empire was totally destroyed. In other words, the moment for rebellion was well chosen, and therefore it also succeeded in the end, when it was joined by other organizations. The Roman Empire, in contrast, was at the peak of its power at the time of the Great Revolt, and continued to rule in Eretz Israel and the environs for yet another 560 years. No conceivable international or internal constellation could have led to the revolt's success.
>
> Is the lesson of all this that it was not worthwhile for the rebellion to break out at all? ... In retrospect one can say that the Revolt fulfilled an important and even essential function in the history of the Jewish People. It gave expression to the mighty vitality innate in the Jewish People, in its religion and culture, which differentiated it from all its neighbours.[12]

The use of 'found objects' – a carpet made as a tribute and a street sign – as points of departure for works by an artist so complex and so much the diplomat as Aroch, obliges the art historian to seek interpretation, even though as conceptual communication at first these motifs appear minor and less relevant to the totality of the picture's plastic language. The attempt to explicate these motifs in their relation to the time and the place – the Jerusalem of the late 1960s, the eve of the Six Day War – constitutes a possibility of seeing the process of Aroch's artistic work in a new light.

MENASHE KADISHMAN

In the course of Kadishman's artistic development, Jerusalem appears as a central motif after a conceptualist-minimalist period, and follows upon works linked to a return to nature in order to preserve and rehabilitate it. At the Symposium on Sculpture at Montevideo (1969), Kadishman for the first time juxtaposed industrialized raw materials with elements in nature, in an environmental presentation in which he affixed sheets of metal painted yellow to tree trunks in the forest. Following this 'personal intervention' in nature there began a chain of artistic events in which he treated the landscape itself as a work of art (for example, a similar activity held in Central Park, Manhattan, after his exhibition at the Jewish Museum in 1970, or the one at Hous Lange Museum in Krefeld, West Germany, as part of his exhibition there in 1972). For his contribution to the exhibition From Landscape to Abstract and from Abstract to Landscape (curator Yona Fisher, one of the events celebrating Israel's 25th anniversary, 1973), Kadishman painted yellow one of the olive trees on the slope that runs down from the Museum to the Valley of the Cross. With this action he was as it were trying to amend something in the sphere of nature, as if to stress, by means of this treatment of nature, that this olive tree is not just a tree growing in a valley, but a symbol imprinted deep in his people's tradition, in the symbols and rituals of the place. Explaining the motif of 'trees' in his work, Kadishman pointed out:

> It began in childhood, with Eretz-Israeli education. To plant trees, the JNF, Tu Bi-shvat. After the conquest of the wilderness, the wilderness had to be planted. I painted a tree next to the Israel Museum, as part of the 25th anniversary exhibition the Museum had organized. There was a bit of a storm about it. People were concerned, maybe the tree would die. The tree is close to my heart, and when I painted it I saw that the same treeish strength which exists above the surface also exists under the surface, in the roots. A strength that is divided between the crown and the ground. I thought of an X-ray photograph, a transparency of the roots. Or of installing mirrors that would 'bring out' the roots, or of upturning the tree, its top in the ground and its roots in the air, producing the same treeish power and splendour. But, how can you do that? I am sentimental, but this works too: the tree is our continuation. Between the tree and us there is an affinity and even a certain equality: the tree is the man of the world of silence, our language is full of trees: man is a tree of the field, the trees die erect, the cedars

of Lebanon, climb another tree. The 'Painted Tree' is an act of love, a kind of personal statement. One stage of a prolonged endeavour to intervene in nature ... Once, years ago, in the Galilee, I found, inside an olive tree, a little Karon which an Arab had hidden there for luck and blessing. It is not easy for me to make declarations about loves, but if in place of love only an intellectual action gets exhibited, that would be imprecise, a bit pompous, and too cold.[13]

FIGURE 2
MENASHE KADISHMAN
The Valley of the Cross with the Israel Museum in the background, 1980. Mixed media on postcard. 10.5 cm × 14.7 cm. Signed upper left: Kadishman 80. Private collection.

Following this documentation of his work, Kadishman was to put out a series of prints in which he continued painting that same tree in the Valley of the Cross, in addition to the yellow, in red, blue and black.

As part of these Landscape Amendments we may see the works done on top of photographs and postcards of Jerusalem in the early 1980s. In his touchings, scratchings and paintings over these landscape photographs, Kadishman intensifies the tension between the natural and the man-made form, thus distancing the 'touristic' sights of the city into some personal-poetic place of reference that links up with a private world of legend and myth of his own.

In this attempt to explain his 'amendment' of the Wailing Wall by painting it in pastels, Kadishman wrote:

> In 'The Wall', every patch of paint is a petition. We do not pray to stones – because one does not ask stones for anything. We place

petitions between the stones and that is 'The Other Wall' – the empty space between the stones. The stones are not holy, but the space around them, which is also part of our feeling, can be holy, and to this joins the Jewish faith that we are part of.[14]

In response to these Landscape Amendments – those lines rich in colour and the rough outlines that scratch and tear the surface of the paper – the landscape awakes to new life, becomes more powerful in its possibilities towards that 'Other City' which is like an echo of the one documented before us in the photograph, as against 'Jerusalem of Below'. 'Even if I walk in Jerusalem,' claims Kadishman, 'then too I am walking to Jerusalem'; and as an artist he accompanies his pilgrimage to the 'Other' by his own means: line and colour.

In recent years Kadishman has dealt, almost obsessively, with the myth of 'The Binding' (of Isaac). His preoccupation with the place of the sacrifice, Mount Moria, aroused further thoughts in him:

> If I stand on Mount Moria and look towards the Mount of Olives – I see all this marvellous pink light – there pass before me scenes from the events of the past: love and sacrifice, Abraham and Isaac, David and Absalom, kingdom and fall. The binding of Isaac occurs in our time, in fact, in every place to which we send our children to wars, but its emblem remains one: Jerusalem – the place where it really happened. I walk on one plane and see another plane which connects to our people's consciousness and to events which occurred here throughout all the generations.

FIGURE 3
MENASHE KADISHMAN
Views in Kidron Valley, 1988. Mixed media (black chalk, black oil pastel, tape).
Signed twice and dated lower left: Kadishman / 88. Lent by the artist.

This poetic-associative flow found expression in a series of drawings done during 1996 on large sheets in black chalk and with tearing and cuttings in the body of the paper. The central scenes all concentrate, indirectly or directly, on the same point in the stream of Kidron, where we see: on the right, Mount Moria, and on its ridge the Wall, with the sealed Gate of Mercy; on the left the way up the slope of the Mount of Olives, the Jewish cemetery, Absalom's Tomb, Jehoshophat's cave and Zechariah's Tomb. In his drawings, Kadishman gives special treatment to the group of monumental tombs, and especially to that of the prophet Zechariah: 'This is the most beautiful sculpture that exists as a structure and it is also part of nature itself.' (Quarried into the rock and still attached to it, the structure is comprised of primary forms of a cube with a pyramid on top – all these endow the sculpture with austerity and power that approach the minimalism of modern sculptural art.) Within the charged boundaries of this high-powered decor, Kadishman plants his figures which continue scenes from his previous series. They are brought together by the force of some ritual act which enables them to float and to unite in the landscape spread out at their feet: 'When you stand on Mount Scopus and look out at Jerusalem on the one side and the Judean desert on the other – you feel that you are floating, you feel part of eternity.' In spite of the myth and the ritual that compose and interlace these works, the drawing retains a kind of primal simplicity and basic archaism which imbue every page of Kadishman's with humanity and credibility.

PINCHAS COHEN GAN

Even when he was a student at Bezalel, Jerusalem had a special significance in many of Pinchas Cohen Gan's works. For the 'Sculpture in Landscape' project at the Academy in 1969, he proposed a 'Garden of Religions in the Valley of the Cross'. The proposal related to the three monotheistic religions to which Jerusalem is sacred, and included extensive research on the symbols connected to this city. The motifs included ritual objects connected to the Temple and the order of worship conducted there: lamp, table, altar, etc.; emblems of the nation and of the tribes: Judah, Priests and Levites; more abstract motifs raised as standards by the city's inhabitants – freedom and fertility, wisdom and kingship, faith and divinity. At the same time, several Christian motifs were studied and attempts were made to consider their sources, as for example the looped cross that is a transformation of the Egyptian symbol of life – the 'Ankh'. Special emphasis was placed on man, on his mate and his family, on the elements of nature and the cosmic systems surrounding him. Out of all these formal, cultural and religious contents, Cohen Gan consolidated a group of tiny bronze casts, models for monumental sculptures for the Garden of Religions. In this series of models, which form a kind of continuum of reductive and conceptual drawings in space, Cohen Gan frees himself of the narrative and syntactic structurality of his symbolic sources, in place of which he presents a set of abstract pictographic signs that attempt to grapple with the charged space of their surroundings.

FIGURE 4
PINCHAS COHEN GAN
Studies for the Garden of Religion, the Valley of the Cross in Jerusalem, 1969.
13 little bronze casts, maximal height 8 cm. Lent by the artist.

In the spring of 1988, Cohen Gan created a series of works in each of which one can identify an element linked to the chain of 'activities' he conducted between 1972 and 1974 – his conceptualist period. During the early 1970s Cohen Gan lived in Jerusalem, and from there set out on journeys 'to travel from one end of the earth to the other, to reach your own end, the end of geography'. His home in Jerusalem, his regional and interregional location with all its social and cultural qualities – all these were tested against other options that the artist created to confront questions of his identity on both physical and spiritual planes. On 10 March 1974 he wrote in his diary:

> The question continues to preoccupy me: a few months after the exhibition in the cowshed, in the summer of 1972, I went to Los Angeles. I wanted to clarity to myself the effect on man of a new environment. I felt the full significance of a return to a natural environment. Today I say: 'natural environment' is a relative concept. A relative homeland, a relative home.

Six days later he added:

> Life in another environment raises problems of hierarchy, of the concepts by which you live – concepts of society, geographical location, your place in Jerusalem, in your home, in the room, yourself.[15]

Cohen Gan's return in 1988 to the activities he had conducted in Jerusalem in the early 1970s is not at all surprising. In fact, and what is very surprising, in those earlier activities Cohen Gan had already grappled with questions that today afflict Israeli politics and society. On 20 March 1974 he wrote in his diary:

> A border is marked on maps as an internal line, and its marking is a visual graphic sign. The limit of our strength is not a geographic border but a cultural border, a border between cultures, the distance between them being much greater than the geographical distance. The points at which you are stopped are the border. These points are not fixed and are subject to different political situations and different conditions each day. The 'Touching the Border' action has a purely spiritual meaning. The border between the populations of Jerusalem is equivalent to the border between the communities in Israel. 'Touching the Border' is the posing of a question.

In each of the nine canvases in this exhibition one finds, *inter alia*, a documentary photograph taken from his activities, like 'Journey to Alaska' (June–August 1973), 'Carrots' (15 March 1974), 'South Africa – the Cape of Good Hope' (30 March to 18 April 1974), and also photographs relating to other activities conducted mainly during his stay in New York.

FIGURE 5
PINCHASCOHEN GAN
The Wailing Wall (detail of 'Jewish Art and Jerusalem'), 1988.

In the central canvas of this series Cohen Gan includes a photograph showing a section of the walls of Jerusalem, taken from the David's Tower area. In the left part of the photograph, where there is a long narrow firing slit, Cohen Gan has cut out the shadow of the slit and in its place pasted a strip of black paper onto the photograph. The attempt at creative work and personal involvement in a connection with a sanctified and historical site is possible for Cohen Gan only in a conceptual way, through a process of dislocation, in exchange for which he is enabled to renew his personal experience. The connotation of this firing slit in Jerusalem's national and military history is long and wearisome, rich and frustrating – but its being opened to quotation of itself opens to the viewer new possibilities and new involvement in many historical situations, some of which have already been defined and are still defined as absurd and lacking any possibility of correct solution. The artist's action has sealed the slit against any passage in or out, both for light or any physical penetration; at the same time one has to remember that the original function of this narrow slit, and perhaps also of many other components of this landscape and of the city's architectural splendour, are long outdated and are of no use except for the value of that aesthetic contemplation which serves as a bridge to the values and messages of this city of many years.

Beside the photographs, one can identify in these canvases elements that have been taken from the cumulative formal lexicon of Cohen Gan's artistic language. Diagrams of flow taken from the series called 'Metaformal Art', human figures taken from 'Atomic Art', constructivistic diagrams recalling earlier series. The nine canvases are built of formal and contextual assemblages of autonomous elements suggestive of a deconstruction which turns into a construction and thus raises the possibility of structure of a new order.

The sense of disquiet, transience and dissociation, change and adaptation, evoked by this series which is dedicated to 'The Art of the Jews and Jerusalem in the Eyes of Heroes and Villains', again and again testifies to the presence of alienation and strangeness as a central motif in the works of Cohen Gan. The status of the refugee and his transient existence was the central topic of the activity in Jericho in 1974:

> The action grew over the last years and especially from now, after the [1973] war. The problem was to give expression to the feeling of a man who is in a continual state of being a refugee. The problem can be approached on a spiritual and on a physical level. The legal attitude towards establishing who is a refugee and/or the United Nations definition of a refugee make no difference to the refugee's actual existence and feelings about the territories he has been in or passed through.

Although this was the third year since Cohen Gan had made Tel-Aviv his place of residence (in June 1985 he presented the project of his parting from Jerusalem at the Hebrew University, in a work entitled 'Jerusalem D.C.'), Jerusalem still serves as a constant metaphor in his works. Through Jerusalem, more than through any other city, he is enabled to define 'the result of equilibrium between different factors in our region and beyond it'. As an example of these factors it is hard to avoid mentioning the 'Infinite Pillar' of Brancusi which was certainly an important reference point for Cohen Gan. In that same album of drawings and sketches of Pinchas Cohen Gan the student, as an additional page towards the 'Garden of Religions in Jerusalem', one finds a page on which he tried to design, by means of computer typesetting, a section from the Song of Songs on a pillar that curves upwards. At the bottom of the page he wrote: 'Brancusi's pillar through the Hebrew Bible'. It is interesting to compare, at the opposite extreme, the way in which exactly the same section was treated by a veteran Bezalel artist like Ze'ev Raban, one of the Academy's founders and first teachers. Raban went out into the streets and markets of Jerusalem, observed the oriental types he met, drew the city's landscapes, the fauna and flora he found there – and with all this returned to his studio at Bezalel and illustrated the verses of the Song of Songs.

Sixty years later Pinchas Cohen Gan would return, on his own initiative, to the Song of Songs, and would convey the message of 'to build Jerusalem' through the minimalistic and conceptualistic inspiration of one of the great sculptors of our century: Constantin Brancusi. Despite the immense difference of visual language, a difference characteristic of the developments that have occured in art between the beginning of the century and now towards its end, the need to reach the endless, the spiritual, remains the same.

NOTES

1. Museum of Modern Art, New York (1965), p. 5.
2. Interview with Yocheved Weinfeld, 'Massa', *La-merhav*, Nov. 1968.
3. Quoted by Yona Fisher in the catalogue *Arie Aroch: Paintings 1953–1968* (Israel Museum, 1968).
4. Interview with Yona Fisher in the catalogue *Arie Aroch: Times, Places, Forms* (Israel Museum, 1976).
5. Ibid.
6. Marcel Duchamp's use of the *objet trouvé*, 'Eau & gaz à tous les étages' (Water and gas on every floor) is surely the first example (1935) of the use of an architectural urbanistic sign for the purpose of building the private mythos of the artist.
7. M. Avi-Yonah, *The Great Revolt: Causes and Circumstances* (Jerusalem, 1983), p. 385.
8. A further close connection with the British and Jewish worlds was between 1942 and 1946 when Aroch served in the British Army, at Sarafend and the Carmel.
9. Heda Boshes, 'The Quests of Arie Aroch', *Ha-aretz*, 26 April 1966.
10. Ibid.
11. Interview with Yona Fisher, 26 June 1974.
12. Nathan Shor, *History of Jerusalem*, Vol. 1 (Jerusalem, 1987), p. 268.
13. Menashe Kadishman, 'Trees', *Musag*, No. 1 (April 1975), p. 47 (Hebrew).
14. This and all subsequent quotations regarding Kadishman are from an interview with the artist by the author, 5 Nov. 1988.
15. All quotations are from the catalogue *Pinchas Cohen Gan: Activities*, Curator Yona Fisher, Israel Museum, Jerusalem (1974).

The Dybbuk Revisited: Images of Religious Jews on the Israeli Stage

SHIMON LEVY

Jewish tradition has rejected theatre not only because of national and historical reasons, well understandable as a wish to differ from the gentile Greeks and Romans, and later from the medieval and Renaissance Christians – in order to avoid their 'pagan' (alternatively 'overly Christian') theatre plays. The cornerstone of Jewish condemnation of theatre, however, may be ascribed to the Second Commandment: 'Thou shalt not make unto thee a graven image nor any manner of likeness, of any thing that is in heaven above, or that is in the earth beneath, or that is in the water under the earth ...' (Exodus 20: 3–4). This commandment led to countless generations of theatrophobia by *halachic* Judaism, but the strong reservation against (re)presentational arts cannot serve alone as an exhaustive explanation of why the highly dramatic elements in the Old Testament and the Mishna, the Talmud and other holy and basic Jewish scriptures, were never actually performed nonetheless.

One must bear in mind that it took some 1400 years for the central and western European Catholic Church to first suffer, then allow and finally harness theatre to its political, ideological and educational purposes, when the drama in/of the ritual emerged beyond the church doors; and mystery, miracle and morality plays were performed in the town squares. Somewhat similarly, it may be observed that so long as the dramatic elements in the Jewish ritual – there is hardly a ritual without dramatic and theatrical elements – were contained within their socioreligious contexts, they were obviously considered 'kosher'. But unlike Christianity, *halachic* Judaism (namely the religious laws) never tolerated theatre's 'threshold position', of observing and presenting religious affairs from a basically non-religious perspective – let alone explicitly secular performances.

Shimon Levy is Associate Professor of Theatre, Tel-Aviv University.

The typical Jewish position of opposing theatre[1] sometimes took the form of drastic warnings against its frivolity, mostly at times when the rabbis, as religious and social leaders, felt that the 'gentile entertainment' offered a genuine and corrupting threat. I believe this principally negative attitude towards theatre to be based on the rabbis' profound understanding of the intrinsic performative aspect of theatricality as such, regardless of whether any particular production, festivity or show 'of the gentiles' was sacrilegious, licentious or even merely bawdy. Following Grotowski's distinction,[2] I suggest that the leaders of the Jewish congregation were much more opposed to the gentile theatre's 'sacred' ability *to create a new reality* than to its 'prostitutional' aspects. Whereas the bawdy 'immoral' aspects can be relatively easily overcome, the performative-creational aspects of theatricality may indeed present a genuine religious threat. It is theatre's potential power to transform matter into spirit, and vice versa, that threatens a real competition to religion. In Judaism the power to create has remained God's exclusive prerogative, and even Catholic transubstantiation, a theological dogma, was only allowed to express itself theatrically from about the fourteenth century. At the same time, one should remember that the transubstantiation is in itself highly theatrical – from the performative point of view, as well as through its sensual appeal to the soul.

It is neither the intention nor within the scope of this essay to analyse the complicated aspects of this thesis, presented only as a brief introduction. Rather, I deal here with a number of principal notions regarding the image of (Orthodox Jewish) religious issues and figures, as they have been portrayed on the Israeli main theatre stages since Hebrew theatre turned professional around the early 1920s: from the well known 'pro-religious' but highly critical *Ha-dybbuk* (1922), through the quasi-religious 'pioneering' plays of the 1930s, and up to the relatively large number of contemporary, blatantly anti-religious productions on the main stages of Israeli theatre in the 1990s.

The birth of professional Hebrew Theatre is closely linked with Vachtangov's international and immensely successful production of *Ha-dybbuk* at the Moscow Art Theatre, performed by an (at the time) only semi-professional Jewish cast. In its very conception, this legendary production (over 1300 performances in Europe and America) reflects a profound and typical tension between Jewish *halachic* tradition and the explicitly secular (in fact quite *non*-Jewish) nature of the show. Vachtangov managed, nevertheless, to bridge the gap between Jewish '*shtetl*' realism' and fictional theatricality with the extensive use of expressionism. The story of An-Ski's play tells of a broken marriage-promise in a Jewish townlet (*shtetl*). Hanan the bridegroom dies and now haunts ('adheres to', as the meaning of the Hebrew verb *lidbok* connotes, physically and in the later spiritual meaning as well) his bride Leah's body and soul.

Whereas ghost stories were well known folkloristic material in east

Europe at the time, this particular story was based on Jewish sources researched by An-Ski, and located in a typically Jewish surrounding. The modes of presenting the story on stage, however, were absolutely non-Jewish. For lack of Jewish (and certainly Hebrew) theatrical traditions (except, perhaps, the *Purimspiel*), this touching melodramatic ghost story demanded other, non-Jewish modes of presentation. Vachtangov indeed used a unique blend of expressionistic theatre styles together with story telling and some 'agitprop' techniques. While not exclusively Jewish in content, *Ha-dybbuk* was totally un-Jewish in its theatricality. Furthermore, as Gershon Shaked notes,[3] the people about whom the play was written and performed would probably be the very last ones to see it. The Orthodox Hasidim, before and after *Ha-dybbuk*, are not theatregoers.

The Dybbuk is a 'threshold play' in more than one sense. Its subtitle 'Between Two Worlds' clearly indicates its author's intention in this respect. The story line deals with the thin, perhaps non-existent line (in the eyes of the characters, at least) between the living and the dead. The play maintains an interesting position in the language war between Hebrew and Yiddish. It was originally written in Yiddish but performed in Haim Nachman Bialik's Hebrew translation, a language the characters themselves understand but most certainly do not speak. Historically, the *Dybbuk* marks yet another schism between the old world of *shtetl* life (the Hasidic Jews of the play) and the new prospects for Enlightenment (*haskala*), and especially the aspirations for a new world order raised by the recent Russian Revolution. Furthermore, the production expressed, dialectically, both nostalgia and criticism of the portrayed on-stage *shtetl* world, even by the Jewish actors themselves – towards their naive, suffering religious brethren. This latter discrepancy may also be described as a gap between the socialistic attitude of presentation and the traditional and folkloristic nature of the material presented.

These tensions certainly put *Ha-dybbuk* in a unique situation. The sociological and artistic aspects of the performance – its text, subtexts and contexts – nurtured one another, but the actual choice to perform *Ha-dybbuk* on stage at all was based on ignoring the anti-theatrical Jewish tradition and breaking the ancient prohibition of the Second Commandment. The harshest tension exists, I maintain, between the central motif of the play – its theatrical *qua* religious usage of the performative function of words to *do* things, especially in the exorcism scene, on the one hand; and its theatrical *qua* anti-Jewish and as such secular aspect, on the other.

It is not only the dead that have kept haunting the Hebrew-Israeli stage since the original *Dybbuk* was released from Leah's body some 80 years ago. The Holocaust and many wars between Israelis and Arabs have added numerous other dead to 'live with'. Clearly, the entire religious theme is still a recurrent one. Whereas the performative aspect is a basic constituent of any theatricality, Hebrew or universal, the particular 'Jewish religious' motif reveals itself as a Dybbuk of sorts too in the modern Israeli theatre. The spirit of Hanan, the young-old religious Jewish dead, is still haunting live (Israeli?) Leah; still claiming moral and emotional debts.

When the Ha-Bimah Group moved from Moscow to Tel-Aviv in the mid-1920s, it continued performing Jewish themes in the new (fictional, dramatic and theatrical *and* real) space – the yearned-for promised land. Ha-Ohel Theatre, with its artistic director Moshe Ha-Levi, made a number of daring attempts to mount Biblical stories, and transform the enormous dramatic potential of the Old Testament, already performed for hundreds of years by the gentiles, into original Hebrew theatrical versions, this time in the very space in which many of the biblical stories and histories really happened. It is important to note that such shows[4] again relied on perceptions and misperceptions of folkloristic Arab, oriental and Jewish-Yemenite sources, especially those relating to modes of pronouncing Hebrew (Sephardi rather than Ashkenazi), as well as costumes ('biblical' sandals, *djellabas* etc.) and stylized dance and movement.

These productions had nothing traditionally religious about them, but they nevertheless regarded the biblical dramatic material with great respect, regarding the scriptures as the obvious foundation of Jewish tradition, now to be truly 'lived' where it all happened. There was, however, a feeling of awe, perhaps even a certain 'almost' religious ardour in the artists' contemporary theatrical approach. Folklore and modern theatricality were a mode of reappropriating Jewish contents in a secular way, an approach that was not filtered through the prohibitions according to the spirit of the Jewish halachic law, but through the newfound links to the soil, the sun, the physical space of the Land of the Bible.

The deliberately secular attempts of the pioneers, from the 1920s to 1940s, to personally connect (and collectively re-collect) themselves as a nation to the land, as Gideon Ofrat rightly observes,[5] are replete with rituals, ecstatic dances, mystical notions concerning a covenant between Sky and Earth. Whole scenes in plays like *Bein I'yim* (Among Ruins), *Adama* (Earth), or *Ha-adama Ha-zot* (This Earth) clearly indicate how playwrights of the period (Sh. Shalom, Ashman, Jaffe, Karmon and others) replaced the old, perhaps dry and no longer relevant *halachic* laws and rites of the Exile Judaism with local, Hebraic ('Israeli') sanctity. Messianic ideology, redemption, and a 'blood covenant' with the Earth – a much more nature-orientated religiosity, dominated the drama of the Yishuv (pre-state) period throughout the years 1910–1948. Even Martin Buber called for a synthesis of Nature with Intellect.[6] Certainly under the influence of European *Blut und Boden* nationalistic notions coupled with socialist 'Narodnaya' ideas, many Hebrew plays could be considered 'religious': albeit not in the institutional sense, but rather in the sense of giving vent to a profound spiritual exhilaration, tinged with magical, romantic yet profoundly critical views of the highly challenging life in the Holy Land.

Whereas a non-Jewish Vachtangov used Jewish life and folklore to shape *The Dybbuk* in an expressionistic style, Jewish playwrights and directors in Eretz Israel, with a greater exposure to the direct influence of a new Space, tended to reshape traditional religious contents into their present Time and Plot of social and ideological ambience.

In the first years after the establishment of the State of Israel in 1948, theatre was little occupied with the religious problem. Later, in the dramatic (following the public) discourse, the quasi- and pseudo-religious rhetoric began to be clearly heard. Nathan Alterman, poet and playwright, wrote the lines 'we are the silver platter on which you were given the State of the Jews...' in his *The Silver Platter* poem, which became an integral part of the public mourning ceremonies in Israel, and found ample echoes in the most important plays that dealt with the War of Liberation, such as *He Walked in the Fields*, *They Will Arrive Tomorrow*, and *In the Plains of the Negev*. In the Israeli consciousness, three years after the Holocaust, hardly any plays had yet been written about the traumatic event. The impact was still too close, too dreadful. The Holocaust happened 'there'. But the dead of the recent War of Independence found an immediate poetic and theatrical commemoration. The religious *Dybbuk* of the early 1920s was transformed and split into the still silent victim of the Holocaust, and the somewhat more talkative dead youngster who had given his life for the State. There is little direct allusion to the traditional Jewish lore of mourning in these dramatic works, as the dominant atmosphere in the young State of Israel was almost explicitly anti-religious. However, inasmuch as *The Dybbuk* had required international theatre traditions in order to express its uniqueness, so too could the secular mourning rituals not possibly avoid at least some cultural and mythical allusions to ancient Jewish Hebrew culture. Of these allusions the most prominent motif is 'The Binding of Isaac' (Genesis 22) that reappeared in many plays. Religious or not in the traditional sense, Yigal Mossinson, for example, describes a scene in *In the Plains of the Negev* in which a father (a character symbolically called Abraham) sends his son to certain death in trying to save other soldiers by breaking through to the besieged kibbutz. The '1948 dramaturgy', as it was often labelled, can hence be seen as reappropriating religious themes into the mostly secular Israeli sociodramatic context. Similar to the period prior to the establishment of the State, when pioneering fervour of a quasi-religious nature replaced the explicitly religious motif, now too the deliberate absence of traditional 'religiosity' in plays bereft of 'pious' notions was filled instead with biblical motifs and much idealistic fervour.

The fourth phase in depicting the Jewish religion and religious figures began in the late 1980s and is continuing today. Many productions dealing with such affairs occupy the main Israeli stages. Both the number and the overall character of these productions indicates a growing anxiety by the (mostly) secular theatre practitioners who are engaged in mounting them. The interesting difference that lies between these later dramatic depictions and the previous phases is marked by a commercial, usually superficial treatment of the image of the 'Religious Jew' rather than coping with the central ideological, spiritual and more profound social issues.

Tikkun Hatzot (Cameri Theatre) by Rami Danon and Amnon Levi (directed and written), is strongly based on the Arieh Deri affair. Deri, a well known religious politician of the Sephardi religious party, was Minister of Interior Affairs, accused of (ab)using public money for party orientated benefits. Deri grew up and studied in an Ashkenazi Yeshiva and consequently has excellent connections with the Ashkenazi religious party (headed by the 100 year old Rabbi Shach). Deri's alleged psychological complexes concerning both his social and emotional status *vis-à-vis* the east European Jewish 'leading *halachic* authorities' (*Gdolei Ha-torah*) and his biography were critically depicted in the show.

Tikkun Hatzot is a semi-documentary, geared to pleasing and teasing the psyched-out taste of a broad common public denominator (typical to the repertoire strategies of Tel-Aviv's municipal Cameri Theatre in many other productions as well). The show is based on a real local political scandal, and is partly influenced by it, but at the same time it adds fuel to the public fire and capitalizes on it. The show received some scathing reviews from the critics: 'since *Tikkun Hatzot* is not a play but a dramatized reportage, there is no real development... The situations and the relationships between the characters are recycled and the whole affair becomes tedious and pretentious...as though the declared analogy between the play's characters and this or that Rabbi or local religious wheeler-dealer may substitute a play...;'[7] 'Folklore Instead of "Kischkes"' (from Yiddish for 'entrails', in the sense of 'the essential') is the headline in Sarit Fuchs's review. '*Tikkun Hatzot* seems a provocation, but whom exactly does it provoke?...It is [no more than] harmless entertainment, teaching us to leave art to the authentically suffering people who are willing to pay a price for spreading out their unpopular truth...'[8]

The most revealing scene in the show is the 'Pulsa deNura' ('Whip of Fire' in Aramaic), a 12 minute long curse-as-exorcism, in which a large group of rabbis engage in a rare and extremely powerful Kabbalistic ritual, frequently reported in Israeli daily papers as a mystical means to achieve political influence. While intending or pretending to show the negative aspects of this God-fearing ceremony, the creators of the production actually indulged in a (conscious?) attempt to infiltrate an indirect, sweet-and-sour pseudo-religious message into their 'awed' audiences. 'This is what this show does: sells the milieu of the "Haredi" (Ultra-Orthodox) world cheaply, like a cheap and ugly picture' (*Ha-aretz*). *Tikkun Hatzot* enables secular Jews to comfort themselves (assisted by the use of sanctimonious kitsch) and mumble: 'If this is how *they* behave as "moral" religious people, then we, as secular people accused by *them* as immoral, are certainly OK.'

An equally superficial but perhaps more painful (to the religious) image of the religious power thirsty Sephardi-'dark' Jew, though without a personal address, can be found in the productions of *Sheindele* and *Fleischer*. *Sheindele*, also by Danon and Levi, at the Cameri Theatre, is the story of a young woman whose husband is given permission by one hundred rabbis to marry a second wife because she herself is barren. The main character, however, is not the young woman herself, but her mother 'The Rebbetzen' , a strong willed influential woman who rules over her particular little sect in the Orthodox world and fights against the religious and political decrees of a rival, male rabbi. While containing authentic elements of conflict between the individual will of the religious Jew, especially Jewish women who by *halachic* law do not have equal rights to men, and the severe rules of 'the tribe', embodied by the leaders, *Sheindele* is still a 'superficial ... voyeuristic melodrama'.[9] A redeeming factor in this particular production was the good acting, which both sold well and served as a figleaf for the show's otherwise caricatured portrayal of issues concerning the religious community.

None of the critics appeared to notice that the main component in the set design was the constant presence of an enormous female sex organ as the backdrop. This was probably intended to serve as the principal on-stage interpreter of the 'meaning'. Here too, while the overt message was a psychopolitical analysis of ultra-Orthodox society, the tacit hidden one was – obviously – latently pornographic. It would appear that the alleged chastity of ultra-Orthodox women encourages, as in the case of Catholic nuns, perhaps, a secular (predominantly male) invading gaze.

Fleischer, by Yigal Even-Or, treats a nasty conflict between the ultra-Orthodox and an elderly couple of Holocaust survivors who have a butcher's shop and sell non-kosher meat. The play sees no possibility for peaceful coexistence between the newly arrived religious family to this petit-bourgeois worker neighbourhood and the old secular residents. *Fleischer* was written with anger against the 'wicked' ultra-Orthodox and their 'dirty tricks' in forcing their lifestyle even upon the dead bodies of non-believers. Even-Or depicts a group of unscrupulous people (Hund = 'dog' is one of them). Fleischer's attempt to use the tactics of 'if you can't fight them – join them' proves unsuccessful. As a Holocaust survivor he compares – implicitly at least – his oppressors (who urge people not to buy his unkosher meat from him) to the Nazis from whom he managed to flee. Both parties in this play are depicted as having no ethical values. Both parties, oppressed secular and oppressing religious Jews, are painted in melodramatically stereotyped black and white. In their attempt to portray the mutually exclusive lifestyles of two kinds of Israelis, playwright Even-Or and director Amit Gazit claimed that they have no enmity for the religious. But the production itself could easily be described as anti-Semitic. Butcher Fleischer's secular anti-religious theology is based both on his Holocaust experiences and on allusions to the book and fate of the biblical Job. However, the metaphysical ramifications hang as high as the sausages in his meat shop.

Three plays by Shmuel Hasfari, *Kiddush*, *Hametz* and *Shiva*, with their explicitly traditional titles, all refer to the lives and tribulations of religious Jews. The first in the trilogy, *Kiddush*, deals with a 'softly' religious family of Holocaust survivors (again!), undergoing a gradual and grotesque emotional decay. The play ends with a mock Kiddush, a sort of sacrilegious Black Mass, in which the bread and wine of the Sabbath are deliberately spilled, quite a shock even for the mildly secular members of the audience. Despite the fact that the atmosphere and the characters belong to the religious sector, Judaism and Jews are dramatically (text) and theatrically (direction) treated by Hasfari 'as though they are no more important than a Rotary Club or a soccer team'.[10] The next two plays, *Hametz* and *Shiva*, try to demythologize and slaughter such Jewish and Israeli holy cows as Massada, the Holocaust and (more understandably) the moral legitimacy of the wars against the Arabs.

Basically, *Hametz*, in its sometimes metaphoric-fantastic approach (directed by Hasfari) attempts to reconstitute the collective Israeli memory. The schizophrenic protagonist of the piece 'burns his *Hametz*' – the 'leavened' bread which is forbidden during the Passover week. Hasfari probably implies that the entire Israeli society destroys its own sanctities and burns them. Arik, a war invalid of the mental kind, moves from one Israeli museum to the next in order to burn them all down. It is not necessarily the playwright-director's task to offer any ideological alternatives to those he allows his hero to destroy. But this play too portrays, in a banal, populistic and simplistic way, that giving up a traditional Jewish identity does not automatically mean receiving a new Israeli one.

The particular Dybbuk in *Hametz* is none other than a neurotic angel, as reflected in the family's name – Mal'ach (angel). The play is neither a parody nor a satire, and most certainly not a serious dramatic attempt to cope with spiritual, historic or social discrepancies between the secular and the religious sectors in Israel – or the many who waver somewhere in between. 'It isn't enough to know how to write notes,' says critic Feingold, 'one should know how to compose'.[11] This *Hametz*, he concludes, is neither kosher nor unkosher. Whereas *Scheindele* and *Fleischer* are both directed in a more or less realistic style, *Hametz* (at least?) is by far more modern in its fantastic postmodern theatrical approach. Its 'Dybbuk', nevertheless, can be described as a mentally sick metamorphosis of the original one, who had at least spiritual aspirations.

The Seder (Passover ceremony) is intensively used in *Memories of a Second Generation* by the Akko Theatre Group under the direction of Dudi Maayan. In their unique and very intimate performance, intended for a participating audience of no more than 24 people at a time, the traditional Seder becomes a vehicle through which Israelis (and Jews) are invited to observe their own 'filters' of Jewishness. Here again similar motifs are used: Holocaust, the Palestinian problem and Israeli nationalism. But Maayan's focus and aim in this unique production is definitely the self-observation and self-reference of his small audience – forced to look at themselves through the mock-ceremony of the Seder.

Dam (Blood) by Bracha Seri is another unique show created by Amir Orian in his studio, seating 14 people, even less than the Akko Group. It employs Orian's 'Open Circle' method, which perceives the here and now of the actor–audience interaction as the most crucial factor in/of the theatrical meeting. *Dam* tells of a woman suffering post-natal trauma who remembers, in a kind of psychotherapeutic session, her religious child-molesting father and her equally religious rapist husband. The production does not particularly emphasize the 'religiousness' of any of its characters, but the audience may still conclude that there exists a fine line between the strict religious milieu and the behaviour of its victims – both molestors and molested.

Va-yomer Va-yelech (And He Said, And He Went, 1996) created by Rina Yerushalmi from many different texts from the Old Testament, is an interesting and most recent attempt to use the ultimate (Jewish) Hebrew text against its religiously Jewish interpreters. Yerushalmi, an experienced director with outstanding ability for clarity, imagination and superb on-stage movement–text relationships, worked with a group of young actors for over a year, finally achieving four hours of biblical mini-dramas. 'The [biblical] text goes to our collective biography. It is not an audience's bond of spectators, but a bond of a common destiny. The Bible is our truly original drama,' says Yerushalmi.[12] The set design is minimalist, the lighting economic, functional and discreet. One outstanding scene is that of the list of different foods that the ancient Hebrews were allowed or forbidden to eat. The actors parodize the kashrut laws and through it the entire religious sector. Unlike *Scheindele* or *Fleischer*, this is a subtle, sharp and witty satire, shedding an ironic light on the ancient, and according to Yerushalmi, irrelevant and superfluous laws of long ago.

In another scene an actress speaks (verbatim) the text of Jephtach's daughter in an increasingly accelerated tempo. The late prime minister Yitzhak Rabin, who saw the play, briefly noted on this highly emotional scene: 'It is not Jewish.' Yerushalmi, nonetheless, gave her audience an often sarcastic collage-like cross-section of the Bible. This, certainly, was intended – but once again the overall impact was one of excellent theatre side by side with great poverty in seriously attempting to challenge more profound spiritual issues, in the Bible itself and later through its Jewish traditional interpreters.

The above productions, and others that have not been mentioned, reveal that Israeli theatre in the 1990s is launching an intensive and interesting cultural war against the exclusive appropriation of what 'Jewishness' means for the religious sector. Contemporary Israeli theatre uses humour, kitsch, parody and satire, but very few dramatic and theatrical arguments of the more belligerent and oppositional kind. Despite being in a minority, the Israeli religious parties have long served as a political balance of power, way beyond their actual electoral power, which has increased considerably following the 1996 elections. These religious parties constitute a relatively large part of the Israeli right wing, whereas many Israeli theatre makers are way to the left of the political centre. After Rabin's assassination and the results of the May 1996 elections, the anti-religious-Jewish trends of the 'betrayed' Israeli Left also found their mark in theatre-reception patterns. Some of the anti-religious productions planned and staged while still under Rabin's Labour government were probably kept alive and kicking because of the anger felt against the aggressive sounds and deeds performed by right-wing religious extremists, with Yigal Amir as the most despicable of 'them'.

In a period when most political violence is carried out by such people, theatre has a pitifully small role to play; but a responsible one nevertheless. Most 'religion orientated' theatre shows in Israel depict a negative image of 'Orthodox Jewishness' and religious Jews. They serve, alas, as superficial propaganda rather than a serious challenge – to either the religious or the secular Israelis. Regarding themselves as exclusively entitled to the one and only 'true' Jewish culture, the religious right-wingers look down on the secular as 'The empty vessel' while perceiving themselves as 'The full vehicle that has the right of way'. One of the more interesting (both ideologically and theatrically) possibilities will be to try and challenge this particular trend of 'spiritual exclusiveness'.

Theatre in Israel today, due to insufficient public subsidies, is in any case far too commercial; anti-religious theatre included. It therefore often casts a charming wink at its audiences – the moderate religious included. The ultra-Orthodox do not come anyway. If some 75 years ago the religious were possessed by a Dybbuk, nowadays it seems that the religious Jews themselves are considered to *be* the Dybbuk in Israeli theatre. Those well versed in Kabbala (Jewish mysticism) know that an unsuccessful act of exorcism may well precipitate the Dybbuk into clinging to its would-be exorcisers.

NOTES

1. Gideon Telpaz, 'Theatre in the Talmudic Literature', *Bama*, 9–10 (1967), pp. 17–26.
2. Jerzy Grotowski, *Towards a Poor Theatre* (New York, 1968), pp. 34 ff.
3. Gershon Shaked, 'The Play as a Way of Cultural Dialoge', *Bama*, 104 (1986), pp. 5–25. See also Freddie Rokem, '*Ha-dybbuk* in Palestine', *Cathedra* (1981), pp. 183–202; Yoram Bilu, from a psychoanthropological point of view, relates to the 'Dybbuk in Judaism as a mental disturbance qua cultural source'.
4. Chaim Shoham, '*Batia by Shatz*: The Staging of Kibbutz – First Stages at the Ohel, The

Workers' Theatre of Israel' (University of Haifa, 1987).
5. Gideon Ofrat, *Earth, Man, Blood* (Tel-Aviv 1980), pp. 128 ff (Hebrew).
6. Martin Buber, 'Reach Your Hand, Ha-bimah', *Bama*, 1 (20), 1939.
7. Feingold, *Ha-tzofe*, 9 May 1996.
8. *Ma'ariv*, 3 May 1996.
9. S. Weitz, *Yediot Aharonot*, 19 Sep. 1993.
10. Jonathan Shahaf, *Ha-ir*, 18 Aug. 1995.
11. *Ha-tzofe*, 2 March 1995.
12. *Yediot Aharonot*, 31 May 1996.

Baalei Teshuva
('Returnees to the Religious Fold')
in Israeli Theatre

DAN URIAN

Baalei teshuva, the newly converted to ultra-Orthodoxy, like the religious who become secular, are 'in between' individuals from both sides of a deep schism in Israeli society. The complex and antagonistic relationship between the secular and the religious in Israel has provided an important role for theatre practitioners. These have variously placed their artistic talents either at the service of religion or against those who have 'returned to the religious fold'.

The religious community (the ultra-Orthodox and the Zionist), living among a secular majority, has in the last decade begun to direct its children into the 'media business' with the aid of the *baalei teshuva* and to create dramatic texts, mainly for television. Their main aims are practical: election propaganda, and video or audio recorded sermons, both for internal reinforcement among the community of believers and to present their viewpoints to the external secular community. The religious camp aims its words directly against the hegemonic group in Israeli society, with its preferential status in Israeli culture, and particularly against what it calls 'the threshold guardians' – the secular leaders and the media which they believe to be controlled by a secular Ashkenazi (Jews of European origin) elite to serve its own needs.[1] The theatrical-religious sermons are directed in the main to an audience of oriental origin, characterized by economic and social and cultural inferiority. The rabbis/preachers exploit the sense of frustration felt by their audience and attack the secular intelligentsia, the politicians, the media and the judiciary. They announce the failure of the Enlightenment movement (the *Haskala*) to achieve its prediction of a Judaism without religion, and proclaim the evil of the Zionist dream in creating a secular Jewish State – an absolute oxymoron from their point of view.

Dan Urian is Associate Professor of Theatre Studies, Tel-Aviv University.

The secular theatre, on its part, is attracted to the subject of conversion to ultra-Orthodoxy by its strangeness, and the sense of threat that it arouses among the secular audience. Proselytization is presented by the secular theatre in a negative light, to no small extent because of its success in attracting youth – many of whom are children of upper middle class parents of western origin.[2] The *baal teshuva* is characterized as one who is motivated by a sense of alienation towards the values of the society in which he lives;[3] his actions are thus also interpreted as harmful to the Zionist 'civil religion' and the secular culture, and as a harsh criticism of this way of life. This situation makes demands upon the theatre, which is perceived by its audience as a sort of 'secular synagogue' and which airs the various problems of concern to its audience.

Teshuva (the return to total observance of the Jewish Law) finds theatrical expression not only in the established theatre but also throughout the entire theatrical 'field'.[4] Any discussion of the subject cannot therefore restrict itself solely to theatre texts but must also examine other aspects, such as actors, entertainers, directors and playwrights.

ACTORS

Theatre artists, particularly actors, have a special place in Israeli society. They are perceived as 'Bohemians'; as a group of celebrities, much talked about, who behave according to their own liberal code. Their 'flamboyant' lifestyles occasionally supply material for newspaper gossip columns and they are depicted as the most secular of all – radical apostates – who repudiate all religion, including the 'civil religion'. Clearly, this image does not provide an accurate reflection of all actors, but there does appear to be a mitigating tendency towards tolerance by many people, who regard actors as an exception to the generally agreed rules of morality, and even accept their transgression of the law. Hanna Rovina, 'mother' of the Israeli theatre, was both an unmarried mother and the quite separate partner of a hard-drinking Bohemian poet. In the puritanical atmosphere of the 1930s, this provided an unending source of popular conversation: 'what no-one would have stood for from any other woman, they were ready to lovingly accept from Rovina'.[5] A later example of this lenient attitude to theatre practitioners is that of Uri Zohar, the noted actor, director and entertainer, who was tried for drug related offences in the 1970s, and whom we shall discuss later in detail. His behaviour in court was relaxed and even jocular and the press gave him favourable coverage.

Because of this image of a 'free life-style', unfettered by the accepted norms and moral code, actors who make the transition from secularity to keeping the religious commandments tend to shock the secular community and arouse their curiosity. The most prominent of such 'transitional' figures is Uri Zohar, who in his time managed to create for himself (in both his films and reality) the image of 'an aging Peter Pan'.[6] Zohar's transition to the 'other' world, in the mid-1980s, still provides a source of interest and amazement, anxiety and outright hostility. The writer and journalist Didi Menussi's reaction is typical: 'Uri Zohar was my friend 25 years ago, and I will never forget what he did to me. War has two situations: one, that you become a deserter; but that's nothing compared to a situation in which you become a traitor.'[7]

The acting profession, and the sensitivity it demands, lends the actors an openness to taking upon themselves other identities as a way of life. One can distinguish between two groups of actors: those who preserve their own identity while being able to adopt others on stage; and those who can only act and are, according to Donald Winnicott, 'completely at a loss when not in a role, and when not appreciated or applauded (acknowledged as existing)'.[8] Actors live under constant stress. They must carry out their 'mission' successfully while being totally exposed on stage to the audience. Their future is uncertain and the majority have no permanent job. This combination of insecurity and freedom of expression leads actors to situations of extremes. Those of them who seek a stable framework as a solution may reach religion, which offers them peace of mind, security and also 'a substitute parent'.[9] This may be a partial or full explanation for the *teshuva* of several well known actors: in the 1980s Uri Zohar, Ika Israeli, Mordechai ('Pupik') Arnon; in the 1990s Irit Sheleg, Shuli Rand, Iris Borer, Shmuel Vilozny and Yehuda Barkan.

The *trajectoire* of Irit Sheleg was meteoric.[10] In 1981, upon completing her studies at the age of 22, she was offered the role of Desdemona by the Cameri Theatre, in a period during which most young actors advanced only very slowly. The press treated her with admiration, also noting her outstanding beauty as a possible reason for her success. To the surprise of many she abandoned the 'safety', as she saw it, of mainstream theatre, for commercial theatre ('in commercial theatre I compete for every ticket').[11] She also gained experience in alternative fringe theatre, took part in several films, and in one of them, *Not for Broadcasting*, directed by Ya'ud Lebanon (1981), she appeared in the nude. Within the theatre Sheleg was perceived as 'unstable', living in a state of constant unease, which progressively worsened, eventually leading to her abandoning her acting career.[12]

Irit Sheleg attempts to explain the change in direction, her conversion to ultra-Orthodoxy, as beginning with her childhood. She describes her secular life as 'beautiful and successful' [and] 'in spite of that I felt a great emptiness and dissatisfaction inside, a constant hunger, and then you begin to ask questions'. She relates to her childhood in several respects: 'I grew up in a home without boundaries. Under such circumstances everything boils over. So you look for a lid.' She mentions a grandfather who for a long period provided a father figure for her and with whom she lived. Sheleg's memories of childhood provide some explanation for her *teshuva*: 'I think that it began at an early age. I remember myself playing truant from school and going to the beach. Sitting on the shore facing the open sea and beginning to feel a sense of yearning. And asking myself what I was yearning for.' She goes on to explain: 'I always remember myself as preoccupied with longings'.[13] Sheleg, who grew up 'in a house in which Judaism did not exist', began to study Judaism during her search for the meaning of longings in other areas – psychology, philosophy, the wisdom of the East. She connects the actual turnabout to a rabbi she met whose words affected her deeply and touched her heart. Listening to him aroused the same sense of yearning within her that she had experienced in her childhood:

> I remember the day ... I remember that moment ... I looked at the man and dropped my glance. *Awed for the first time in my life* [emphasis added]. He began to talk and he spoke and spoke ... he spoke about the immanence of the Torah. I did not understand a single word he said, but my soul must have understood every word. I simply felt that I was sitting there when suddenly a tap was turned on within me and I was crying and crying. Without knowing why I was crying. I wanted time to stand still and for me to go on listening to the rabbi. Those same *yearnings* [emphasis added] that I used to feel as a child on the seashore, I felt at that very moment.

Sheleg's description is similar to many other descriptions of situations in which, for similar reasons, a return to the religious fold is expedited by means of a key figure – a chosen agent – who may 'replace' the real parents. John Bowlby speaks of the 'attachment figure' as one's trusted companions:

> Human beings of all ages are happiest and able to deploy their talents to best advantage, when they are confident that, standing behind them, there are one or more trusted persons who will come to their aid should difficulties arise. The person trusted, also known as an attachment figure, can be considered as providing his (or her) companion with a secure base from which to operate.[14]

This attachment figure can be God himself (substituting for a father figure or a mother figure), but also an 'intermediary' figure – a preacher, priest, rabbi – who demonstrates by his faith the 'higher ideal in life'.[15] Uri Zohar describes such an attachment figure: 'This Jew to whom I owe my life', as an important figure in the change he underwent.[16] Yehuda Barkan, entertainer, actor and director, who was particularly famous for his candid camera films, which included pornographic scenes, also arrived at a stage of (partial) *teshuva* under the influence of the rabbis.[17]

Teshuva provides the actor with a protective framework, like a family, possibly as an answer to unsatisfied childhood needs, and particularly to a lifestyle devoid of any security. To supply these needs, shared by many secularists, the proselytizers employ the texts of their theatrical homilies and sermons as a strategy aimed at such 'conversions'.

THE DRAMATIC MARKETING OF *TESHUVA*

Proselytizers include among their persuasive techniques those of a dramatic nature.[18] In addition to booklets, posters and cassettes, they hold meetings in people's homes and give seminars and sermons to large audiences before which the most famous *baalei teshuva* appear, such as Uri Zohar, or the seekers of a Jewish way of life, such as Yehuda Barkan, who provide personal examples of a successful path. The actors appear in 'uniform', attesting to their choice – the full ultra-Orthodox garb in Zohar's case; beard, white skullcap and *tfillin* (phylacteries) for Barkan – publicly demonstrating their faith in their new path. 'Until today I was an actor, far from the Most Holy, blessed be He. Today I am an actor who believes in the Most Holy, and in the Creator of the Universe,' stated Barkan at one such gathering.[19] The choice of actor for such gatherings is frequently made according to the principle of casting for a theatre play.[20]

The majority of the texts used by the proselytizers set out from a standpoint close to that of their addressees and thus use the semiotic vocabulary and concepts of their audience. They organize group simulation games, a distinctly dramatic activity, during which the rabbis, lecturers and other team members play secular roles, while the secular participants represent the religious factor. The temporarily 'secular' rabbi tries to 'persuade' the genuinely secular person who is playing a religious role that it is permitted to travel on the Sabbath, while the secular person in his new role must marshal his arguments to the defence of religion. After all have reverted to their own identities, the path to persuasion is far easier.[21]

During such games the secular identity adopted by the proselytizer is generally one which does not disguise his religiosity. He may also play the role of a dramatic figure, adopting more sophisticated theatrical techniques.[22] Rabbi Benjy Levene, for example, from the 'Gesher' (bridge) organization, has been appearing in the play *The Four Faces of Israel* since 1978. He plays and manipulates fictitious characters before a mixed secular and religious audience. The play is didactic, of a comic-educational nature ('An Educational Comedy of Jewish Identity'). It is followed by discussion groups led by instructors. Rabbi Levene rationalizes the problematic and even forbidden choice (from the point of view of religious law) of the theatre medium, by his desire to introduce serious questions relating to the essence of the Jewish identity and to guide the spectators into considering and clarifying their viewpoints. He does not 'seek a comic performance'.[23] The contradiction in his approach, between his liberal attitude and his aim of proselytization, demonstrates the tension between the religious message and the theatrical frame associated with secularism.

Levene is not a self-declared proselytizer. He defines his activities and his organization as aimed at slowing down assimilation and as a barrier against 'corrupt western culture'.[24] While the play has no explicit appeal for *teshuva*, its aims are not far from those of a gathering directly intended as such. His comedy creates a renewed hierarchy of archetypes representing different value perspectives in Jewish Israeli society. The four figures in the play are: an elderly ultra-Orthodox man from Mea Shearim (an ultra-Orthodox neighbourhood in Jerusalem); a bus driver (representing the secular Israeli); an American tourist from the Jewish National Fund; and an assimilated Jewish artist of French origin living in Zefat and married to a Christian woman. The emphasis is on the positive nature of the religious figure and the ridiculous and lost nature of the other three. The play helps its religious audience to reinforce their directed beliefs, and its secular audience towards a 'soft' *teshuva*.

The play evolves as a series of interviews. One of the (female) instructors interviews Rabbi Levene in his four different roles. The order of appearance of the characters is significant. The first figure, presented in a positive light, is that of the ultra-Orthodox Jew; he is followed by the secular figures who represent disappointing alternatives.

The most problematic character from Levene's point of view is that of Jean-Paul Simon, the assimilated artist, because secular youth tend to identify with him. Levene accordingly frequently eliminates him from the performance. Jean-Paul offers a world vision that is cosmopolitan, anti-religious, peace loving, caring for all mankind – characteristics more likely to attract sympathy than to repulse. For Levene this is a threatening and frustrating character; a monster he himself has created. Levene succeeds in 'reducing' the artist by presenting him as someone who creates confused, unintelligible paintings, and who wears unusual attire – beret, socks with holes, a flamboyant belt.

The self-censorship reveals the difficulty faced by religious preachers when using dramatic techniques. These, by their very nature, are open to different readings, and different audiences may interpret them in a different way to that intended by the author; a deviation which may impede their effective instrumental use. It is thus possible that the videocassettes made by the proselytes, such as those in which Uri Zohar attacks the 'free' world vision, may be perceived by their secular spectators as simply an entertaining curiosity, as inarticulate texts, or even as a threat. They may, therefore, actually reinforce the secular and anti-religious viewpoint.

IDEOLOGICAL CONFLICT

Religious Jewish groups generally take a negative attitude to the theatre, neither making nor watching theatre unless for a 'didactic' or political purpose. Uri Zohar relates to his artistic past as an 'optical illusion':

The spectator sees on the stage that for others too life is full of contradictions and lack of meaning, and he leaves satisfied. This identification and release finds its expression – on another level – also on the football field or in a pornographic magazine. Shakespeare only adds philosophy, ideas and emotions. This approach is clearly anti-Torah and I will therefore not support it. Not as a spectator and not as a creative artist. The Torah deals with quite the opposite: man must discard the trivial and unessential and concentrate only on himself.[25]

Uri Zohar at first related sceptically to the possibility that he might harness his acting and directing talents for religious ends, through fear that he might not have an audience. His approach to the subject later changed and he currently makes frequent public appearances, mostly of a theatrical nature. His public sermons are recorded and edited on tape (audio and video) and he uses them to disseminate matters of *teshuva*. In contrast and opposition to such sermons, the secular theatre has staged various plays: *Trumpeldor 85* (1985) by Shimon Zimmer; *The Last Secularist* (1986) by Shmuel Hasfari; *In Reverse* (1986) by B. Michael, a religious journalist – the play is a sort of 'deconstruction' of a *teshuva* discourse; and *Entertainment as Halacha* (1994), a stand-up comedy show which includes a critical attitude to religious conversion, performed by two young religious-Zionist women. These plays reveal the objections raised to such conversions among both the secular and the religious-Zionist groups.

As an entertainer, Uri Zohar won great acclaim, more for his acting talent than for his humorous material. 'Uri Zohar,' wrote Yeshyahu Ben-Porat, 'his personal charm, his talent for acting and mimicry – is able to transmit across the stage even corny old jokes ... and he has the ability, as an individual, to elicit not only waves of laughter and thunderous applause, but something far more important and rare: a good mood and a tolerant one.'[26] As a preacher too, Zohar does not excel in interesting texts. 'His sermons are full of outworn clichés,' noted the religious writer Haim Be'er.[27] Zohar himself is aware of the effect of the publicity from his past. In his homilies, as in his films, he interweaves his own image into the text. The subject matter of his films deals with biographical occurrences contemporary to the time of each film.[28] Among those who watch his video *The Birth Pangs of Redemption*, and see Rabbi Uri Zohar garbed and hatted in black, there are possibly some who recognize the actor Uri Zohar, whose films are still frequently screened, displaying a naked upper torso, short pants and outrageous tricks. Zohar uses this tension between then and now, between the past 'sinner' whose pleasure seeking and flippancy are well documented, and the body language and rhetoric of an angry prophet publicly reproaching the sinful.

Most of the videotape of *The Birth Pangs of Redemption*[29] is taken up with Uri Zohar's appearance before an audience. He uses this appearance to appeal to two types of spectators – those in the auditorium and those watching the tape at home. The laughter and applause were edited onto the tape later. The accepted practice when filming a speech is usually to provide a view of the assembled audience. For the tape in question, however, the particular audience was not filmed in order to 'broaden' Zohar's appeal to a far wider audience.

The contents are directed at a working class audience of oriental origin. It is important to note in this connection that the secular Uri Zohar had been one of the most prominent representatives of that same elite Ashkenazi culture that had suppressed, according to his present version of events, those from an oriental background. From the first moment, Zohar teaches that we 'are living in terrible times' caused by the poisoning of souls by the 'guardians of the threshold'. The source of all evil, as pinpointed by all these homilies, is those secular Ashkenazis who are ashamed of their Jewishness; they and their failed Zionist religion, which is a later development of the Jewish Enlightenment. This dangerous situation will lead to assimilation and to destruction. However, there is a solution: *teshuva*, which will also lead to redemption.

One of the secular theatre's first reactions to the proselytic activity could be seen in *Trumpeldor 85* (1985) by Shimon Zimmer, directed by Yosef Karmon. In this satire the Minister of Defence appears at the home of a family who lost their son in the 1973 Yom Kippur War; he bemoans his troubles: a new war is about to break out and he does not have enough soldiers. The few who are left no longer have any ideals. He proposes to restore their son to life for one night, on condition that the following day the son will be prepared to set off once more for war 'with his former ideals'. The parents consent to the proposal and the son agrees to die once more. One of the characters in the play is a proselytizer who attempts to persuade the son to enter a Yeshiva (college of Torah education) instead of re-enlisting in the army; to choose Judaism over fulfilling the commands of the Zionist 'civil religion'. His speech is a parody of one of Uri Zohar's sermons:

> Shalom Jewish sinners ... shalom to the many sons with their parents ... the many parents with their sons ... shalom to a neighbourhood of sin ... to those fed up with hearing lectures on acupuncture... to those fed up with hearing about the hemispheres and meditation ... to those fed up with hearing about the holistic approach to healing chronic illness, to those fed up with hearing about herpes ... come, approach me, ye holy flock ... come and listen to me ye misguided souls ... I too was a secular pig ... I too was in the pit of sin and drugs ... I too smoked the sweet weed ... I too spilled my hot seed on vile pictures ... O God ... you have forsaken us. Abandoned in the rain ... I close my eyes ... and there is America ... on the shores of the Mississippi ... with greying beard – stands Herzl ... the man

who dreamed us ... the man who stood 100 years ago on the banks of the river in Vienna ... I look at him and his eyes touch mine ... and in his hand the broken Zionist dream ... assimilation ... and where he wished to take us before it all began ... to Uganda ...yes, to be Negroes ...

The new religiosity of conversion to ultra-Orthodoxy was written about by B. Michael (a religious journalist who lived among secular Jews), in a play aimed at 'revealing' the manipulation and ignorance of those with pretensions to 'knowing the right path'. *In Reverse* is an anti-sermon or stand-up comedy that mocks religious conversion, its arguments and the jargon of its emissaries and followers.

The proselytizer in the play is depicted as 'a magician who performs his magic tricks, but immediately reveals how he does them'.[30] The character refers to Uri Zohar, and to quotes from interviews with him. Zohar's mention of his secular past: 'I was okay, just as Adam and Eve were okay before they tasted the apple',[31] is developed in the play into a speech:

Tell me about drugs! I was there. Tell me about lechery! I was there. Tell me about profligacy, money, entertainment, alcohol, tomfoolery, publicity, high society — all those wonderful things that it takes to fill your lives nowadays — I was there! I've tasted that poison! You can't teach me anything new! And only now, from the place I'm at right now, can I see all these things in the right perspective: all is vanity! Folly! Misery! All the parties in the world, and all the money, and all the material pleasure that exists — are not worth even half of one Sabbath spent according to *halacha* in a Jewish house. That is true happiness. Perfect. Complete.

The methods used by the proselytizers are shown up by B. Michael, who critically breaks down the 'logic' of one of Zohar's sermons:

Perhaps you know Rabbi Uri Zohar — one of our great proselytizers. In an interview he once gave he said that the proof, which I shall now present to you, is one of the principal proofs which led to his own *teshuva*. It goes like this: In Leviticus Ch. 11 the Bible enumerates those animals which it is permitted to eat and those which are forbidden ... It is permitted to eat those which chew the cud and have cloven hoofs and forbidden to eat those which do not. These are things which even you know. Now, something interesting occurs there: the Bible determines that in all the world there are only three animals which chew the cud but do not have cloven hoofs: the camel, the coney and the hare ... So can you explain to me how Moses could establish this with such certainty? ... Only one being could provide such a guarantee: a superhuman being — the Creator of the World.

It's true – there is a small problem here; the rabbit and hare do not chew the cud ... so could it be possible that the Torah is mistaken? That Uri Zohar is mistaken? No! The rabbit and the hare are mistaken! They're simply felons.

The ending to *In Reverse* reveals conversion to ultra-Orthodoxy as a self-contradictory phenomenon and presents its messages as false:

If you simply remember what we have learned here today – that coercion – is love. A secularist – is a coward. Freedom – is rubbish. Science – is nonsense. Progress – is regression. Forward – is backward. And the main thing – there is only an answer where there are no questions – if you remember all that – I can relax. You, *all of you* [emphasis in the original], will eventually reach us ...

In Reverse attempts to reveal the 'pseudo-intellect' and 'pseudo-logic' employed by the proselytizers through their distortion of facts, misquotations and deliberately forced *gematria* (a form of numerology) games. Exposure of this deception reinforces the secular audience's objections; an audience which is well aware that efforts at *teshuva* are being directed at it and its values, and which fears the possible effect. For this audience, plays that ridicule religious conversion constitute a sort of exorcism ritual. Such a ritual can be found in the pointed satire by Shmuel Hasfari, *The Last Secularist* (1986), directed by the playwright at the Cameri Theatre. The events take place in an ultra-Orthodox state founded upon the ruins of the secular State of Israel. One of the scenes features a proselyte, a former entertainer, who needs to 'repent his dubious past' and who must 'turn a new page in a new artistic career' by farting the tune of *Ha-tikva*, the anthem of the Zionist State. Chupchik, the entertainer, has difficulty in producing farts. In order to help him, the ultra-Orthodox employ Pavlovian stimuli: they show him the flag of Israel and sound the siren for Remembrance Day.[32]

The ultra-Orthodox group has its own reservations regarding the *baalei teshuva*, and its attitude towards them is discriminatory.[33] A similar attitude, albeit more moderate, is shown by the religious Zionists.[34] One expression of this can be found in a stand-up comedy performance by two young religious women, Noya Shuster and Nurit Hadar, graduates of the Bnei Akiva youth movement, religious schooling and army service. They are exceptional in having undertaken graduate theatre studies and in performing before mixed audiences in stand-up comedy – a 'secular yuppie' genre. While the actresses themselves serve as 'intermediaries', thanks to their secular training and skill in this new (for the religiously observant) profession, they also take care to express their reservations regarding the *baalei teshuva*. Noya Shuster criticizes the religious conversion of the oriental Jews which, as she sees it, involves a payment, and finds even greater fault with the proselytizers. Her opinion on the subject of Uri Zohar is explicit: she sees him as a former secularist who following 'conversion' is now convinced that only he possesses the key to truth.[35] The two women present the entire attempt at proselytism as ridiculous and false, with one of them speaking as a *baal teshuva*:

> Lord, Lord of ... what's that? You've moved to here? You've been discovered by fans, they've come to ask for your autograph? Right. It really is better here. Fresh air, scenery ... Lord, is it alright for me to talk to you like this? After all, I've been a *baal teshuva* for one week ... but there are two sides to this two-way route. I've done my share, and you – what? Hear O Israel ... that's your name isn't it? Okay, you don't need to get upset, we've known each other for a week! Take care of the matter for me and I'll carry out the commandments for you, you've never seen anything like it ... the Ten Commandments? Big deal! Honour thy father – honoured. I'll honour my mother too. Thou shalt not kill – won't kill. Thou shalt not steal – I'll try ... Thou shalt not commit adultery – I haven't adulterated ... with the neighbour it's not adultery? Listen, your writing's not too clear! Okay, this evening for the last time. So what's to become of me? What shall I do? ... To come to you? No, thank you, no, no, I like to be close to earth, and I'm also afraid of heights.

The play was performed many times before religious-Zionist audiences who, according to the two actresses, did not appear to have any reservations about the monologue. The rabbis, too, who gave their blessing for the show, did not demand any form of censorship, which is informative regarding the suspicions and double-standard approach of the religious audience to the *baal teshuva* and his motives.

SEMIOTIC CONFLICT: LANGUAGE, BODY LANGUAGE, COSTUME, PLACE AND ACCESSORIES

The proselyte alters his language, clothing and habits, and a change also takes places in his personal standards and values. Accommodating to a new language reflects 'a deeper process of socialization'.[36] It constitutes an important element in the ideo-semiotic conflict between the two camps, also noticeable in their changed attitude to the body and in an altered use of body language, clothing and other accessories.

Uri Zohar displays a diminishing awareness of the type of style required to create a link with the audience, and perhaps also a diminished sense of value regarding one important achievement of Zionism – rebirth of the Hebrew language. There is a degree of protest in the choice of language used by the proselytes, particularly in the adoption of Yiddish, or the deliberately incorrect use of language.[37] In the secular plays, this mixture of styles and languages as part of a character design is used to depict the proselytizer as ridiculous and a cheat. The jargon that Yehoshua Sobol places in the mouth of the eponymous 'hero' in his translation of *Tartuffe* is that used by the proselytizers. The change of language and its fluctuations, the mixture of high and low styles, and religious and secular vocabularies, creates a new and self-contradictory language.

Tartuffe by Molière, staged by the Haifa Municipal Theatre (1985), was translated by Sobol into the language of proselytism during a period which witnessed the height of this phenomenon in Israel. The translator's overt attack on the proselytizers was 'served up' in Cleant's speech (*Tartuffe* I, 5):

> These people who with the fervour of *hypocritical messianity* [translator's addition, D.U.] rush around / to make a fortune, please God, and don't forget to demand / their pleasures between their prayers ... / These people who know how to suit their religion to their needs and desires, these are the scoundrels, the bearers of grudges, the peddlers of faith, the plotters / In their bitterness and wrath they endanger humanity / for no weapon sickens them / including the cynical use of the religious feelings of the people / and so they murder the soul of mankind in the most methodical way / *Recently* [emphasis mine, D.U.] the counterfeit types have become increasingly common.[38]

'If one chooses to stage *Tartuffe* today,' explains Sobol, 'it is because life in Israel is in the grip of madness, of religious sanctimoniousness and hypocrisy.' Regarding language, he notes: 'In translating, I set out from this reality and go towards Molière, with my ears echoing with the language of Shapira, Goren and Porush [noted rabbis and religious politicians in the 1980s]: "Kashrut supervisors", "sacrificial hen", "God be blessed", etc. Tartuffe interests me as a proselytizer, as a candidate for the Rabbinate, as a rabbi.'[39] Orgon, as a *baal teshuva*, in Sobol's version, adopts the language of the ultra-Orthodox, employing such expressions as 'a blessing for every deed', 'he has a watchful, wary and ultra-Orthodox eye', 'blessed be the Lord', 'as God wills', etc. This satiric depiction of Tartuffe reached its heights in the play in the courtship of Elmire. Tartuffe undresses before having intercourse with the wife of his friend, a pious man, and remains on stage with only his loins barely covered – and a skullcap on his head. In order to seduce Elmire into believing that they are not breaking any religious law, he tells her (in the Hebrew version): 'If you will become *teshuva*, I'll introduce you to the orchards of the Jewish law. I'll lead you by degrees to the practice and reveal to you the secret – if you only let me guide you in the way of the flesh' (80–81).

At the close of the twentieth century, which worships the body, it is the spirit or soul that presents a problem for the body,[40] in contrast to both Christian and Jewish religious concepts, which perceive the body as a restricting obstacle, a confining vessel whose desires must be overcome.[41] The contrasting perceptions of the body by the secular and the religious are featured in *Boochie* (1984) by Yosef Bar-Yosef, staged at the Haifa Municipal Theatre under the direction of Gedalia Besser, and adapted for television (1991) by Gilad Evron, directed by Ram Levy. The religious characters in the play cover up their bodies and obscure their physical and sexual identities, hiding behind black suits, voluminous dresses and head coverings. Baruch (Boochie) the son, who has suddenly returned to his father's house from the outside (secular) world, to seek refuge from his creditors, uncovers the hidden physical sexuality. When Boochie sings in the shower, his ultra-Orthodox brother-in-law says of the secular: 'Their bodies make them happy.'[42] His sister, ultra-Orthodox and married, confesses to Boochie her love for another man: 'With him I feel naked,' she repeats several times, raising her voice: 'Naked! Naked! Naked!' And he shushes her: 'Enough. Naked is only once. It's not Holy, Holy, Holy!' (91). Boochie's encounter with a young ultra-Orthodox woman, who wants to cross over to secularism, almost ends in lovemaking. She displays her body to him, rolls down her black stockings and hikes up her dress. Boochie: 'Here too they take off their clothes for me. What am I, a shower?' (94).

The first theatre text to present the feminine aspect of proselytism was *One Hundred New Apples Including VAT* (1996) by Ora Morag and Israel Gurion. It is the story of a secular woman coerced into *teshuva* by her husband. She recounts her story after separating from her husband and religious life. The play was staged by a commercial theatre with the apparent aim of pure entertainment. However, every peek by critical secular eyes into the ultra-Orthodox world heightens the conflict between the two worlds and discloses the clash of ideologies.

The play is a humorous report on the phenomenon of 'following the husband's footsteps' and to a great extent also the footsteps of a tyranny which increases with proselytism. The woman is forced to adapt to a new world which condemns her. In addition to the obligation of providing a livelihood, she must also adjust to the hard labour of housework in a home which upholds all the commandments of Judaism. She must come to terms with a husband who has altered all his habits and begun to speak Yiddish. The most extreme change takes place in the attitude to the body and sex. She wears clothing that suffocates her: 'I'm hot. I'm hot – inside the clothes.' However, one good point that she finds in the ultra-Orthodox way of life is that the man does not need to overcome his bodily urges – his new religion does not permit him to do so: 'Whoever wants to quit – please do so, there is Christianity! ... but no need to struggle in Judaism. You must be with a woman – and lustily. The commandment says: sow thy seed and multiply and pleasure thy wife.' Most of the scenes in the play disclose the sexual urges and physicality beneath the trappings of religious conversion, and the legitimization of 'quickie sex'. A deliberate tension is created between the constant attempt on the part of the husband and the Orthodox community to compel modesty and head to foot clothing – in one scene the husband demands that his wife wear a long skirt and not pants, returning repeatedly to button up her shirt – and between an intensive sex life on the other hand ('highly advisable for she who wants to invigorate her sex life'). The wife reiterates how she achieved a compromise with her husband over the commandment of immersion in the *mikveh* (ritual bath) – a walk to the sea and a naked dip followed by making love: 'This isn't the man I married. Such a wild animal! Such urges!' Like other theatre texts, this play too deliberately exposes the physical weaknesses of those who hide beneath the trappings of religion, in order to refute the uniqueness of their beliefs.

Covering up the head and body is highly important in the ultra-Orthodox world and is featured as such on the secular stage. The *teshuva* of Boochie too in Bar-Yossef's play is accompanied by a change of clothing. In the television version, after he moves into the Orthodox neighbourhood, he begins to wear a skullcap and exchanges his jeans and red-flowered shirt for the Orthodox black garb, but with a glimpse of his former clothing still showing. In contrast to the skullcap that he puts on, his sister removes her head covering when confessing her forbidden love for another man (91). Boochie, who is marking his change in identity by means of his black garb, has previously referred to the prayer chanting, ultra-Orthodox Jews who accompany his dying father as 'three stinking black coats' (72). Leah, the young ultra-Orthodox girl, half questions, half determines: 'You're not really going to wear this coat are you? It's just Purim? …' (93), and he avoids answering.

Body language also serves in the conflict between the two camps on the stages of both preacher and actor. The body language of Uri Zohar in the videotape *The Birth Pangs of Redemption* is characterized by a great deal of gesticulation with the hands. Movement of the body, particularly the hands and mainly the index finger, draws attention, indicating and warning. Body movements accompanying references to the secular world are filmed from a low angle. In contrast, hand gestures accompanying references to religious belief are raised high with fingers curved at head height, forming a sort of dome or roof. The gesture accompanying the words 'we are with the Lord' reaches its climax with the final word, and is maintained frozen for several seconds. Zohar thus confers upon the word 'Lord' an aura of tremendous protection. In the final scene of the video, Zohar offers *teshuva* as a recipe for redemption and asks his listeners to take his words and make something of them. He extends the palms of his hands to his audience as if to say 'Take!', repeating this gesture several times, and then clenches his fists while saying 'with the help of God'. He ends with a gesture of throwing a ball into the audience, as if handing them God's will.

In contrast, and opposition, to Uri Zohar, the play *In Reverse* offers Alex Ansky, a well known actor and extremely popular radio presenter. Ansky wears for the purpose Uri Zohar's 'clothes' – beard, black hat, black coat and pants and white shirt. The role necessitated the secular actor becoming acquainted with a new body language, as can be learned from a description of one of the rehearsals:

> Ansky ... wears the expression of a professional proselytizer on his face. The face becomes as soft as jelly but eyes are burning with fire. The weight of the body is centered on the stomach. One hand strokes the beard. The change is quite startling. B. Michael, who is sitting at the side is called urgently when Ansky, out of secular bad habit, hooks a finger into the front of his trouser belt. 'Either behind your back', corrects B. Michael, 'or on the beard'.[43]

Desecration by Chonni Ha-meagel, staged at the Akko Festival of Fringe Theatre (1994), made semiotic use of the entire system of theatre signs in order to demonstrate the ridiculous nature of the *teshuva* gatherings. This was an experimental performance that critically examined religious ritual, particularly in Judaism. Prior to the performance the spectators were given two booklets: one was 'The Modern Testament' – a collection of selected texts from the *Shulhan Aruch* (codification of Jewish law compiled by Yossef Karo, first printed in 1565), including the rules governing the prohibition of the idle spilling of one's seed, the law of celibacy prior to a woman's menstrual period, toilet procedures and laws of atonement on the eve of Yom Kippur. In addition to the programme notes, a catalogue of swimsuits by a well known Israeli designer was also provided. Chonni Ha-meagel, himself from an ultra-Orthodox family, referred to the particular choice of text and audience:

> Each time I try to reach that same level of banality and naivete found in the Torah. It contains so many foolish and stupid things, not to mention immoral, to the extent that I think the Torah should be made illegal.... . The principal part of the play is the audience itself ... I tie them to their chairs, hand out *tallithot* [ritual prayer shawls], burn incense, give a few pills to intoxicate them and fly them high into the air with all my music.[44]

The theatre space, a Crusader Hall, was designed as a church-cum-synagogue. The spectators were asked to remove their shoes which were collected by one of the actresses, while another actor handed out *tfillin* (phylacteries). Both were dressed in robes reminiscent of the Hare Krishna sect. Various holy artefacts were scattered around, particularly on the dais in the front on which was set a Holy Ark with drawn curtains and candles, above which an illuminated sign displayed the prohibition 'Thou shalt not commit adultery'. Television screens showed scenes from Uri Zohar's secular films as well as videotapes by Zohar the proselytizer. The textual blend of the sacred and the secular in *Desecration*, the range of scenes dealing with the *halachic* attitude to various personal matters, and particularly the choice of videoclips of Uri Zohar, combined to form a sort of lexicon of desecration; the complete opposite of the religious semiotic 'dictionary' used by the proselytizers in their appearances. The actors read out the passages from 'The Modern Testament'; actresses strode about attired in the fashionable swimsuits from the catalogue; from time to time a voice could be heard giving instructions to airline passengers; a nun passed by and stood next to the Holy Ark; the Ten Commandments were screened on an electronic board; actresses performed a striptease and one of them masturbated in front of the audience. All this was accompanied by heavy rock music. One scene that particularly focused audience attention was a 'number' performed by a preacher/magician who succeeded first in pulling a dove out of the Holy Scripture and releasing it, and then slaughtered a chicken in a cruel ritual of atonement – 'angering' one of the actresses who played an enraged member of the audience.

One play featuring an especially vehement objection to proselytism was *Dinner* by Amir Orian, which ran for one year (1985–86) at the Heder (room) Theatre, to an audience numbering only fourteen. It was subtitled 'A Lesson in *Shulhan Aruch* to an Audience of Forced Proselytes'. (The Hebrew word *be-koach* [forced] in this case acquires the double meaning of possibility and coercion.) In the course of the evening 'the company of actors taught the audience the correct way to be good Jews'.[45] According to Orian, this was an extremely difficult performance for both actors and audience, particularly the scene of ritual slaughter of the hen, which was then cooked and served to the spectators.

Amir Orian designed his play to 'counterattack' Israeli culture and its theatre of the 1980s; a culture which he sees as being pseudo-religious nationalist.[46] He perceives the *teshuva* phenomenon as one indication of this trend, which during the 1980s reached a peak in the number of new *baalei teshuva*.[47] Every possible theatrical means was enlisted in his play to highlight the more repugnant elements of the religious ritual. Orian explains his approach to religion and ritual (taking in *teshuva* along the way) using a Freudian interpretation, principally the distinction between the 'death' of the individual personality necessitated by religious life, and that of a 'free', secular way of life:

> The ritual tool symbolizing the spirit of the group is the totem, at which are directed all the commandments and prohibitions connected with the ceremony. In this case, the hen is the totem and the taboo concerning what is permitted or forbidden relates to it. It is a father figure, a god, authority, the manifestation of all these fundamentals ... the spirit of the totem is assimilated into the body of the believer and becomes part of him. The believer can discharge the totem, or reject it. He can continue to identify with the totem until death. Assimilation in this case means identification. Rejection is non-identification. If the players/believers go all the way in the

direction of identification, they will also have to accept, during the process of assimilation, the fact of the death of the totem within themselves. They must either die or cease the ceremony. In other words: *the religious ritual is a form of death*, [emphasis mine, D.U.] the death of the personality and its entry into an accumulated situation that is locked in and sealed. Another possibility is to cease the ritual in order to preserve a situation in which life flows freely without predetermined fixed borders.[48]

The main part of the event takes place at its end, during which the spectators 'are programmed' to choose rejection of the religious ritual, by rejecting death of the individual personality. To achieve this, a process of 'deconstruction' of the ritual act is suggested, aided by the verses that have accompanied the play: 'Everything spoken by the actors has been taken from various holy scriptures. The pieces will be collected together and used according to existing conditions on the spot at any moment. The text is not fixed' (28). The slaughter of the hen is particularly hard to take, carried out according to all the requirements of the laws of kosher slaughtering. A tray, bowl for the blood, chopping board, knife – all the accessories of ritual slaughter are provided. The scene mainly emphasizes the contrast between the secular and religious viewpoints and rejects any illusion of compromise:

> The man/son says: 'this is our atonement', and slaughters the hen ... The audience appears to belong to the community of those who have totally lost their way, and the standard slaughter procedure may be interpreted by them as inhumane, and possibly is so from their viewpoint. However, as one knows, between humane thinking and kosher slaughtering or any other ritual act ... any similarity is purely coincidental ... The women [proselytes, D.U.] are in fact given the task of directing the secular audience's attention to the more acceptable and convenient characteristics. They are charged with pimping for religion. (32)

The secular theatre, in these and similar plays, offers the audience a means of auto-immunization against *teshuva*. The secular approach holds the view of sober and independent confrontation with reality and rejects religion as a totalitarian authority. The conflict between religious and secular texts is thus mainly reflected in either the need for such texts or the open rejection of any authority that could be termed 'parental'.

A LACK OF PATERNAL AFFECTION

Freud perceived a belief in God and religion as a fixated longing for the all-protective father figure, an expression of a desire for help. Psychoanalysis, in contrast, aims at helping one to rely only on one's own strength, intelligence and skills. Freud clarified his ideas in one of his later lectures:

[It] is easy to understand how it is that the comforting promises of protection and the severe ethical commands are found together with the cosmogony. For the same individual to whom the child owes its own existence, the father (or, more correctly, the parental function which is composed of the father and the mother) has protected and watched over the weak and helpless child, exposed as it is to all the dangers which threaten in the external world; in its father's care it felt itself safe. Even the grown man, though he may know that he possesses greater strength, and though he has greater insight into the dangers of life, rightly feels that fundamentally he is just as helpless and unprotected as he was in childhood and that in relation to the external world he is still a child. Even now, therefore, he cannot give up the protection which he has enjoyed as a child. But he has long ago realized that his father is a being with strictly limited powers and by no means endowed with every desirable attribute. He therefore looks back to the memory-image of the overrated father of his childhood, exalts it into a Deity, and brings it into the present and into reality. The emotional strength of this memory-image and the lasting nature of his need for protection are the two supports of his belief in God.[49]

Changing one's religious beliefs may have causal links with the family history of the proselytes. The choice of God, with or without the mediation of a proselytizer, in many instances effectively provides a parental substitute. In Israeli culture such a choice of 'parent' contrasts utterly with the secular parents who have abandoned the religious path and Jewish tradition. One interesting expression of this is exemplified in Yariv Ben-Aharon, son of Yitzhak Ben-Aharon, one of the leaders of the Ha-kibbutz Ha-meuhad Movement and the Zionist-Socialist Worker's Movement. Yariv criticizes his father's exchange of Judaism for socialism and has returned to the perception of the world and the study – albeit without fulfilling the *mitzvot* (commandments incumbent upon Jews to perform) – of the Jewish texts of his grandfather. In a novel he wrote, Yariv describes his difficulties:

Peleg wonders: Did his father, who in his heart abolished the Diaspora, banish at the same moment God from the land? Did he distance God from his son in order to rule him with his own god of integrity, or did all this happen simply to distance him from the God of his grandfather?[50]

This pattern includes the 'grandfather' figure employed by Rabbi Benjy Levene from Mea Shearim. By using such a figure, Levene circumvents the father figure who has become secular and 'returns' the secular spectator to the grandfather he may have had. Other proselytizers too cultivate the authoritative characteristics of a father figure.[51] In contrast to such figures are the prominent caricatures of frightening and even emasculating father figures in secular plays such as *In Reverse* and *Dinner*.

Yosef Bar-Yosef remembers how his ultra-Orthodox father, the writer Yehoshua Bar-Yosef, looked before he became an apostate: 'I remember him dimly, wearing a long coat, hat, beard, sidelocks. I myself had already spent two years studying in a *heder*.'[52] The father, newly secular, worked for a newspaper and the family moved to live in the socialist-Zionist Borochov neighbourhood of Tel-Aviv. Yosef was transferred from the Jerusalem *heder* to a school in Borochov. Like the character of the young girl Leah in *Boochie*, he too mumbled 'there is no God', to see whether the skies would tremble. His mother remained religious. The child grew up between these two worlds, eventually joining Ha-shomer Ha-tzair (a left wing youth movement): 'My statement is not against religion or secularism,' explains the playwright,

> for between the extremes of religious law practiced by the father, and the mendacious frivolity of the son, there are other ways of existence. As a religious and a secular being, this time I chose a conflict. If there is any statement here at all, it is about the seriousness of both sides. Each side needs to know that it pays a price, for it chooses its own side and not the other.[53]

At one of the turning points in *Boochie*, the protagonist says (in amazement or irony or both): 'I really will return to the fold one day' (39). His *teshuva* is linked to his confused relationship with his sick and dying ultra-Orthodox father. Boochie, who has got into bad company, left his parents' home twelve years ago and has now returned, afraid of his pursuing creditors. He wants his inheritance as well as to solve his relationship with his father. Bar-Yosef explains: 'My play about the Orthodox is about a son seeking his father's love.'[54] The play features many aspects of father–son relationships, particularly that between Boochie and his father, but also between Boochie and his own son, as well as between Boochie's father Eliyahu and his father. The various comparisons heighten the gap. Eliyahu's father says about Eliyahu that 'he knows what he's doing, you can rely on him' (97), and Boochie reacts sorrowfully: 'My father never said anything like that to me' (ibid.). And, following this line of thought, Boochie speaks about his own son: 'I've left the children. A week ago my son stood opposite me with a breadknife, like this! You remember? Like I stood opposite you, with a breadknife!' (99).

The father–son relationships in *Boochie* attain a 'theological' dimension when Boochie's brother-in-law Nissan explains why the creation of the world by God is preferable to Darwin's theory of evolution: 'Why choose an ape father when one can choose our Father in Heaven? It's true that a great and terrible father is more difficult; the more possessions one has the more one worries. But does anyone throw out his possessions because of the difficulty?' (69). In this way, he also bestows upon Eliyahu his father-in-law as 'a great and terrible father' – a sort of god-like image. And indeed, Boochie recalls resentfully, 'when did he ever tell us such stories when we were kids? When did he ever hold our hands?' (85). 'When my skullcap fell off I was afraid he'd hear it in his room. A disaster' (92). 'We never talked,' he tells his father sorrowfully,

> you only asked me: Where did you pray? Now too. I am not a small child any longer. Your father said about you 'you can rely on him'. You never ever trusted me. Before I even opened my mouth you said 'go on, start lying!' I lied ... I deserve a father, any father, don't I? Why me, why is my father my father only together with God, with the synagogue? I don't believe, I can't, simply can't, it's too much for me, you must understand this. I've nowhere to go but to you, not there, not here, only you still remain. (99)

Only death makes peace between them: 'When you die you embrace me, dead, only dead can I embrace you' (100). Bar-Yosef comments on Boochie's *teshuva*: 'All the "conversions" that we witness, are by the nature of things due to a deep *lack*' (emphasis added).[55] However, religious conversion, in this version, does not heal the pain caused by a father's lack of paternal affection.

In theatre, in its widest sense, two contrasting viewpoints come into conflict: the secular and the religious. The 'vocabulary' of this theatre is a restricted one; the characters, arguments and judgements delivered repeat themselves. One particularly prominent feature is the need for a strong father (=god) figure on the one side and a need to free oneself from such a figure on the other side. There are many for whom Judaism is identified with the grandfather from the Diaspora; this may awaken nostalgic yearnings, but also criticism and even aversion or 'self-hatred'. The father figure who became secular upon his immigration to Eretz Israel plays a central role in this connection. He represents the possibilities of a life unencumbered by any transcendent authority, through negating the illusions found in religion, and affirming the validity of dealing with human reality with all its difficulties, on one's own. It is no coincidence that the proselytizers have much dealing with grandfather–father–son relationships. Uri Zohar 'remembers' his grandfather, who perished in the holocaust, 'because of those clothes. Because of the skullcap'. Although he is 'not angry' with his father who became secular, he does note with satisfaction that his father eventually followed in his footsteps and 'at the age of 70 chose the *teshuva*'. He praises in particular his own son, 'who turned me into a father' and customarily rises in his presence to show respect.

The proselytizers lead their followers, by means of public appearances and gatherings, away from the postmodern world in which there has occurred what Jean-François Lyotard calls an 'incredulity regarding meta-narratives',[56] towards a safe reality in which sons need a 'father' and such fatherhood is ritually manifested. In contrast, the theatre reinforces the secular identity while uncovering what it perceives as a ridiculous and false path back to Judaism, and the pitiful weakness of those who are in need of an authoritative father figure.

NOTES

1. Tamar El-Or, '"*Tinokot she-nishbu*": Perception of Secularity among the Ultra-Orthodox', *Megemot*, Vol. 34, No. 1 (1991), especially pp. 113–16.
2. Yehudit El-Dor, 'Types of Perspective and Attitudes regarding Teshuva among High School Students', MA Thesis, Tel-Aviv University, 1985 (Hebrew).
3. Shaul Meizlish, *Return to Judaism* (Givatayin, 1984) (Hebrew); Janet Aviad, *Return to Judaism: A Religious Renewal in Israel* (Chicago and London, 1983).
4. The term 'field' (*champ*) was coined by Pierre Bourdieu. Bourdieu's concept *champ* is a complex one. It can nonetheless be characterized as a collection of common factors and strategies in a particular connection – like an economic, political or religious field – influenced by other fields: political social, economic, artistic, etc. The field is delineated by both positive and negative factors. In connection with the theatre, for example, the constant competition between mainstream theatre and experimental or 'alternative' theatre has worked to shape both competitors. One advantage to Bourdieu's concept lies in bringing the cultural products close to the field of production. He includes in the 'field' all those same factors that other theories (excluding that of Richard Schechner) still hesitate to incorporate, such as: the playwright's, director's or actors' social biographies; the historical and economic circumstances under which the text was created; the audience and its social characteristics; means of materializing the text; marketing, public relations, advertising etc. All these play an important and possibly decisive part in the creation of 'cultural products' – artistic works and theatrical performances. Pierre Bourdieu, *Les Règles de l'Art* (Paris, Seuil, 1992), pp. 201–45, 249–91.
5. Carmit Gai, *Hanna Rovina* (Tel-Aviv, 1995), p. 186 (Hebrew).
6. Renan Shor, 'Aging Children', *Kolnoa 75* (April–May 1975), 4–17 (Hebrew).
7. Yirmy Amir, 'Every morning I connect with the *tfillin* to the Most Holy Blessed Be He', *Yediot Aharonot, 7 Yamim*, 1 March 1996 (Hebrew).
8. D.W. Winnicott, 'Ego Distortion in Terms of True and False Self', *The Maturational Process and the Facilitation Environment: Studies in the Theory of Emotional Development* (London, 1990), p. 150.
9. Antti Oksanen, *Religious Conversion: A Meta-Analytical Study* (Lund, 1994), pp. 29–30.
10. I use the term *trajectoire* as distinct from biography, in the meaning given by Pierre Bourdieu (*Les Regles de l'Art*, pp. 359–63).
11. Author's interview with Irit Sheleg on 9 Jan. 1996. All further quotations are taken from the same interview.
12. Amalia Argaman-Barnea, 'Returning to Herself', *Yediot Aharonot*, 3 Aug. 1988 (Hebrew).
13. The decisive role played by parents in their children's tending toward religion can be learned from the actor Shuli Rand. Rand was born into a religious home and at a very young age became secular, following two family tragedies: his older brother died and shortly afterwards a sister was born with Down's Syndrome. His parents explained these tragedies to him, according to their religious reasoning, as God taking back for himself the good children. Shuli Rand, the child who feared that God would take him too, began secretly to avoid carrying out the religious commandments, removing his skullcap, turning on the lights on the Sabbath – until reaching secularity. He is currently undergoing religious conversion, which he explains as a return to those sources to which he belongs; from an interview with Cobi Midan, 'Nocturnal Meeting', Israeli Television, Channel 2, 30 Jan. 1996.
14. John Bowlby, *Making and Breaking of Affectional Bonds* (London, 1979), p. 103.
15. Research by Antti Oksanen into religious conversion has revealed hundreds of such

cases linked to John Bowlby's attachment theory. A key figure in the process of religious conversion according to Oksanen is 'the attachment figure' who may 'replace' the parents. According to this theory, individuals of any age are happier and better able to utilize their talents if they believe that another (or several other) figures will come to their help in times of difficulty (*Religious Conversion*, pp. 129–58).
16. From an interview with Yael Dan, 'Personal Story', Israeli Television, Channel 1, 5 May 1996.
17. Amir, 'Every Morning'.
18. On the uses of advanced modern technologies for reinforcing traditional religious values, see David Chaney, *Fictions of Collective Life* (London and New York, 1993), p. 177. See also reference by Ali Yassif to audio and video tapes as 'an example of proselytization strategy: using recognized symbols from the secular world – radio and television – in order to bring about their destruction'. Ali Yassif, 'Tales of Religious Conversion: Rhetoric, Folklore and Ideology in Israeli Reality', *Pages for Literary Research*, 9 (1993–94), p. 128 (Hebrew). He goes on to study 'dramatic-theatrical techniques' of one of the proselytizers (p. 142).
19. Amir, 'Every Morning'.
20. Michael Quinn claims that 'there is something in the dramatic performance that causes the spectator to seek information about the personal life of the actor and to store this "life" in a celebrity box'. Moreover, the famous figure, the celebrity, may be an agent for the strategy of a certain ideological approach; see M.L. Quinn, 'Celebrity and the Semiotics of Acting', *New Theatre Quarterly*, 22 May 1990, pp. 4–161.
21. Meizlish, *Return to Judaism*, p. 160.
22. Yassif, 'Tales of Religious Conversion'.
23. From an interview in the *Jerusalem Post*, 30 Dec. 1988. Meizlish, a supporter of *teshuva*, includes the Gesher organization among the proselytizing bodies; see Meizlish, *Return to Judaism*, pp. 26, 148.
24. From the programme notes to Levene's show *The Four Faces of Israel*.
25. Meizlish, *Return to Judaism*, pp. 47–8.
26. Yeshayahu Ben-Porat, 'Uri Zohar Vilified and Enchanted Me', *La-isha*, 25 June 1963 (Hebrew).
27. Haim Be'er, 'Local Hero', *Davar*, 2 December 1983.
28. Renan Shor, 'The Cinematic Experience – the *Tsabar* Image in Uri Zohar's films', *Kolnoa* 78, No. 15–16 (1978), p. 41.
29. I would like to thank my students Lenny Shahaf and Erez Gottlieb of the Theatre Department of Tel-Aviv University who introduced me to the tape. Several of the analytic elements are taken from work carried out by them under my instruction.
30. From an interview with my student Osnat Ganor, 8 May 1995.
31. Meizlish, *Return to Judaism*, p. 44.
32. This scene aroused a stormy public debate; it was also censored. The official Board of Censors for Film and Theatre, which initially banned the entire play, eventually restricted itself to eliminating certain scenes including the above. The Board was convinced that the play 'greatly damages the basic values and feelings of a wide section of the public, both religious and secular', and is 'an inciting satire that may stir up hatred' (*Davar*, 1 Dec. 1986).
33. Elor, 'Tinokot She-nishbu', pp. 118–19.
34. Meizlish, *Return to Judaism*, pp. 168–9.
35. From an interview with Noya Shuster, 28 Jan. 1996.
36. Mordechai Rottenberg, *Seventy Faces of Life: A Sermonizing Biography as Personal Psychotherapy*, trans. from the English by Yitzhak Komem (Jerusalem, 1994), p. 205 (Hebrew).
37. Yassif ('Tales', p. 142) notes that the style of Nissim Yagen, a proselytizing sermonizer, tends towards 'sub-standard Hebrew ... he deliberately uses expressions and a vocabulary or broken language ... that speak to the less educated stratum of the population'. This is also the style used by Rabbi Amnon Yitzhak, who is also a proselytizer: 'When I was in a secular school, the biology teacher told me that my ancestors were apes. *Inteh wa abuk* (Arabic: you and your father) are monkeys, I told him (audience laughs). Then he showed me drawings of how such a little monkey becomes a lawyer (laughter). The next day the Bible teacher told me that God created us. I told him: Just a moment, yesterday the biology teacher said that I came from an

ape, who is right? Free choice, he told me. Okay, I understood. But during recess where do we play – on the ground or on the trees? (the audience is rocking in the aisles).' Gai Ben-Porat, 'He Takes Their Children', *Ha-ir*, 3 May 1996.
38. Molière, *Tartuffe*, Hebrew version: Yehoshua Sobol (Tel-Aviv, 1985), p. 21. Sobol retained Molière's text for the major part, only altering a few details. Nonetheless, the translation is in the main Jewish-Israeli and 'equivalent' expressions to the French change their meaning and anchor the play in its Israeli connection. Thus, for example, 'Lately' is the translator's addition that brings the play closer to the phenomenon of *teshuva*, which reached one of its high points in the middle of the 1980s.
39. Hanna Rosenthal, 'Tartuffe as a proselytizer', *Al Ha-mishmar*, 21 March 1985.
40. Anthony Synnott, *The Body Social: Symbolism, Self and Society* (London and New York, 1993), pp. 34, 36.
41. David Biale, *Eros and the Jews* (Tel-Aviv, 1994), p. 13 (Hebrew).
42. Yossef Bar-Yossef, 'Boochie', *Difficult People: Four Plays* (Tel-Aviv, 1986), p. 66 (Hebrew).
43. Michal Kapra, 'Or Revers Yeshiva', *Ma'ariv*, 7 Nov. 1987 (Hebrew).
44. *Telegraph*, Haifa and the North, Journal of the Festival, 22–23 Sep. 1994 (Hebrew).
45. From an interview with Amir Orian, 30 Jan. 1996.
46. Among the texts that accompanied the play were verses from the book of Genesis (15: 18–21), the covenant between Abraham and God which gave the theatrical event political significance, especially during the 1980s when the right wing government policymakers tended towards a vision of Greater Israel.
47. Meizlish, *Return to Judaism*, p. 14. In 1983 their numbers reached 11,000. The first half of the 1990s has seen a rise in the number of *baalei teshuva* (no precise numbers available).
48. Amir Orian, *The Heder [room] Theatre. A New Definition of a Theatrical Term: 'Dinner'* (Tel-Aviv, 1985), pp. 24–5 (Hebrew).
49. Sigmund Freud, 'A Philosophy of Life', *New Introductory Lectures on Psycho-Analysis*, trans. W.J. Sprott (London, 1949), pp. 208–9.
50. Yariv Ben-Aharon, *Peleg* (Tel-Aviv, 1993), p. 70; see also pp. 97–8 (Hebrew).
51. Yassif ('Tales', p. 144), introduces a sermon by Yagen which brings two father figures into confrontation: one, ridiculous, a secular father who is a professor ('threshold guardian') and his son who disparages him; the other, a noted rabbi whose son respects and honours him.
52. Emanuel Bar-Kedma, 'About People Who Wasted Their Lives', interview with Yossef Bar-Yossef, *Yediot Aharonot*, 24 Nov. 1989.
53. Sarit Fuchs, 'He Returned with No Answer', *Ma'ariv*, 2 Nov. 1984.
54. Seamus Finnegan, *James Joyce and the Israelites and Dialogues in Exile* (London, 1995), p. 71.
55. Hannah Rosenthal, 'There Is No God – Thank God', *Al Ha-mishmar*, 2 Nov. 1984.
56. Jean-François Lyotard, *The Postmodern Condition: A Report on Knowledge* trans. Geoffrey Bennington and Brian Massumi (Manchester, 1984), p. 46.

From Rejection to Recognition: Israeli Art and the Holocaust

DALIA MANOR

The absence of Israeli artists from an international exhibition that presented responses to the Holocaust by contemporary visual artists, mainly Jewish, may serve as a point of departure for this essay. This absence from the exhibition shown in London and entitled *After Auschwitz: Responses to the Holocaust in Contemporary Art*[1] can be construed as no more than the personal decision of one curator. But it may also signify the absence of the Holocaust from Israeli art, at least until very recently. Looking at a much wider review of the influence of the Holocaust on the visual arts such as the monumental survey by Ziva Amishai-Maisels (1993), one finds that Israeli artists represent around 15 per cent of the total discussed in the book.[2] However, many of these artists have only a minor impact on the Israeli art scene. Others have dealt with the Holocaust only on a limited scale. Some artists have dealt extensively with the Holocaust and are thus widely discussed in the book, most notably Mordechai Ardon, Shmuel Bak, Naftali Bezem and Yosl Bergner. Yet these artists, in spite of the respect and success they have gained in certain circles in Israel and abroad, have been rejected by mainstream Israeli art and the art establishment and have been marginalized in Israeli art history. Consequently, the presence of Holocaust related subjects in Israeli art has been minimal.

An illustration of this situation is the retrospective exhibition of Ardon held at the Tel-Aviv Museum of Art in 1985.[3] Ardon was 89 at the time and this was only his second one-man show in Israel since his arrival in the country in 1933. Just seven out of over 100 paintings in the exhibition came from public collections in Israel. One that came from abroad was Ardon's major work on the Holocaust, the triptych *Missa Dura* (1958–60) which includes a Hebrew text (Psalms 69) and thus was

---

Dalia Manor is a London-based art historian and critic.

said to be directed towards the Israeli public.⁴ This work has been in the collection of the Tate Gallery in London since 1963. In 1963, sometime before his first one-man show in Israel, Ardon was asked why he had previously refrained from exhibiting in Israel after living there for 30 years and holding such posts as the Director of Bezalel School of Art and the Artistic Adviser to the Ministry of Education and Culture. Ardon evaded answering but elsewhere in the interview he said: 'I have the feeling sometimes that I am isolated here [in Israel]. The artists here, as in Europe and maybe in America ... do not ask the questions that I ask. So I am a little isolated here ...'.⁵ Two years afterwards he moved to Paris to find a more understanding atmosphere.

In the story of Israeli art, Ardon was often given the role of 'Leader of the Opposition', the ultimate antagonist to the Abstract movement led by Yosef Zaritsky. Other members of this 'salon de refusés' are often overlooked even when the Holocaust in art is discussed.

In an article dedicated to Israeli artists in the catalogue of the exhibition held in Washington and titled *Burnt Whole: Contemporary Artists Reflect upon the Holocaust*, Sarit Shapira describes how the theme of the Holocaust has infiltrated Israeli art. She uses the word 'infiltrated' because, as she explains, 'at least in the most interesting work, it tends to appear as something that guides, even forces, associations with that tragedy yet avoids depiction, allegory, or metaphor for it'.⁶ Shapira here ignores the art that has treated the Holocaust directly or used allegory or metaphor and dismisses it as being either of no interest or no relevance, while clearly preferring works in which the memory of the Holocaust may exist in a hidden way, 'lying subliminally in their textures, distorting their "normalcy"'.⁷ This is not merely a question of personal choice, for Shapira follows a well established tendency in the historiography and criticism of Israeli art that gives preference to form over narrative and to language over symbol. Thus the artists who took a different path are dispossessed from history even in their own, so to speak, natural territory.

It is not my purpose here to defend these artists; they have their own defenders. Nor do I intend to analyze or judge the merit of their work. Rather, what I am after is the hows and whys of this rejection. What sort of ideological, political and cultural mechanism enabled Israeli art to establish itself in constant opposition to the problems aroused by the Holocaust? And how is this process reflected in the self-image of Israeli art *vis-à-vis* Jewish art and Jewish identity? The latter part of the essay will deal with the change of attitude towards the subject since the 1980s and the emergence of a new generation of artists who tackle it.

Why one looks for artistic responses to the Holocaust in Israel is, I think, self-explanatory, considering the importance of the Holocaust to the very existence of Israel. The fact that every official guest to Israel is taken to visit Yad Va-shem, the national Holocaust memorial, points to the concept that the acknowledgement of the tragedy of the destruction of European Jewry 50 years ago will create an understanding, hopefully a sympathetic one, as to the current problems of the State of Israel. This connection was made explicit in the Declaration of Independence in which the Holocaust serves as a major justification for Zionism and for the establishment of the State of Israel. Later on, the State had endowed the six million murdered Jews with a commemorative Israeli citizenship and consequently assumed the right to speak for the dead and represent the victims in the reparation agreement and most notably in the Eichmann trial, whereas the denial of the Holocaust was perceived as undermining the existence of Israel and legislation concerning this offence was issued by the Knesset in 1981.[8] According to 'revisionist' historian Tom Segev, the influence of the Holocaust affected some of the most crucial decisions in the history of Israel: the mass immigrations, the nuclear project in Dimona and the Six Day War of 1967.[9] While this may be somewhat of an overstatement, there is little doubt that the Holocaust has exacerbated Israel's inherent sense of vulnerability *vis-à-vis* its Arab neighbours.[10]

The way in which the connection between the State of Israel and the Holocaust is perceived in daily life is best exemplified by the act of commemoration: the proximity of the Days of Remembrance, one to the victims of the Holocaust and the other to Israelis who have fallen in the Arab–Israeli wars – one week separates the two days – and the growing similarity between the ceremonies of the two create not only a continuous time of bereavement and memorial but also a strong affinity between the dead.

The location of Yad Va-shem on Mount Herzl near the central military cemetery has similar implications, as do those monuments that associate the Holocaust with 'heroism'.[11] Holocaust museums exhibits that conclude the course of display with the establishment of the State of Israel, or monuments that bear the title of Holocaust and Revival (such as the Tel-Aviv monument by Igael Tumarkin), all point in the same direction.

All this notwithstanding, the Holocaust was for a long time Israel's greatest taboo. The literary response existed for many years on the periphery of literary life in Israel while the leading figures in Hebrew literature hardly broached the subject.[12] When they did, in poetry more that in prose, most importantly by Natan Altherman and Avraham Shlonsky, the form of a declamatory poem was used. The poet would then take the role of a leader who gives voice to the people as they have done with regards to other topics that concerned the Israeli society.[13] Elsewhere, the motifs of lament, protest and revenge had a strong presence in Hebrew poetry long before the Second World War. The work by survivors both in poetry and prose remained for the most part separated from mainstream literature,[14] whereas the native born writers, particularly the generation of the War of Independence, treated the

Holocaust in a superficial and stereotypical manner, unable to understand and often with a sense of shame, guilt and even loathing.[15]

In the field of drama a few plays in the 1950s put the Holocaust at the centre of the theatrical activity, usually focusing on themes of struggle and heroism such as the story of the female parachutist Hana Senesh or the Warsaw Ghetto revolt or different dramas that reflected the Israeli experience and point of view. Apart from a few exceptions in the 1960s, the subject disappeared from the stage until the 1980s when the new interest in it was characterized by confronting the taboos and challenging conventions in accordance with the tendency of political theatre that was prevalent at the time.[16] Politicizing the Holocaust however was not unique to the theatre, which often reacted against the growing use of the Holocaust as an argument in political debate. This attitude became widespread after the change of government in 1977 from Labour to Likud.[17]

Since the 1980s the Holocaust has had a constant presence in Israel's cultural agenda, whether in the increased number of academic research on various aspects of the subject or by artistic expression in theatre, cinema, television, literature, and even in popular music. The visual arts somehow have not kept pace, and despite the wide acknowledgement of the tremendous impact of the Holocaust on life in contemporary Israel the subject has remained relatively marginal in the art even within the context of relevant issues of anxiety and identity.[18] Before the 1980s, artists who dealt with the Holocaust were even more marginalized and disregarded almost to the extent of non-existence. 'They were not modern', an influential figure in the Israeli art scene told me when I mentioned that there were few artists who treated the Holocaust in the early days. What does it mean, 'They were not modern' – this short and clear judgement that presumably put everything in its proper place? One is tempted to interpret it literally, namely, that being 'modern' was in contrast to working on themes of the Holocaust, which stood for something 'old' and out of date. Yet the statement 'They were not modern' apparently reflects the old debate of the 1940s and 1950s in Israeli art between figurative and abstract art. These artists were figurative and narrative whilst the cutting edge of Israeli modern art was abstract, or so it claimed to be. Later on when these figurative artists became commercially successful in the 1960s and 1970s they were even despised by the then young and rising conceptual artists and their supporters.[19]

Undoubtedly what was at stake could be described in artistic terms as a struggle between the avant-garde and conservatism: on one side there were progressive artists who wanted to free art from previous artistic and social conventions through changes and innovations in language and form. On the other, there were artists who were concerned above all with the message conveying moral issues and subject matter including traditional themes. And this is indeed how the big divide between Zaritsky and his followers on one hand, and Ardon and his followers on the other, has been usually described by historians and writers.[20] An interesting exception to this simplistic division is Igael Tumarkin, one of the most influential artists in Israel since the early 1960s. The fact that he deals with the Holocaust in a 'modern' way – that is, in semi-abstract compositions and expressive assemblages – strengthens the argument that the rejection of artists who painted Holocaust subjects was grounded essentially in stylistic and artistic principles.

Tumarkin was modern and therefore was accepted. However, it should be noted that Tumarkin's Holocaust themes were not interpreted as such, particularly when combined with other images of war and violence or incorporated in the recurrent motif of the Crucifixion in his work.[21] Since the 1980s, Tumarkin has expressed a more direct attitude towards the subject in his work, often employing a characteristic Holocaust symbol such as the rail track and even entitling some of his sculptures *Shoah* (not to be confused with his memorials to the Holocaust). Nevertheless, the interpretation of Tumarkin's art in relation to the trauma of the Holocaust is still rare.[22]

Apart from the artistic nature of the dispute mentioned above, it is no secret that an important part of it was the struggle between its two central protagonists, Zaritsky and Ardon. Similarly, the New Horizons group founded by Zaritsky in 1948 and often referred to as the most influential group of painters in Israel[23] is now understood to be a pressure group that demanded hegemony in the artistic field and fought for prestigious status for its members rather than for a particularly defined artistic belief, especially in the early years of its existence.[24]

Art politics and power games are often disguised by supreme values and progressive ideas. In this particular case there is more to it, and the core of the matter can be found in the way in which Israeli art is often defined: as a constant tension between the two poles, the Local and the Universal, or 'here' versus 'there'. As the discourse of Israeli art is so conveniently organized around this binary system, other options such as the issue of the Jewish identity of the artists is forgotten, or indeed pushed outside the system altogether and with it Jewish history and culture.[25] What is suggested here is that in the course of defining its own identity, a process which accompanies Israeli art from its very beginning, a partial 'solution' was found by repressing its Jewish affinity and by focusing on the local-universal concepts aiming to achieve both authenticity and acceptability. Through the concept of locality, Israeli art seeks its identity and uniqueness by emphasizing its relation to the place, the Land of Israel, and in particular to its physical properties such as the light, the climate and the landscape. The quest for the universal generally means the desire of the artists to belong to western modernism, both by following its current artistic trends and by considering themselves to be part of these trends. The conception of Israeli art as a kind of 'distant extension though close in time and spirit to European twentieth-century art', as Benjamin Tammuz put it,[26] has been accepted in one version or another by almost all interpreters of Israeli art. Yet not all of twentieth century art was suitable for adoption, and through a continuous process of selection Israeli art absorbed a specific 'French accent'. For many artists, in particular for the New Horizons group, the 'world' simply meant Paris.[27]

It is possible that the very question of identity in art and literature is in itself a Jewish characteristic, as the writer A.B. Yehoshua has suggested.[28] But in the historical account of Israeli art the question of what distinguishes Israeli art as such is declared to be totally separated from the question of what characterizes Jewish art.[29] No wonder that artists who were excluded from this discourse had also rejected its premises. Ardon said: 'I don't like to distinguish between Jewish and Israel. We say "Jewish" and mean the Diaspora, the negative side of our life, and "Israel" – the new type of Jew, the positive type. For me Jewish is an eternal conception, and for me Israel and Jewish are the same thing.'[30] Ardon here points to the central element in Zionist ideology which set its seal on most of Israeli culture. It is the attempt to create an alternative culture other than in the Diaspora in order to renew the nation and create the new Jew, the authentic Hebrew person, the opposite of the Diaspora Jew. The Hebrew term *Gola* or *Galut* (exile) with its negative connotations was in common use until not long ago in referring to the Diaspora. Hence the concept of *Shelilat Ha-galut* (negation of exile) is essential to the self-identity of Israeli Jews. The Holocaust strengthened the received stereotype of the passive Jews in exile who went like 'sheep to the slaughter', unlike the new Israeli Jews who would fight courageously to defend their homeland and their national independence.[31] Thus the tension between Israeli and Jewish existence is inseparable from the attitude of Israelis towards the Holocaust.

It is true that in the visual arts these notions are not as directly and explicitly manifested as in Hebrew literature. They exist, though sometimes under the surface, and may be reflected in different aspects of artistic life such as preferences in how and what to exhibit, criticism, interpretation and the status in the art field. It is worth mentioning that when historical or critical texts on Israeli art are written by non-Israeli writers the sharp edged polarity put by Zionist ideology between the Israeli and the Jewish is blunted or even disregarded. They would often prefer to put Israeli art within the context of Jewish art.

The very beginning of Israeli art is rooted in the Zionist enterprise – that is, the establishment of Bezalel Art School in Jerusalem in 1906. In the 1920s a young generation of artists, many of whom were previously Bezalel students, introduced a kind of oriental 'localism' which was different from the official Bezalel art. This was often called (by the artists themselves and subsequently by historians) the 'revolt' against Bezalel and referred to as the clash between Modernism and tradition. Yigal Zalmona describes the process as 'a fervent wish by the Modernists to create an original Jewish culture which would be antithetical to that of the art produced by Jews living in the Diaspora'.[32] Here Modernism is directly equated with Zionism and the claim for originality is based on the assumption that the work of Diaspora Jews belongs to the past, to a declining culture. The considerable contribution of Jewish artists in Europe and Russia to the Modernist movement at the time was either ignored or unknown, and in any case did not affect the unfavourable image of the *Galut* as promoted by Zionist ideology, and as has been absorbed and is still held by artists and writers. More than any specific style, the concept of negation of exile prevails in the art of the 1920s with the depiction in bright colours of the country's landscape and inhabitants and the favouring of a primitivist style and idealization of the Orient.

This art by painters such as Reuven Rubin, Nahum Gutman and others was soon rejected as romantic and nostalgic and not modern but the idea has not disappeared. It has re-emerged in the late 1930s and the 1940s with different accent on a regional identity based on the ancient cultures of the Near East by a group of writers and artists known as The Canaanites, who emphasized the schism between Judaism and 'Israelism'.[33]

Again, developments in the art are described in direct link to the ideology of negation of exile. When the extent of the Holocaust began to be known, writes Zalmona, 'the search for roots in the ancient Near East was given further impetus, fed by the desire to sever all ties with Europe'.[34] It was the age of myths; ancient myths were sought and a new myth emerged – that of the original new Jew, the native born Sabra, the healthy and proud deeply rooted youth also identified as the fierce fighter of the units of the PALMACH; in short, the ultimate contrast to the Diaspora Jew.

This was no atmosphere in which to accept imagery from the Holocaust. Marcel Janco had a first hand encounter with this rejection when trying to show drawings he made following the shocking events he experienced during the pogrom in Bucharest in 1941, shortly before his emigration. He also made drawings based on stories of survivors. As Janco attested later, when he showed these drawings to some fellow artists in Israel 'they all told me to leave it alone, that no Jew wanted to look at that'.[35] So he did, and concentrated on subjects of immigration, settlement and struggle for independence – typical themes in the history of modern Israel – before turning later on to abstraction.

For a short period in the 1930s, artists of Eretz Israel came under the influence of the Jewish School of Paris and its expressionistic manner, perhaps the outcome of disillusionment from the Orientalism of the 1920s and the hope for reconnection to the Jewish identity. At the same time German Expressionism was introduced by artists who came from Germany and central Europe following the rise of Nazism. Like many of their fellow German immigrants they confronted immense difficulties in absorption, refusing to give up values and culture they brought with them and of which they were proud, or to accept the cultural supremacy of the veteran population, mainly of east European origin, who already dominated the political and cultural power centres in Jewish Palestine.[36] In the history of Israeli art this conflict is known as the divide between the 'French School' of Israeli painting and the 'German School'. So much so that in the most comprehensive book so far on Israeli art the decade of the 1930s is split between two chapters by two different writers, one dedicated to the French influence and the other to the German influence.[37] Thus art historical writing perpetuates and justifies what was in fact a matter of social conflict between 'new' and 'old' immigrants who had different views of their own cultural identity. What other than the continuous dominance of the east European 'French' tendency in Israeli art can explain the inclusion in one chapter of this book of artists as diverse as Anna Ticho, who came from Vienna to Jerusalem in 1912 and made mostly landscape drawings, and the Polish born Holocaust survivor Osias Hofstatter, who immigrated in 1957 and painted distorted suffering figures; all under the title of the German influence of the 1930s! In a similar way, Amnon Barzel includes in the chapter on that era artists of a later period who dealt with the Holocaust and themes of immigration and refugees such as Bezem, Bak, Bergner, Ofek, Hofstatter and others.[38]

One may conclude that writers do not always know what to do with artists who do not fit the historical pattern dictated by the ideas of predominant groups and thus prefer to put all the odd ones together. It is most revealing, however, that in the art books the Holocaust is located within the period of the 1930s – before it actually happened – and it is directly related to the German Jews as if it was their problem alone.

Moreover, the subject is discussed as briefly as possible before moving on to the modernist movement of abstraction – the New Horizons group founded shortly after the establishment of the State. The enclosure of the Holocaust and the art related to it in the pre-State pre-modern period makes it easier to treat it as a separate event of another era, not really relevant to Israeli culture and history. At times these artists are discussed in later chapters, usually without going into too much detail, and in spite of the difference between them in styles and subjects they are always mentioned together as in a little ghetto outside history. Needless to say most of the rejected artists immigrated shortly before, during or after the Second World War, whereas the dominant groups consisted of established artists who had settled in the 1920s.

The appearance of the New Horizons group in 1948, writes Amnon Barzel, 'marked a meaningful schism between national, local, Jewish, figurative art, and the new idiom, which was universal and abstract'.[39] It was indeed significant that by now identity has shifted to another geography, packing together the local and the Jewish, and both are thrown away in favour of the new universalism. This image of the makers of 'the new idiom, which was universal and abstract' is undoubtedly what the group has chosen to put forward, not necessarily in accordance with reality as evident in the variety of styles and artistic beliefs among the group members. Moreover, they had not reached real abstract art until much later towards the end of the 1950s. Unlike Hebrew literature, Israeli visual art has not admitted to be in the service of ideology and the building of a new culture. To the present the New Horizon group is considered as the manifestation of art that is the expression of the individual and at the same time universal and modern. Nonetheless, the debates that accompanied the group's activity and above all the discussions on what distinguishes Israeli painting reveal how deep and urgent was the need to define the identity of Israeli art in national terms.

Progress was the keynote and in the words of Zaritsky 'the development in human society' and 'advance in science and technology changed the rhythm of our life and our point of view' and thus 'imposes on the artist new forms and new means of expression'.[40] 'Our life' for that matter had nothing to do with the reality of Israel in the 1950s as much as the conception of 'the development in human society' was detached from the horrors of recent history. Art for Zaritsky was autonomous and timeless, yearning to exist beyond permutations of life and time and at the same time to be part of an ideal vision of modernity, and should be judged only in terms of quality of pictorial language. Not all artists shared these convictions and some of them left the group, but the idea that abstract art is 'the new expression of the new man of our time', as Marcel Janco put it, an international language that does not need any literary subject,[41] had by the mid-1960s a strong hold in Israeli art.

The success of abstract art as a major trend in European and American art since the late 1940s through the 1950s and 1960s may be explained as a tendency to distance oneself from recent events of the Holocaust and to concentrate on 'pure' art.[42] Although this may well be true with regard to the rise of abstraction in Israeli art, it is also quite clear that the rejection of Holocaust related art had its roots elsewhere and was accompanied by the objection to all sorts of Jewish subject matter. Moreover, support for modern, abstract art was accompanied by continuous denouncing not only of representational art but also of the use of symbols and Jewish consciousness, as evident from the manifesto of the newly founded group Tatspit in 1964.[43] The possibility of the abstract and the Jewish in art as compatible concepts was not considered at the time,[44] nor was any notion of Jewish tradition as a source for universalism. Modern art was understood as a kind of Esperanto and it was the task of Israeli art to speak it fluently and professionally, perhaps with a local dialect, in order to be recognized and accepted in the international art scene. Never was this state of being challenged. Israeli art seems to have accepted its peripheral position where it is tuned to and measured by values determined out there in the centre. This acceptance nevertheless does not lack a certain degree of complaint.[45]

A young generation of artists, many of them native born, set out in the late 1960s and 1970s to make art by non-painterly conceptual means of collage, found objects, installation and performance, borrowing from current trends in American art and supported by the art establishment. The flag of universal avant-gardism was raised again but the content was often local: social and political issues, territorial disputes, the history and mythology of the country, environment and language. All these topics were approached with a strong sense of urgency and responsibility. With few exceptions, Israeli art of the 1970s was concerned with Israeliness, with collective identity and memory. It was, though, the identity and memory as built and perceived by the dominant group in the social and cultural structure of Israel, and up to 1977 also in its political system. The collective identity reflected in the avant-garde art of the 1970s was rooted in the ideas and values of what is known as the Zionist Left, or the Labour movement, that go back to the formative years of the Yishuv in the Second and Third Aliya.

An interesting case is the individualistic art of Yocheved Weinfeld that stems from her own experience. Weinfeld's performances and body art gained her a unique position in the art of the 1970s, but an important aspect of her work was overlooked at the time. She was the first Israeli artist to deal with the female body, body fluids and sexual politics. She also dealt with the Holocaust. It is rather surprising to see no mention of it in the catalogue of her solo exhibition at the Israel Museum in 1979 in which memories of her childhood were the sources of the images; a childhood in Poland were she was born in 1947 to Holocaust survivors.

Instead, the curator insists that 'the real subject of the exhibition is the process of image information, the complex operation in which visual images take shape and exist in the artist's mind'.[46] Reading her work in terms of process and formal language continues the way of modernist interpretation which was favoured by mainstream Israeli art. It was also a convenient means to evade confrontation with the images and their significance. One of Weinfeld's most powerful works points out the status of women in the concentration camps who as sexual slaves were both victims and victimizers. The artist's own memories of childhood combined with imagined memories of herself as a victim, the focusing on the body and sexuality and the use of photographs and objects were to become later on distinctive features in the work of other artist who are children of survivors.

THE HOLOCAUST IN ISRAELI ART 263

A considerable change in attitude towards issues of Jewish identity in Israeli art was apparent by the early 1980s. It was led by Moshe Gershuni, a prominent figure in the Conceptual art trend of the 1970s. The turning point in Gershuni's art occurred when he started to paint expressionistic paintings in violent gestures and crude colours that included written statements; many of them had a personal nature, figurative images, Jewish symbols and quotation from psalms, prayers and poems. The possibility of literary content in painting, previously unthinkable, was now eagerly adopted. This transition echoed a wider tendency in western contemporary art of the return to painting and the development of Neo-expressionism together with an interest in national and cultural identity. This trend and particularly its manifestation in the new German art was highly appreciated in Israel.[47]

In 1982 a special issue of the Israeli art magazine *Kav* was dedicated to the subject of locality and local identity in Israeli art. Gershuni who was born in Tel-Aviv in 1936 contributed a statement that opened with the words: 'I am a Jew! Yes, with all the mystique that it may imply. I am Israeli because I am Jewish, otherwise there is no need for me to be precisely here.'[48] Gershuni continues with the demand for a new interpretation of what is it to be a Jew in Israel, a question that became acute for many secular Israelis at the time.

FIGURE 1
MOSHE GERSHUNI
Justice Shall Walk Before Him, 1988. Painted dishes, 60 × 65 cm.

Gershuni's art does not refer to the Holocaust in any direct sense, and the Jewish elements in his work emerged as part of a complex process of confronting his own identity, including his sexual identity. Nonetheless themes of memorial, lament, comfort and forgiveness in his work suggest a constant presence of mourning and suffering in the Jewish culture, whereas Christian texts and symbols refer to the allurement to the rival culture. Above all, Gershuni is attracted to the most forbidden of all: the swastika, the symbol of supreme evil. In several works of the 1980s Gershuni incorporated the swastika and in some of them put it as the main image that dominates the painting. Through its immediate recognition as the symbol of Nazism, and consequently of the Holocaust, the swastika becomes in a kind of perverted way also the symbol of Jewish fate and history not unlike the (yellow) Star of David that features in many of Gershuni's paintings. The work *Justice Shall Walk before Him* (1988) consisted of four old dishes and combines these two Holocaust symbols. Gershuni painted the swastika on two dishes and wrote the Hebrew words 'Tzedek Le-fanav Yehalech' (Justice Shall Walk before Him) on the other two together with two Stars of David, one black and one yellow. The words (Psalms 85: 14) are part of a prayer recited at Jewish funeral processions. When written on the dishes a change of function is suggested from food dishes to vessels used in the rituals of Purification of the dead.[49] The straightforward juxtaposition of the Hebrew words and Star of David with the swastikas is startling at first, implying a dubious connection between the idea of justice and the notion of absolute evil. Is it not that the concept of justice in the acts of God has been utterly shattered, or at least seriously questioned in view of the Holocaust? And is it not that in the name of justice to the memory of the victims some unacceptable things are done?

Gershuni's work certainly does not offer any answer or clear statement. Rather it points to the mutability of concepts, values and symbols; that nothing is steady or in its place – even justice is on the move – and the past is inseparable from the present and from the future. Gershuni touches the issue of the Holocaust through one concentrated statement (the swastika), a single abstract sign, as if admitting this event to be so immense and thus beyond reasoning, comprehending or representation. It is obvious, though, that the subject can no longer be pushed to the far past and to the history of the Diaspora Jews as once many Israelis believed. Judging from the immediate positive responses to Gershuni's art one can conclude that he touched a sensitive nerve in Israeli society and expressed concerns of identity that were shared by many.

In the opened up atmosphere towards Holocaust related images that was created in the 1980s, much of it thanks to the prestigious status of Gershuni, the work of Osias Hofstatter now met a receptive attitude. Hofstatter was a survivor born in 1905 and immigrated in 1957. During the 1980s and 1990s he enjoyed a growing public recognition in

FIGURE 2
OSIAS HOFSTATTER
Grief, 1974. Ink on paper, 41 × 28 cm.

exhibitions, prizes, catalogues and films. His expressionistic style and the fact that his tormented grotesque figures have no direct Holocaust implications made his art more acceptable, though he always remained sideways.

The threat of a nuclear disaster brought artists from various countries to turn to the traumas of the past as indication to the future. The work of native born Aviva Uri, a prominent artist since the 1960s, underwent a certain change in the 1980s when her drawings became more wildly expressionistic, some representational images were added to her otherwise abstract style, and the theme of a catastrophe and total destruction obsessively occupied her. In a text about drawing she wrote: 'The line of our present days ... is a different line, completely different. It is hard for this line to be "pure", "beautiful", "clean"; the line of which Auschwitz and Hiroshima are his past and missiles of havoc his future.'[50] In some of her drawings Uri clearly indicates through signs such as the Star of David or Hebrew words the Jewish identity of the victim of such a disaster. Thus she suggests a more personal meaning to this worldwide angst, though not necessarily connected to the Holocaust. The theme of the victim can also be understood in Israel in relation to a sense of insecurity after many wars and continuous terrorism. Similarly, the motif

FIGURE 3
AVIVA URI
The Victim, 1985. Mixed media on paper, 148 × 102 cm. Private collection, Herzliya.

of the Aqedah, the Sacrifice of Isaac, that became rather frequent in Israeli art of the 1980s is interpreted in the context of either the Holocaust or the wars of Israel or both.[51]

For children of survivors the issue of the victim bears a closer and more personal meaning than the biblical myth. As the offsprings of victims they might have internalized the experience of their parents so that the Holocaust becomes part of their own biography. Artists who are children of survivors treat the subject in various ways. Yet there are common motifs that characterize the identity of children of survivors in general, as psychotherapist Dina Wardi has outlined: the identification with death; the identification with the victim and the aggressor; and the problem of sexual identity and self-esteem.[52]

In 1979 Yocheved Weinfeld made a series of ten wall collages consisting of photographs, objects and texts that were shown at the Israel Museum. A year earlier she said: 'Lately it has occurred to me that the two most important things that direct our life here are the Holocaust and Zionism. I have not sensed either of them personally... . I am now trying to find out how these two things affected me. This is the subject of my next show.'[53] Weinfeld may have attempted to connect the two but

FIGURE 4
YOCHEVED WEINFELD
Visual Images #8 (Detail), 1979. Mixed media, 162.5 × 307 cm.
The Israel Museum, Jerusalem

eventually her childhood experience of anti-semitism, of shame, fear and displacement feature in the majority of the works. One of the works related directly to the Holocaust, though to an issue hardly discussed since it involves no heroism, no meaningful sacrifice. In this work Yocheved Weinfeld put herself in a position of identification with the victim-aggressor, in this case the same women, through staged photographs of herself in the role of one of these women. The text to this work reads: 'In the concentration camps where all the Jews were dirty and hungry there were also beautiful women who the Germans loved. So the women would beat Jews and get food. Now they are being punished. Their heads are shaven.'[54]

As already mentioned, the signification of Weinfeld's act was not elaborated in the catalogue of her exhibition. Perhaps it was considered to be implicit. There may also be another reason: questions of self-identity have not been part of the discourse of Israeli art. In fact it was always the 'we' rather than the 'I' that was heard in Israeli society and culture, and what mattered was the collective identity – be it Israeli, Jewish or artistic. 'Art' was always beyond the self; it was supposed to be universal rather than particular, to refer to artistic issues by and large rather than to mirror any private experience. Moreover, the ongoing preference in Israeli art of criticism based on formal criteria, together with the constant effort to define Israeli art in relation to the country, to the Jewish people and to the art world, left little space for the voice of the individual. This is also true for artists like Ardon or Bezem who painted Holocaust themes through sets of symbols while refraining from any personal or emotional confrontation.

Combining the personal and the collective memory characterizes much of Haim Maor's work. A son of survivors who was born in Israel in 1951, Maor has dealt consistently with the Holocaust as a major theme in his work since the early 1980s. He approaches the issue of identity from the traditional point of portraiture both in painting and

FIGURE 5
HAIM MAOR
Self Portrait with Father's Face. Triptych, 1986–87.
Superlac and laquer on wood, 350 × 80 cm.

photography, in art and documentation. Images of his own face and body, his parents, a female German friend and her parents, as well as other people, Israelis and Germans, occupied a series of work entitled *The Face of Race and Memory* that was shown at the Israel Museum in 1988 and continues to be part of his work since. The use of visual conventions of the frontal or profile view brings to mind classic examples of Renaissance portraits and at the same time police photos or the kind of photographs made in Nazi camps. They raise the question to what extent these images represent the people behind them; what is there for us the viewers in these images beyond sheer identification? And above all, what is it that we identify or classify when we see these faces? The recurrence of the number 78446 in Maor's work, which is the number that was tattooed on his father's arm, similarly implies the gap between identification and identity. Maor uses private and personal material but his work is concerned with wider social phenomena such as racist attitudes – his works may turn out to be a 'test' for the viewers. He deals with patterns of commemoration, forgetting and denial and the function of language and information in representing the Holocaust, as in his project *The Forbidden Library* shown at HCAK in Haag in 1993 and in several venues in Israel during 1994–95.

An important aspect of Maor's work is its organization in spatial terms as an installation built as one way route with different stations along which the viewers experience the work. The artist acts almost like a director who intends to lead and control the spectator's observations, emotional reactions and conclusions. An earlier installation entitled *A Message from Auschwitz-Birkenau to Tel Hai* was held in 1983 in a bomb shelter in Tel Hai in the Galilee, a place that in the Israeli collective memory is the ultimate symbol of heroism, sacrifice and settlement.[55] Maor set there a track along empty rooms and a dark narrow corridor leading to the shelter where a silhouette of the entrance to Auschwitz was put on the wall connected by rail tracks to a black eagle on the opposite side. One could see the showers on the way out. It was a distressing experience. This was Maor's first work that was consciously related to the Holocaust and followed a visit to Poland including Auschwitz earlier that year which affected him deeply. In later works he has avoided acting so aggressively towards the viewers, leaving more space for contemplation and conceptualization without totally abandoning the theatrical effects.

Visits to Germany and Poland in the early 1990s also marked a turning point in the work of Simcha Shirman, an established artist-photographer who was born in Germany in 1947 to Holocaust survivors of Polish origin and a year later settled with his family in Israel. These journeys were part of a process begun when Shirman turned 40 and started to investigate the effect of his parents' traumatic experience on his own behaviour, his world view, his relationship with his parents and the nature of his work. There are some similarities with the work of Haim Maor in the use of images of himself (either the face or the naked body) and of his own family and in the choice to present the work in a complex installation where images, objects and text are combined and organized to fit a given space. In the work of both artists the Holocaust is not the subject but the background, and its communicative power is conditioned by the viewer's ability and readiness to decipher the codes and embark on the journey offered by the artists. In Shirman's work there is no fixed route and images of the real are mixed with fabricated images and accompanied by texts, at times documentary, at others fictitious myths. Fantasy is almost part of reality in Shirman's work: an invented character, the One Armed Rider, gives the title to a series of work whereas the use of the letters SS and attached number as the artist's signature evokes fearful associations, though these are actually the artist's initials and date of birth. As a photographer Shirman finds photography the fundamental element for both collecting material for his work and constructing his identity, in the process of which he

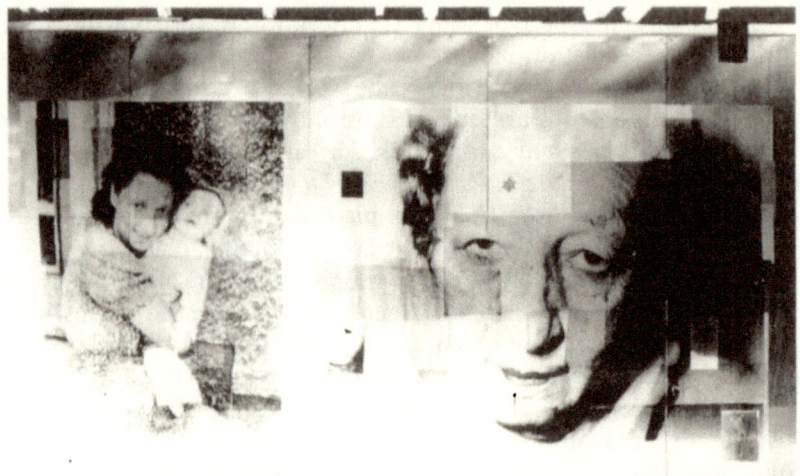

FIGURE 6
SIMCHA SHIRMAN
Someone Else's Mother, or A Hug of a Woman that I Don't Know,
S.S. 470430-940430 [375 × 625cm, 1994]

explores the family album and attempts to reconstruct unknown pictures in lost albums. Memory and lack of memory, fact and fiction, experience and dreams are the material of Shirman's art.

Manipulating and fabricating images often in a most horrific manner marks the work of Honi Ha-meagel, who practises diverse media such as photography, performance, film and video and keeps a special place in the fringe of Israeli art from the early 1980s. Many of his works refer directly to the Holocaust, and others deal with different kinds of cruelty rituals, manifestations of madness or with political questions regarding Jewish identity. Honi, who sees himself as 'an echo of the dead', set out to protest, to testify and to influence, and his work is extremely provocative, revolting and designed to both fascinate and shock in the tradition of Dada, anti-Art, Pop and drag culture. In dressing up in clothes of the camps while emphasizing their specific aesthetic he goes beyond the identification with the victim and the aggressor. Just the same, the fictional biography that he invented for himself as a survivor consisted of many absurd details including his own death.

The growing interest in the Holocaust in Israel in the last decade opened the way for artists, usually children of survivors, to explore through their art via their own experience some of the major issues generated by the Holocaust. In the early photographs of Gilad Ofir images typical to Holocaust iconography such as railway tracks or symbols of demonic power were clearly evident, whereas in the paintings of Varda Gezow and Hanna Shir Holocaust memories are evoked in association and through the emotional content of their work rather than in any direct representation. Nevertheless, the Holocaust has remained rather marginal in Israeli art. Occasionally, an established artist pushes it to the stage centre for a while, as happened in the case of Moshe Gershuni who by the late 1980s and early 1990s moved to a more abstract imagery dealing less and less with Jewish symbols and identity. In recent years some Israeli sculptors were involved in several commemoration projects outside Israel. Micha Ullman's *Bibliothek* of 1995 in Bebel Platz, Berlin, was built in commemoration of the burning of books of Jewish writers in May 1933 in the same spot. It is an empty library dug into the ground and seen through a glass window at the square level. In spite of being literally buried under the surface of the ground this anti-monument has immense impact on the viewers. It belongs to a current tendency in Holocaust memorials to tackle the issue of memory and the act of commemoration in abstract, minimalist and even invisible forms.

Dani Karavan completed in 1994 in Port Bou, Spain, a monument entitled *Passages* in memory of Walter Benjamin, the German-Jewish philosopher and writer who died there in 1940 while escaping. Another memorial by Karavan entitled *Way of Human Rights* (1993) is in the German National Museum, Nuremberg. In a temporary exhibition in 1989 entitled *Dialogue Düsseldorf–Duisburg* held in these two German cities at the same time, Karavan used one of the most recognizable symbols of the Holocaust – railway track. Indeed this work is often interpreted in this context,[56] yet Karavan preferred to interpret this object in a formal mode and in context of his other works while refusing to connect it to the Holocaust.[57] 'I am not a Shoah artist,' he insists, emphasizing the bad reputation that this possible liaison has.[58]

By the second half of the 1990s the Holocaust is no longer rejected in Israeli art and has a certain legitimacy within the work of the so-called Second Generation. This graduate recognition is, perhaps, what allowed established artist Yitzhak Livneh to admit publicly for the first time that his painting might have something to do with his experience as a son of survivors. Nevertheless he resists any direct connection and is anxious about the type of labelling this connection might imply. 'I have never though I would make a painting which is related directly to the Holocaust', he said. 'Some Israeli painters try to touch it. Perhaps it is possible; I cannot... . It is so much inside me, so much part of me that I cannot treat it.'[59]

The difficulty and pain involved in dealing with this trauma, not only for survivors but also for their children, may offer an explanation for the silence of Israeli art concerning the Holocaust. However, as shown earlier, the continuous exclusion of this issue from the discourse of

FIGURE 7
ROEE ROSEN
Live & Die as Eva Braun #2, 1995. Mixed media on paper, 27.5 × 16.9 cm

Israeli art has its ideological origins in the attempt to construct a distinct Israeli identity, different from the Diasporic one. For Israeli artists to this very day, the term 'Shoah artist' entails a negative connotation of kitsch, sentimentality and anachronism – and above all, of exclusion from the boundaries of acceptability in Israeli art that had been defined a long time ago. As the visual art in Israel is still dominated by concepts developed in the 1950s and the 1970s, whereby art's supreme concern is art itself, its form and language, any expression of individual experience of life (or death) should be either performed in abstract gestures or be well hidden under the surface. As a result, memories of the Holocaust and consequently the exposure of a private world are still an unfavourable subject for artists in Israel. Moreover, no serious discussion on the possibility of representing the trauma, as well as on its moral, theoretical and political implications, has ever taken place in Israeli art.

In the winter of 1997–98, the artistic representation of the Holocaust suddenly entered the public arena in a controversy around an exhibition at the Israel Museum in Jerusalem. Young and up-and-coming artist Roee Rosen (born 1963) exhibited an installation of texts and 60 paintings entitled *Live & Die as Eva Braun*. The texts invited the viewer to take the role of Hitler's mistress Eva Braun and gave imagined description of the sexual activity of the couple in the bunker in Berlin shortly before their suicide, while the paintings showed a mixture of childhood imagery, references from German art, computer games, Nazi symbols and erotic images. The scandal was inevitable, rife with condemnations of 'obscenity' and demands to ban the exhibition. For Rosen, who acknowledges the influence of Gershuni's work of the 1980s, the project had a very personal significance. 'My identity in all its levels is scarred by the Holocaust,' he said.[60]

As in the work of Yocheved Weinfeld and other children of survivors, themes of identification with the aggressor and sexual fantasies are dominant in this project. Like Haim Maor and Simcha Shirman, Rosen incorporates in his works pictures of himself and his family including a self-portrait as a child with a little Hitler moustache. And like Maor, Rosen directs the spectator along a series of scenes in a fixed route, assuming a disciplined and cooperative viewer who is capable of deciphering all the clues and who would follow the instructions to reach the desirable conclusion. Rosen, however, uses humour and irony in addition to shock and pornography and the conclusions are far from being decisive. Despite the very private character that the treatment of the subject suggests, it seems to me that Roee Rosen here embarked on a wider mission to reinstate the Holocaust in contemporary art in Israel as a legitimate and relevant issue. It is an art project aimed at generating a discussion on the notion of identity – Israeli, Jewish and personal identity, on commemoration and representation of loss and of evil – what is appropriate and what is not, and on the function and contribution of art to this process. Whether Rosen's ambitious project will stay a one-off event or help to break the seal of silence around the Holocaust in Israeli art remains to be seen.

NOTES

1. The exhibition *After Auschwitz: Responses to the Holocaust in Contemporary Art* comprising the work of 20 artists was shown from February to April 1995 at the Royal Festival Hall in London and later travelled to other venues in the UK and Germany. The 'After Auschwitz' Symposium, in which this article was first presented, was organized by the curator of the exhibition Monica Bohm-Duchen together with Sarah Wilson of the Courtauld Institute and was held at the Courtauld Institute of Art, University of London, on 5–6 April 1995. By the term 'Israeli artists' I refer to artists who actually participate in the artistic life in Israel.
2. Ziva Amishai-Maisels, *Depiction and Interpretation: The Influence of the Holocaust on Visual Arts* (Oxford, 1993). The calculation is based on the number of artists (a total of 250) who are mentioned individually in the bibliography given at the end of the book.
3. Marc Scheps, *Ardon: A Retrospective* (Tel-Aviv Museum, 1985).
4. Amishai-Maisels, *Depiction*, pp. 314–15. For a detailed description of the work see pp. 259–60, and Ziva Amishai-Maisels, 'Where the Past Meets the Present: The Art of Ardon', in *Ardon: A Retrospective*.
5. Carl Katz, 'Ardon', *Ariel*, 5 (Summer 1963), pp. 13–14.

6. Sarit Shapira, 'Scorched Link', in *Burnt Whole: Contemporary Artists Reflect upon the Holocaust* (Washington DC, 1994), p. 4.
7. Ibid.
8. Dina Porat, 'Attitudes to the Young State of Israel towards the Holocaust and Its Survivors: A Debate over Identity and Values', in L.S. Silberstein (ed.), *New Perspectives on Israeli History* (New York, 1991), p. 169; Tom Segev, *Ha-million Ha-shvi'i* (The Seventh Million: Israelis and the Holocaust) (Jerusalem, 1991), pp. 313–15, 335, 400.
9. Ibid., pp. 9, 109, 346, 364.
10. In his fierce criticism of Segev's book, Tuvia Friling argues against the connection made between the Holocaust and Israel's conception of national security, claiming that Israelis are not unique in their responses to real threats to their national existence compared to other nations, and that ancient heritage also influences these responses. Tuvia Friling, 'The Zionist Movement' March of Folly and *The Seventh Million*', *Journal of Israeli History*, Vol. 16, No. 2 (Summer 1995), pp.133–58. However, various scholars find a direct link between the wars of Israel and Holocaust-related expressions in the media, as well as the growing academic and personal interest in the Holocaust. See Nurith Gertz, 'The Impact of the Holocaust on Israeli Ideological Models', in Yehuda Bauer (ed.), *Remembering for the Future: Working Papers and Addenda* (Oxford, 1989), Vol. 3, pp. 2442–8; Dina Porat, 'Teaching the Holocaust to Israeli Students, 1974–1987', in ibid., Vol. 3, pp. 2692–7; Nili Keren, 'Ideologies, Attitudes and Holocaust Teaching in the State of Israel – History and Recent Development', in ibid., Vol.1, pp. 1029–37. On the Holocaust in the public rhetoric during the Gulf War see Moshe Zuckermann, *Shoah Ba-heder Ha-atum: Ha-'shoah' Ba-itonut Ha-israelit Bi-tkufat Milhemet Ha-mifratz* (Shoah in the Sealed Room: The 'Holocaust' in the Israeli Press during the Gulf War) (Tel-Aviv, 1993), especially Chs 6, 8, 10, 12, 17.
11. Esti Rein, 'From General to Individual Commemoration: Holocaust Memorials in Israel', *Gesher*, 126 (Winter 1992/1993), pp. 78–80.
12. A.B. Yehoshua, 'Aesthetic Impediments of Holocaust Literature', in *Ha-kir Ve-hahar: Metsiouto Ha-lo Sifrutit Shel Ha-sofer Be-israel* (The Wall and the Mountain: The Extra-Literary Reality of the Writer in Israel) (Tel-Aviv, 1989), p. 140; Gershon Shaked, *Gal Hadash Ba-siporet Ha-ivrit* (New Wave in Hebrew Fiction) (Jerusalem, 1971), p. 71; Hillel Barzel, 'Holocaust Poetry', in N. Gross, I. Yaoz Kest and R. Kalinov (eds), *Ha-shoah Ba-shira Ha-ivrit: Mivhar* (The Holocaust in Hebrew Poetry: A Selection) (Jerusalem, 1974), p. 10.
13. Barzel, 'Holocaust Poetry', p. 19.
14. This situation is said to have changed since the 1960s and more so since the 1980s. See Dan Laor, 'The Changing Image of the Holocaust in Israeli Literature', *Cathedra*, 69 (Sep. 1993), pp. 160–3; Avner Holtzman, 'Trends in Israeli Holocaust Fiction in the 1980s', *Modern Hebrew Literature* (Tel-Aviv), 8–9 (Spring/Fall 1992), pp. 23–8. On the other hand it is argued that even the most successful and widely discussed writer among the survivors, Aharon Appelfeld, does not represent Israeli literature at large and that Israeli Holocaust literature at its most is not written by those who experienced it. See Yael S. Feldman, 'Whose Story Is It Anyway ? Ideology and Psychology in the Representation of the Shoah in Israeli Literature', in Saul Friedlander (ed.), *Probing the Limits of Representation: Nazism and the 'Final Solution'* (Cambridge MA, 1992), p. 229.
15. Shaked, *Gal Hadash*, pp. 72–3; Yehoshua, *Ha-kir Ve-hahar*, p. 141.
16. Ben-Ami Feingold, *Ha-Shoah Ba-drama Ha-ivrit* (The Holocaust in Hebrew Drama) (Tel-Aviv, 1989), pp. 11–13, 75, 199; Feldman, 'Whose Story Is It?', pp. 223–6.
17. Segev, *Ha-million Ha-shvi'i*, pp. 371–82. For criticism of the political use of the Holocaust see Boas Evron, 'The Holocaust: Learning the Wrong Lesson', *Journal of Palestine Studies*, 10 (Spring 1981), pp. 16–26.
18. For example, the exhibition *Harada* (Anxiety) curated by Miriam Tovia-Boneh and Ilana Tenenbaum at the Museum of Israeli Art, Ramat Gan, 1994. Whereas the catalogue points to the immense influence of the Holocaust on political and social life in Israel, only two out of the 32 exhibiting artists deal directly with the Holocaust. A more specific pursuit of the issue was the exhibition *Postscripts: 'End' Representations in Contemporary Israeli Art* curated by Tami Katz-Freiman at the Genia Schreiber

University Art Gallery, Tel-Aviv University, 1992. Here also only two out of 16 artists treat the Holocaust directly.
19. Liah Greenfeld, *Different Worlds: A Sociological Study of Taste, Choice and Success in Art* (Cambridge, 1989), pp. 26, 80–3, 105, 138–9, 114–24.
20. Ran Shechori, 'Zaritsky', *Mussag*, 9 (Feb. 1976), p. 39; Amnon Barzel, *Art in Israel* (Milan, 1988), pp. 56 ff. It is worth mentioning that stylistically the work of Ardon is no less abstract than that of Zaritsky. But it is not based on impressions of nature, as Zaritsky's paintings are, and incorporates symbols from kabbala.
21. For example, a text by the poet Nathan Zach (1961) that manages to bypass symbols such as barbed wire or crosses, or a text by critic Sara Breitberg (1982) using generalizations rather than any direct interpretation, both printed in *Tumarkin: In the Centre of the Margins* (Tel-Aviv, 1985), pp. 16–18, 210. Similarly, art historian Posèq identifies Holocaust content in Tumarkin's work only when explicitly stressed by titles or symbols. See Avigdor Posèq, 'Four Types of Scream in the Work of Igael Tumarkin', *Motar*, No. 1 (July 1993), pp.101–6. In her essay in the catalogue of Tumarkin's recent retrospective, Ellen Ginton discusses the motif of death, including violent death, in Tumarkin's work as a major theme. However, she hardly mentions the impact of the Holocaust on Tumarkin, a son of a Jewish mother and a German father, as a possible origin for this concern. She also argues that the avoidance of literal analysis by writers and critics was due to the artist's own emphasis on formalist interpretation of his work. Ellen Ginton, 'His Name Begins with a T: From *The Gates of Hell* to *The Gate of the Kiss*: On the Birth of Art out of Death in the Work of Tumarkin', in *Tumarkin: Sculptures, 1957–1992* (Tel-Aviv Museum of Art, 1992), not paginated.
22. For Holocaust reading of Tumarkin see Amishai-Maisels, *Depiction*, pp. 280–3, 345–50. The announcement of Yad Va-shem early in 1998 of their intention to award Tumarkin a prize was probably the first official recognition of Tumarkin's preoccupation with Holocaust themes.
23. Barzel, *Art in Israel*, p. 56; Gila Ballas, *Ofakim Hadashim* (New Horizons) (Tel-Aviv, 1980), p. 11.
24. Graciela M. Trajtenberg, 'Stratification Process in the Artistic Field – The "New Horizons" Group', MA Thesis in Social Sciences, Tel-Aviv University, 1990; Yigal Zalmona, 'New Horizons – the Impresario Experience', *Kav*, No. 1 (June 1980), pp. 79–82.
25. Sarah Chinsky points out that between the two categories of the Local (Zionist) and the Universal (European) 'other worlds' are absent from the discourse. However, she totally ignores the Jewish 'world' as she directs her argument to the oriental and Arab 'other': Sarah Chinsky, 'Silence of the Fish: The Local versus the Universal in Israeli Discourse on Art', *Teoria U-vikoret*, No. 4 (Fall 1993), pp. 114 ff.
26. Benjamin Tammuz (ed.), *Sipura Shel Omanut Israel* (The Story of Israel's Art) (Ramat-Gan, 1980), p. 11.
27. Ballas, *Ofakim*, p. 14.
28. A.B. Yehoshua, 'The Dilemma at the Heart of Israeli Culture after Forty Years', in *In the Shadow of Conflict: Israeli Art 1980–1989* (New York, 1989), p. 10.
29. Tammuz, *Omanut Israel*, p. 10.
30. Katz, 'Ardon', p. 28.
31. Amnon Raz-Krakotzkin, 'Exile within Sovereignty: Toward a Critique of the "Negation of Exile" in Israeli Culture (Part II)', *Teoria U-vikoret*, 5 (Fall 1994), pp. 118–24; Segev, *Ha-million Ha-shvi'i*, pp. 261-3.
32. Yigal Zalmona, 'History and Identity', in *Artists of Israel: 1920–1980* (New York, 1981), p. 30.
33. According to Shavit there are crucial differences between Hebraism of the 1920s and Canaanism of the 1940s in spite of some points of similarity in insisting on secular culture and the attitude towards the Diaspora Jew. These cause confusions and inaccurate use of the term 'Canaanite' (as indeed occurs in referring to Canaanism in art). Yaacov Shavit, *The New Hebrew Nation: A Study in Heresy and Fantasy* (London, 1987), p. 4.
34. Zalmona, 'History and Identity', p. 40.
35. Quoted in *Marcel Janco: On the Edge, Drawings of the Holocaust* (Ein Hod, 1990), p. 24. In a conversation in 1983 Janco made a direct link between the Holocaust drawings and the theme of the wounded soldier repeated in his work after 1948. See

Gideon Ofrat, *1948, Dor Tashah Be-omanut Israel* (The 1948 Generation in Israeli Art) (Haifa University Gallery, 1984), not paginated.
36. M. Getter, 'Immigration from Germany, 1933–1939', *Cathedra*, 12 (July 1979), pp. 125–47, especially p. 146.
37. Tammuz, *Omanut Israel*, Ch. 3 by Doreet LeVitté and Ch. 4 by Gideon Ofrat.
38. Barzel, *Art in Israel*, pp. 47–52.
39. Ibid., p. 57.
40. In a letter to *Massa* newspaper of January 1958, quoted in Ballas, *Ofakim*, p. 71.
41. In an interview in *Ma'ariv*, April 1965, quoted in ibid., p. 129. Janco, a founding member of New Horizons, left the group in 1956, probably because of friction with Zaritsky.
42. Amishai-Maisels, *Depiction*; the chapter 'Distance through Abstraction'.
43. Ballas, *Ofakim*, p. 95. The group consisted of veteran New Horizons artists and younger artists. The joint rejection of narrative art and Jewish subject matter is often taken as a matter of course. In his description of Zaritsky's attitude towards Chagall's imagery, Omer claims that it 'stood in absolute contradiction to the perception of the Israeli artist, who detested any "anecdotes" and strived to purify painting from its "literalness"'. Mordechai Omer, *Zaritsky: Retrospectiva* (Zaritsky: A Retrospective) (Tel-Aviv Museum, 1984), p. 144.
44. The conception that Jewish art is abstract art was proposed by Pincus-Witten who also mentioned some Israeli abstract artists who emerged in the 1970s. Robert Pincus-Witten, 'Six Propositions on Jewish Art', *Arts Magazine*, 50 (Dec. 1975), pp. 66–9.
45. In 1964 the sculptor Itzhak Danziger wrote: 'There is something almost tragic about living in this country [Israel]. One feels as though one is living off the side, not at the centre of things ... Yet living out there is not the solution either ... You lose your local identity. And so you live here but your attention is elsewhere' (quoted in Sara Breitberg-Semel, *The Want of the Matter: A Quality in Israeli Art* (Tel-Aviv Museum, 1986), p. 181). The absence of the visual tradition of Classical and Christian Europe is referred to as problematic, mainly by native born artists. Tamar Getter, 'Thoughts on Paintings, 1976–1989', *Kav*, 10 (July 1990), pp. 43–6.
46. Stephanie Rachum, *Yocheved Weinfeld* (Jerusalem, 1979).
47. The attraction of Israeli artists to German art since the mid-1970s and especially during the 1980s is an issue that deserves separate discussion. For interpretation of Gershuni's work in this light see Sarit Shapira, *Routes of Wandering: Nomadism, Journeys and Transitions in Contemporary Israeli Art* (Jerusalem, 1991), pp. 206–7.
48. Moshe Gershuni, *Kav*, 4/5 (Nov. 1982), p. 18. No other artist of the contributors to this issue identified himself in such a way.
49. Alec Mishori, 'Broken Vessels: Purification Motifs in the Ceramic Works of Moshe Gershuni', *Studio* (Tel-Aviv), 17 (Dec. 1990), p. 17; Itamar Levi, *Moshe Gershuni: Works 1987–1990* (Tel-Aviv Museum of Art, 1990), No. 32.
50. Aviva Uri, 'Ha-Kav' (The Line), Postscript in Doreet LeVitté, *Aviva Uri* (Jerusalem, 1986), p. 119.
51. Gideon Ofrat, *Aqedat Yitzhak Ba-omanut Ha-israelit* (The Sacrifice of Isaac in Israeli Art) (Ramat-Gan, 1988).
52. Dina Wardi, 'Memorial Candles: Reflection of the Holocaust in the Art of the Second Generation', *Studio*, 17 (Dec. 1990), pp. 40–6. For a full discussion of the subject see Dina Wardi, *Memorial Candles: Children of the Holocaust* (London, 1992).
53. Ruth Debel (compiler), 'What Does It Mean To Be an Israeli Artist ?', *Art News*, No. 77 (May 1978), p. 56.
54. For a detailed interpretation of this work see Amishai-Maisels, *Depiction*, pp. 362–3.
55. In March 1920 the commander Yosef Trumpeldor and other members of the little settlement of Tel Hai were killed in an Arab attack, acquiring pride of a place in Israeli historiography. See Yael Zerubavel, 'New Beginning, Old Past: The Collective Memory of Pioneering in Israeli Culture', in Silberstein (ed.), *New Perspectives*, pp. 193–215. In the history of Israeli art this event has a special place due to Melnikov's sculpture of the Roaring Lion that was erected in Tel Hai as a memorial to the fallen. In 1980 the college at Tel Hai and curator Amnon Barzel organized there an international sculpture symposium. Maor's work was made for the second symposium, Tel Hai, 1983.
56. Amishai-Maisels, *Depiction*, p. 424, n.164.
57. In an interview with Miriam Tovia-Boneh, *Studio* (Tel-Aviv), No. 3/4 (Sep.–Oct. 1989),

p. 12, Karavan links this work to his previous works with railway tracks as a formal device. He offers, however, an explanation to the number he wrote in pencil on the wall as part of the railway track installation – the number 14897 of the last transport from the Jewish ghetto of Lodz to Auschwitz.
58. In an interview with Joseph Croitoru, *Studio*, 38 (Nov. 1992), p. 35, Karavan denied again that the work with the railway track in Düsseldorf has any connection to the Holocaust. He also explained why he has refused commissions from the Germans to design memorials directly related to the Holocaust. Later on he changed his mind and in 1994 submitted a proposal to the international competition for The Monument in Memory of Jews Murdered in the Holocaust in Berlin. Recently he seems to have changed his mind further, and in an exhibition at Tel-Aviv Museum of Art in winter 1997/98 dedicated to the memorial to Walter Benjamin in Port Bou, Karavan also showed a video documentation of his work in Düsseldorf–Duisburg that focuses on the number written on the wall as well as a new installation in which the railway track is the main element. It is impossible not to interpret these works in the context of the Holocaust.
59. Quoted by Tali Tamir, 'Painting as a Living Dead: On the Paintings of Yitzhak Livneh', *Studio*, No. 73 (June–July 1996), p. 15.
60. In an interview with Galia Yahav in *Studio*, No. 88 (Dec. 1997), p. 26.

Index

Ackerman, Shmuel 200
Aderet, Avraham 120
Agnon, Shai 143
Agudat Israel 57, 87, 96, 98
Alexander, Hanan 152
Algeria 49, 163
Alon, Yigal 109
Allon, Eli 139, 145
Altherman, Natan 255
Altneuland 74
Amichai, Yehuda 4
Amir, Yigal 228
Ansky, Alex 243
Arab–Israeli conflict 167–8
Arab–Israeli wars 221, 255
Aran, Zalman 17, 68, 91, 149
Ardon, Mordechai 232, 253
Aristotle 163
Aroch, Arie 201, 205, 208
Ashkenazi Jews 3, 63, 84, 222, 224, 237
Auschwitz 88, 265, 269
Avineri, Shlomo 68
Avi-Yonah, Michael 207
Azaryahu, Maoz 69

Baalei teshuva 230–31, 234, 239–40, 245
Babel, Isaac 76
Bak, Shmuel 253
Balfour Declaration (1917) 142, 207
Barak, Aharon 35
Barak, Ehud 37
Barkan, Yehuda 232–4
Bar-Lev, Mordechai 48, 69
Bartov, Hanoch 105
Bar-Yosef, Yehoshua 248
Bar-Yosef, Yosef 242–3, 248–9
Barzel, Amnon 260

Bashevis-Singer, Isaac 81
Batlle, Georgette 200
Bedouins 65, 194
Be'er, Haim 236
Begin, Menachem 91, 98
Bellow, Saul 81
Ben-Aharon, Yariv 137, 139, 142, 144–5, 247
Ben-Aharon, Yitzhak 247
Ben-Ari, Eyal 71
Ben-Gurion, David 1, 38–9, 98–9, 108, 121–2, 128, 178
Ben-Haim, Paul 78
Benjamin Walter, 271
Ben-Porat, Yeshyahu 236
Ben-Yehuda, Baruch 149
Ben-Yehuda, Netiva 118
Bergen-Belsen 180
Bergman, Menachem 127
Bergmann, Samuel Hugo 133
Bergner, Yosl 253
Besser, Gedalia 242
Bezem, Naftali 253
Bhabha, Homi 176, 178, 196
Bialik, Haim Nahman 4, 79–81, 93–4, 96, 126, 147–9, 221
Bible 16, 50, 60, 80, 144, 147–8, 152, 160, 227, 238
Bilu, Yoram 71
Borer, Iris 232
Borochov Berl, 93
Brancusi, Constantin 218
Braun, Eva 273
Brenner, Yosef Haif 4, 74, 88, 93–5, 142, 144
Buber, Martin 133–4, 144–5, 222
Buchenwald 180

Camp David Accords 67

Canaani, David 142, 145
Carmel Institute 36, 40
Carnoy, Martin 49, 67
Circassians 65
Clausen, Christopher 31, 46
Clifford, James 176
Cohen, Erik 67
Cohen, Geula 89
Cohen Gan, Pinchas 201, 214–18

Dan, Yosef 40, 47
Danon, Rami 224
Danziger, Yitzhak 126, 201, 204
Dayan, Moshe 92, 109
Deri, Arieh 98, 224
Deshen, Shlomo 42
Dinur, Ben-Zion 80
Don-Yehiya, Eliezer 36, 47, 68, 127
Druzes 65

Edingen, Angelica 163
Egypt 49
   and Camp David Accords 67
Eichmann, Adolf 19, 168
Elboim-Dror, Rachel 103, 127
Eldad-Sheib, Israel 91, 97
Eliav, Lova 4
Eretz Israel 107–8, 110–16, 119–22, 124–5, 132, 142, 186, 223, 249, 259
Erter, Yitzhak 88
Ethiopia 83
Euripides 160–62, 164–5, 167–8, 171–2
Even-Or, Yigal 225
Even-Zohar, Itamar 78
Evron, Boaz 29, 46
Evron, Gilad 242

First World War 95, 107
Fischer-Lichte, Erika 172
Fisher, Yona 211
Fleischer 29, 225, 227
France 2
Freud, Sigmund 76
Freytag, Holk 163–4, 166, 168–9
Friedman, Menachem 56, 69
Front de Liberation Nationale (FLN) 163
Fuchs, Sarit 224
Furstenberg, Rochelle 40

Gamlielit, Esther 78
Gaon, Yitzhak 200
Gassler Elizabeth 204
Gavison, Ruth 35, 47
Gaza Strip 2–3, 65, 165
Gazit, Amit 225
Gefen, Aviv 41
Germany 50, 95, 269
Gershuni, Moshe 263–4, 271, 273

Gertz, Nurit 5
Gezow, Varda 271
Ginsburg, Asher (see Ahad Ha-am)
Gitlin, Michael 200
Glickson, Moshe 734, 85
Gliksberg, Haim, 208
Golah Ve-nechar 29
Goldman, Eliezer 69
Gordon, A.D. 4, 75, 77, 116, 134, 142
Gramsci, Antonio 49, 67
Greenberg, Moshe 47
Greenberg, Uri Zvi 75, 91, 96–7, 99
Grobman, Michail 200
Grossman, David 4, 44, 48, 71
Grotowski, Jerzy 228
Gurewitz, Adolph 96
Guri, Haim 104, 123–6, 131
Gurion, Israel 242
Gush Emunim 58, 95
Gutman, Nahum 78, 259
Guttman Institute 22, 29, 34, 40
Guttman Report 41

Ha-am, Ahad 4, 74, 79, 84, 94, 147–9
Habibi, Emil 65, 71
Hadar, Nurit 239
Hagana 104, 176
Haifa 61, 133, 203
Halacha, 21, 24–5, 34–5, 52, 53, 61, 80, 91 147
Ha-Levi, Moshe 222
Halkin, Shimon 126
halutzim (pioneers) 35, 146
Ha-meagel, Chonni 244, 270
Ha-Meiri, Avigdor 97
Hametz 29, 37, 226
Hammer, Zevulun 151
Hanoch, Gershon 77
Ha-poel Ha-tzair (Young Workers Party) 92, 134, 143
Har-Even, Shulamit 137
Har-Even, Y. 97
haredi, (Ultra-Orthodox Jews) 3–4, 56, 86, 224
Harpoz, Yoram 125
Hasfari Shmuel 29, 37, 226, 236, 239
Haskala 230
Ha-shomer Ha-tzair 92, 116–17
Hazaz, H. 73
Hebrew culture 9–11, 14, 27, 33, 35, 39, 42, 45, 54, 60, 97
Hebrew language 3, 16, 20, 44, 60, 63, 78, 104, 123, 125, 147–8, 160, 240
Helman, Sara 69
Herut 93
Herzl, Theodore 92–3
Hiroshima 265

INDEX

Histadrut 14, 107, 121
Hofstatter, Osias 260, 264–5
Holocaust 14, 18–20, 37, 42, 51–3, 56–7, 60, 87, 95, 113, 148, 175–82, 185, 188–9, 191, 195, 221, 223, 225–6, 249, 253–62, 264, 270–73
Holocaust Remembrance Day 18, 148–9
Holy Land 56–57
Horgin, Yaakov 97
Horowitz, Dan 68, 71, 111–12, 116
Horowitz, David 77
Hungary 95

Inbar, Efraim 37
India 83
Intifada 37
Iran 50, 82
Irgun 103
Israel
  and accords with the Palestinians 37, 58, 67, 177–8, 189–90
  and Arab citizens 1, 52–3, 64–6, 178
  and Arab culture in 54
  and Communist Party 65
  and culture 3–4, 9, 12, 14, 17, 26, 40–41, 54, 61, 80, 144, 160, 190, 245
  and cultural elite in 39, 42
  and defence forces (IDF) 14, 17–18, 37, 165–6
  and Diaspora relations 42
  and Independence Day 18, 38, 52, 148
  and Jerusalem Liberation Day 18
  and Jewish identity 2, 12, 17, 20, 85, 254
  and Jewish Zionist identity 24–5, 194
  and memorial day for the fallen of the IDF 18, 148
  and Palestinian economic interdependence with 2
  and peace with Egypt 67
  and secular Judaism in 29, 33, 43, 45
  and society 2, 4, 51, 61, 66, 176, 267
  Armenians in 111
  Art in 253–73
  Chief Rabbinate in 56
  Cinema in 175–97
  Civil Rights Movement Party in 61
  Declaration of Independence 10, 255
  Druze in 111
  Fiftieth Anniversary of 1, 146
  Jewish Studies in 135, 151, 153

Kibbutz movement 5, 34
Land of 2, 27, 51, 57, 74–7, 79, 83, 87, 92, 103, 147, 160, 180–2, 191, 257
State of 9, 13–14, 17–18, 20, 23, 26, 29, 56, 80, 107, 111, 223, 254–5
Theatre in 159 227–8
War of Independence (1947–49) 14, 64, 103–5, 110, 133, 187, 195
Israeli, Ika 232
Italy 50

Jabotinsky, Ari 96
Jabotinsky, Ze'ev 92–3, 96
Janco, Marcel, 259 261
Jerusalem 42, 90, 115, 133, 150, 181, 186–7, 200–206, 209, 212–14, 217–18, 248, 258, 260
Jewish Culture 30–34, 36, 39, 42, 44, 76, 78, 108, 114, 149–50, 159, 173, 217, 228
Jewish Diaspora 1–2, 17–19, 26–7, 80, 84, 94–5, 103, 106, 112, 122, 126, 135, 146, 149, 175, 177, 181–2, 186, 249, 258–9, 264
Jewish identity 16, 178, 265
Jewish National Fund (JNF) 81, 175, 211, 235
Jewish People 17–19, 56, 59, 74, 76, 93, 106, 142, 209
Jewish State 28, 30, 52, 66
Judea and Samaria (see also West Bank) 2–3, 57

Kadishman, Menashe 201, 212–14, 218
Kaniuk, Yoram 4
Karavan, Dani 271
Karmon, Yosef 237
Karni, Y. 74
Karo, Rabbi Joseph 54, 244
Katz, Elihu 34, 46–7
Katznelson, Berl 80, 92–3, 99, 139, 143
Kaufman, Yehezkel 29
Kenan, Amos 108
Keren Ha-yesod 175
Kimmerling, Baruch 5, 29, 46, 67–8, 70
Klausner, Yosef 96, 147
Knaz, Yehoshua 4
Knesset 20–21, 25, 82, 167, 255
Kook, Rabbi Abraham Isaac 55, 57–8, 88, 95, 143
Kretzmer, David 68, 71
Ktuvim Group 77
Kulturkampf 4, 20, 49, 66

Labour Party 42, 61, 93, 98, 147, 228

Lamdan, Y. 75
Lamm, Zvi 116
Laor Yitzhak 68
Lapid, Yosef 167
Laqueur, Walter 68
Larsky, Helmar 183
Lasch, Christopher 43, 45–6, 48
Law of Return 3, 25
Lebanon 37, 172
Lebanon War (1982) 3, 53, 165, 167
Lebanon, Ya'ud 232
LEHI 103, 210
Leibowitz, Yeshayahu 69
Leslau, Avraham 48
Levene, Rabbi Benjy 234–5, 247
Levi, Amnon 224
Levin, Itche Meir 96
Levinsohn, Hanna 46
Levy, Ram 242
Levy, Shimon 5
Levy, Shlomit 46
Liebman, Charles S. 5, 47, 68, 127
Likud 88, 91–3, 98
Lilker, Shalom 47
Lissak, Moshe 67
Lithuania 87
Livneh, Yitzhak 271
Lulav, Omri 136, 145
Lundberg G.A. 46
Lustik, Ian 71
Luz, Ehud 69
Lyotard, Jean-Francois 249

Maayan, Dudi 226
MAFDAL (National Religious Party) 151
Maimon, Yehuda Leib (Fishman) 38–9
Maimonides 53
Malkin, Ahuvia 119–20
Manor, Dalia 5
Maor, Haim 267–9, 273
Ma'oz, Moshe 72
MAPAI 38, 53, 68, 96, 98, 118, 121
MAPAM 38, 72
Margalit, Dan 37
Marks, Gerald 200
Masada 226
Mea Shearim 97, 235, 247
Mead, Margaret 31
Meged, Aaron 105
Meletz, Raffi 105
Menussi, Didi 232
MERETZ 42, 151
Michael, B. 236, 238
Migdal, Joel, S. 69
Miron, Dan 5
Mizrahiim 53
Morag, Ora 242
Mordechai, Yizhak 37
Morris, Benny 68

Moscow 222
Mossinson, Yigal 105, 223

NAHAL 133
Nardi, Nahum 78
Nazis 3, 176, 181, 225
Nazism 50, 260, 263
Netanyahu, Benjamin 86, 98
Neustein, Joshua 200
New Testament 64
Nikel, Leah 208
Nitzan, Shlomo 105
Nordau, Max 93
Novak, Hava 174

October 1973 War 3, 17, 53, 105, 133, 135, 237
Ofek, Avraham 200
Ofir, Gilad 270
Ofrat, Gideon 222, 229
Old Testament 50–51, 59
Omer, Mordechai 5
Onslow, Herbert Charles 208
Oral Torah 16
Orian, Amir 245
Oslo Agreement 65
Oz, Amos 4, 44, 127, 134

Palestine (in the mandatory era) 87, 195
    Arab population of 53, 188, 208
    British rule in 103
    Jewish community in 78
    Jewish immigration into 60, 179
    partition of 2
Palestinians 2, 51–2, 65, 89, 165, 173, 184, 190, 194
Palestinian Liberation Organization (PLO) 72, 167
PALMACH 97, 103, 110, 112, 118, 123, 125, 137, 202, 259
Peace Process (see also Oslo Accords, Camp David Accords) 67
Peled, Yoav 68
Peloponnesian Wars 160, 170
Peres, Shimon 86, 88, 98–9
Peretz, Rabbi Yitzhak 99
Perl, Joseph 88
Pilsudski, Josef 96
Pingaud, Bernard 173
Poland 78, 83, 86–7, 262, 269
Porat, Orna 163
Porath, Yehoshua 68

Raban, Ze'ev 218
Rabikowitz, Dalia 4, 62, 71
Rabin, Yitzhak 42, 65, 99, 227–8
Rabinovitch, A.Z. 142
Rabinowitz, Jacob 76, 85
Rand, Shuli 232
RATZ Party 72

INDEX 283

Ratosh, Yonatan 78–9, 97
Rauschenberg, Robert 208
Reches, Eli 71
Reform Judaism 32, 67
Reuveni, A. 96–7
Rieff, Philip 45
Rivers, Larry 209
Romania 78
Rosen, Roee 272–3
Rosen-Zvi, Ariel 47
Roth, Joseph 81
Roth, Philip 81
Rovina, Hanna 231
Rozik-Rosen Eli 5, 173
Rubenstein, Amnon 151
Rubin, Nisan 48, 127
Rubin, Reuven 259
Rudner, Amos 136
Russia 78
Russian Revolution 221

Sabra and Shatilla 165
Samet, Gideon 39–40
Samuel, Herbert Louis 207–8
Sartre, Jean-Paul 163–4, 169
Schaltz, Shaul, 200
Scholem, Gershom 128, 133
Schwebel, Ivan 200
Schweid, Eliezer 5, 29, 33, 39–40, 42, 47, 110–11, 128
Second Aliyah 94–5, 97, 141–4, 262
Second World War 11, 13, 18, 27, 133, 168, 172, 176, 202–3, 255, 260,
Secular Judaism 33–6, 43–4, 46
Segev, Tom 255
Senesh, Hana 256
Seri, Bracha 227
Shabtai, Jacob 114, 128
Shach, Rabbi 63, 83, 86–91, 98–9, 224
Shahaf, Jonathan 229
Shahak, Amnon 37
Shaked, Gershon 3–5, 105, 127, 196, 221, 228
Shalom, S. 75
Shamir, Moshe 79–80, 105, 112, 128
Shamir, Yitzhak 98
Shapira, Anita 68, 128
Shapira, Avraham 5, 96, 133–4, 144
Shapira, Sarit 254
Shapiro, Yonathan 44, 48
Sharon, Ariel 89
Shas Party 3, 63–4, 88
Shazar, Zalman 31, 92
Shdemot Circle 133, 135–6, 138–43
Shelah-Ratosh Uriel , 96
Sheleg, Irit 232–3
Shenhar Commission 17, 42, 151
Shir, Hanna 271
Shirman, Simcha 269, 273

Shlahin, Ofer 163
Shlonsky, Avraham 74–6, 255
Shnerson, Rabbi Zalman 58, 90
Shnitzler, Arthur 76
Shoham, Chaim 228
Shor, Nathan 210, 218
Shulhan Aruch 53, 88, 90, 245
Shuster, Noya 239
Simon, Ernst 133
Simon, Jean-Paul 235
Six Day War (1967) 2–3, 14, 17, 19, 53, 57, 133–5, 139, 255
Smilansky, Yizhar (see S. Yizhar)
Smooha, Sammy 71
Sobol, Yehoshua 241
Sokolow, Nahum 93
Soviet Union 23, 61, 73, 149
Stern, Avraham 97
Stern, Yair 91
Sternhall, Zeev 68
Sudan 50
Suslov, Mikhail 31

Talkowski, Zvi 200
Tammuz, Benjamin 258
Taylor, Charles 152
Tel-Aviv 51, 61, 79, 83, 190, 202–3, 209, 217, 222, 224, 248, 253, 263
Telpaz, Gideon 228
Tumarkin, Yigael 208, 257
Tzefira, Bracha 78
Tzur, Muki 138, 140, 144–5

Ufaz, Gad 5, 145
Ullman, Micha 271
United Nations 51
United States 13, 28, 32, 85, 143
Uri, Aviva 265
Urian, Dan 5, 46, 174

Vilozny, Shmuel 232

Wardi, Dina 266
Warsaw Ghetto 256
Wasserstein, Bernard 46
Weinfeld, Yocheved 262, 266–7, 273
Weitz, Yechiam 115, 197
Weizmann, Chaim 93
West Bank (see also Judea and Samaria) 2–3, 57, 65, 165
Wolfsohn, David 93
World Zionist Organization 51
Ya'ari, Meir 77, 92
Yad Va-shem 254–5
Yehoshua, A.B. 44, 71, 258
Yelin-Mor, Natan 97
Yerushalmi, Rina 227
Yevin, Yehoshua Heshl 96
Yishuv 9–11, 13, 25, 34–5, 51, 82, 85, 106–7, 113–17, 120, 146–9,

153, 184, 262
Yizhar, S. 4, 82, 105, 108–9, 115, 128, 180
Yom Kippur War (see October 1973 War)
Yosef, Rabbi Ovadia 63–4, 98

Zach, Nathan 4
Zalmona, Yigal 259
Zaritsky, Yosef 201, 254
Zemach, Shlomo 143

Zerubavel, Yael 70
Zimmer, Shimon 236–7
Zimmerman, Barry 144
Zionism 1, 13–14, 16, 18, 24, 33, 38, 50, 55, 82, 84, 87–8, 91–2, 107–8, 123, 141, 146, 240
Zionist movement 3
Zisenwine, David 5
Zohar, Uri 231–3, 235–40, 243–4, 249

Selected Titles from the Cass Series in Israeli History, Politics and Society

Providing a multidisciplinary examination in all aspects, the series serves as a means of communication between the various communities interested in Israel: academics, policy-makers, practitioners, journalists and the informed public.

ISSN 1368–4795

PEACE IN THE MIDDLE EAST
The Challenge for Israel
Efraim Karsh (Ed)

The State of Israel seems closer than ever to its professed loftiest ideal: contractual peace with its Arab neighbours, first and foremost the Palestinians. What are the implications of peace for Israel? How would it affect the country's political and economic systems and its national security? What would peace mean for Israel's regional and international standing and for its relations with world Jewry? A distinguished group of specialists from Israel, Europe and the United States address these crucial issues.

168 pages   1994
0 7146 4614 8 cloth   0 7146 4141 3 paper

FRANK CASS PUBLISHERS
Newbury House, 900 Eastern Avenue, Newbury Park, Ilford, Essex, IG2 7HH
Tel: +44 (0)181 599 8866 Fax: +44 (0)181 599 0984
NORTH AMERICA
c/o ISBS, 5804 NE Hassalo Street, Portland OR 97213 3644
Tel: (800) 944 6190 Fax: (503) 280 8832 E-mail: cass@isbs.com
Website: http://www.frankcass.com

THE SHAPING OF ISRAELI IDENTITY
Myth, Memory and Trauma
Robert Wistrich and David Ohana (Eds)

The essays in this volume examine in an original, provocative and critical perspective the fundamental myths, symbols and historical memories that have played an active role in shaping the development of Israeli society. How does Zionism relate to the Jewish religious tradition; to the Diaspora; to the Holocaust – to the mystique of the land; to the reality of war; to its own dead and captured soldiers; to the geopolitical isolation of Israel; to its own localisation in time and space after centuries of Jewish wanderings in exile?

256 pages 1995
0 7146 4641 5 cloth   0 7146 4163 4 paper

BETWEEN WAR AND PEACE
Dilemmas of Israeli Security
Efraim Karsh (Ed)

> 'Karsh has outlined in one volume the contemporary dilemmas of Israeli security in the widest sense. Indeed, he has produced a work that constitutes a comprehensive survey of those dilemmas and does much to elucidate them. Between War and Peace *is a timely and useful work which this reviewer strongly recommends.*'
>
> **F H Toase,** *Royal Military Academy, Sandhurst*

304 pages 1996
0 7146 4711 X cloth   0 7146 4256 8 paper

FRANK CASS PUBLISHERS
Newbury House, 900 Eastern Avenue, Newbury Park, Ilford, Essex, IG2 7HH
Tel: +44 (0)181 599 8866 Fax: +44 (0)181 599 0984
NORTH AMERICA
c/o ISBS, 5804 NE Hassalo Street, Portland OR 97213 3644
Tel: (800) 944 6190 Fax: (503) 280 8832 E-mail: cass@isbs.com
Website: http://www.frankcass.com

U.S.-ISRAELI RELATIONS AT THE CROSSROADS

Gabriel Sheffer (Ed)

The U.S.-Israeli 'special relationship' is viewed as, one of the most solid and stable bilateral relationships. Yet the new international and domestic reality in both the U.S. and Israel warrants a thorough re-examination.

The essays in this collection deal with, among other things, the general global setting and its implications for this relationship; with 'hard' strategic factors; and less tangible aspects, such as American images of Israel, the attitudes of other American religious denominations, and the situation of the American Jewish community.

248 pages   1997
0 7146 4747 0 cloth   0 7146 4305 X paper

FROM RABIN TO NETANYAHU
Israel's Troubled Agenda

Efraim Karsh (Ed)

The May 1996 election of Benjamin Netanyahu, the leader of the right-wing Likud Party, as Israel's youngest ever prime minister provides further proof of the volatility of Israeli politics. What are the sources of Netanyahu's victory and what are its domestic and external implications? Does it spell the demise of the nascent peace process between Israel and the Palestinians? Or will Netanyahu be the leader to rally the Israeli public behind the territorial concessions attending the attainment of comprehensive peace? A distinguished group of specialists from Israel, Great Britain and the United States address these questions.

328 pages   1997
0 7146 4831 0 cloth   0 7146 4383 1 paper

FRANK CASS PUBLISHERS
Newbury House, 900 Eastern Avenue, Newbury Park, Ilford, Essex, IG2 7HH
Tel: +44 (0)181 599 8866 Fax: +44 (0)181 599 0984
NORTH AMERICA
c/o ISBS, 5804 NE Hassalo Street, Portland OR 97213 3644
Tel: (800) 944 6190 Fax: (503) 280 8832 E-mail: cass@isbs.com
Website: http://www.frankcass.com

ISRAEL AT THE POLLS, 1996
Daniel J Elazar and Shmuel Sandler (Eds)

The 1996 Israeli elections were the first elections by direct vote for the position of prime minister in which a newcomer – Binyamin Netanyahu – defeated the most veteran Israeli politician, Shimon Peres. The result indicated not only a transition of power from the left-centre to the right-centre, but also the decline of the major parties and the ascendance of the smaller parties. *Israel at the Polls, 1996* looks at the parties, election campaigns and the processes that determined this outcome. Major issues such as religion and politics, Israel as a Jewish state, the peace process, and the 'new politics' are analysed by outstanding Israeli political scientists.

288 pages 1998
0 7146 4864 7 cloth   0 7146 4421 8 paper

FRANK CASS PUBLISHERS
Newbury House, 900 Eastern Avenue, Newbury Park, Ilford, Essex, IG2 7HH
Tel: +44 (0)181 599 8866 Fax: +44 (0)181 599 0984
NORTH AMERICA
c/o ISBS, 5804 NE Hassalo Street, Portland OR 97213 3644
Tel: (800) 944 6190 Fax: (503) 280 8832 E-mail: cass@isbs.com
Website: http://www.frankcass.com

For Product Safety Concerns and Information please contact our EU
representative GPSR@taylorandfrancis.com
Taylor & Francis Verlag GmbH, Kaufingerstraße 24, 80331 München, Germany

www.ingramcontent.com/pod-product-compliance
Lightning Source LLC
Chambersburg PA
CBHW030108010526
44116CB00005B/151